李志强　主编

Legal Research on Investment and Financing of Chinese Enterprises in the Overseas Countries

中国企业海外投融资法律研究

中国金融出版社

责任编辑：贾　真
责任校对：张志文
责任印制：丁淮宾

图书在版编目（CIP）数据

中国企业海外投融资法律研究 / 李志强主编 . —北京：中国金融出版社，2019.1

ISBN 978-7-5049-9925-2

Ⅰ. ①中…　Ⅱ. ①李…　Ⅲ. ①对外投资 — 涉外经济法 — 研究 — 中国 ②融资 — 涉外经济法 — 研究 — 中国　Ⅳ. ① D922.295.4

中国版本图书馆 CIP 数据核字（2018）第 303543 号

中国企业海外投融资法律研究
Zhongguo Qiye Haiwai tou Rongzi Falü Yanjiu

出版发行　中国金融出版社

社址　北京市丰台区益泽路 2 号
市场开发部　（010）63266347，63805472，63439533（传真）
网 上 书 店　http：//www. chinafph. com
（010）63286832，63365686（传真）
读者服务部　（010）66070833，62568380
邮编　100071
经销　新华书店
印刷　北京市松源印刷有限公司
尺寸　169 毫米 ×239 毫米
插页　10
印张　25.25
字数　400 千
版次　2019 年 1 月第 1 版
印次　2019 年 1 月第 1 次印刷
定价　60.00 元
ISBN 978-7-5049-9925-2
如出现印装错误本社负责调换　联系电话（010）63263947

中國企業海外投融資法律研究系列叢書

鄒瑜

全国人大宪法和法律委员会主任李飞（前排右二）和著名法学家李昌道教授（前排左二）等出席高端智库举办的法律研讨会

新西兰前总督（中）及环太平洋律师协会时任主席丹尼斯（左一）与李志强律师在奥克兰合影

环太平洋律师协会 2018 年中理事会后的亚洲区域会议上，泰国副总理 Vissanu Krea-ngam 先生（中）与环太平洋律师协会候任主席弗朗西斯（右一）、副主席李志强（左二）及泰国著名国际律师合影留念

德高望重的司法部原部长邹瑜与李志强律师合影

上海市人民政府市长应勇在第三十次上海市市长国际企业家咨询会议上与环太平洋律师协会副主席李志强一级律师、仲裁员合影留念

全国人大宪法和法律委员会主任委员李飞与环太平洋律师协会候任主席弗朗西斯和副主席李志强律师合影留念

上海市人大常委会主任殷一璀与金茂凯德律师事务所李志强律师合影

出席中国企业赴比荷卢投融资法律研讨会的专家合影，从左到右为李志强、刘辉、Bart、张宁、陈卓夫、周汉民、Peter Corne、钱衡和杨冬雨

民建中央副主席、上海市政协副主席周汉民教授在中国企业赴大洋洲投融资法律研讨会上发表主旨演讲

上海市政协副主席徐逸波在中国企业海外投融资第十次系列法律研讨会上致辞

著名法学家李昌道教授（右）和著名国际法学家周汉民（左）为 G20 律师服务联盟揭牌

著名法学家李昌道教授（右）和上海市商务委员会副主任申卫华（左）为“一带一路”法律研究与服务中心揭牌

上海市司法局局长陆卫东会见环太平洋律师协会主席白培坤并合影，从左到右为张婷婷、忻峰、王协、陆卫东、白培坤、俞卫峰、李志强、陈说

中国十大杰出青年法学家、上海市司法局副局长罗培新教授为东方证券董事会秘书王如富赠中企海外投融资系列法律研究丛书

出席中国企业赴亚洲投融资法律研讨会的专家合影，从左到右为李志强、钱衡、刘晓红、吕南停、王桂埙、张宁、马屹、刘辉、吴根宝、陈功

上海市人民政府侨务办公室主任徐力（左）和著名法学家李昌道（右）教授出席“一带一路”法律研究与服务中心印度站揭牌仪式

著名法学家李昌道教授与金砖国家律师服务联盟中印律师合影

环太平洋律师协会 2017 年伦敦年中理事会上一致表决 2020 年年会花落中国上海，图为与会理事合影

李志强律师在 2016 年环太平洋律师协会布鲁塞尔区域会议上就“一带一路”法治内涵发表英文演讲

“一带一路”法律研究与服务中心英国站的中英两国研究员在伦敦合影

“一带一路”法律研究与服务中心设立意大利站暨金茂凯德律师事务所罗马代表处

2018 年 9 月 28 日，环太平洋律师协会副主席李志强在拉美区域会议上就外国仲裁裁决在中国执行的最新发展发表演讲

参加中国企业赴大洋洲投融资法律研讨会的中外专家合影，从左到右为李志强、叶必丰、钱衡、徐静琳、周伟、申卫华、池洪、黄柏兴、马屹、杨冬雨和钟可慰

“一带一路”法律研究与服务中心阿根廷站和墨西哥站的研究员合影

“一带一路”法律研究与服务中心墨西哥站的中墨两国律师研究员合影

李志强律师在伦敦女王玛丽大学和华东政法大学国际法学院联合主办的人民币国际化——风险与挑战研讨会上发表英文演讲

2017 年 11 月 12 日，环太平洋律师协会在伦敦举行理事会，审议 2020 年年会举办城市，时任中国理事的李志强律师向理事会作陈述发言

时任环太平洋律师协会中国理事李志强律师在伦敦区域会议上就“一带一路”倡议的法治内涵发表演讲

编委会

撰 稿 人 Nicholas Towers（Selborne Chambers）（英国）

Studio Legale Associato Simonetti Persico Scivoletto 律师事务所（意大利）

Luca Simonetti　Corrado Scivoletto　Giuseppe Persico（意大利）

Giuseppe Schiavello　Stibbe 律师事务所　Jan Bogaert（比利时）

Wintertaling 律师事务所（荷兰）

GéraldOriger　Sarah-Nada Arfa（卢森堡）

Hesketh Henry 律师事务所（新西兰）　Hak Jun Lee（新西兰）

Majmudar& Partners 律师事务所（印度）

Prof. Dr. N. L. Mitra, Partner - Fox Mandal & Associates（印度）

Fox Mandal & Associates 律师事务所（印度）

Estudio Beccar Varela 律师事务所（阿根廷）

Rivadeneyra,Treviño Y De Campo, S.C. 律师事务所（墨西哥）

Viktoria Von Mirbach　G. Angelica Juárez（墨西哥）

翻　　译 李　建　欧　龙　陈　说　杨子安　孙晨怡　崔　源　张承宜

邱泽龙　龚嘉驰　潘金涛　游　广　张博文　李屹民

Editorial Committee

Liu Hong　Liu Ying　Xiao Bing　Yang Hui　Lu Quefei　Zhang Xing
Zhang Li　Zhang Zhihong　Zhang Ming　Yu Xiao　Chen Fuyong
Chen Zhichao　Ou Long　Jin Wenzhong　Zheng Yujian　Zhao Siyuan
Zhao Guorong　Zhong Kewei　Jiang Chengjun　Xu Yigang
Huang Jinlun　Huang Baixing　Huang Aiwu　Liang Jiawei　Dong Ying
Chu Qinhua　Pan Yingfang　Bart Kasteleijn　Jan Bogaert　James Jung
L. Augusto Vechio　Vidaur Mora

Author　Nicholas Towers (Selborne Chambers) (UK)
Studio Legale Associato Simonetti Persico Scivoletto Law Firm (Italy)
Luca Simonetti　Corrado Scivoletto　Giuseppe Persico (Italy)
Giuseppe Schiavello
Stibbe Law Firm Jan Bogaert (Belgium)　Wintertaling Law Firm (the Netherlands)
GéraldOriger　Sarah-Nada Arfa (Luxembourg)
Hesketh Henry Law Firm (New Zealand)
Hak Jun Lee (New Zealand)
Majmudar& Partners Law Firm (India)
Prof. Dr. N. L. Mitra, Partner - Fox Mandal & Associates (India)
Fox Mandal & Associates Law Firm (India)
Estudio Beccar Varela Law Firm (Argentina)
Rivadeneyra, Treviño Y De Campo, S.C. Law Firm (Mexico)
Viktoria Von Mirbach　G. Angelica Juárez (Mexico)

Translator　Li Jian　Ou Long　Chen Shuo　Yang Zi'an　Sun Chenyi
Cui Yuan　Zhang Chengyi　Qiu Zelong　Gong Jiachi　Pan Jintao
You Guang　Zhang Bowen　Li Yimin (Adam Li)

总序

习近平总书记提出“新丝绸之路经济带”和“21世纪海上丝绸之路”，即“一带一路”倡议，是在新的全球治理背景下提出的新思维，是推动全球合作发展的新理念。它依靠中国与有关国家既有的双边和多边机制，借助既有的行之有效的区域合作平台，旨在借用古代丝绸之路的历史符号，高举和平发展的旗帜，主动地发展与沿线国家的经济合作伙伴关系，共同打造政治互信、经济融合、文化包容的利益共同体、命运共同体和责任共同体。

2016年5月20日，习近平总书记主持召开了中央全面深化改革领导小组第24次会议，提出要发展涉外法律服务业，要适应构建对外开放型经济新体制要求，围绕服务我国外交工作大局和国家重大发展战略，健全完善扶持保障政策，进一步建设涉外法律服务机构，发展壮大涉外法律服务队伍，健全涉外法律服务方式，提高涉外法律服务质量，稳步推进法律服务业开放，更好地维护我国公民、法人在海外及外国公民、法人在我国的正当权益。

在实施“一带一路”倡议过程中，中国企业“走出去”参与全球投资和融资活动亟须法制保障，亟须优质高效的专业法律服务，亟须开展深入细致的法律研究。由金茂凯德律师事务所“一带一路”法律研究与服务中心发起汇集全球优质法律资源组织相关国家的著名律师和法律专家将相关国家和地区的法律进行分类研究，在此基础上出版中国企业海外投融资法律研究系列丛书，着实做了一件十分有意义的工作。该丛书由蜚声海内外的著名法学家、曾参与《中华人民共和国香港特别行政区基本法》制定工作的李昌道教授审定，国际律师协会和环太平洋律师协会理事李志强一级律师主编，一批国内外知名的专家、学者和企业家、金融家担任该丛书指导和编委。我相信，该丛书的出版发行将有利于我国企业更好地参与国际经济贸易和金融活动，有利于推动中外法律文化交流与合作，也有利于提供我国参与全球治理的智力支持和法制保障。

李飞

2016 年 12 月 28 日

General Preface

The New Silk Road Economic Belt and the 21st Century Maritime Silk Road, i.e. the " Belt and Road "initiative, proposed by Xi Jinping, General Secretary, are new ideas put forward under the background of new global governance and a new concept to promote global cooperation and development. It relies on the existing bilateral and multilateral mechanisms of China and the countries concerned, with the help of existing effective regional cooperation platforms, aims to, under the historical symbols of the ancient Silk Road, hold high the banner of peaceful development, actively develop the economic partnership with countries along the route, work together to create a community of interests, a community of destiny and a community of responsibility of political mutual trust, economic integration, and cultural inclusion.

On May 20, 2016, General Secretary Xi Jinping presided over the 24th meeting of the Central Comprehensive Deepening Reform Leading Group, proposing to develop foreign-related legal services, adapting to the requirements of building a new open economic system, and focusing on serving the overall situation of China's diplomatic work and national major development strategy, develop and improve support policies, further develop foreign-related legal service institutions, develop and strengthen foreign-related legal service teams, improve foreign-related legal service methods, improve the quality of foreign-related legal services, steadily promote the opening of legal services industry and better protect the legitimate rights and interests of our citizens and legal persons and those of foreign citizens and legal persons in China.

In the implementation of the "Belt and Road" Initiative, when the Chinese enterprises going out to participate in the global investment and financing activities, they urgently need legal safeguarding, quality and efficient professional legal services and intensive and detailed legal research. The " Belt and Road " Legal Research and Service Center, established by Jin Mao Partners, published serial books on the overseas investment and financing for Chinese enterprises on the basis of legal research on related different countries and regions by famous lawyers and legal experts from relevant countries under the organization of Jin Mao Partners. It is a pretty meaningful work. The series was examined by professor Li Changdao, the renowned jurist at home and abroad, who has participated in the formulation of the Basic Law of the Hong Kong Special Administrative Region of the People's Republic of China. Li Zhiqiang (Jack Li), councilor of the International Bar Association and Inter-Pacific Bar Association, and grade A lawyer, is the chief editor. A number of experts, scholars and entrepreneurs, financiers acted as directors and editors of the series. The publication of this series, I believe, will help Chinese enterprises to better participate in the international economic, trade and financial activities, facilitate the promotion of the communication of legal and cultural cooperation between China and foreign countries, and help to provide intellectual support and legal guarantee for Chinese participation in global governance.

Li Fei

December 28, 2016

序

《中国企业海外投融资法律研究》是“中国企业海外投融资法律研究”系列丛书第四部著作。本书聚集赴英国、意大利、比利时、荷兰、卢森堡、新西兰、印度、阿根廷和墨西哥投融资法律研究和实务操作，为中国企业赴上述九国进行投融资活动提供了重要的法律参考和法律指南。

英国是西方大国，也是亚洲基础设施投资银行的重要投资参与国，中英两国正在构建面向21世纪的全球全面战略伙伴关系，虽然两国“地处亚欧两端，却长期彼此吸引”。伦敦作为英国首都，是国际金融中心城市，2018年底，沪伦通即将起航，伦敦成为最具活力和最重要的人民币交易中心和离岸人民币市场之一。

古丝绸之路始于中国长安，终于意大利罗马。两千多年后的今天，“一带一路”倡议使这条古丝绸之路再次焕发勃勃生机。作为“一带一路”的交汇点，中企投资马可波罗的故乡方兴未艾。

中国和比利时于1971年建交，比利时是最早同中国建立产业合作基金的国家。2007年两国又签署中比直接股权投资基金谅解备忘录。中比两国科技混委会自1979年成立以来已召开18次会议，签订了涉及农业、能源、地质、环保、生物、信息、纳米科技等领域近400个政府间科技合作项目。

中国和荷兰互联互通关系紧密。荷兰是中国在欧盟第三大贸易伙伴、第一大投资目的地国和第三大外资来源国。荷兰地理位置优越，物流业发达，转口贸易是荷兰对外贸易的主要支点，中国大量出口需要通过荷兰转运至世界其他国家和地区。

卢森堡金融地位特殊，传统优势显著。2018年9月28日，中国建设银行在卢森堡证券交易所发行首笔境外绿色债券，两国金融领域合作广泛。

中国和新西兰于1972年建交，1997年8月，新西兰在西方国家中率先与中国就中国加入世界贸易组织双边市场准入问题达成协议，并于2004年4月正式承认中国完全市场经济地位。2008年4月，中新两国签署自由贸易协定，新西兰成为第一个与中国达成双边自由贸易协定的发达国家。2017年4月，双方举行中新自贸协定首轮升级谈判，新西兰成为首个同中国举行自贸协定升级谈判的西方发达国家。2017年3月，中新签署关于加强“一带一路”倡议合作的安排备忘录，新西兰又成为首个与中国签署类似合作文件的西方发达国家。中国是新西兰第一大货物贸易伙伴、出口市场和进口来源地。

中国和印度于1950年建交，两国是和平共处五项原则这一当代国家法原则的主要提出国。双方在上海合作组织、金砖国家领导人合作机制等多边合作平台开展互利合作。总部位于中国上海的金砖国家新开发银行的首位行长由印度籍人士担任。

中国和阿根廷于1972年建交。2017年5月，阿根廷总统马克里来中国出席首届“一带一路”国际合作高峰论坛，两国建立了全面战略伙伴关系，中国是阿根廷第三大全球贸易伙伴。

中国与墨西哥于1972年建交，中国是墨西哥第二大贸易伙伴，墨西哥是中国在拉丁美洲的第二大贸易伙伴。

中国企业赴上述九国投融资潜力巨大，中国与上述九国法学法律界人士交流合作日益频繁，为我国企业家和金融家提供了优质高效的跨国跨境法律研究与服务。

党的十九大提出了习近平新时代中国特色社会主义思想，丰富和发展了马克思主义中国化最新理论成果。习近平主席指出，中国坚持对外开放的基本国策，坚持打开国门搞建设，积极促进“一带一路”国际合作。“一带一路”倡议是中国世纪大战略，是新时代中国开放的主方向。努力实现政策沟通、设施联通、贸易畅通、资金融通、民心相通，打造国际合作新平台，增添共同发展新动力。中国开放的大门不会关闭，只会越开越大。要以“一带一路”倡议为重点，坚持引进来和“走出去”并重，遵循共商、共建、共享原则，加强创新能力开放合作，形成陆海内外联动、东西双向互济的开放格局。这些重要论断为新时代中国企业“走出去”参与国际投融资活动提供了路径和方向。

“一带一路”倡议需要良好的法制环境，它集政治环境、经济环境、文化环境、社会环境、生态环境等之大成。我们一定要关注多边法律框架、双边国际合作规范，关注法律服务和金融服务的关联性，以及争端解决机制研究等，推动中国企业走向世界，世界企业走向中国，这是我们义不容辞的职责。

1990 年夏，我的研究生、忘年交李志强开始从事律师工作，作为当年首位到民办律师机构工作的上海高校优秀毕业生，他不忘初心，钟爱事业，在为中外当事人提供优质高效法律服务的同时，长期注重前沿课题研究，2001 年李志强当选上海市第八届“十大杰出青年”，成为这一奖项设立以来首位获此殊荣的专职律师。2012 年他获评一级律师。2017 年 10 月李志强受聘担任“上海会议大使”，成为上海 110 名会议大使中首位法律人，积极推动有影响的国际组织来华、来沪举办国际会议。2018 年 3 月在菲律宾首都马尼拉举行的环太平洋律师协会第 28 届年会上李志强当选环太平洋律师协会副主席，成为上海自 1843 年开埠以来首位在国际律师组织中担任领导人的上海律师。李志强律师充分发挥他的特长和优势，广结海内外朋友，数十次在国际多边法律论坛就“一带一路”倡议的法治内涵和中国改革开放 40 年来法治文明的巨大成就发表演讲，传播中国法律制度和法律文化的正能量，并积极研究港澳台地区和各国法律，为中企海外投融资活动提供法治保障。

自习近平主席提出“一带一路”倡议以来，金茂凯德律师事务所开启了“一带一路”法律研究与服务中心，并先后于 2015 年 11 月 28 日和 2018 年 2 月 21 日获准注册“金茂凯德”和“Jin Mao Partners”中英文商标，先后发起成立了 G20 律师服务联盟、金砖国家律师服务联盟、上海合作组织律师服务联盟、金砖 + 律师服务联盟和东盟律师服务联盟，在港澳台地区和五大洲等数十个国家和地区设立了 56 个站点。加强对中国企业海外投融资相关法律研究和实践，将有助于中外法律文化交流互鉴，有利于中外法律人沟通合作，有益于中国企业更好、更稳、更快地融入“一带一路”倡议伟业，也是法律界参与“一带一路”倡议和构建人类命运共同体的伟大实践。

近代以来久经磨难的中华民族迎来了实现中华民族伟大复兴的光明前景，将建成富强民主文明和谐美丽的社会主义现代化强国。作为一名从事法学教学科研、立法执法、法治宣传、法律服务和参政议政等工作已达 60 多年的老法律人，我衷心祝愿更多的法律人投身国家依法治国的宏伟事业，投身“一带一路”倡议的伟大事业，在中华民族伟大复兴的中国梦征程中实现自身的人生梦。

2018 年 10 月 1 日

Preface

Legal Research on Investment and Financing for Chinese Enterprises in the Overseas Countries is the fourth series of *Legal Research on overseas Investment and Financing for Chinese Enterprises*. This book focuses on the legal research and practices in the United Kingdom, Italy, Belgium, the Netherlands, Luxembourg, New Zealand, India, Argentina and Mexico, providing an important legal reference and guidance for the investment and financing in the aforementioned nine countries for Chinese enterprises.

The United Kingdom is a major Western country and an important investment participant in the Asian Infrastructure Investment Bank. China and the United Kingdom are building a global comprehensive strategic partnership for the 21st century. Although the two countries are located at both ends of Asia and Europe, they have long attracted by each other. As the capital of the UK, London is an international financial center. At the end of 2018, Shanghai-London Line is about to open to sail. London has become one of the most dynamic and important RMB trading centers and offshore RMB markets.

The ancient Silk Road began in Chang' an and ended in Rome. Today, more than two thousand years after, the "Belt and Road" Initiative has brought this ancient Silk Road to life again. As the meeting point of the "Belt and Road", the hometown of Marco Polo, is in the ascendant with the investment of Chinese enterprises.

China and Belgium established diplomatic relations in 1971, and Belgium was the first country to establish an industrial cooperation fund with China. In 2007, the two countries signed a memorandum of understanding on the China-Belgium Direct Equity Investment Fund.

China and the Netherlands have close interconnections. The location of the Netherlands is excellent with developed the logistics industry.The transit trade is the main support of the foreign trade of the Netherlands. A large number of Chinese exports need to be transferred to other countries and regions through the

Netherlands.

Luxembourg has a special financial position and a significant traditional advantage. On September 28, 2018, China Construction Bank issued the first overseas green bond on the Luxembourg Stock Exchange. The two countries have extensive cooperation in the financial sector.

China and New Zealand established diplomatic relations since 1972. In August 1997, New Zealand is the first in reaching an agreement with China on China's accession to the World Trade Organization bilateral market. In April 2004, it officially recognized China's full market economy status. In April 2008, China and New Zealand signed a free trade agreement, and New Zealand became the first developed country to reach a bilateral free trade agreement with China. In April 2017, the two sides held the first round of the China-New Zealand FTA negotiations, and New Zealand became the first western developed country to hold a free trade agreement with China. In March 2017, China and New Zealand signed a memorandum of understanding on strengthening the cooperation of the "Belt and Road" Initiative, and New Zealand became the first Western developed country to sign similar cooperation documents with China. China is the largest trading partner, export market and source of imports of New Zealand.

China and India established diplomatic relations in 1950, and the two countries are the main proposing countries of the principle of peaceful coexistence, the principle of contemporary inter-country law. The two sides will carry out mutually beneficial cooperation in multilateral cooperation platforms such as the Shanghai Cooperation Organization and the BRICS Leadership Cooperation Mechanism. The first president of the BRICS New Development Bank, headquartered in Shanghai, China, is an Indian.

China and Argentina established diplomatic relations in 1972. Macri, President of Argentine, came to China to attend the first "Belt and Road" Form for International Cooperation in May 2017. The two countries have established a comprehensive strategic partnership. China is the third largest global trading partner of Argentina.

China and Mexico established diplomatic relations in 1972, China is the second largest trading partner of Mexico, and Mexico is China's second largest trading partner in Latin America.

Chinese enterprises have great potential for investment and financing in the above-mentioned nine countries. China has increasingly exchanged and cooperated with the legal and law circles of the above-mentioned nine countries, providing high-quality and efficient cross-border legal research and services for Chinese entrepreneurs and financiers.

The 19th National Congress of the Communist Party of China put forward "Xi Jinping's Thought on Socialism with Chinese Characteristics for a New Era", enriching and developing the latest theoretical achievements of Marxism in China. President Xi Jinping pointed out that China adheres to the basic national policy of opening to the outside world, insists on opening the country to engage in construction, and actively promotes the international cooperation of the "Belt and Road" Initiative. The "Belt and Road" Initiative is an important strategy in the new century and the main direction of China's opening up policy in the new era. China strives to achieve policy communication, facility connectivity, trade smooth, financing and people connectivity,create a new platform for international cooperation, and the door opening to the world will never close with the new power of common development. Quite contrary, it will only open wider. We must focus on the development of the "Belt and Road" Initiative, adhere to the principle of bringing in and "going out", follow the principle of joint construction and sharing, strengthen the open cooperation of innovation capabilities, and form an open pattern of linkage between the land and the sea and mutual assistance between the east and the west. These important theories provide a path and direction for Chinese enterprises to go global to participate in international investment and financing activities in the new era.

The "Belt and Road" Initiative requires a good legal environment, which integrates political, economic, cultural, social and ecological environments. We must pay attention to the multilateral legal framework, bilateral international cooperation norms, pay attention to the relevance of legal services and financial services, and research on dispute resolution mechanisms, etc. It is our unshakable duty to promote Chinese enterprises to the world and world enterprises to China.

In the summer of 1990, Jack Li(Li Zhiqiang), my graduate student and bosom friend, began his work as a lawyer. As the first outstanding graduate from Shanghai University to work as a lawyer in private law firm, he did not forget his true heart and love his career. While providing high-quality and efficient legal services for Chinese and foreign parties, he paid great attention to the research on frontier issues. In 2001, he was elected as the eighth Top Ten Outstanding Youth in Shanghai, becoming the first full-time lawyer to receive this honor since the establishment of this award. In 2012 he was awarded a grade A lawyer. He was appointed as the Shanghai Conference Ambassador in October 2017, the first lawyer among the 110 conference ambassadors in Shanghai. He actively promoted influential international associations to hold international conferences in China or Shanghai. He was elected as the Vice President of the Inter-Pacific Bar Association at the 28th annual meeting and conference in March 2018, the first Shanghai lawyer to become the leader of the international bar associations since the opening up of Shanghai in 1843. He gives full play to his strengths and advantages, and makes friends from home and abroad. He gave speeches dozens of times in the international multilateral legal forum on the rule of law of the "Belt and Road" Initiative and the great achievements of the rule of law in China's 40 years of reform and opening up policy. He activelydisseminate the positive energy of the legal system and legal culture, and actively study the laws of Hong Kong SAR, Macao SAR and Taiwan region and countries to provide legal protection for the overseas investment and financing activities of Chinese enterprises.

Since President Xi Jinping proposed the Belt Road Initiative, Jin Mao Partners has established the "Belt and Road" Initiative Legal Research and Service Center, registered the Chinese and English trademark of " 金茂凯德 " and "Jin Mao Partners" on November 28, 2015 and February 21, 2018 respectively, establishment of the G20 Lawyer Service Alliance, the BRICS Lawyer Service Alliance, the Shanghai

Cooperation Organization Lawyer Service Alliance, the BRICS + Lawyer Service Alliance and the ASEAN Lawyer Service Alliance, and established up to 56 stations in Hong Kong, Macao and Taiwan and the five continents. Strengthening the legal research and practice on overseas investment and financing of Chinese enterprises will help the communication and mutual understanding of Chinese and foreign legal cultural, facilitate the Chinese and foreign legal persons to communicate and cooperate, and help Chinese enterprises to integrate better into the Belt Road Initiative smoothly. It is also a great practice for the legal industry to participate in the "Belt and Road" Initiative and build a community of shared future for human.

The Chinese nation, which has been suffering since the modern times, has ushered in a bright future for realizing the great rejuvenation of the Chinese nation, and will build a strong, democratic, civilized, harmonious and beautiful modern socialist country. As a law senior, being engaged in law teaching and research, legislation, law enforcement, propaganda of rule of law, legal services, and political participation and suggestion, I sincerely hope that more law people will join the national grand undertaking of governing the country according to law and join the great cause of the "Belt and Road" Initiative to realize the dream of life in the development of Chinese dream of the great rejuvenation of the Chinese nation.

Li Changdao

October, 1, 2018

目 录

Contents

“一带一路”领航篇

“一带一路”创新之路与人工智能

李昌道

在从事法律工作的许多年里，我书写了许多故事，我当过故事的主角，也做过陪衬的绿叶。我不得不说，许多事情是自己应该做的，很多是被人安排做的。但我最想说的是，这些工作，大多也都是我自己乐于做的。一个法律工作者，仅仅从业远远不够，只有敬业、乐业才能成就一番事业。现在有些经过归纳、提炼、升华以后的我人生的故事，提高了我的形象，每每听闻这些话语，我既为自己而高兴，也难免有点惭愧。

其实，如果一定要为我戴一顶帽子的话，我希望加的是这三个字：法学家。我就是一个法学家，而且法学家面前还要加两个字：上海。因为我做的许多工作，都是希望为上海的法律实务和理论的结合，实实在在地做一些事。我一直觉得，只有虚心学习、学以致用、与时俱进的法律工作者，才能真正为社会作出杰出的贡献。我固然是一名老师，但又何尝不是一位虚心求学的学子呢？陷于自我满足、自我陶醉的人，终究难以获得长足的发展。只有认清自己、认清实际、认清趋势的人，才能真正把握住核心问题、关键问题。我认为，当前就有许多急需探讨的新兴法律课题，“一带一路”框架下的人工智能法律问题就是其一。

2017年5月，国家主席习近平在“一带一路”国际合作高峰论坛开幕式上发表主旨演讲时强调，要将“一带一路”建成创新之路。习近平主席明确指出，创新是推动发展的重要力量。要坚持创新驱动发展，进一步发展在数字经济、人工智能、纳米技术、量子计算机等前沿领域的合作，推动大数据、云计算、智慧城市建设，努力构建成21世纪的数字丝绸之路。“一带一路”沿线的建设，不仅是传统商贸往来的关系，还有新兴信息技术的交融，并且，这两者之间必将相互依托、共同发展。

技术在发展，法律也需要进步。针对人工智能当前实践情况以及未来可能发生的问题，我愿作一些阐述。

首先，人工智能将会对很多法学的重要原理产生一定影响。我举一个例子，今年年初，在美国亚利桑那州，无人驾驶汽车撞死了人，到现在还没有判决。在法学领域里有一个很重要的原理就是无罪推定，以及谁主张谁举证的原则。那么，无人驾驶汽车如何适用无罪推定呢？对于人工智能是否要采取无罪推定呢？我们都知道，无罪推定在罗马法的时候已经制定了，在国法大全上也都确定。现在这一原则面临颠覆性的情况变化，其中是非曲直，值得我们探究。

其次，人工智能对法律的完备充实提出了更高的要求。我们过去讲的法律，从罗马法开始都是自然人，现在有机械人、机器人了，行为主体就发生了变化，对此是否要制定法律呢？如何调整法律呢？有材料声称欧盟在2018年底要召开会议，讨论机器人的权利法案。不同主体之间的异同，如何在法律上更好地得到体现，也需要长期广泛的研究。

再次，人工智能还会对法律工作者的结构产生影响。众所周知，任何一项工作包括律师也好，都有一个基础和中层、顶层的工作，最基础的工作，比如法律、案例、咨询、审查，那都是基础性的。这些工作很多地方的事务所都已经可以或者即将可以由人工智能完成了。针对这种越来越近的深刻变化，我们整个法律服务业也需要早做准备。有些中层的工作，比如诉讼胜负的决策，还有诉讼策略的选择，很多地方也已经通过人工智能来做了。此外，关于顶层工作的问题，据说有的地方已经做过试验，机器人跟名律师法庭辩论，和下围棋一样，结果怎么样呢？还是机器人赢了。所以现在有许多人讲，有了人工智能律师就不要了，为什么？因为都能够用人工智能做了。我对此持反对意见，人工智能是我们律师新的工具，而不能代替我们律师。如何利用、善用人工智能技术的同时保护律师的传统竞争优势，又是一个与我们法律从业者自身息息相关的话题。

最后，我还想对金茂凯德律师事务所的创始合伙人李志强先生为建设“一带一路”法律服务事业，尤其是针对“一带一路”中新兴法律问题的探究所作出的贡献表示感谢。正是许许多多保持谦虚、不懂就学、与时俱进、积极奉献的中国法律人，才使我国的法律服务事业紧紧贴合人民渴求、社会需求、国家要求，真正做到了造福于大众。

祝愿各位朋友，和中国的法律服务事业一样，时刻进步，勇攀高峰，收获满满。

（本文是著名法学家、原上海市人民政府参事室主任、上海市高级人民法院副院长、上海仲裁委员会副主任、上海市法学会副会长、复旦大学法学院院长、九三学社中央法制委员会顾问李昌道教授在“一带一路”法律研究与服务中心2018年中秋国庆茶话会暨《法学宗师李昌道》首映式上的演讲）

The "Belt and Road", Hand in Hand

李志强（Jack Li）

This ideal and plan is the "Belt and Road" initiative.

Some of you here may not know much about the "Belt and Road". It refers to the Silk Road Economic Belt and the 21st Century Maritime Silk Road, a cooperation initiative proposed by the Chinese president in 2013. The initiative invites countries, with the help of established and effective regional cooperation platforms, to take good advantage of the existing bilateral and multilateral mechanisms, actively develop economic cooperation partnership with the countries along the route peacefully, and work together to build political trust, economic integration, cultural inclusion of interests' community, destiny community and responsibility community.

Although the Belt and Road has been proposed for only a few years, it possesses hundreds of years of history and inheritance. The Silk Road was an ancient land trade route that originated in ancient China, connecting Asia, Africa and Europe. Its initial role was to transport goods such as silk and porcelain produced in ancient China, and later it became an important way of economic, political and cultural exchanges between the East and the West in ancient times.

In 1877, the German geographer Richthofen named this road "the Silk road" because it worked as the way of the silk trade between China, India and the central Asia from 114 BC to 127 AD. This name was soon accepted by academia and the public, and formally used. After that, in another book the Ancient Silk Road between

China and Syria, which was published at the beginning of the 20th century, German historian Haulmann further extended the Silk Road to the western Mediterranean Sea and Asia minor, based on newly discovered archaeological materials. It defined the basic connotation of the Silk Road, that is, it was the channel of land trade connecting China with South Asia, West Asia, Europe and North Africa through Central Asia in ancient times.

It could be said that hundreds of years ago, along the way, there have been a number of travelers and caravans who have made far-reaching contributions for the East-West cultural and economic exchanges. At that time, it was with such a hard, precious bond that gave the people of the countries far away from each other the chance to understand and learn from each other, thus promoting the development of their own civilizations.

Time flies, after hundreds of years, today we have been able to use all kinds of technology to communicate freely, and many ancient roads have been abandoned. However, the“Belt and Road” still has a strong vitality, because the new era of the world pattern has given it a unique significance and new role. In this ever-changing era, the historical accumulation of the “ Belt and Road” has taken on a new meaning. It is not just for the benefit of some countries along one route, but for the development of a broader, freer, mutually beneficial new model of international cooperation.

Complex and profound changes are taking place in the world today. The deep impact of the international financial crisis continues to manifest, the world economy recovers slowly, development is divided and the pattern of international investment and trade, including the rules of multilateral investment trade are in the process of profound readjustment. The development problems disturbing all countries are still severe. Especially in recent years, the trade frictions between China and the United States have aroused great concern from the international community, and both sides have taken a lot of economic and trade restrictions on each other.

I know that many people are discussing the right and wrong. I just want to quote what Premier Zhu Rongji said in 1999 to show my view. When the Chinese former premier visited Washington, D.C., he told President Clinton: There is no problem between China and the United States which cannot be resolved through friendly negotiation. There do exist some divergence between us. But only friends who can show different opinions are the best friends. Only a candid friend is a real friend. I believe that the current relationship between China and the United States is a microcosm of the world international relations. We should always bear in mind that confrontation can only hurt both sides, and only win-win is the best way. The "Belt and Road" is such a road to resolve contradictions and promote common development.

The following figure and data from 14 aspects makes a vivid demonstration to the fruitful outcome that the Belt and Road has achieved:

1. Up to now, more than 100 countries and international organizations have actively supported and participated in the construction of the "Belt and Road". Resolutions of UN General Assembly and the UN Security Council have also included the content of the "Belt and Road".

2. Up to now, with 103 countries and international organizations have signed 118 cooperation agreements under Belt and Road initiative.

3. More than 30 countries in China have signed capacity cooperation agreements.

4. Together with more than 20 countries along the "Belt and Road", 75 overseas cooperation zones have been built.

5. Chinese companies have invested more than US$70 billion, creating 250000 jobs and 2.3 billion US dollars in taxes.

6. The Asian Infrastructure Investment Bank is officially operating and 87 countries and regions are actively involved.

7. China annually sponsors 10000 new students from countries along the "Belt and Road" to study in China.

8. From January to April 2018, bilateral trade volume involving China and countries along the "Belt and Road" has exceeded US$389.1 billion, which has increased by 19.2% compared to last year.

9. From January to April 2018, the direct investment brought out by Chinese enterprises towards the countries along the “Belt and Road” was US$4.67 billion, which has increased by 17.3% compared to last year. The turnover of foreign contracted projects was US$24.2 billion, whose year-on-year increase reaches to 27.7%.

10. The “Belt and Road” countries invested more than US$8.2 billion to China in 2017, a year-on-year increase of 25%.

11. According to the statistics of the China Railway Corporation, by the end of August 2018, the China-Europe trains have operated with more than 10000 lines, reaching 15 countries and 43 cities in Europe. The total value of goods shipped each year increased from less than $600 million in 2011 to the $14.5 billion in current year.

12. In 2017, China signed 4 new free trade agreements and accumulated 16 free trade agreements involving 24 countries and regions. In 2018, 10 free trade agreement negotiations will be promoted. As an important starting point for the “Belt and Road” economic and trade cooperation, the building-up of overseas economic and trade cooperation zones have been promoting. At present, Chinese enterprises have promoted 75 overseas economic and trade cooperation zones along the “Belt and Road” countries, with a total investment of more than 27 billion US dollars, attracting nearly 3500 enterprises in the zone.

13. 356 international road passenger and cargo transportation routes has been operated, and 403 direct flights were carried out reaching to 43 countries along the “Belt and Road”—which means approximately 4500 direct flights per week.

In my opinion, to truly enjoy the benefits of the“Belt and Road”, the following are essential.

Firstly, we should further develop open, inclusive regional cooperation system. I believe that only by opening up can we discover opportunities, seize them well, create opportunities on our own initiative, and finally achieve our country’s goal. The “Belt and Road” initiative is to turn the world’s opportunities into China’s, China’s opportunities into the world’s. It is based on the perception and vision that the "Belt and Road" is open oriented, aiming at solving the economic growth and balance problem by promoting the orderly and free flow of economic elements, strengthening connectivity in infrastructure such as transport, energy and networks; improving allocation of resources and the deep integration of the market and developing a greater scope, higher level, deeper regional cooperation, in order to create an open, inclusive, balanced framework of regional economic cooperation.

Secondly, we shall insist on the definition of the "Belt and Road" platform as a pragmatic cooperation and refuse to turn it into a geopolitical tool for either side. The spirit of "peaceful cooperation, openness and tolerance, mutual learning and mutual benefit, mutual benefit and win-win" has become the historical wealth shared by mankind. The "Belt and Road" is an important initiative of the present era put forward by adhering to this spirit and principle. By strengthening the all-round and multilevel exchange and cooperation among the countries concerned, we can give full play to the potential and comparative advantages of each country, forming a mutually beneficial and win-win regional interest community, a destiny community and a responsible community. In this mechanism, countries are equal participants, contributors and beneficiaries. Therefore, the "Belt and Road" emphasizes the equality and peace from the beginning. Equality is an important international standard that China adheres to and a key foundation for the construction of Belt and Road. Only cooperation based on this can be sustained and mutually beneficial. Equality and inclusiveness lightens the resistance, enhances the efficiency of co-construction and helps international cooperation to take root and the construction of the "Belt and Road" is inseparable from the peaceful international environment and regional environment. Peace is the essential attribute of the construction, and it is also a pivotal factor to ensure its smooth progress. This determines that the "Belt and Road" should not and cannot become a tool of great power politics or repeat the old geopolitical game.

Thirdly, we shall attach importance to the joint construction and sharing of joint development initiatives. The "Belt and Road" construction is carried out through specific projects on the basis of bilateral or multilateral linkage, It is a development initiatives and planning resulted from full policy communication, strategic docking and market operations. Joint Communique of the Leaders Round table of the "Belt and Road" Forum for International Cooperation emphasized the basic principles of building the "Belt and Road", including the market principle, that is to fully understand the role of the market and the main role of enterprises, to ensure that the government plays an appropriate role. Government procurement procedures should be open, transparent, and non-discriminatory. It can be seen that the core main body and supporting force of the "Belt and Road" construction is not in the government, but in the enterprise. The fundamental method is to follow the market law and realize the interests of all parties involved through the market-oriented operation mode. The government exerts the leading and service function of constructing platform, establishing mechanism and policy guidance.

Fourthly, the "Belt and Road" is not a substitute of the existing mechanisms. The comparative advantage of relevant countries is different but complementary.

Some countries are rich in energy resources but poor in depth of development, some have abundant labor force but lack of job opportunities, some have broad market space but weak industrial foundation, and others have strong demand for infrastructure construction but lack of funds. Our country is the second largest economy in the world, with the largest foreign exchange reserves in the world, more and more superior industries, rich experience in infrastructure construction, strong equipment manufacturing capability, good quality, high performance-to-price ratio, capital, technology, talent, management and other comprehensive advantages. This provides a realistic need and a great opportunity for China and the other parties to achieve industrial docking and complementary advantages.

Therefore, the core content of the "Belt and Road" is to promote infrastructure construction and interconnection, to connect policies and development strategies of various countries, to deepen pragmatic cooperation, to promote coordinated and coordinated development and to achieve common prosperity.

It is clear that the "Belt and Road" is not intended to replace existing regional cooperation mechanisms, but to complement existing ones. In fact, the construction of the "Belt and Road" has been in the cooperation with the Russian-Eurasian Economic Union, the development plan of Indonesia's global ocean fulcrum, the economic development strategy of Kazakhstan's bright road, the Mongolian grassland path initiative, the European Investment Plan of the European Union and the Egypt's Suez Canal Corridor development plan, forming a number of landmark projects, such as Sino-Kazakhstan (Lianyungang) logistics cooperation base construction. As one of the achievements in the construction of the economic corridor of the new Eurasian Continental Bridge, the logistics cooperative base of China and Kazakhstan (Lianyungang) has initially realized the seamless docking of deep water port, ocean-going trunk line, China-EU railway and logistics station. This project and Kazakhstan "Bright Road" development strategy is highly compatible. President of Kazakhstan's "Bright Road" party, Peru Asev, said that the "Belt and Road" initiative effectively promoted the economic development of Kazakhstan and the entire Central Asian region in the connection with the "Bright Road" new economic policy. It has opened up broad space and created more opportunities for countries to cooperate in economic, cultural and other fields.

Finally, the construction of the "Belt and Road" should attach importance to the development of cross-border legal services. With the deepening of the "Belt and Road" construction, the amount of investment and financing is increasing. The demand of the legal services about the project compliance and dispute resolution of is also expanding.

As the founder of Jinmao Partners in Shanghai, I also feel the various opportunities of legal affairs in the development of the "Belt and Road". As one of the main force of the "Belt and Road" legal service, my firm has set up more than 50 the "Belt and Road" legal research and service centers since its establishment, including Mexico Station and Italy Station in order to promote the "Belt and Road" legal service construction and broaden the channels of legal exchanges. Just a few weeks ago, I also organized a seminar on Chinese companies' investment and financing in Russia. I hope that in the near future, I will be able to hold more meetings with all of you here.

In addition, the Chinese government also strongly supports the construction of cross-border legal services. For example, recently, eight Shanghai government departments, including the Municipal Judicial Bureau, Development and Reform Commission, Economic and Commercial Commission, Education Commission, Foreign Affairs Office has jointly issued Opinions on the Implementation of the Development of Foreign-related Legal Services in Shanghai. The policy document clearly states: “We strongly support the convening of The Inter-Pacific Bar Association the in Shanghai in 2020 to attract overseas enterprises to Shanghai for providing a new opportunity for development.” Ladies and Gentlemen, the development of cross-border legal services is always done by two or more countries together, and we are waiting for you to join us.

Facts speak louder than words. Although the “Belt and Road” initiative has been around for only five years, people from China and other countries, both East and West, have produced remarkable results.

In the area of people-to-people exchanges, the Chinese Government and the countries concerned carry out various cultural cooperation projects, such as the year of Culture, the year of Tourism, the Festival of Arts, and other cultural cooperation projects. Each year, the Chinese Government provides 10000 government scholarships. Nearly half of the overseas students studying in China come from countries along the “Belt and Road”.

Ladies and Gentlemen, the “Belt and Road” is a peaceful and friendly path to promote common development and achieve common prosperity. We welcome everyone from all over the world to join us to paint a bright future for the world.

（此文是李志强律师在 2018 年 9 月 20 日环太平洋律师协会洛杉矶北美区域会议上的主旨演讲）

New Trends in Enforcement of Arbitral Awards in China

李志强（Jack Li）

The "Belt and Road" initiative is likely to significantly boost outbound investment by Chinese companies and their trading partners in their the "Belt and Road" investments. How to enforce foreign arbitral awards in the people's Republic of China (PRC) will become a particularly important issue.

In 1987, China joined the New York Convention on the Recognition and Enforcement of Foreign Arbitral Awards (New York Convention). On April 10, 1987, the Supreme People's Court of China (Supreme Court) issued Notice of the Supreme People's Court on Implementing the Convention on the Recognition and Enforcement of Foreign Arbitral Awards Acceded to by China (the Supreme Law Notice), describing the issues related to the enforcement of foreign arbitral awards under the New York Convention. On December 26, 2017, the Supreme People's Court promulgated Relevant Provisions of the Supreme People's Court on Issues concerning Applications for Verification of Arbitration Cases under Judicial Review (Law [2017] No. 21, hereinafter referred to as "Provisions on Applications for Verification of Arbitration Cases") and Provisions of the Supreme People's Court on Several Issues concerning Trying Cases of Arbitration-Related Judicial Review (Law [2017] No. 22) (hereinafter referred to as "Judicial Review Provisions"). The above two provisions are the judicial interpretations of the application of the arbitration law and the judicial review of arbitrations issued by the Supreme People's Court in the form of normative documents since the promulgation of the law, named Interpretation on the Application of the Arbitration Law of the people's Republic of China (interpretation of Law [2006] No. 7) (hereinafter referred to as "Judicial interpretation of the Arbitration Law") in 2006.

On February 23, 2018, the Supreme People's Court issued three judicial interpretations on implementation issues. Among them, Provisions of the Supreme People's Court on Several Issues Concerning the Handling of Cases in the Arbitration of Arbitral Awards by the People's Court (hereinafter referred to as the "Rules for the Implementation of the Awards"), and Regulations on Reporting and Verification of Arbitration Judicial Review Cases just issued two months ago, together with the Arbitration Law and its judicial interpretation, jointly depict China's regulatory framework for the revoked and unimplemented arbitral awards. As stated by the Supreme People's Court at the press conference, As stated by the Supreme People's Court at the press conference, arbitration has become contractual, autonomous, non-governmental and quasi-judicial because of its own characteristics, such as autonomy, flexibility, convenience, and as well, it is final and binding. It has become an important way to resolve disputes. The Supreme People's Court has intensively issued relevant judicial interpretations, which reflects judicial supervision and support for arbitration.

Jinmao Partners, as a legal service center in the first batch of professional service trade units in Shanghai confirmed by the Shanghai Municipal Commission of Commerce and the Shanghai Municipal Bureau of Justice, since the establishment of the "Belt and Road Legal Research and Service Center" on February 18, 2016, has been committed to the "Belt and Road" foreign-related legal services. We have held a series of seminars on overseas investment and financing, and invited a large number of well-known entrepreneurs, financiers and legal experts from home and abroad to attend, which greatly promoted the exchange and cooperation between Chinese and foreign entrepreneurs, financiers and legal experts. In addition, the "Belt and Road" facilitation team, led by founding partner Jack Li, the first class lawyer in China, has visited overseas many times and has established long-term friendly cooperative relations with numerous top law firms in countries along the "Belt and Road" line. At the same time, Jinmao Partners has set up workstations or representative offices in Japan, the United States, India, Malaysia, Belgium, the Netherlands, Luxembourg, Italy, Brazil, New Zealand, Australia, Argentina, and Thailand, and accumulated a large amount of foreign legal practical experience. This paper selects the substantive and procedural issues related to the recognition and enforcement of arbitral awards in the three provisions, and briefly analyzes the new judicial direction reflected in these three new judicial interpretations and regulations.

1. Compliance with New York Convention Enforcement Obligations to Create a Quality Rule of Law Environment in the Free-trade Pilot Area

On September 23, 2005, Shanghai Golden Landmark and Siemens signed a contract for the supply of goods by tender, stipulating that Siemens should ship the equipment to the site by February 15, 2006 and disputes shall be submitted to the Singapore International Arbitration Centre for arbitration. The two parties have disputes in the performance of the contract. Shanghai Golden Landmark filed an arbitration at the Singapore International Arbitration Center to terminate the contract and stop paying the purchase price. In the arbitration process, Siemens filed a counterclaim requesting payment of all purchases, interest and compensation for other losses. In November 2011, the Singapore International Arbitration Center issued a ruling rejecting the arbitration request of Shanghai Golden Landmark and supporting the arbitration counterclaim of Siemens. Shanghai Golden Landmark paid a portion of the amount, and the outstanding payment and interest under the arbitral award were RMB 5133872.3. Based on the Convention on the Recognition and Enforcement of Foreign Arbitral Awards, the New York Convention, Siemens has requested the first Intermediate people's Court of Shanghai to recognize and implement the arbitral award made by the Singapore International Arbitration

Center. Shanghai Golden Landmark defended that the arbitral award should not be recognized and enforced on the grounds that both parties are Chinese legal persons and that the place of performance of the contract is also in China, so the civil relationship involved in the case has no foreign factors. The agreement to submit the dispute to a foreign arbitration agency is null and void, and recognition and enforcement of the award would be contrary to China's public policy.

After reporting to the Supreme people's Court and receiving a reply, the first Intermediate people's Court of Shanghai concluded that, in accordance with the provisions of the New York Convention, the arbitration award involved should be recognized and enforced. Looking at the actual situation of the subject and performance characteristics involved in the contract of this case, according to the fifth provisions of Article 1 of Interpretations of the Supreme People's Court on Several Issues Concerning Application of the Law of the People's Republic of China on Choice of Law for Foreign-Related Civil Relationships (I), it can be concluded that the contractual relationship is a foreign-related civil legal relationship. The specific reasons are as follows: First, although Siemens and Shanghai Golden Landmark are both Chinese legal persons, their registered places are all within the Shanghai Free Trade Zone, and their nature is wholly foreign-owned and are closely related to their foreign investors. Second, the characteristics of the performance of the contract in this case have foreign factors. The equipment involved in the case was first transported from outside China to the free trade experimental area for bonded supervision, and then, according to the need for the performance of the contract, timely customs clearance and customs clearance procedures were carried out, and transferred from the region to the outside. At this point, the import procedures have been completed, so the transfer of the subject matter of the contract also has certain characteristics of international goods sale. The arbitration clause in the case is valid. And the content of the arbitral award does not conflict with China's public policy, so the recognition and enforcement of the arbitral award is not contrary to Chinese public policy. At the same time, the ruling also pointed out that Shanghai Golden Landmark actually participated in the entire arbitration proceedings, argued that the arbitration clause is valid, and partially fulfilled the obligations established in the award after the award was made. In this case it claims to reject the application for recognition and enforcement of the arbitration award involved in the case on the grounds that the arbitration clause is invalid does not conform to the generally accepted legal principles of estoppel, good faith, fairness and reasonableness, so its claim should not be claimed.

The Pilot Free Trade Zone (FATZ) is the basic platform, important node and strategic support for China to promote the "Belt and Road" construction. Connecting international practices, supporting the development of free trade pilot zones, improving international arbitration and other non-litigation dispute resolution mechanisms will help strengthen the international credibility and influence of the rule of law in China. The ruling of this case is based on the reform of the investment and trade facilitation in the Pilot Free Trade Zone. In the case of contract disputes between wholly foreign-owned enterprises in the Pilot Free Trade Zone, the identification of foreign-related factors is emphasized, and it confirmed that the arbitration clause is valid and clarified that "anti-expression is prohibited". This ruling fulfills the "New York Convention" concept of "favorable to the implementation of the ruling" and reflects China's basic position of abide by international treaty obligations. At the same time, the case promoted the breakthrough reform of enterprises in the Pilot Free Trade Zone to choose overseas arbitration. The judicial experience in this case can be replicated and be promoted is a successful example in the Pilot Free Trade Zone. In January 2017, the Supreme People's Court issued the Opinions of the Supreme People's Court on Providing Judicial Guarantee for the Building of Pilot Free Trade Zones, stipulating that if the foreign-funded enterprises registered in the Pilot Free Trade Zone have agreed to submit commercial disputes to the extraterritorial arbitration, the relevant arbitration agreement shall not be invalidated only on the grounds that the dispute does not have foreign-related factors. It also stipulates that if one or both parties are foreign-invested enterprises registered in the Pilot Free Trade Zone, and agrees to submit the commercial disputes to the extraterritorial arbitration, People's court shall not support the claim if one party submits the dispute to an extraterritorial arbitration and claims that the arbitration agreement is invalid after the relevant award has been made, or the other party does not object to the validity of the arbitration agreement in the arbitration proceedings, and claims that the arbitration agreement is invalid on the grounds that the arbitration agreement is invalid after the relevant award has been made. This helps to build a more stable and predictable the "Belt and Road" legal environment for doing business.

2. Create a System of the Outsider's Applying for Not Executing the Arbitral Award

Articles 9 and 18 of the Several Provisions of the Higher People's Court of Guangdong Province on Handling Cases about a Petition for Not Enforcing an Arbitral Award (for Trial Implementation) refer to the system for the third party to apply for refusal to execute an arbitral award.

The Zhuhai Intermediate People's Court of Guangdong Province initiated the system for the applicant to apply for refusal to execute the arbitral award, and clarified the following relief procedures: if the outsider files an enforcement objection during the enforcement of the case, if the Executive Board has examined that the arbitral award may be wrong, the objection will be submitted to the Judicial Committee for discussion; if the Judicial Committee considers that the ruling violates the public interest and it is necessary to initiate the examination mechanism, the filing court shall decide to file the case, and the fourth court shall be responsible for the examination; if the fourth court considers that the arbitration award is wrong after examination, it shall not enforce the arbitral award. The basis for the establishment of the system is Article 237, paragraph 3, of the The Civil Procedure Law of the People's Republic of China, "if the people's court determines that the enforcement of the award is contrary to the public interest, it shall not enforce it." From the start and connection of the procedure, the standard of non-enforcement, and the handling of the ruling, the system has made a clear breakthrough in applying the law.

In the No.203 case, Jiangsu Higher People's Court also similarly applied the third paragraph of Article 58 of the Arbitration Law of the People's Republic of China and the second paragraph of Article 237 of the Civil Procedure Law. It stipulates that the arbitral award shall be judicially examined ex officio and that the ruling shall not be deemed to be effective if it violates the public interest.

The application for non-executive system by outsiders is an innovative provision made by the Supreme People's Court to prevent false arbitration. However, there are certain drawbacks.

First of all, Arbitration Law and Civil Procedure Law stipulate that the subject who applies for revocation and non-enforcement can only be the parties. The above regulations conflict with the current law of our country.

Secondly, the provision does not limit the scope of the subject of the outsider who has the right to apply for non-enforcement. The provisions on the conditions for the non-existing application of the case are too principled and broad, which may cause abuse of rights by persons unrelated to the arbitration case, delay the enforcement of procedures, result in a decline in the efficiency of judicial and arbitration, and affect the credibility of the court and arbitration.

Finally, according to the theory of res judicata, the res judicata has relativity. Even if there is an effective judging document, it does not affect the third party to sue separately, and defends its own rights and interests in accordance with the provisions of the substantive law, not necessarily by negating the validity of an effective judicial instrument. In addition, from the practical experience of civil litigation, the effect of the third party's revocation is not satisfactory.

It is undeniable that in practice there is a situation in which the interests of the outsiders in the case are damaged by false arbitration cases, and this phenomenon really needs judicial supervision by the court to protect the interested parties. China's criminal law also provides corresponding provisions for false litigation and arbitration. After the above-mentioned judicial interpretation is made, it is also necessary to strengthen the understanding of the relevant theories such as res judicata, follow up and improve the supporting system, and further clarify the identification and corresponding conditions of the subject identity who applies for not executing the arbitral award. Whether the system can effectively combat false arbitration is still left to the test of time.

3. Uniform Review Criteria for Non-enforceable Cases

The Provision on the Enforcement of the Award is more detailed than the Interpretation of the Arbitration Law and other relevant provisions in respect of the statutory reasons for non-enforcement of the arbitral award. We believe that although both non-enforcement and revocation are judicial reviews of arbitral awards and the two systems have the same ground, the emphasis should be different. The revocation of an arbitral award is a review of the arbitral award and the impartiality of the arbitral proceedings. The court may conduct a comprehensive review or a formal review. However, the non-enforcement of the arbitral award is to deal with the enforcement objection of the executor, whose purpose is to avoid the enforcement error, and should be more inclined to safeguard the enforcement procedure, so the examination should be limited to the “mild” formal review.

In any case, the judicial authority that revokes the arbitral award is the people’s court where the arbitral institution is located, and the judicial organ that is not enforced may be the people’s court in any place in the country. Detailed regulations are of great benefit to the harmonization of standards for non-enforcement cases.

Among them, some articles are in line with the internationally accepted philosophy. For example, Article 14, paragraph 3, provides for a dissent system:

Where the applicable arbitration procedure or arbitration rules are specially prompted, the parties know or should know that the statutory arbitration proceedings or the chosen arbitration rules have not been complied with, if the parties still participate in or continue to participate in the arbitration proceedings and have not raised any objection, the people’s court shall not support the application for not enforcing the arbitral award on the grounds of violating the legal procedure after the award has been made.

There was no such provision in the Provisions for the Enforcement of the Award (Consultation Paper). When soliciting opinions, an organization proposed that abandoning objections is not only a common practice of international commercial arbitration, but also a requirement of the principle of good faith, which can promote the parties to exercise their procedural rights in a timely manner. This opinion was accepted in the final judicial interpretation.

The Supreme People's Court emphasized in the press conference that there is a precondition for the waiver of the objection, that is, "the situation that requires violation of the procedural rules must be specifically prompted with the parties." The arbitral tribunal is required to ask the parties whether there is any objection to the arbitral proceedings that have already taken place at the end of the trial.

4. Connection of Set-aside and Non-enforcement

According to the provisions of the Arbitration Law, China has applied for the revocation and non-enforcement of domestic arbitral awards, adopting a two-track parallel system of these two remedies, and the legal reasons for the two are basically the same. The parallel system in practice leads to the abuse of judicial procedure by the executor to hinder the enforcement, and repeated review results in the waste of judicial resources and other adverse consequences.

On May 4, 2017, the Intermediate People's Court of Yanbian Korean Autonomous Prefecture of Jilin Province applied for a case in which an application for not enforcing the arbitral award is made after the application for revoking the arbitral award is rejected. On August 26, 2015, the Yanbian Arbitration Commission accepted the construction contract dispute between Hengsheng Company and Hongfeng Company. On January 4, 2017, the Yanbian Arbitration Commission made a (2015) Yan Zhongzi No. 1055 ruling on the construction contract dispute between Hengsheng and Hongfeng. Hongfeng company was not satisfied with the result and it applied to the Yanbian Intermediate People's Court to revoke the above ruling. On March 20, 2017, the Yanbian Intermediate People's Court (Civil Trial 2nd Chamber) made a (2017) Ji 24 Min Te No. 4 civil ruling and rejected the application of Hongfeng Company. Later, in the enforcement of the procedure, Hongfeng Company requested not to enforce the Yanbian Arbitration Commission (2015) Yan Zhongzi No. 1055 ruling on the grounds of that " The arbitral tribunal's judgment deprived the parties of their right to appeal. The arbitral tribunal did not serve the notice of the court in accordance with the law. Due to objective reasons, it was unable to participate in the trial and the arbitral tribunal did not support its request to have an extension of the trial. The arbitral tribunal did not give a statutory defense period for the arbitration request for the change, which was a procedural violation."

After reviewing by the Yanbian Intermediate People's Court, the organ (arbitral tribunal) that made the legal document in force in this case did not serve the notice of the court in accordance with the relevant provisions. The legal representative of Hongfeng Company was far away from the field, and the request for extension of the trial was not allowed under legitimate reasons. Hongfeng Company did not participate in the court normally. It was not allowed to conduct cross-examination and certification of the evidence in court, and it lost the right to defend the evidence and reached a level of fairness that would affect the outcome of the arbitration. Hongfeng Company's reasons for not enforcing the arbitration award were established, which were supported by the Court.

The relationship between revocation and non-enforcement of arbitral reward, and if the parties have the right to apply for not enforcing the arbitral award after the application for revoking the arbitral award is rejected, and in addition, when the court that accepts the application for revocation is inconsistent with the execution court, how to deal with the completely different conclusions of the two courts' determination of the revocation/non-enforcement are always difficult points in practice. The Enforcement Regulations attempt to clarify the convergence of the two procedures in order to simplify the process of judicial review of arbitration. In the Articles 10 and 20, the rules are as follows:

If both applications exist in one case, revocation shall be reviewed first. If the executor withdraws the application for revoking the arbitral award, it shall be deemed to have withdrawn the application for non-enforcement at the same time.

Non-enforcement should follow the one-off application principle, except for new evidence. The reason for the application for non-enforcement shall not be the same as the one be rejected in the former application for non-enforcement.

The above provisions embody the Supreme People's Court's efforts to eliminate conflicts or duplication of the two procedures on the basis of the existing two-track system, which objectively helps the parties and the outsiders to have more relief opportunities. But in the long run, the unification of judicial review of arbitration still requires reform at the legislative level.

In addition, there are several aspects of the Executive Regulations that are worth mentioning:

Clarify the scope of the arbitration mediation as non-enforcement (Article 1)

Clearly clarify the handling of unclear implementation content (Articles 3 to 5)

Defining the finality of the ruling and its exceptions (Articles 22 and 5)

5. Expanding the Scope of System of Application for Verification Concerning the Arbitration Cases

For civil litigation cases involving the validity of the arbitration agreement outside the arbitration judicial review case, if the case is not appealed to the first-instance civil ruling, the application for the review system shall also apply. Different from the arbitration judicial review cases, the civil litigation cases accepted by some courts also involve the determination of the validity of the arbitration agreement. If the people's court is dissatisfied with the ruling of dissent, dismissal, and jurisdictional objection due to the effectiveness of the arbitration agreement, the parties may appeal in accordance with the law. Article 7 of the Provisions on Applications for Verification of Arbitration Cases also clearly stipulates that different types of appeal systems should be applied in accordance with foreign-related and non-foreign-related cases. However, the regulation does not make clear the non-foreign (Hong Kong, Macao and Taiwan) cases need to apply the “party cross-provincial administrative region” and “social public interest” exceptions in accordance with Article 3 of it. However, we believe that non-foreign civil litigation cases should in principle be subject to the “three-tier court” reporting system in which exceptions are applied in accordance with Article 3.

Provisions on Applications for Verification of Arbitration Cases stipulates the reporting and verifying system for both foreign (Hong Kong, Macao, and Taiwan) and non-foreign (Hong Kong, Macao, and Taiwan) arbitration judicial review cases to the higher or Supreme people’s Court, and a unified standard for the discretion of arbitration judicial review cases, which has played a positive role in respecting the parties’ will to arbitrate, avoiding the arbitration agreement or award being denied at will, maintaining the finality and authority of arbitration at home and abroad.

6. Clearly Stipulates the Principle of Confirmation of Foreign-related Factors in the Judicial Review of Arbitration Cases

In the past, judicial interpretation, including the determination of foreign arbitration judicial review cases in the Civil Procedure Law, many of them adopted the standard of whether the arbitration institution is a foreign arbitration institution or not. However, in fact, whether the arbitration institution is foreign-related is not necessarily an inevitable guarantee for the case. In reply No. 2 of the Supreme Court (2012), there was a case in which the parties entered into an arbitration clause in the Trade Agreement, stipulating that the disputes may be submitted to the International Chamber of Commerce for arbitration in Beijing. The Supreme People’s Court believes that both parties to the “Trade Agreement” are Chinese legal persons, the subject matter is in China, and the agreement is also concluded and implemented in China. There is no component of foreign-related civil relations, and the agreement does not belong to foreign-related contracts. Since the jurisdiction of arbitration is a power conferred by law, and the law of our country does not stipulate that the parties may submit disputes not involving foreign factors to an overseas arbitration institution or temporarily arbitrate outside China. Therefore, there is no legal basis for the two parties in this case to submit the dispute to the International Chamber of Commerce for arbitration. This case should not be a foreign-related case.

In Judicial Review Provision, it is made clear that where the arbitration agreement or arbitral award has the circumstances specified in Article 1 of Interpretations of the Supreme People's Court on Several Issues Concerning Application of the Law of the People's Republic of China on Choice of Law for Foreign-Related Civil Relationships (I), it shall be the foreign-related arbitration agreement or the foreign-related arbitration award. That is to say, according to the subject, object, legal fact, subject matter and other aspects of the relevant civil legal relationship, there are foreign factors to determine whether the civil legal relationship is foreign. In addition, in accordance with the relevant legal principles of civil litigation, Judicial Review Provisions stipulates that applications for confirmation of the validity of arbitration agreements involving the Hong Kong Special Administrative Region, the Macao Special Administrative Region, and the Taiwan Region, and applications for enforcement or revocation of a case involving an arbitral award of the Hong Kong Special Administrative Region, the Macao Special Administrative Region, and the Taiwan Region by an arbitration institution in China, shall be reviewed in accordance with the provisions applicable to judicial review cases involving foreign-related arbitration.

7. Three-level Principle for Confirming the Application of the Law on the Validity of Foreign-related Arbitration Agreements

The principles for the application of the law for the confirmation of the validity of foreign-related arbitration agreements in Article 16 of 2006 Judicial interpretation of the Arbitration Law are three-leveled principles: The law stipulated by the parties, the law of the place of arbitration, and the law of the courts (lexfori); and Article 18 of the Law of the People's Republic of China on Choice of Law for

Foreign-Related Civil Relationships, which was implemented in 2011, supplements that if the partied have not agreed on the law applicable, they may apply the law of the place of arbitration or the law of the place where the arbitration institution is located. Judicial Review Provisions further confirms and supplements some issues on the basis of adhering to the above-mentioned three-level law application principles:

（1）It is necessary to choose the applicable law of arbitration agreement clearly: if the parties agree to choose the law applicable to confirm the validity of the arbitration agreement concerning foreign affairs, they should make a clear expression of intention. The law applicable to the contract only cannot be regarded as the law applicable to the confirmation of the validity of the arbitration clause in the contract;

（2）The law of the place where the arbitration institution is effective or of the place of arbitration is preferred: if the parties have not chosen the applicable law, and if the applicable law of the place where the arbitration institution is located and the law of the applicable place of arbitration make different determinations of the validity of the arbitration agreement, the people's court shall apply the law that confirms the validity of the arbitration agreement;

（3）The arbitration institution or place of arbitration may be determined by the arbitration rules: if the arbitration institution or place of arbitration is not agreed upon in the arbitration agreement, but the arbitration institution or place of arbitration may be determined according to the arbitration rules agreed upon in the arbitration agreement, then the arbitration institution or place of arbitration be determined according to the rules shall be regarded as an arbitration institution or place of arbitration as stipulated in Article 18 of the Law of the People's Republic of China on Choice of Law for Foreign-Related Civil Relationships.

8. Law Applicable to the Review of the Effect of an Arbitration Agreement on a Foreign Award under the New York Convention

When a people's court applies the Convention on the Recognition and Enforcement of Foreign Arbitral Awards to examine a case in which a party applies for recognition and enforcement of a foreign arbitral award, the respondent raises a plea on the grounds that the arbitration agreement is invalid, the people's court shall, in accordance with the provisions of paragraph 1 (a) of Article 5 of the Convention, determine the law applicable to the confirmation of the validity of the arbitration agreement, that is, determine the capacity of the parties to act according to the law applicable to the parties to the award, and then determine the validity of the arbitration agreement; or determine the validity of the arbitration agreement based on the law chosen by the parties. If the parties have no choice, the validity of the arbitration agreement shall be determined in accordance with the law of the country making the award (arbitration place). Unlike the applicable legal provisions confirming the validity of an arbitration agreement, the applicable law under the Convention does not include lexfori, since a foreign award has been made and should have the place where the award was made.

On this point, an relatively instructive case is Hyundai Glovis Company's applying to the Ningbo Intermediate People's Court of Zhejiang Province for recognition and enforcement of the Singapore International Arbitration Center (SIAC) 004 Arbitration Award in 2015. On July 13, 2012, Hyundai Glovis and Zhejiang Qiying Energy Chemical Company signed a "sales and purchase agreement", stipulating that Qiying Energy Chemical will purchase about 55916 metric tons of bulk Indonesian thermal coal (mixed) from Hyundai Glovis at a unit price of 57 US dollars per metric ton, and the port of unloading shall be Ningde, the time when the ship arrives at the anchorage port of discharge shall not be later than July 16, 2012. Any disputes between the parties relating to the agreement shall be finally settled by the three arbitrators appointed in accordance with the Arbitration Rules of the Singapore International Arbitration Centre (hereinafter referred to as the SIAC Rules), and the place of arbitration shall be Singapore.

After the above agreement was signed, Hyundai Glovis fulfilled all obligations and delivered 55922 metric tons of coal to the port of discharge on July 14, 2012. Qiying Energy Chemical unloaded and received all of the above coal. But later, Qiying Energy Chemical did not pay the full amount of the contract. After repeated calls by Hyundai Glovis, Qiying Energy Chemical still owed $146755.30. According to the arbitration clause in the Sale and Purchase Agreement, Hyundai Glovis filed an arbitration application with SIAC on January 23, 2014. SIAC accepted the case and according to the SIAC Rules, duly perform the service, notice and other obligations to Qiying Energy Chemical at the address and mailbox agreed upon in the Sale and Purchase Agreement. Qiying Energy Chemical has not raised any objection or participated in the arbitration as required. On September 18, 2015, Hyundai Glovis applied to the Ningbo Intermediate People's Court of Zhejiang Province for recognition and enforcement of SIAC 2015 arbitral award.

The court found that the case was a party applying for recognition of a foreign arbitral award. Since the arbitral award in this case was made by SIAC in Singapore, and both China and Singapore are members of the New York Convention, the relevant provisions of the Civil Procedure Law of the People's Republic of China and the New York Convention should be applied for review. The court found that the 004 arbitral award submitted by Hyundai Glovis and the Agreement for Sale and purchase have been notarized and certified in form in accordance with the provisions of Article 4 of the New York Convention, and the court examined whether Qiying Energy Chemical has received appropriate notice of the appointment of arbitrators and the conduct of arbitration proceedings; whether the arbitration clause agreed by the parties is invalid; whether the arbitration proceedings and the composition of the arbitral tribunal are in violation of the agreement of the parties and the SIAC rules. After all these examinations, the court found that Award 004 does not Contains relevant circumstances under article 5 of the New York Convention, which would cause non-recognition or non-enforcement, nor does it violate the terms of the reservations made by China when it acceded to the Convention. Thus, the award should be recognized and enforced.

9. Clearly Stipulate that the People's Courts Shall Implement the Awards of the Mainland Arbitration Institutions by Applying Different Provisions of the Civil Procedure Law in Accordance with the Non-foreign Rulings and Foreign-related Rulings, and No Longer Based on Whether the Arbitration Institution is Domestic or Foreign

Article 17 of the Judicial Review Provisions adjusts the scope of application of Article 274 of the Civil Procedure Law, and clearly stipulates that the people's courts shall examine the application for the enforcement of not only not only the arbitral awards made by foreign-related arbitration institutions, but also foreign-related arbitration awards made by the arbitration institutions in China in accordance to Article 274 of the Civil Procedure Law. This regulation has been adapted to the development trend of arbitration institutions in China. At present, domestic arbitration institutions, including the China International Economic and Trade Arbitration Commission and the China Maritime Arbitration Commission, which were first established in the China Council for the Promotion of International Trade, have not stipulated that they only accept foreign-related or domestic cases. There is no distinction between the scopes of the arbitration institutions, and there is no separate division of domestic arbitration institutions or foreign arbitration institutions now. Article 17 of the Judicial Review Provisions harmonizes the differences on foreign-related arbitration in the various legal provisions of the Arbitration Law, and is easy to implement in practice.

10. Reaffirm the Right to Appeal

Article 20 of Judicial Review Provisions stipulates that the ruling made by the people's court in the arbitration judicial review case shall have legal effect once it is served, except for the ones on dismissal of the case, rejection of the application and jurisdiction objection. Where a party applies for reconsideration, appeals or applies for retrial, the people's court shall not accept, unless otherwise provided by law and judicial interpretation. This provision fully complies with Article 154 of the Civil Procedure Law on civil rulings.

The Supreme people's Court issued three judicial interpretations in just a few short months, which greatly encouraged the arbitration community. Twenty years ago, the Arbitration Law was promulgated. And since Interpretations on Arbitration-Related Judicial Review Cases being issued in 2006, changes have been made a lot in regulations and provisions of arbitration. There are two amendments to the Civil Procedure Law, in 2007 and 2012, and Interpretation of the Supreme People's Court on the Application of the Civil Procedure Law of the People's Republic of China in 2015. The procedures and standards for judicial review of arbitration have been constantly changing. The Supreme Law now makes three consecutive new judicial interpretations and regulations to meet the needs of the increasingly developing domestic and foreign situation of arbitration, by making regulations and innovative adjustments to some new circumstances. It provides important new legal guidelines for arbitration centers on the handling of domestic arbitration and related cases. Those interpretations and provisions are worth further studying.

That brings to the end of my speech. Thank you!

（此文是李志强律师在 2018 年 9 月 28 日环太平洋律师协会智利首都圣地亚哥举行的拉美区域会议上的主旨演讲）

英国投融资法律研究篇

伦敦证券交易所规制

杨子安　孙晨怡

一、简介

伦敦证券交易所是世界四大证券交易所之一，作为世界上最国际化的金融中心，伦敦不仅是欧洲债券及外汇交易领域的全球领先者，还受理超过三分之二的国际股票承销业务。伦敦的规模与位置，意味着它为世界各地的公司及投资者提供了一个通往欧洲的理想门户。在保持伦敦的领先地位方面，伦敦证券交易所扮演着中心角色，它运作世界上最强的股票市场，其外国股票的交易超过其他任何证券交易所。

伦敦证券交易所于1986年10月进行了重大改革，例如，改革固定佣金制；允许大公司直接进入交易所进行交易；放宽对会员的资格审查；允许批发商与经纪人兼营；证券交易全部实现电脑化，与纽约、东京交易所连机，实现24小时全球交易。这些改革措施使英国证券市场发生了根本性的变化，巩固了其在国际证券市场中的地位。

总体而言，英国证券市场的自律监管传统基本上一直运作良好，维持了市场的公平、公正和高效。与其他国家的证监会监管不同，英国更加注重自律监管的理念，将所有金融监管纳入金融行为监管局的统一监管之下，并特别强调交易所自律监管的效用。与其他国家证券交易所的自律机制相比，英国证券交易所对其会员的自律更具约束力和强制执行力，证券交易所被赋予了其他国家的证券交易所不享有的自律权力（如许可权）。

二、伦敦证券交易所上市标准

（一）主板上市的“黄金标准”

（1）上市文件由英国上市管理局审查。

（2）遵守“上市规则”中的上市原则。

（3）聘用保荐人。

（4）75% 的业务有营业收入记录。

（5）控制公司的大部分资产。

（6）清晰的营运资本表。

（7）遵守关于公司治理的“联合准则”。

（8）最少 25% 的公众股比例。

（9）最低市场 70 万英镑。

（10）3 年经审计的财务信息。

（11）股票完全可转让。

（12）遵守伦交所的“准入及披露标准”。

（二）AIM（替代市场）上市的基本要求

（1）必须委派一位指定保荐人和指定经纪人。

（2）合法成立的公众公司和同类公司。

（3）公司的会计账目符合英国或美国的通用会计准则。

（4）具有两年主营业务盈利记录；否则董事和雇员需保证进入 AIM 后的一年内不出售所持股份。

（5）自有资金满足未来一年的发展需要。

（6）虽无盈利指标，但一般的：过去一年的净利润要在 200 万英镑以上；融资额不低于 2000 万英镑；年增长率不低于 20%。

三、伦敦证券交易所上市途径

（一）股票

外国公司可在伦敦证券交易所的主板市场（作为首要上市或第二上市）直接上市发股。无论公司申请哪一类上市，英国上市管理署（UKLA）——英国金融服务管理局分管在伦敦上市的部门——都有一系列在批准上市和伦敦证券交易所接受股票交易之前必须达到的基本要求。

对希望在伦敦上市发股的公司的要求包括保荐人、经营记录、由公众持有的股票、控股股东、招股说明书、持续性义务。

（二）存股证

专业类DR仅由机构投资者交易，因此UKLA对此类DR的上市要求相对比较宽松。相反，零售类DR可由包括私人在内的任何投资者交易。因此，零售类DR业务需要更高水平的投资者保护，其上市要求也更严格——基本上与直接上市发股一致。

对希望在伦敦上市存股证（DR）的公司的要求包括上市代理人、经营记录、由公众持有的存股证、上市说明书、存托银行、持续性义务。

（三）债券

希望在伦敦上市债券的发行者必须达到的主要要求包括上市代理人、两年经营和财务记录、申请上市可转换证券的公司通常应有至少3年的经营记录、上市文件、可转让性、市值、同一类的所有证券均须上市、可转换证券。

四、伦敦交易所规则

（一）规则体系

从伦敦证券交易所的规则体系上看，分类管理的特色较为明显：一是伦交所规则依据其针对的对象进行了显著区分，划分为针对会员单位的规则、针对上市公司的规则以及针对不同市场的规则三大部分；二是在每部分的规则中也进行了清晰的分类判别，如在会员单位的规则中，对会员单位进行分类并作出不同的规定。

1. 针对会员单位的规则

相对我国台湾地区或日本的单行规则或专门规则居多，较为分散化的体系不同，伦敦证券交易所的会员规则经过编纂，以类法典的形式进行规范，共分为八大部分，包括定义、核心规则、订单簿交易规则、非订单簿交易规则、做市规则以及清决算规则六个部分基础规则，以及合规、违约两个部分特别规则。此外，需要注意的是，由于2007年欧盟《金融工具市场指令》开始施行，在交易透明度、多边交易机制、利益冲突防制以及最佳实践等问题上均提出了欧盟标准，因此伦敦证券交易所也对其规则进行了大范围的修改以符合欧盟条例的要求。

（1）定义。定义部分是伦敦证券交易所规则较有特色的部分，与其他交易所的规则通常在各个单行规则中进行术语定义不同，伦敦证券交易所将所有规则涉及的术语集中在规则开篇进行了非常详细的界定，并在伦敦证券交易所规则上产生效力，如无特别规定，所有的规则中提到的术语均应以开篇定义为准。从规则所称的“人”、工作日，至罚款、大宗交易等共149项各类称谓、缩略语、交易用语，均作出了细致的界定，并会根据市场的变化进行及时修正。

例如：

承认交易：允许在交易所的市场上交易。

代理：以代理身份代表客户的会员公司（修订N37/09-2009年8月19日生效）。

投标价格：会员公司准备购买证券的价格（修订N09/17-2018年1月3日生效）。

工作日：交易所开放交易的任何一天。

MiFID：金融工具市场指令2014/65/EU（修订N09/17-2018年1月3日生效）。

（2）核心规则。核心规则部分详细规定了伦敦证券交易所所有会员的具体权利义务，总共包括会员单位的分类规则、提供的服务分类规则、合规及强制执行规则、收费规则、行为规则及交易系统规则六部分，共60条。其中，行为规则对券商受到禁止的行为进行了规定，包括误导性行为、错误实践以及股价操纵等；交易系统规则则针对券商的交易系统问题、强制停止交易、处置问题时的市场状况等问题作出了规定。

例如，根据规则条文，在会员单位的授权方面，交易所可以承认一个法人实体，如果该法人实体是：①根据指令 2014/65/EU 定义的投资公司，在该指令的含义范围内被授权或允许在其所在州进行受监管活动，或相当于受监管活动；②根据指示 2013/36/EU 的定义，在该指示的含义范围内被授权或允许在其所在州进行受监管活动的信贷机构；③任何其他人士：声誉良好；具备足够的交易能力、权利和经验；足够的组织安排（如适用），以及有足够资源履行其职责，并在适当情况下进行清算和结算安排。

交易所对个人申请入会的评估可包括但不限于：其授权或适用豁免的范围，包括在相关情况下，根据受规管活动令及任何适用的本地法律或规例，以及申请人的财务资源、健康、廉洁及遵守第 1020 条的证明文件。如交易所认为有必要保护交易所市场的完整性，可根据第 1015 条采取行动，而无须事先通知有关会员公司。

在会员服务方面，该规则第 1100 条规定会员公司可担任结算代理，或使用其服务在交易所进行结算。本条含义为会员公司必须自行安排在交易所进行交易。会员公司可雇用一名或数名结算代理人，其中可包括其一般结算会员，但无须雇用。个别结算会员也可另设结算代理人。

另外，对于收费规则，有四条关于交易费用的规定。具体为第 1300 条规定："会员公司须向交易所付款：在有关交易所价目表内列出的所有适用的认购、收费或其他款项；根据交易所与会员公司之间的相关合同应交的所有其他款项；和交易所通知的所有其他款项。"第 1301 条规定："除非交易所另有规定，任何认购、收费或其他到期款项均应在收到发票后 30 个日历日内全额支付。"第 1302 条规定："为了支付应付给交易所的费用和款项，交易所可要求会员公司在联合王国的银行账户上执行并维持以交易所为受益人的直接借记授权。"第 1303 条规定："除正当争议外，如会员公司未能按本规则缴付会费，交易所可终止其会员资格，但不影响交易所可采取的任何其他行动。"

（3）订单簿交易规则与非订单簿交易规则。该部分的规则主要与交易系统和交易机制相关，其中订单簿交易规则规定了更高的交易标准和系统参数。

第2000条规则定义认为，如果交易在交易所订单簿上自动生效，则该交易认为是订单簿交易。该条指导规则还说明，如果在规则第3000条中详述的订单簿之外进行交易，也可以认为是订单簿交易。

第3000条规则规定：如果交易双方中有一方或双方为会员公司，且该交易已生效，则该交易为外汇交易：3000.1在证券交易所市场上进行交易的证券，除了规则3000.2中规定的证券（详见参数），并且成员公司及其客户或交易对手在交易时或之前达成协议，即受制于交易规则；或3000.2未在另一个欧盟受监管市场上列出的AIM证券（详见参数），除非成员公司及其客户或交易对手在交易时或之前达成协议，否则它应为非订单簿交易：①符合AIM主要市场注册机构的要求；或②符合AIM二级市场注册机构的要求，并按照该组织的要求向其报告；或③如果会员公司通过非AIM一级市场注册机构或AIM二级市场注册机构的机制进行交易，则会员公司须以非公开形式实时向交易所报告交易情况。

（4）做市规则。做市规则与上述订单簿和非订单簿交易规则相关，主要分为以下几个部分：做市商的注册规则、订单驱动证券做市商的义务规则及例外、报价驱动证券做市商的义务规则及例外、报价驱动证券做市商的活动规则、金边债券做市商规则以及固定利率做市商规则。根据该部分规则，券商可以选择注册何种做市商，但必须遵守其相应的做市商角色规则。

第4101条规则规定，做市商必须维持一个可执行的报价，或出价，并在其注册的每种证券中提供指定的订单。维持可执行的报价或指定的订单必须符合以下几个条件：在强制期内至少维持90%的常规交易；订单必须维持持续至拍卖结束时，包括任何延期；订单必须在FTSE指数交易日内的拍卖期间维持在相关位置，包括任何延期期间；维持在相关位置，仅允许在预定的一级拍卖期间进行拍卖，包括任何延期期间；必须保持与交易所在零售债券订购簿或那些做市商只提供交易所市场框架内最低规模的投标价格的固定收益证券订单簿上指定的某些证券的联系。

第4102条规则指出，交易所可应市场庄家的要求，暂停或更改做市商的契约内容。在具体实践中，当证券价格大幅波动时，该交易所偶尔允许做市商放宽利差。这是非常罕见的，通常不会持续一天。为了在价格大幅波动时放松做市商的价差义务，该交易所可能暂时将最大利差制度提高到现有价差。

例如，将5%的安全范围移动到10%、15%或25%的容忍度，而不是提供全面的豁免。

第4103条规则则意在保障信息披露的真实性，其明确指出，如果做市商及其客户或交易对方在远离交易系统的情况下进行场内交易，做市商必须至少按其显示的价格和规模进行交易。此外，第4110条规则同样从反面列举了做市商没有义务维持其可执行的报价或指定的订单的具体情形：在开场拍卖期间的证券交易中，或者由于价格监控违规而引发的非预定日内拍卖情形的；在结束拍卖期间的证券零售债券的订单；备兑认股权证届满时；在有关市场上正处于公共假期的证券或作为该证券基础的证券；在证券或以该证券为基础的证券中，在相关市场上出现交易暂停的情况。市场庄家在恢复交易时必须重新输入其可执行的报价或指定的订单；在交易所交易基金或交易所交易产品中，在构成交易所交易基金或交易所交易产品的基础证券或工具中，至少有10%没有固定价格的情况下。

在此规则下的实践中，做市商不仅负有规范做市的相关要求，同时也对严格按照规范程序停止做市负有义务。当规定情形发生时，做市商应负责通知交易所，并通过与市场监督部门联系，向交易所通报和寻求暂停做市义务的许可，在该部门认为交易所交易基金或交易所交易产品中10%或10%以上的标的证券或工具没有固定价格时，如果获得相关部门批准，暂停做市将适用于适用于所有做市商在特定的交易所交易基金或交易所交易产品。这项暂时停牌只适用于有关日期，如有需要，市场庄家必须每天分别提出要求。

（5）清算结算规则。该部分规则是会员规则中较为重要的部分，包括清算结算规则、交割时间、中央对手方规则等相关规定，共82条。伦敦证券交易所2001年开始使用伦敦清算所作为SETS的中央对手方。伦敦证券交易所为其成员公司提供多个中央对手的选择权，中央对手选择的引入，旨在通过中央对手之间的公开竞争，为成员提供更多的选择，以确保中央对手服务质量最高，价格最低。

第5000条规则开篇明义地指出，伦敦证券交易所会员须确保其所进行的每一项伦敦证券交易所交易均获妥为结算。具体而言，会员公司负责确保在议定的交割到期日交付其所有在交易所业务的证券，不管该成员公司是否以代理人或委托人的身份出售。结算可以是毛额的，也可以是净额的。在没有达成相反的协议的情况下，应假定进行全面结算。之所以列入这条规则，是为了确保交易所市场的有序运作，而且因为根据 FCA 的承诺，交易所有义务为使用交易所设施进行的所有交易作出安排。成员公司有义务确保以其名义进行的交易得到结算。即使不结算的原因是由于客户或交易对手未能结算和/或成员公司仅仅作为代理人时，这一义务也并未灭失。

第 5020 条规则强调，伦敦证券交易所会员只有在其交易时随时可获得股票的情况下，才能进行“保证交付”的交易。为了确保“保证交付”的效力，该规则要求，如果交易是根据第 5020 条规则进行的，卖方应提高保证交付交易的结算优先权（或采取其他同等行动）至任何其他未处理、应在同一天结算的未保证交付交易。

在结算过程方式上，伦敦证券交易所在第 5025 条规则中也提出了要求，即进行销售的伦交所会员应确保应在交易系统上依据自动执行而执行交付的证券在交易的预定结算日期或之前以电子形式记录。

第 5030 条规则指出，伦敦证券交易所会员应在交易时商定交割地，但若未商定，则应在证券或市场的“标准”交割地结算交易。这条规则只适用于双边贸易。中央交易将服从相关中央交易对手方的规则和程序。交易应当按照所使用的清算和结算制度的规则和程序进行结算。与贸易结算有关的任何特殊条款或条件，应在交易进行之时或之前商定，并应在贸易确认后予以明确说明和说明。未经行业双方事先同意，不允许部分结算，但须遵守相关结算系统经营者的程序。

第 5040 条规则规定，凡在发行人已经开始持续关闭清盘登记册的情况下，买方会员须在交付转让证明书或核证转让时付款，但须附有注册持有人向清盘人发出的授权书，说明清盘人须向买方或其客户或对手方支付任何资本回报。在实践中，往往会根据买方和卖方之间的协议，由卖方向买方递交一份“保证函”，承诺将由清算人进行任何分配，以取代第 5040 条规则下产生的文件。

第 5042 条规则规定，如因法院、行政或监管命令或因影响此类证券发行人的破产事件而无法达成中央交易方合同，则该中央对手方合同应按照中央对手方的规则处理。

在延迟清算方面，伦敦证券交易所也作出了详尽的规定。

第 5060 条规则对交付失败的定性已经明确：每一位伦敦证券交易所成员

都同意，某一行业的一方未能在到期日交付证券或支付证券价款的情况本身并不是该交易的任何一方将该交易视为被拒绝接受的理由。

第 5061 条规则指出，买方不得仅仅因为证券迟于到期日交付而声称没有支付证券的义务。上述两条规则意在充分保障各类交易遭遇交割风险的情况下交易自身的稳定性，有助于稳定市场态势。

第 5071 条规则规定，如要求方未能在交易所设定的最后期限前撤回收购要求，则求购方必须接受并支付交易所因买入交易而交付的任何证券所产生的费用。

第 5074 条规则指出，交易所应将购买交易的细节通知责任方，在此之后，责任方必须立即将交割指令与交易所通知的其他结算系统中的交割指令相匹配。

在责任归属方面，伦敦证券交易所制定了两条规则：第 5080 条规则指出，要求在交易所购买证券的会员对其请求中的任何错误或遗漏负有责任，交易所对任何此类错误或遗漏不负责任。第 5079 条规则指出，除部分例外情况，负法律责任的一方须就交易所因执行购货要求而招致的任何费用或损失，向交易所弥偿任何及全部法律责任。

在通过中央交易对手进行清算方面，伦敦证券交易所规则如下：第 5100 条规则指出，结算成员只有在与相关的中央交易对手方签订清算成员协议的情况下，才能清算或同意清算某一特定中央对手方证券的交易。结算会员必须遵守与其订立结算会员协议的中央交易对手所施加的规则及规例及任何合理条件。第 5101 条规则指出，除非与交易所达成下列安排，否则会员不得在交易系统内输入中央交易对手证券的命令：会员是一个非清算成员或结算成员，是一个当前有效的清算协议的中一方，协议另一方是一个单独的、将清算任何由此产生的交易的一般清算成员；它本身是结算会员，该指令具有本金、无风险本金或匹配的本金容量。

在该规则下，所有代理交易必须由一个与交易一方的会员公司分开的一般清算成员进行清算。本身是结算会员的会员公司，只能清算其本身的本金、无风险本金或匹配的本金业务，并需要为其代理业务作出单独的清算安排。个体结算会员只能自行结算。

在结算服务的终止方面，伦敦证券交易所也制定了规则：第 5110 条规则明确：一般结算会员必须提前通知交易所，然后才能暂停其作为结算会员的服务给任何会员公司。

实践中，一般结算会员必须致电通知市场监管部门，并以书面确认。在此情况下，交易所须在议定的时间，或在合理的切实可行范围内，尽快暂停该成员商号就所有中央交易对手证券提交命令，并删除该成员商号在该交易系统内的任何现有指令。一般结算会员仍须对交易所完成这些程序前所执行的涉及会员公司的所有交易负责。

（6）特别规则。特别规则部分包括执行规则和违约规则两部分内容。在执行规则中对会员单位的违法违规行为的处罚作出了规定，依据规则，伦敦证券交易所可以采用施加罚款、出具警示函等处罚手段，或者将相关问题提交执行小组或纪律委员会。执行小组能够作出不超过 5 万英镑的罚款，并可继续将相关事项提交纪律委员会审查。纪律委员会则是伦敦证券交易所处罚的最高机构，有权作出无上限的罚款、恢复原状、中止会员资格以及开除等严厉处罚。

违约规则部分则适用于会员发生违约时的处理，包括清算违约、交割违约等情形，以及违约所应承担的相应后果。

规则规定，如交易所认为会员公司违反交易所规则，交易所可对该会员商号采取纪律处分。交易所可施加定额罚款、发出警告通知及 / 或将纪律事宜交由执行小组或纪律委员会处理。在适当的情况下（包括在执行小组授权的更大的制裁被执行小组认为是适当的情况下），执行小组可将案件提交纪律委员会。执行小组是由交易所工作经验丰富的高级成员组成的小组，其还审议针对定额罚款的上诉。执行小组的任何最终决定（将决定提交纪律委员会的决定除外），均可向上诉委员会提出上诉，临时决定不能上诉。纪律委员会成员来自经验丰富（非交易所）人士，可以施加比执行小组更广泛的制裁，并有权自行公布其调查结果。纪律委员会的任何最终决定均可向上诉委员会提出上诉，同样，其临时决定不能上诉。

在考虑针对违规行为采取何种纪律行动时，交易所考虑的因素有很多，如违反规则的严重性、规模和性质，违规行为是如何被曝光的，违反规则的实际或潜在市场影响以及任何其他影响，违反规则的程度是故意还是过失的，成员公司的一般合规历史以及有关违规的具体历史，规则的一致和公平应用

（以前类似规则违反的任何先例），会员公司对调查事项的反应和行动。

表 1 总结了交易所的纪律程序。

表 1　伦敦证券交易所的纪律程序

过程	一般使用于	组成	上诉机构
警告通知	规则漏洞	（没有听证）	
固定惩罚	有固定罚款通知的违规行为	（没有听证）	执行小组
执行小组	纪律方面的问题； 反对定额罚款的上诉	交易所高级人员	上诉委员会
纪律委员会	纪律问题	适当的有经验（非交易所）人员	上诉委员会
上诉委员会	针对执行小组调查结果的纪律申诉； 针对纪律申诉委员会的调查结果	适当的有经验（非交易所）人员	

表 2 总结了交易所对违反规则的处罚。

表 2　伦敦证券交易所对违反规则的处罚

过程	可用的制裁	上诉机构
警告通知	可以规定所需的纠正措施； 成员公司案例历史的正式行动记录	
定额罚款	如任何适用的定额罚款通知所述	执行小组
执行小组	以下之一： 私人非难； 每次违规罚款最高可达 50000 英镑； 转介给纪律委员会事项	上诉委员会
纪律委员会	以下一个或多个： 私人非难； 公开非难； 无上限罚款； 暂停活动； 恢复原状； 中止会员资格	上诉委员会
上诉委员会	执行小组推荐： 执行小组可适用的任何制裁	
	纪律委员会转介： 纪律委员会可以采取的任何制裁措施	

2. 针对上市公司的规则

由于伦敦证券交易所不同的市场板块区分较为显著，因此在上市公司的规则上也同样采取了分块规制的思路，主要分为主板上市公司规则、另类投资市场规则、专业证券市场规则以及专业基金市场规则四大部分。

主板市场方面由于英国金融市场发展历史悠久，相关的法律法规制度较为完善，因此在涉及上市公司规则方面，伦敦证券交易所并没有选择进行全面规范，而是仅就上市公司的上市及信息披露标准作出规定。该部分规则共包括上市标准、信息披露规则、上市申请程序、持续义务、合规及处罚措施五大部分，其中合规及处罚措施占据了超过一半的篇幅，详细规定了上市公司合规要求、执行小组、处罚委员会以及上诉委员会的职责与处理程序。

相对于主板市场的详细规则，伦敦证券交易所其他的市场板块如另类投资市场、专业证券市场与专业基金市场的规则较为简单，以指引为主，其中专业基金市场还指定了相应的信息披露标准规则。

（二）规则修订

根据英国 2012 年《金融服务法》的规定，该法既承认公认投资交易所的自律地位，也确认金融行为监管局对证券交易所的核准和监督。因此，尽管伦敦证券交易所有着较强的自律地位，其规则修订仍然需要通过金融行为监管局的核准。

伦敦证券交易所规则的修改通常在确定规则需要修改时，首先会将提案进行公告发布，向社会及各利益相关方进行征询。在获得各方对提案的反馈之后，伦敦证券交易所将考虑和综合各方面的意见对提案进行修正，并作出最终文本发布。确认公告会对修改的原因、依据以及获得反馈的情况进行简单说明，并附上最终确认的规则修改提案。在最终确认无异议之后，伦敦证券交易所即会发布规则修改公告，正式宣告其规则的修改，简单说明本次修改的情况，并对某些重要条文的修改作出提示，并规定修正后条文的生效时间。

英国的替代性争端解决办法

Nicholas Towers

替代性争端解决办法是一个总体概括性术语，指的是除诉诸法院之外，还可以通过不同的方式解决争端。在英国，人们积极鼓励当事人在不提起诉讼的情况下解决他们的纠纷，而且有许多方法可供当事人使用。替代争端解决的主要目标是帮助各方更快、更私密和更方便地解决争端，而不是通过诉讼程序。英国法官在独立性和能力方面享有很高的声誉，这使英国成为许多国际争端的目标地。然而，重要的是，在英国，法院诉讼通常是公开的。当事人必须假定法庭诉讼程序，特别是审判程序将是公开的。此外，任何不是诉讼当事方的人仍然可以从法庭记录中获得案件陈述和任何判决，只需支付少量费用。

一、谈判

第一种也是最常见的方法是协商。这意味着双方之间可能通过信件或会议达成和解。如果能够达成私人和解协议，当事人的律师可以起草一份协议，该协议将是一份具有约束力的合同，其中规定了和解的条件。如果已经在法院提起诉讼，可以将和解协议记录在同意令或 Tomlin 命令中，从而结束诉讼程序。该命令不必包括和解条款，只需提及和解协议文件即可。

私人谈判的一个巨大优势是确定性，如果当事方之间的争端不能得到解决，那么他们就必须将裁决交给法官或仲裁员，这种做法（对任意一方而言）总是有失败的危险。投资者应该警惕任何声称某案件有 100% 胜诉机会的英国律师。

谈判另一个主要的方面是，它将对未来的工作机会产生鼓励作用，而且谈判比上法庭具有更高的灵活性。在法庭上法官只处理他们面前的事实和法律问题，然而当事各方才是充分了解各自商业目的和需要的人。

在英国，为真正解决争端而进行的谈判自然地“不带偏见”，不能用来对付在法庭上提出请求的一方。只有在法官或仲裁员就费用作出主要决定后才能提及。在谈判中提出的提议可能会对成本产生影响。例如，A 起诉要求 B 给付 20 万英镑，B 在谈判中提出支付 15 万英镑，但 A 拒绝了这个提议，并接受了审判。A 赢得了审判，但法官只判了 10 万英镑。然后，B 可以向法官证明他曾在谈判中愿意支付 15 万英镑，并争辩说 A 本应该接受这一提议。这可能导致判给 A 的法定费用要远低于预期水平，即使 A 赢得了审判。

为了鼓励当事人接受合理的和解要约，有一种争议解决工具，其被称为第 36 部分要约（以“民事诉讼规则”中出现的部分命名）。如果原告提出第 36 部分要约建议，而被告拒绝接受，但原告在审讯后获得更多的损害赔偿，则产生的后果之一是被告须额外支付 10% 的损害赔偿，以及损害赔偿及讼费的利息，年率为 10%。

二、调解

调解与谈判非常相似，只是更有条理，各方将在中立的地点开会，由独立的第三方充当调解人，努力帮助各方解决争端。调解中发生的事情是保密的；规定调解条件和调解人费用安排的调解协议通常将保密作为一个条件。

调停没有固定的形式。通常会有一次开幕会议，调解人允许各方在进入不同的会议室之前作简短的开幕词。调解人的作用是帮助各方正视其案件的现实，中立地提出问题，鼓励各方与对方沟通，反思其在该案件的长处和弱点。在这种情况下，当事人往往只从律师那里得到片面的建议，案件中的弱点会被淡化。

调解人将秘密地讨论每一方的情况，并将任何提议或让步传达给对方。调解人只能在明确许可的情况下与对方沟通。即使在双方关系很差的处境中，争端也是可以被调解的。

调解不在于输赢，而在于找到双方都能接受的解决办法，并保护双方保持未来关系的可能性。在调解中，当事人可以作出他们能想到的任何形式的交易。例如，在有关未付款发票的争议中，法院只会决定发票是否应支付。在调解中，当事人可以同意接受较低数额的发票金额，以换取未来合同的授予。这样，争端就解决了，并且这也为今后的工作达成了协议，双方就可以节省诉讼费用。

当调解达成和解时，可以在法庭上将其记录为同意令，和解条款仍将保密。调解的主要缺点首先是要求当事各方支付调解人和律师出庭的费用；持续一两天而不成功的调解费用可能相当昂贵。此外，调解人无权强迫各方解决争端，因此无法保证争端得到解决。然而，如果调解取得成功，费用将只占诉讼调解费用的一小部分。调解即使是在审判前不久，也可以随时进行。法院大力鼓励调解，对于不合理地拒绝调解的一方，法庭将会通过在审判中判令其支付对方的法律费用，或判令不得将法律费交付给不合理一方的方式来惩罚他们。如果审判法官裁定某一方不合理地拒绝调解，那么即使他们赢得了审判，他们仍然可以受到费用令的惩罚。

三、裁断

在建筑工程领域，裁断是目前解决纠纷的一种非常普遍的方式。根据1996年《住房补助、建造和重建法》，如果建筑合同中有付款争议，任何一方都可以坚持要求作出裁断。这是一个非常迅速的过程，在28天内将争端提交一个称为裁决人的独立第三方做出裁断。裁决人的决定对当事各方具有约束力，因为它必须支付费用，但最终各方还是可以通过诉诸法院或仲裁来解决争端。裁断决定很少受到败诉方的质疑，因为上法庭要付出相当高的成本。裁断的主要优点是它是一个非常迅速的过程，但这可能使它不适合非常复杂的争议。

四、仲裁

仲裁是一种解决争端的合同型机制，通过这种机制，双方当事人（通常在合同中或较少在单独的文件中）达成仲裁协议，而不是进行诉讼。

仲裁协议可涵盖合同引起的所有争议，也可限于某些问题，如付款争议或所提供货物的质量。如果仲裁协议具有约束力并适用于有关争端，当事各方将被要求遵循该协议规定的机制（或双方随后同意的机制），指定一个仲裁庭并遵守所规定的程序规则［例如，“贸易法委员会规则”或国际商会、伦敦国际仲裁法院、特许仲裁委员会（CIArb）或塞尔伯恩商会仲裁处的仲裁规则］。

仲裁协议通常规定指定 1 名或 3 名仲裁员。如果只有一名仲裁员，他们通常将由一个独立的机构，如 LCIA 或 CIArb 进行指定。如果有 3 名仲裁员，每一方通常指定 1 名仲裁员，两名仲裁员选择第三名仲裁员担任主席。虽然理论上仲裁可以比诉讼便宜，但在实践中它一般不会便宜很多。仲裁协议通常规定仲裁的地点、仲裁的法律、合同的管辖法律和仲裁的时限。可以在世界上任何地方同意仲裁，虽然合同规定适用的法律可以是英国或中国法律，但当事各方可以同意仲裁听证会将在一个中立地点举行（如在阿拉伯联合酋长国）。

五、法庭协助

英国是仲裁的坚定支持者，仲裁受 1996 年《仲裁法》管辖。如果有效仲裁协议的一方当事人试图在法院提起诉讼，希望进行仲裁的另一方当事人可以向法院申请，除非仲裁协议无效，否则法院必须中止该请求。然而，这一申请必须在诉讼程序中采取任何步骤回答主要索赔之前提出。一般来说，这意味着在对索赔提出书面抗辩之前。

当然，如果双方当事人都同意他们宁愿诉诸法院而不是仲裁，他们仍然可以这样做，而且法院不会拒绝审理索赔要求。法院还将采取宽松的口径解释仲裁协议，并将尽量避免认定仲裁协议因不确定性无效。即使是那些含糊不清，只申明是“伦敦仲裁”的仲裁协议也得到了支持。高等法院拥有比仲裁员更广泛的权力，并随时协助当事各方进行仲裁。仲裁当事人可能会担心的一个问题是，他们如何坚持让某人参加仲裁以提供证人证据。因为如果该人不是仲裁协议的当事方，仲裁员不能强迫他们出席。然而，根据 1996 年《仲裁法》，高等法院可以协助下达命令，要求该人作证。此外，高等法院也可以下令保存证据，或对财产进行检查。高等法院也可以下达禁令，保留资产。这些被称为“冻结令”，可以防止命令的目标在判决之前处置特定的资产。

六、仲裁程序

在英国，法院为处理案件制定了严格和可预测的程序时间表。在披露文件、提供估计法律费用预算和听证方面都有默认要求。在大型项目和大型纠纷中，这些活动的成本可能很高。此外，法官们经常很忙，这可能意味着审判开始前的长时间拖延。仲裁的好处是当事人可以根据自己的需要自由调整程序；他们可以跳过成本预算，或者安排一个定制的披露程序。他们可以同意审判在一天中的特定时间，甚至在周末进行。然而，由于需要让律师参与仲裁，程序通常模仿诉讼。此外，在有 3 名仲裁员的情况下，审判必须在适合所有仲裁员的时间进行，这可能造成延误。

七、仲裁裁决

英国是 1958 年《承认及执行外国仲裁裁决公约》的签署国，该公约通常被称为《纽约公约》。这意味着即使该仲裁听证会不是在伦敦进行的，它将承认并执行国际仲裁裁决。在伦敦仲裁的一个强大优势是很难撤销仲裁裁决，因为提出质疑的理由有限。第一个理由是对裁决提出质疑，理由是仲裁庭没有管辖权。然而，如果当事人参加了仲裁，尽管他们知道或本应知道质疑管辖权的理由，但在仲裁中没有对管辖权提出质疑，他们就不能采取这一理由。

质疑的第二个理由是影响法庭、诉讼程序或裁决的严重违规行为。违规行为必须是对申请人造成“实质不公正”的行为，所以不可能是微不足道的违规行为。这一申诉理由可以包括以下几种类型：（1）就它无权决定的问题做出裁决；（2）不决定它必须作出决定的所有问题；（3）不采取行动公平、公正地在当事人之间作出裁决，未给予每一方合理的机会提出己方的判例，并应对处理其对手提出的判例；（4）作出欺诈或违反公共政策的裁决。

质疑的第三个理由是就法律问题提出的上诉。当事人的协议可以排除这一理由，而且常常在仲裁协议中列入排除这一质疑理由的规定。

上诉的理由不包括以仲裁员误解事实为依据的上诉。如果仅仅是仲裁员不相信某一证人在证据中所说的话，就不能仅以此为理由对这一裁决提出质疑。

八、混合程序

在英国，在替代性争端解决方面有许多创新之处。其中，最受欢迎的是仲裁和调解的结合。它有时被称为“arb-med”，它旨在解决调解的主要问题，即没有解决的保证。它还试图解决仲裁的僵化问题，因为仲裁不具有调解的灵活性。

程序通常包括先举行仲裁听证会。在聆讯后，仲裁员不会立即作出决定。然后各方将进行调解。调解人通常不是仲裁员。当事各方将听取证据和意见，以及仲裁员的反应，并能对他们的案件进行评估。然后，他们可以试图达成一项解决协议。如果达成协议，仲裁员将不提供决定。如果调解中未达成协议，则仲裁员将作出裁决。

这种方法的优点在于它允许当事人使用调解的灵活性，也为纠纷提供了明确的结果。主要的缺点是，这种方法将相当昂贵，因为仲裁和仲裁员以及调解员的费用必须支付。这种方法通常更适用于不超过 1 天的法庭或仲裁时间的小纠纷。这种方法并不真正适用于诸如审判可能会持续几天或几周的大规模纠纷。

意大利投融资法律研究篇

意大利投融资法律研究

Luca Simonetti
Corrado Scivoletto
Giuseppe Persico
Giuseppe Schiavello

一、意大利基本概况

意大利是南欧国家，它是地中海的一个半岛，由阿尔卑斯山脉连接起欧洲的其他地方。其领土面积约 30.1 万平方公里。意大利首都是罗马（约 300 万人），其他最大的几个城市分别为米兰、都灵、那不勒斯、热那亚、佛罗伦萨、博洛尼亚和巴勒莫。总人口约为 6000 万人。

意大利的历史以及其在景观和经济资源方面的广泛差异决定了其强大的自治制度。意大利是世界上城市化程度最高的国家之一（约 8000 个市镇，其中 141 个人口超过 5 万人，其中 46 个市镇超过 10 万人），但一些南部地区有强大的犯罪组织（国际知名的黑社会，如黑手党和克莫拉）。意大利各地区在礼仪、文化、生活方式和收入以及信念方面有着很大的差异。即使是意大利语，也经过了一个世纪的斗争（从 1860 年半岛的政治统一到 1960 年前后通过电视扩散开始），才取代了原有的地方性方言。

尽管从 2000 年开始，经济危机强劲，但意大利仍然是世界上最大的经济体之一（欧洲第四大、全球第八大经济体），国民生产总值为 18157.57 亿美元，人均收入为 29866 美元（2015 年数据），其人类发展指数也很高（2014 年为世界第 27 位）。

（一）宪法和政治框架

意大利是共和国（根据 1946 年举行的全民投票决定）。更确切地说，意大利是一个议会共和国：立法权属于议会，由众议院和参议院组成。两院拥有对等的权力，这也意味着任何一个立法措施都需要得到两院的批准。参议院、众议院两院议员每届任职五年。

议会也有权给予政府信任或否决。总理（称为部长理事会主席更佳，简称内阁）由共和国总统按照议会的指示任命，但总理必须前往议会取得两会的信任投票，一旦他 / 她失去信任投票，就将被迫退出。

尽管只以废除的形式（全民投票是为了废除或确认现有规则），全民公投是众所周知并广泛使用的（自 1946 年以来已经举行了 70 多场全民公投）。相反，公民投票以咨询的方式是非常罕见的（公民投票是为了征询对现有提议的意见），并以宪法的形式被禁止（当公民投票是为了引进新的立法时）。

议会还任命共和国总统（国家元首），其权力类似于国王在现代的君主立宪制中所持有的权力。每任总统任职七年。

法律的合宪性审查是委托给宪法法院来处理的，但与美国最高法院不同的是，不能直接由法院来采取行动：事实上，法官在判决一方提交的案件时，只有认为有必要就一项既定规则（对决定案件至关重要的情形）是否违背《宪法》作出初步决定，宪法法院才会被要求作出决定。如果宪法法院裁定该规则违反宪法，则该规则被废除，不能再适用。

低于政治层面的行政机构（从属于政府和各部门高层，由政府任命的主管任职）主要由公职人员运行，公职人员需要通过公务员考试才能被录用，并且终身任用，没有正当理由不能被随意调职或解雇。行政行为应当遵循公正和有序的两项原则（《宪法》第 97 条），这意味着意大利的官僚主义遵循现代欧洲行政国家的模式，如法国、德国和英国。除此之外，意大利各级行政当局还必须遵循法治。

然而，许多事情都得由当地机构决定和管理：市、区和片区在许多重要事项上的管理都是一致的（而且常常是排他性的），它们也拥有自己的人事部门；市、区主要通过收取地方税来获取资源。而各省正在解散，将其权力向下移交给市政府或地区。

司法权力是完全自主、独立于政府的。法官（荣誉法官除外）通过公开考试选取，终身受雇于司法机关，除有正当理由不得调职或解雇；此外，他们的职业生涯由意大利法官自治组织（司法机构高级司法委员会）负责监督和决定，以保证司法权力与政治权力完全独立。

（二）经济

意大利的官方货币是欧洲货币，即欧元（经过一段时间与欧洲主要货币的融合后，于 2002 年引入；意大利以前的货币是里拉）。

意大利是一个高度工业化的国家（在全球排名第七位），但其产业却遭受了 21 世纪的危机。

意大利是一个承认商品和资产私有，同时也存在国有资产的国家。私人财产可能因公共利益而被征用，但国家（一般）必须根据资产的市场价值对财产所有人进行补偿。

因此，私营企业和上市公司同时存在，尽管从 20 世纪 80 年代开始，大多数上市公司都是私有化的。尽管如此，国家持有大量在许多由经济部门经营的公司的股份（或以其他方式控制）。

经过一段时期的经济规划（主要在 20 世纪六七十年代），如今政府放弃了任何将经济发展带到一个或者另一个方向的意图，而主要通过经济政策的常规手段来管理经济，如公共支出、税收等。但是，由于进入欧盟，特别是由于采用欧元作为货币，这些手段已经被削弱了。事实上，欧盟会限制每个会员国出现赤字的可能性，欧元不能由成员国单方面作出决定而贬值，而应要求欧洲中央银行作出决定。另外，贴现率计算的权利保留给欧洲中央银行，而不再由成员国酌情决定。这对意大利处理经济危机的能力是个特别严格的限制，并且由于意大利公共债务巨大（2015 年占国民生产总值的 132.7%），导致意大利解决在千禧年发生的危机方面面临很大困难。

外汇管制在 1990 年大幅度消除。外国人购买意大利资产的唯一重大限制是房地产，房产可以被外国人购买，但只能在互惠制下购买（该外国人的国家也允许意大利居民在那里购买房产）。

（三）社会结构

意大利是一个没有重要种族和宗教冲突的国家。这主要是由于几个世纪以来意大利的少数民族都很少，非洲和其他非欧洲国家的移民直到最近也互不相干。然而，经济危机、北非的政治和宗教动乱以及近东大大增加了移民的数量，导致了不宽容、种族主义和对移民进行隔绝和阻碍的强烈要求的浪潮。相同的例子还有很多，由于类似的原因欧盟其他国家（和美国）也在发生类似的事。

（四）法律环境

意大利法律是传统罗马法律制度的样板，理论上法律由议会制定，法官只能将其适用于手头的具体案件，而不能自己“创造”法律。当然，现实与理论有所差别，法官作出的解释也是非常重要的。此外，从19世纪开始，意大利像法国和德国这样传统的罗马法国家一样，也开始进入了法典编纂阶段。因此，目前大多数意大利民法和商业法都载于《民法典》；刑法载于《刑法典》；程序法载于《民事诉讼程序》《刑事诉讼程序》和《行政诉讼法典》；甚至税法都趋向于以《法典》形式呈现，或法律重述（唯一文本）。

意大利是联合国及北约的成员，尤其还是欧盟的创始成员。在后者方面，意大利一定会尊重和遵守欧盟发布的所有规则；尽管意大利经常被欧洲法院谴责其拖延执行欧盟规则，但意大利颁布了很多来源于欧盟的立法，并且导致其显著修改内部法律。

意大利作为欧盟的成员，无论是意大利还是其他欧盟成员国，在欧盟的层面上习俗和贸易事项更容易达成一致。此外，意大利方面还没有定下移民政策，但在布鲁塞尔已经定下来了。

二、投资

（一）银行和金融活动概述

众所周知，欧盟银行业形势正在从监管的角度进行划时代的转变。事实上，虽然经过了以重大变化为特征的30多年，但始终与以往的情况有相对的联系，就《巴塞尔协议Ⅱ》和《巴塞尔协议Ⅲ》而言，从2014年11月起，单一监督机制SSM和单一解决机制SRM的引入，代表了银行监管历史性发展的一步。SSM和SRM实际上是欧洲银行业联盟的两大支柱，是对金融全球危机的回应。

具体到意大利银行体系，尽管经济持续衰退，但其表现出了良好的恢复力。虽然它主要面向传统的贷款活动，但总体上来说，尽管非常困难，它还是阻挡了经济危机对个人机构的影响。

意大利银行监管制度根据新的欧洲监管制度成形，且已经适应了国际监管中的市场紧缩。然而，2014—2015年，经济金融危机的持续不仅明显加重了部分银行的困难，而且还将银行资产负债表不良贷款余额增加到高于其他发达经济体的平均水平。不良贷款的总余额应考虑到债务人的抵押品覆盖率，而意大利比其他国家高得多。国际间的比较恰当地代表了意大利银行的健康状况：事实上，意大利银行对于其他欧元区国家的银行来说处于优势地位，如高度接触的新兴市场目前正面临经济困难。

众所周知，由于银行不良贷款大幅增加，将遗留资产带入了持续的欧洲政策争议之中。2008年以来观察到的不良贷款的快速增长可能正严重剥夺欧洲经济在信贷方面的急剧需求，如果贷款质量下降阻碍银行贷款，从2008年开始不良贷款的增长将在削减欧洲经济急需的信誉中起到至关重要的作用，将使经济复苏更加困难。意大利的情况就是一个检测这种可能性的有趣的案例：2008—2015年，意大利银行的总不良贷款率翻了一番，信贷紧缩，而在这个银行和企业之间的结构性关系众所周知的紧密的国家里，经历了两次明显的衰退。

退一步说，在意大利法律体系中，《银行业统一法》（*Testo Unico Bancario*，TUB）在基本层面上从银行业务定义的角度定义了银行。TUB第10条规定，银行业务包含于联合收取公众储蓄和各种形式的信贷中，并且与欧洲立法一致，银行可以进行任何未明确保留至其他主体的财务活动，而适当银行业务（定义）只保留给银行。根据TUB第13条的规定，意大利银行和意大利境内设立的欧洲子公司需要由意大利银行适当的注册。此外，根据第14条的规定，它们行使银行业务需要据一个意大利银行的提案获得BCE授权。

先从欧洲成员国的银行说起，它们可以根据SSM规定的程序在意大利境内设立子公司，或者根据 TUB（如果欧盟成员国不参加 SSM），或者它们可以在共和国境内进行银行业务，而不设立子公司，条件是所属成员国的主管当局通知意大利银行。

另外，非欧盟银行，没有设立子公司，就只有在获得意大利银行决定将其与 CONSOB（意大利当局负责管理意大利金融市场）一起提供投资服务的正式授权之后，才能在意大利经营。

虽然不完全，考虑意大利法律允许它们在意大利领土上提供专业能力的信贷，意大利主要金融机构的框架需要与金融中介完成。但在 2015 年 7 月，TUB 第 5 号改革生效，因此现在，意大利银行授权金融中介机构以任何形式提供融资，包括发行担保，并且在收到意大利银行的授权后，将其输入 TUB（第 141/2010 号修订的立法法令）第 106 条规定的登记册。实际上，所有这些实体都要遵循一种审慎的监管制度，略等同于适用银行的监管机制，目的是实现金融稳定，维护良好和谨慎的管理。

值得注意的是，对于非意大利金融中介机构，对这些中介机构的监管在欧盟一级并不统一，因此，当涉及非意大利（但基于欧盟）的中介机构的控股股东由其主要营业地的一个或多个欧盟银行持有的相关金融中介机构的同一成员国持有时，只有在欧盟金融中介机构控制股权的情况下，TUB（第 18 条）才建立相互承认机制。

在我们刚刚描述的相互承认的情况下，有关非意大利金融中介机构的一般规则是在 TUB 第 114 条中规定的，其中规定经济和财政部应对在外国注册办事处的企业在意大利领土内行使第 106 条所述活动进行规范。为此目的颁布的《参考法令》是 2015 年 4 月 2 日颁布的第 53 号法令，规定了外国机构进行财务活动的条件，区分不被允许相互承认的欧盟金融中介机构和非欧盟实体。欧盟实体可以通过在意大利设立一个“常设机构”。（一个分支机构），进行融资活动（连带和辅助活动）。在这种情况下，除意大利银行根据 TUB 第 107 条和根据第 106 条登记的登记册的授权外，还有法令 n.53/2015 号的第 6 条所规定的附加条件将被适用。

相反，非欧盟金融中介机构只能通过在意大利设立一家公司进行融资活动，该公司由意大利银行根据 TUB 第 107 条授权和第 106 条注册。

意大利外资银行和中介机构的框架相当复杂，涉及地理来源、结算方案和提供的产品和服务范围，主要外资银行包括全球银行业金融集团。而中介机构人员在其原籍国以及包括意大利在内的国际层面都担任领导职务。

外资银行的大部分在意大利的业务都通过设立一个办事处完成，还有一些中介机构则通过分行网络加强了在该国的实体业务，主要是为了提高与零售客户的关系质量和订单数量。对于大多数银行来说，除附属公司外，还报告了属于主要外国集团的其他法律机构的存在，在大多数情况下，这些法律实体是专门从事资产管理和信托活动的金融公司。

在意大利境内建立的最根深蒂固的欧盟银行主要有德意志银行 SpA、荷兰商业银行、巴克莱银行、工银欧洲、德国商业银行、荷兰银行、阿瑞尔银行、ABC 国际银行公司、毕尔巴鄂比斯开银行（BBVA）、德国巴伐利亚银行、法国巴黎银行、法国巴黎银行证券服务、农业信用投资银行、瑞士信贷、德意志银行 AG、汇丰银行、德国工业银行、工银（欧洲）、苏格兰皇家银行。

近年已经有几个亚洲国家，特别是中国和日本的银行及机构在意大利设立了分支机构。三菱东京日联银行有限公司是一个例外，因为它在1963年就设立了代表处，并在1972年开始全面运作。它是日本最古老的银行，自成立以来在国内经营不间断。近年来，野村国际公司意大利分行也已在意大利设立，亚洲的中国建设银行也通过其欧洲分公司瑞穗银行有限公司开设意大利分行。

（二）合并和收购

民营企业可以被组织或运营为独资企业或合伙企业，或者是公司的形式。公司可分为限责任公司和股份有限公司。传统意义上，意大利的公司属于小型的或中型的公司（90% 以上的意大利公司只有 9 名以下的员工），然而，也有很多大公司，并且意大利的股票市场高度发达。

为了进行并购操作，根据手头的税务问题和并购后的业务实体，很多方式被运用。主要有以下几点：分享或购买配额；持续经营或部分转让；合并和分立。

公司都可以提出各种不同的问题，任何并购操作，不论其法律形式如何，都可根据其规模大小，产生竞争问题。此外，有关跨境并购可能会受到欧盟指令 2005/56/EC 号的约束。

（三）竞争监管

1. 部门竞争监管

意大利有关反垄断问题的法律的出台是在 1990 年。从此以后，所有企业竞争问题都由反垄断局处理。在竞争案件中，反垄断局的决定可以在拉齐奥行政法庭上提出上诉，并在更大程度上向国务院提出上诉。

反垄断局对于诱导性广告也有类似的职能，这些诱导性广告一般是由传统法庭和自律机构处理的，即所谓的广告自律评委。

不公平竞争一般是普通法庭的权属范围。

意大利反垄断的规定，从实践角度来看，与欧盟的制定趋同。它们有一个一般性的原则，在意大利《反垄断法》中，要求反垄断局和意大利法官根据欧盟（特别是欧洲法院）的原则来解释意大利反垄断规则，甚至在案件与欧盟有利害关系时直接参照欧盟法条。

对于意大利和欧盟的竞争条款之间的关系，一个基本原则就是意大利对于与欧盟没有利益关系的案件有处理的权力，也就是说，如果意大利认为一个案件涉及欧盟利益，则它们必须马上通知欧盟委员会并且除非欧盟委员会允许，否则停止有关的调查。另外，一旦欧盟委员会决定调查一个案件，意大利反垄断局则不能继续调查。但是，在集中的时候，与意大利的权力和欧盟的利益相关的案件之间的区别比较容易，对于卡特尔和滥用行为来说，区分是复杂的。实际上，发生的事情更类似于各种各样的原则（国家一级和欧盟一级）的认同以及有关各方（管理局、欧盟委员会和其他欧盟成员国的反垄断执法机构）之间的合作。

2. 竞争法简介

（1）集中。集中，如合并、收购等，如发生以下情况需要提前通知反垄断局：所有相关企业（计划运营前的最后一年）的总营业额高于 4.95 亿欧元；目标实体（计划经营前的最后一年）营业额高于 5000 万欧元。这些阈值每年更新一次。

对于银行，营业额被认为相当于活跃资产的十分之一（不包括备忘录账户）；对于保险公司而言，被视为相当于兑现的总保费。事先未通知反垄断局将受到罚款处罚（高达总营业额的 1%）。收到通知后，如果反垄断局认为有必要，应在（收到通知后 30 天内）开通调查，这一调查可以在开通后 45 天内通过决议的方式决定关闭拒绝或有条件授权（这个期限在特殊复杂的情况下可以被延长）。

如果行动在通知之前已经完成，反垄断局可以发出必要的命令，重新建立竞争条件并消除扭曲：违反这种命令的行为将被处以总营业额的最低 1% 最高 10% 的罚款。如果在主管当局作出否定的决定后进行操作，情况也会如此。

（2）纵向和横向协议。卡特尔，或者一般来说，企业之间的纵向或横向协议一律被禁止，因此在其范围内具有或消除，限制或一致地改变国内市场或相关部门竞争的效力无效。例如，通过

① 固定价格或其他交易条件；

② 限制或控制生产，市场准入，投资或技术开发；

③ 分享市场或供应来源；

④ 对不同方面的同等交易应用不同的条件，使其处于竞争劣势；

⑤ 缔结合同，由其他各方接受与此类合同主体无关的补充义务。

协议如果对消费者有用，可能会由反垄断局特别授权，但协议是有期间限制的。

（3）滥用支配地位。当一个或多个企业在意大利市场或其相关部分占据主导地位时，不能滥用市场力量，尤其是不能

① 固定价格或其他交易条件；

② 限制或控制生产，市场准入，投资或技术开发；

③ 分享市场或供应来源；

④ 对不同方面的同等交易应用不同的条件，使其处于竞争劣势；

⑤ 缔结合同，由其他各方接受与此类合同主体无关的补充义务。

（4）协议和侵权行为常见的规则。关于协议和侵权行为的调查可以由反垄断局根据其自主收集的信息或通过谴责（一般来自竞争对手）开始。在协议的情况下，一些利益相关企业可能提前向反垄断局提交协议以获得其放行。在后一种情况（双方达成协议的通知）中，反垄断局必须在通知后的 120 天内开展调查，否则反垄断局失去干预的权力，除非通知不完整或虚假。有关各方可以参加调查，由反垄断局听取，并提交文件和简报。反垄断局认为有紧急停止或中止协议或滥用，有权在调查结束前发出冻结令；如果当事人不

遵守命令，他们可能会被罚款营业额的 3%。

在调查期间（但不得迟于开放后 3 个月），有关各方可提出（以承诺的形式）能够消除协议或被调查行为的反竞争特征的安排。如果反垄断局认定这样的承诺足以重新建立竞争，就可以接受这些承诺，并对当事各方强制执行，在没有确定任何违规行为的情况下关闭调查。但是，如果情况发生变化，反垄断局可以依法重新开放调查，或者当事人不履行其承诺（在这种情况下，罚款最多可达到其营业额的 10%），或者最终如果双方提供的信息是错误的或误导。

调查后，反垄断局必须发出其决定（在调查开始时，反垄断局本身所指明的期限内）。如果认定协议或行为实际上违法，则命令各方采取必要措施重新建立真正的竞争，并且如果侵权是严重的，也适用罚款（高达每一方的营业额的 10%）。如果当事人不遵守管理局的命令，同样适用此罚款。

（四）税

1. 税收管理

意大利税收制度由意大利税收机构 Agenzia delle Entrate 管理。Agenzia delle Entrate 有自己的结构和不同的部门（控制、诉讼等）。Agenzia 发行文件解释税法（所谓的 Circolari），或提出其对税收实践（Risoluzioni）产生的具体案件的意见。这些文件可以从 Agenzia 的网站下载（www.agenziaentrate.gov.it/wps/portal/entrate/home）。

在某些情况下，纳税人可以向 Agenzia 申请特别裁决。Agenzia delle Entrate 还负责管理某些地方税，并负责相应分配这些资金。

税收征收目前委托给特别机构 Equitalia。然而，在 2016 年通过的重组过程中，Equireia 从 2017 年 7 月起被纳入 Agenzia delle Entrate；因此，Agenzia delle Entrate 将负责税收管理和税收征收。

在纳税人不同意 Agenzia delle Entrate 或 Equitalia 所作出的决定的情况下，他们首先可以进入省税法院（Commissione Tributaria Provinciale）。如果纳税人（或税务机关）对回复不满意，可以向区域税务法庭（委托代理地区）提出上诉。最高上诉的例子是最高上诉法庭（Cortedi Cassazione），任何一方都可以提出最后的上诉。Cortedi Cassazione 裁决法律问题，而不是事实，因此，

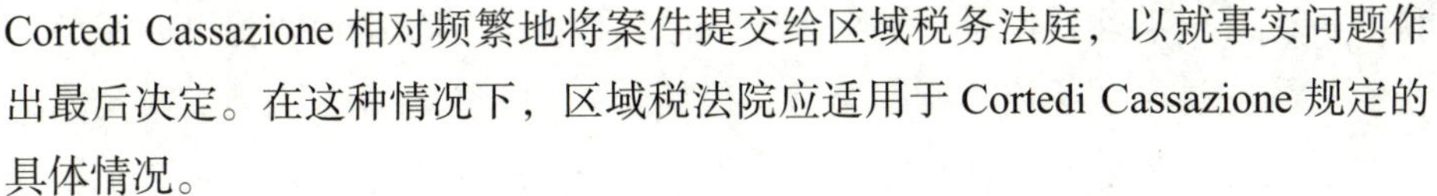

Cortedi Cassazione 相对频繁地将案件提交给区域税务法庭，以就事实问题作出最后决定。在这种情况下，区域税法院应适用于 Cortedi Cassazione 规定的具体情况。

2. 税制

关于税收制度，应当在个人与公司之间对税收居留进行初步区分。

在以下情况下，个人应视为意大利的税务居民：

（1）个人在居民人口登记册中登记大部分的纳税年度（公历年）；

（2）个人或经济利益或惯常居所在的大部分税金年度位于意大利。

大部分纳税年度一般定义为公历年至少 183 天。但是，为了达到这个标准，纳税人不需要连续出现在意大利。个人税收制度，根据这些规则，居住在意大利的个人将根据其全球收入进行评估，而非居民个人将仅根据他 / 她的意大利来源收入进行评估。

如果有下列情形，一家公司将被认为是意大利的纳税居民：

（1）其注册办事处在意大利，或者其行政办公室在意大利，所有战略决策都在意大利进行；

（2）其活动的主要目的是在意大利。发现在意大利征税的实体在全球收入中受意大利企业所得税的影响。税制，指非居民用于税务目的的实体仅对意大利来源地收入（归属于意大利常设单位的收入）承担法人所得税。

3. 税务规则

关于税收规定，应特别提及 PAYE（Pay-as-You-earn）规则，特别适用于就业收入。一般来说，雇主应当注册预扣税，将从雇员的定期支付（工资）中扣除个人所得税的一笔款项，代表雇员缴纳给 Agenzia delle Entrate。扣除工资的金额将按照雇员的个人所得税税率计算，员工每期将获得适当计算的净额（毛收入扣除税收）。

税收抵扣。如果超额税已经支付（如扣缴的税款超过员工的总税额），纳税人可能并不是要求退回超额税费，要求退还其他未偿还的税务负债，不仅垂直扣除（有关相同的税），而且横向（对其他税收的负债），具体限制适用。这是有权获得税收抵免的纳税人的实际补救办法，作为复杂和耗时的退税的替代办法。

反避税规则。根据 2015 年推出的新一般反避税规则（GAAR），意大利税务机关有权消除任何源于无有效经济原因以及希望获得税收优惠或避免承担税负的交易。这适用于所有交易，包括合并和分立的业务交易，新实体的并入以及资产和金融工具的出售和转让。新的 GAAR 规则有效地在法定形式上实施了欧洲法院最初在增值税环境中制定的滥用法理原则。

转让定价规则。意大利对相关居民和非居民公司之间的交易实施转移定价规则。根据这些规定，内部交易必须按公平原则进行，以防止将税基任意转移到其他司法管辖区。一般来说，适用经合组织转让定价指南。原则上，意大利转让定价规则不适用于国内交易；然而，根据判例法，这些交易中的价格严重不足可以根据滥用情况进行调整（例如，纳税人与另一家公司之间的交易在清算边缘净营业亏损）。如果意大利公司符合意大利转让定价文件要求，允许以跨国公司原则确定跨国企业设定的转移价格的一致性，则转让定价调整的结果将不予罚款。

4. 主要分类

意大利税收相当复杂，涵盖广泛的收入来源和资产。形成意大利税收制度里程碑的最重要的类别是：个人所得税、企业所得税、区域生产活动税、增值税、继承和赠与税、注册税。

个人所得税。个人所得税按以下个人所得收入计算：工资和工资收入（就业收入）、自营职业收入、房地产租赁收入、营业收入、资本收入（如股息收入）、其他收入，如彩票收入。

个人所得税税率。个人所得税是以累进税率征收的。第一级应纳税所得额（首次为15000欧元）的税率为23%；第二级为13000欧元，税率是27%；第三级为27000欧元，税率为38%；第四级为20000欧元，税率为41%；第五级为75000欧元以上，税率为43%。最重要的是，纳税人的地域附加费约为1%～3%。每个地方当局和省设置的市级和省级附加费可能达到0.9%。

企业所得税通常适用于排除个人的纳税人。一般来说，企业所得税是根据企业在一个标准财年，用 1 月 1 日至 12 月 31 日的运营结果进行计算，根据适用的税率加减调整。可扣税费用的例子包括：业务形成成本，利息支出（受限制），支付的特许权使用费，支付的工资和津贴，社会保障金，汽车费用（受限制），坏账（受限制），行政费用，广告、办公支出和佣金，娱乐费用（受限制），资产折旧（受限制）。《意大利税法》规定了对利息支出的可抵扣性的具体限制。支付的利息扣除受到以下更大的限制：利息收入；EBITDA的30%（利息、税前折旧和摊销前的收益）。超过上限的任何利息支出可以在后期财政年度结转，但受限于相同的限制。

企业所得税税率。从2017年1月1日起，企业所得税按实体应纳税所得额的24%的固定利率计算。然而，如果公司被视为休眠，企业所得税的适用税率为34.5%，以资产和投资的最低收益为基础收取。

区域生产活动税。区域生产活动税的税基与企业所得税有所不同。从广义上来说，区域生产活动税收取生产价值，即应纳税净营业收入。区域生产活动税不考虑利息和其他财务收入和支出，转移经常性担保的资本损益、工资费用（例外）和非常收入项目。

区域生产活动税税率。标准率为3.9%，地方当局可以在规定的范围内增加或减少标准费率。

增值税。与欧盟其他地方一样，增值税通常是在意大利供应地的货物或服务的供应方面收取的，无论客户是私人还是企业。因此，它是在产品周期的每个阶段收取的多阶段税收，但最终由终端用户（最终消费者）承担。欧盟以外的货物进口也被征收增值税。税收的总体框架是根据欧盟立法规定的增值税指令（2006/112/EC，经修订）以及相关的指令和法规。这些允许成员国几个应用税收的选择，而不是设定利率的权力（在某些广泛的范围内）。用品可能要纳税，免除（有或没有扣除进项增值税的权利）或超出范围。免除用品扣除进项增值税的权利有时被称为“零评级”。完全应税或零评估用品的企业通常有资格全额扣除进项增值税（在供应品上产生的增值税）。专门免征供应品的企业没有扣除权，不符合扣除进项增值税的资格。混合豁免物资的企业没有扣除和应税或零利用的物资的权利，可以全额扣除直接在应纳税或零额度供应上产生的进项增值税。部分扣除将用于间接成本。豁免物品没有扣除权，包括银行、金融和保险服务；为个人提供医疗保健；出售和出租不动产。所有实体，如个人或公司进行经营时必须注册增值税。为注册增值税，应纳税人必须申请增值税登记号码（PartitaIVA）。

增值税税率。除非以零或减免的税率征收，所有用品均以标准税率征收增值税，即22%。意大利也有两个减税税率：10%和4%。10%的税率适用于以下用品：住宅物业的维护和修理、某些食品、客运、接受文化活动、酒店和餐厅服务。4% 的税率适用于：维修、修理和销售第一居所，某些食品和饮料，书籍和报纸，残疾人士的某些用品。零等级税率（免税）适用于欧盟内部大多数跨境货物和服务供应，并向第三国出口。

继承和赠与税。虽然税收由受让人承担，但转让时转让人的身份完全决定被转让的权利或财产是否须缴纳税款。如果转让人在转移时是意大利居民（无论是在死亡还是在转让人的一生），那么转让人的全球财产都是需要缴税的。另外，如果转让人是非居民，那就只有位于意大利的财产才需要缴税。受让人的住所是无关紧要的。以下是免税的：配偶、直系后代（如子女和孙子女）或直系前辈（如父母和祖父母）的首次 100 万欧元以内转移；100 万欧元以内转移给兄弟姐妹；除上述之外，150 万欧元以内的转让给残疾受让人的。

继承和赠与税率。这取决于转让人与受让人之间的血缘关系程度。配偶、直系后裔和直系前辈税率为 4%，兄弟姐妹和近亲被征税 6%，其他承受人的税率为 8%。

注册税。具体行为和合同必须在签字或者具体情况发生时向当地注册税务局提交，并且必须支付相关税费。

注册税率。根据合同和作为合同对象的资产的性质，以合同的形式，将注册税征收为固定金额或占货物价值的百分比和 / 或作为合同对象的权利。作为一般规定，在交易受到增值税影响的情况下，不得按比例征收注册税。

5. 纳税申报

一般来说，意大利税收制度是以自我评估为基础的。因此，责任在于有关人员准备和提交报税表并计算自己的税收责任。纳税年度应在规定的日期结束后提交。延迟填报会受到很大的惩罚。

从 2015 年起，一些纳税人已经能够选择税务机关在就业和养老金收入方面预先填写的纳税申报单。选择此选项的纳税人可以直接接受网上的纳税申报单，也可以在规定的时间内在线修改。使用预先填写的申报单是可选的，纳税人可以自由地以正常方式提交自己的申报单。

根据 2016 年和随后的税收年度新法规，意大利税务机关可以在提交报税年度之后第五年的 12 月 31 日（有些例外情况）之前审核一个人的纳税申报单。举例来说，2016 年税收年度评估将开放至 2022 年 12 月 31 日。

自我评估原则也适用于继承和赠与税，但是，当遗产资产的价值低于 10

万欧元且死者不拥有任何房地产时，则不得追缴遗产税。

6. 优惠税制

专利盒制度。截至 2015 年，对通过使用合格无形资产（如专利、品牌、专有技术等知识产权）产生的收入实行优惠税收制度。执行与这种无形资产有关的活动的纳税人可以选择将企业所得税和区域生产活动税税基减少为相对于使用这一无形资产所得收入的 30%（2015 年）、40%（2016 年）和 50%（2017 年和未来几年）的资格资产。该豁免适用于知识产权许可和资产直接剥削所产生的收入。在大多数情况下，提前作出裁决是进入专利盒制度的先决条件。如果在处置之后的第二个会计年度终止之前至少 90% 的处置收到的现金用于维持或开发其他合格无形资产，处理合格资产取得的资本利得可以被免除。这个制度在选举之后的 5 个财政年度有效。

新税务居民个人。《2017 财政法》提出了可能吸引高净值群体的特殊税务法规。新税务居民可以对该制度行使选择权，如果他们在行使该选择权之前的 10 个税期之中至少 9 个不是意大利的税务居民；按照先进的裁决程序取得意大利税务机关的批准。该选择在原则上 15 年内是有效的，无论公民身份如何，所有人都可以使用该选项。

选择这一制度的个人仍然以通常方式根据在意大利的收入缴纳意大利税。但是，如果纳税人每年缴纳 10 万欧元，并向意大利当局披露所有相关信息，则其外国收入和收益将避免缴纳意大利税收。这项豁免可以扩大到家庭成员，每名成员的费用为 25000 欧元。

（五）贸易

1. 简介

意大利是欧盟（EU）、世界贸易组织（WTO）、经济合作与发展组织（OECD）、欧洲安全与合作组织（欧安组织）和北大西洋公约组织（NATO）的成员国，并适用这些机构签署的国际协议。

欧盟成员国之间形成关税同盟和大型统一市场，成为自由贸易区。它对来自非欧盟国家如美国、日本和中国的进口产品征收共同关税。

正如欧盟所有成员，意大利采取共同的贸易政策。某些产品需要符合特定的质量标准，特别是玩具、机械、电磁兼容性、电信终端设备、有源植入式医疗设备、医疗设备、非自动称重设备、建筑产品、防爆电气设备、低压电气设备、简单压力容器、个人防护装备和燃气用具。合格产品必须携带“CE”标志以显示其兼容性，由制造商或进口商贴在产品上作为自我承诺的声明。

2. 部门监督贸易与贸易促进机构

经济发展部是负责监督贸易和确定增加出口以及意大利企业国际化战略的政府部门。在经济发展部内，国际化政策总局和国际商业政策总局负责贸易和商业政策。

作为与经济发展部独立的部门，意大利贸易促进局（ICE）是根据经济发展部制定的战略，促进意大利公司国际化的政府机构。ICE 向意大利和外国公司提供信息、支持和建议。

除了罗马总部，ICE 还通过与意大利大使馆和领事馆相关的贸易促进办事处的网络在全球范围运营，并与当地政府和企业合作。

ICE 在海外提供广泛的服务来帮助意大利和外国企业相互联系，特别是：

（1）识别可能的业务伙伴；

（2）与意大利公司举行双边贸易会议；

（3）代表团访问意大利；

（4）正式参加本地展览会；

（5）与意大利专家进行论坛和研讨会。

3. 部门监督海关

海关问题监督机构是海关署，一个以与经济和财政部签订的协议为框架的实体。海关署执行控制活动，评估和事后追回与货物流通有关的征收责任，包括消费税。但是，海关署的活动范围并不限于海关关税。此外，海关署也阻止违法的非法贸易冒牌产品或不符合健康安全立法、武器、毒品、文化遗产、非法贩运废物以及受《华盛顿公约》保护的濒危动物和植物物种的国际贸易活动。在烟草制造领域，海关署负责监督与消费税有关的程序。它还控制零售销售关税和烟草商网络，并执行保证这些产品符合国家和社区立法所需的技术验证。

截至 2012 年，海关署与国家垄断独立行政部门合并成海关和垄断机构。海关主管部门在中央和区域方向以指导、协调和控制等功能被组织。组织图还包括 15 个化学实验室，负责分析产品样品，通常旨在对每个进口商品征收税收的职责进行正确的分类和验证。

4. 海关规定

海关关税适用于进口欧盟地区的货物。进口关税的金额取决于进口货物的价值和性质。特别是对于每个商品，欧盟关税规定了对进口商品的价值或数量适用的税率。

一般来说，海关规定由欧盟集中发行，并直接在包括意大利在内的所有会员国适用。但是，有些地区由国家当局自行决定，特别是在实际执行规则方面，因此不能安全地假定海关规则在整个欧盟范围内同样地被解释和适用。

进入意大利后，非欧盟货物应附有欧共体同一单证（SAD），由进口商提交的一份声明，用于为海关识别和描述货物。所有欧盟成员国的 SAD 均有效，其中所包含的信息受到海关总署的审查。

任何人员可以任命一位代表与海关署进行海关规定制定的活动和手续。这种代表权可能是直接的，在这种情况下，代表应以委托人的名义行事；或是间接的，在这种情况下，代表应以自己的名义行事，而代表委托人。

经济运营商在意大利引进货物时，货物的正确分类是一个关键问题。不正确的分类可能会引起更高的关税，经营者可能面临不必要的税收负担；或者应用较低的关税，可能引起意大利海关当局的税务评估。

一般来说，货物的价值由交易价值表示，因此，出口到欧盟关税地区的货物实际支付或可支付的价格。在确定交易价值是否可以接受时，买方和卖方相关的事实本身并不足以忽略交易价值。对销售情况在必要时进行检查，如果关系不影响价格，交易价值就被接受。实际支付或可支付的价格是进口货物的总金额，包括为履行卖方义务，买方向卖方或买方向第三方支付的所有作为出售进口货物的条件的费用。

在确定海关完税价格时，就以下项目是由买方引起且未被包含进价款来说，它们应被加入价款（未穷尽所有情况）：佣金和经纪费；使用费和许可费；进口货物的保险费用。

同时，假如货物到达欧盟关税地区后的运输费用以及其他具体项目与实际支付或实际支付的价格分开列示，则不得包含在海关完税价格中。

当进口货物来自优惠原产地时，进口减免税率或零税率适用。优惠原产地取决于欧盟与其他非欧盟国家之间的商业协议的存在或欧盟向非欧盟国家单方面提供的福利。减免税率或零税率的适用还可能取决于优惠关税待遇的存在或法律规定的特定豁免的存在。

5. 消费税

以下商品须缴纳消费税：

（1）能源和类似货物（如汽油、瓦斯油、天然气、电力、煤炭）；

（2）酒精和酒精饮料（如葡萄酒、啤酒、乙醇）；

（3）加工烟草（如雪茄、香烟、烟草）。

一般而言，关于一个月内为消费而发布的消费品，相关消费税应在下个月的 16 日内支付。关于进口的消费品，就程序和时间线而言，适用海关规定。

一般来说，消费品的生产、加工和持有须通过财政仓库进行暂停执行。为了管理财政仓库，有必要取得意大利海关当局颁发的许可证；财政仓库的所有者需要服从具体的义务（如提供保证、保存存储商品的特定会计系统、受要求的意大利海关总署进行的控制）。

在某些情况下，如果最终产品没有在意大利被消费，则向发布消费品的运营商退回税款。

三、劳动

（一）劳动法律法规简介

1. 适用于意大利就业合同的规定

雇佣关系主要由法定规则（其中许多是强制性规则），特别是意大利《宪法》《民法典》《工人权利法案》，以及涵盖特定受关注领域的额外的草案来规定。

《宪法》规定了有关劳工事务的一般原则，而《民法典》和《工人权利法案》则载有适用于雇佣关系的相当详细的规则。

意大利是欧盟成员国，并且不需要通过当地立法（欧盟条例）执行就可立即适用或要求在地方执行（欧盟指令）的欧洲法律强制性规定的阐释者也是一样的。欧洲法律规定了若干就业问题的统一标准。最显著的欧盟指令是关于工作时间、集体解雇、在转让企业时维护雇员权利的指令。

除此之外，雇佣关系还可能受到国家集体谈判协议和公司协议（在规定的雇主和雇员工作委员会之间签订）的约束，主要用更多详细的方式，规定了适用于特定类别的雇员和 / 或特定类型的行业或商业部门的具体条款和条件。

（1）意大利《宪法》。意大利《宪法》第 35 条至第 40 条规定的主要原则是：

① 雇员享有适当的工资，每周休息和每年度假的权利；

② 男女工作上的平等；

③ 雇员有足够的养老金和社会保障覆盖的权利（如涉及工作中的事故、疾病、残疾、失业）；

④ 组织和参加工会的自由；

⑤ 罢工权。

（2）《工人权利法案》和其他关于雇佣关系的实质性法律

《工人权利法案》（1970 年 5 月 20 日第 300 号法案）是关于劳工问题的最重要的框架立法。其主要目的是保护工人的自由和尊严，特别保障了员工的言论自由、政治或宗教观点和信仰、参加工会和从事工会活动等的权利。

《工人人权法案》还和1990年7月15日第604号、1990年5月11日第108号，以及2015年3月4日第23号法令一起管理个人解雇的问题。1991年7月23日第223号法律规定了集体解雇的问题。

2015年6月15日第81号法令包含了关于所有主要类型的就业合同的条文。

（3）国家集体谈判协议（CBAs）

雇佣关系的几个方面由 CBAs 管理。这些协议是适用于在特定工业部门工作的特定类别的雇员的私人合同，并由代表有关雇员的工会与相应商业部门的雇主协会谈判达成。

CBAs 的应用不是强制性的。原则上，CBAs 实际上仅限于那些属于企业家协会成员的雇主，他们进入或遵守特定的 CBAs，或者那些特别提到在个人就业合同的框架下特定 CBAs 的雇主。

事实上，当他们必须解决 CBAs 没有明确管辖的雇佣合同有关的有争议的事项（特别是在最低工资方面）时，任何给定的 CBAs 的某些条款也被用作劳动法庭的基准。

当 CBAs 适用时，其规定不能仅仅为了利益而被修改为对雇员的损害。CBAs 规范了工作分类、最低工资（根据不同的就业水平）、资历、试用期、通知期、工作时间、假期、病假和病假工资、补充福利计划、加班费等工作。

（4）适用法律

根据意大利的法律，国际就业合同由 2008 年 6 月 17 日的 EC 第 593 号条例管辖。EC 第 593 号条例第 8 条规定，个人雇佣合同应受当事人选择的法律管辖。然而，这样的法律选择可能不会导致雇员丧失由不能被按照在没有选择的情况下可适用的法律制定的协议减损的条文提供的保护。

适用顺序为：雇主惯常通过履行合同进行工作的国家的法律；如果以前的原则不适用，雇员所在营业地所在国家的法律；如果从整体情况看，合同与上述国家以外的另一国家的法律更为密切相关。

2. 员工类别

根据意大利《民法典》，员工主要分为蓝领（工人）、白领（科员）、高级白领（精英）、高管。

CBAs 一般是根据每个工作类别、工作水平（职称和职务的排名）以及相关的最低工资来确定。

特别地，高级白领不属于高管的类别，而是那些需要专业知识和技能来开展相关重要活动的员工。根据高级白领的行为准则，他们拥有广泛的自主权，但也应当在较高的层级来作出决定。

高管是一群被赋予广泛自主权力和职能的高级职员，但也具有相应的责任；他们的活动旨在促进、协调整体管理企业的业务活动或其中的一部分。

因此，高管实际上管理着公司的业务（在董事会的监督下），并且在公司的结构层级中一般归属于总经理（总经理也是一种高管），当然，其他人，如董事会也可以承担这一职责，而所有其他类别的员工都是从属于他们的。一般来说，高管具有广泛的自主权，主要涉及全部或部分业务的决策。

3. 任务与职责

在招聘的时候，员工必须谨记公司根据法律与合同分配给他 / 她的任务与职责。此后，除非直接影响员工工作角色的业务结构发生变化，否则员工不能被降职并进行重新分配，当然员工同意降职以维护其工作（而不是被解雇）或为了达到不同的专业背景的情形除外。如果员工被降级违反了法律规定，他有权要求辞职，或者要求恢复以前的职责，并要求赔偿损害赔偿。

在雇佣关系进行的过程中，员工也可以被分配到其他任务和职责，条件是新职责与之前的职责属于同一职业类别，并且具有与之前相同的正式等级等。

如果一名雇员被指定承担了高于6个连续月份的高级职务，则除非他/她放弃这项权利，否则他/她应当被视为已经被明确地分配到与此类职务相对应的较高职类，有权享受更高级别的相关报酬和福利。

4. 招聘

各类员工一般从直接招聘中产生。在某些情况下，雇主不得不招募一些“受保护类别”的雇员，如寡妇、孤儿、难民和残疾人。

非欧盟国家应当遵守移民规则。

通常，雇主通过设定一些包含关键条款和条件的合同来雇用雇员，即聘用日期、就业状况和期限、工作地点、职位、职责和报酬。此外，就业函还应包括试用期、工作时间、假期、附带福利和通知期间（当这些事项不受CBA规定的情况下）。

5. 合同类型和持续时间

（1）开放式就业合同。这份合同是标准的劳动合同，没有特别的正式要求（原则上，一个不限制的雇佣合同甚至不需要书面形式）。

（2）定期就业合同。这个合同代表的是开放式就业关系的例外。

与同一名雇员可以订立多个固定期限合同，履行相同类别和职级的职责或职务，不论这几个合同之间的时间如何，其最长期限为36个月。如果超过这样的期限，合同将根据法律规定自动变为开放式的。

最初签订的少于36个月的固定期限合同可以在员工同意的情况下延长最多5次，总共持续时间不得超过36个月。

每个雇主可以签订的固定期限合同具有一定的数量上限。一般来说，雇主可以签订一定数量的固定期限合约，但不得超过1月1日生效的开放式合同数量的20%。

雇用一些固定期限的雇员，没有上限，以便开办新的活动（在这种情况下，定期合同的最长期限为12个月）；替代缺席但有权恢复的雇员（如病假或产假或育儿假期间的雇员）；雇用50岁以上的雇员。

上述规定不适用于与高管签订的期限为五年的定期合同。无论如何，高管有权在合同期三年后结束合同。

（3）其他类型的就业合同。意大利法律还规定了其他类型的雇佣合同，其中主要的是学徒合同，这是一项雇佣初期学徒的开放式合同，合同到期后雇主可以自由退出。

学徒合同还允许雇主支付较低的社会保障费用；作为交换，合同要求雇主向学徒提供合同条款所要求的培训（理论和工作）。

6. 试用期

员工最初的就业期可以是试用期。任何试用期的协议必须以书面形式签订。试用期的最长法定期限为 6 个月。所有 CBAs 可以根据员工的工作水平调整此类期间的持续时间（平均期限为 20 个工作日至 6 个月）。

在试用期内，除了非常有限的例外情况，任何一方均可随意终止协议，无须另行通知或者赔偿。

7. 工资

意大利《宪法》保证员工获得公平工资的权利。CBAs 据此提出了适用的最低工资和福利以及强制性的加薪。

工资可以在协商的基础上从最低工资（所谓的最低限度）开始增加：这种增加可以授予个人（通常奖励他 / 她的具体技能和经验的雇员）（或在此情况下，最低限度的工资可以抵消 CBA 中商定的任何基薪）。

全球范围内雇员的总薪酬包括最低工资及其之外的额外项目，例如，在 CBAs 中列出的附加项目和 / 或附带福利（实物补偿）的金额等价物，如午餐券、公司车辆私用等。

通常，年薪在 12 个月内支付，第十三次在每个日历年 12 月支付。某些 CBAs 还提供了第十四次（在某些情况下是第十五次）的分期付款。

8. 工作时间

普通工作时间由法律规定，每周 40 个小时。CBAs 可以减少这种持续时间，并可以根据业务需要制定灵活的工作时间表。无论如何，7 天工作时间表的任何平均持续时间不能超过 48 个小时（包括加班）。此外，员工有权每 24 个小时连续休息 11 个小时，其结果是，原则上最高每日工作时间不能超过 13 个小时。

加班工作主要由 CBAs 的规定进行管理：如果没有达成这样的集体协议，雇主和雇员之间可以事先商定超时工作的事宜，但必须在每年 250 个小时以内。

加班工作也需要给以特别的补充报酬。

上述工作时间的限制原则上不适用于可以自行决定日常安排时间的主管和雇员（如家庭办公人员和远程工作人员）。

9. 兼职就业

所有类型的就业合同都可以采取全日制或兼职。兼职工作时间表不能单方面的由雇主修改。但可以在兼职合同中插入具体条款，以便不时地调整工作时间表，以及在每天或每周的工作时间表中引入一定的灵活性。根据员工原有的协议，增加超过最初商定的数额的工资或者根据不同的工作时间表计算。

兼职员工具有与全职员工相同的权利，尽管某些权利（度假、病假）可以与提供给雇主的工作量成正比。

10. 假期

根据意大利《宪法》，工人每星期有权休息 1 天（通常是星期日），在已有的宗教和法定节假日（通常为 11 天，在某些地方为 12 天）可以远离工作，而且也有一段带薪假期，一般这个期限至少为每年 4 个星期。

休假的权利通常由 CBAs 来进行规定，其中会给予一些员工超过最低法定标准的假期，这主要取决于员工的工作水平和工作资历。

雇员每年享有至少两个星期的假期（在与雇主约定的期限内，并符合后者的业务需要），其余两个星期在该假期累积的历年的到期日起 18 个月内。

未经使用的假期不能被没收，并在终止雇用后支付报酬。

11. 病假及病假工资

在有病历文件的情况下，雇佣关系暂停一段时间，这个期限通常由 CBAs 确定，持续时间不得低于 3 个月。

在病假期间，雇员可以从国家社会保障机构获得补偿，但根据几乎所有的 CBAs 规定，雇员同时有权从雇主处收到剩余款项，从而使收取的款项达到总付款的 75% ~ 100%。

在病假期间，除正当事由之外，员工不能被解雇，只有在病假结束之后，员工仍然无法恢复正常工作时，才能予以解雇。

12. 工作地点和转移

在雇用时，必须将雇员分配到合同规定的工作场所。雇主不能随意搬迁；

相反，搬迁必须通过客观的技术、组织和 / 或生产性原因来证明。

搬迁时依据上述合法理由，不能拒绝；如果员工未充分考虑到搬迁问题，可将其重新分配到以前的工作地点。

员工的搬迁应当以公平的方式通知给他 / 她，通常在 CBA 中规定，雇主应承担搬迁和转移费用。

13. 发明

雇员在雇佣关系中创造的发明，如果与雇佣合同中定义的任务相关，属于雇主，并相应补偿（发明任务是雇员职责的一部分）。如果发明超出了分配给员工的职责，但是在履行职业义务的同时与业务活动相关的事项发生的，则发明属于雇主，但雇员有权获得适当的赔偿。如果发明超出了雇佣关系的范围，但仍然与雇主的业务活动有关，则雇主有权利选择使用发明或申请专利，通过向该专利支付费用或版税。在所有情况下，员工都保留被视为发明人的道德权利。

14. 惩戒措施和制裁

在雇佣关系中，雇员必须遵守雇主的指示，并遵守雇主的层级组织。

不遵守这些规定，或未能适当履行合同义务，雇主有权激活纪律处分程序。

这种程序要求，员工的错误及时以书面形式通知给他 / 她，并给予雇员至少 5 天的时间提交其意见和辩护；随之而来的纪律措施（如果有的话）必须与过错相称，必须及时传达给雇员。

如果雇主适用纪律守则，则在每个生产单位附上相应的副本。如果雇主不适用任何CBAs（通常包括纪律守则），也没有自己的守则，根据司法先例，允许雇主对违反所谓最低限度的错误实行制裁的道德规范，即根据集体所共有的道德价值观或与刑事规定相违背的行为标准，使任何人都能将其视为“错误”。

纪律制裁是：口头或书面谴责、罚款（最多 4 个小时工资）、暂停无薪（最多 10 天工作）、解雇。

在纪律程序中，雇员也可以以暂停薪酬的方式，作为预防措施，以在评估雇员责任所需的时间内保护雇主的利益。

15. 竞争和保密

根据意大利《民法典》，员工在其雇用期间不得与雇主进行业务竞争，不得泄露有关该承诺或生产方法的机密或秘密信息，或使用此类信息给雇主造成损失。

非竞争性义务仅限于在雇主经营的同一类业务中，除非在双方当事人之间签订了具体的非竞争性协议，否则在雇佣关系终止后不能生效。

所述非竞争性协议仅在以下情况下可强制执行：以书面形式订立；它规定了适当的赔偿；对象 / 范围、持续时间（管理人员不超过 5 年，其他员工 3 年）和地理区域有限。

16. 解雇

根据意大利的法律，不允许雇佣关系终止（除少数情况外）。

因此，一旦各方签订了开放式的劳动合同，试用期到期，雇主无权单方解雇雇员，相反只有在有正当理由终止（非常严重违反合同或任何其他类型的行为，损害雇主与雇员之间的信任关系），在这种情况下，解雇可以恕不另行通知；或主观上合理的理由（有关的不履行合同归属于雇员的合同，如表现不佳、疏忽等），在这种情况下，解雇是可执行的，但须经通知；或存在客观合理的理由（任何不归于雇员的原因，而不是雇主的经济或组织或生产性需求，如营业缩减、营业额下降等），其中案件解除可强制执行，但须注意。

所有以雇员身份出现问题为由的解雇都应在纪律程序之前进行。

除正当理由之外，在以下情况下，劳动关系永远不会被终止：产假（如果在小孩第一年之前通知，解雇是无效的）；结婚妇女（婚姻第一年届满前通知解雇是无效的）；临时不在病假（在整个病期内）的雇员。

以固定期限雇用的员工只能因正当理由（或者终止雇主的所有业务）而被解雇。

不符合法律规定对所有其他雇员提供法律保护的高管人员有不同的规定，原则上可以随意解雇。如果 CBAs 适用于其雇佣关系，要求解雇是合理的，管理人员将被保护免于被解雇。

根据司法先例，合理解雇的概念相当广泛。这是因为一个主管人员（由于他的高层次的等级职位）必须通过强大的信任关系与雇主挂钩。因此，即使没有理由解雇其他类别的雇员的轻微错误也可能是解雇主管人员的理由。

原则上，当主管人员在履行职能标准方面的作用似乎不足以使雇主能够合理地期待实现这一点时，主管人员的解雇可以被认为是合理的，而且主管人员的解雇可以很容易地执行。例如，主管人员不同意雇主决定的主要业务指导方针，或者当主管部门的工作职位在新的业务需求方面变得不足或证明是不经济的时候，或者当角色变得多余时，主管人员都可以被解雇。

17. 选择性解雇

雇主打算在同一个生产单位或同一境内的同一生产单位或多个生产单位的平均超过15名以上雇员中解雇至少5名雇员时，解雇被视为集体解雇。集体解雇之前必须有一个强制性程序，需要向雇主提供工会书面通知：（1）裁员的原因；（2）妨碍采取可能阻止这种冗员的替代措施的技术、组织或生产性原因；（3）要解雇的雇员的数量、工厂配置和工作情况以及目前就业人员的总人数；（4）计划执行设想的解雇的时间安排；（5）雇主预见的措施，如果有的话，以应付所述解雇的社会影响；（6）适用于计算雇员被解雇的任何赔偿或奖励措施的方法（法律规定的除外）。通信的副本也必须涉及适用的就业机构。

应工会要求，对被设想的解雇进行联合审查，以评估裁员的原因以及避免集体解雇的可能性。如果工会在落实集体解雇方面不同意，应在政府机构的面前进行额外的咨询。咨询程序可能持续7 ~ 75天。

与程序最相关的问题是，雇主不得自行决定哪些雇员被解雇（没有“樱桃采摘”）。相反，这种选择应与工会所述的冗余理由相一致，并应通过适用法律规定的标准（共同适用）：（1）家庭收费；（2）工作资历；（3）雇主的技术、生产和组织需求。如果与工会达成协议，法律标准可以被其他标准所取代（如自愿申请提前终止雇佣关系、考虑雇主支付货币激励、接近退休年龄等）。

18. 通知期限

正当理由以外的解雇应当给予合理的通知期限。

通知的期限由集体谈判协议约定，但随着工作年限和熟练程度而变化（对员工而言，通知期限平均从20日到6个月不等，对于管理人员可能会达12个月）。

通知期限也可以由赔偿金替代，不再给予通知。

19. 经济赔偿金

不论劳动合同终止的原因或者理由，任何员工都有权获得一定数额的经济赔偿金。

具体而言，经济赔偿金的金额为雇员每年的总工资除以 13.5（大约全年工资的 7.4%，不能从工资中扣除，但可以上限计算）。经济赔偿金每年都会评估并以法定利率为基数增加。

经济赔偿金与解雇赔偿不同，后者在非法解雇时也可以给予员工。在适当的时候，除了给予经济赔偿金，员工还会得到解雇费。

20. 社会保障费用及养老计划

雇用员工时，企业应当向有关社会保障机构登记所有员工信息（没有登记员工的社会保障信息及 / 或者支付法定社会保障金的，将会受到罚款，情节严重的，还会追究刑事责任）。

外国公司在意大利雇用员工，不必设立分公司、分支机构或者代表处等固定场所。外国公司只需要一个社会保障代理即可，该代理机构会处理所有行政机关要求的法定文件、费用和登记等事项。社会保障费用主要用来支付国家法定的养老计划，同时也会用来支付特定的为患病、失业和生育等提供保障的公共基金。

社会保障费用由企业按员工全年工资的 30% ~ 35% 缴纳（可以上限缴纳）和员工按工资的 8% ~ 9% 缴纳（在任何情况下，该部分费用由企业支付，按每月的工资数额代缴）。

员工也可以加入补充养老基金，补充养老基金主要由每年的经济赔偿金利息支付。另外，员工无义务以工资缴纳补充养老基金。集体谈判协议也可以规定企业为加入补充养老基金的员工应缴纳的额外部分的数额。

21. 卫生和安全义务

如果员工从事法律规定的特定活动、必须使用机械设备的活动或者使用电气或高温设备，企业必须在意大利工伤卫生署为员工投保事故险，并支付由意大利工伤卫生署依据员工从事活动的性质而规定的保险金。如果发生工伤事故，意大利工伤卫生署将会向员工（员工死亡时，向其继承人）提供医疗服务和经济补偿金。

如果员工缴纳了工伤和职业疾病保险，那么企业可以免于承担民事责任，但是企业因其违法行为承担了刑事责任而引起事故或者职业疾病的除外。在后者情况发生时，员工可以对企业提起诉讼，请求对超过意大利工伤卫生署的补偿之外所遭受的损失进行赔偿，同时，意大利工伤卫生署可以起诉企业，对其向员工支付的补偿进行追偿。除了为员工缴纳保险，企业还有义务遵守有关工作场所的卫生和安全标准。

根据员工职务活动的性质，企业还应当采取一切必要的措施来保护员工的身体和精神健康。具体而言，依据《卫生与安全法案》，企业应当对员工的卫生和安全风险进行全面的评估，并且形成书面文件列明并评估所有的风险。该书面文件应当包括集体风险评估、可能遭受特别风险的员工的类别、工作压力、怀孕员工的风险以及与年龄差别相关的风险。

风险评估报告应当列明，用来评估潜在风险的标准、采取的安全和预防措施、处理具体风险所采取的预防方法、不定时提高工作场所安全性的安全措施计划以及实施安全措施的程序。企业还应当指定专人负责“预防及保护系统”，并培训专门的安全人员。

另外，由于物理介质（噪声、机械振动、光辐射）、手工处理物料、接触某些化学产品、使用计算机终端设备，使员工遭受安全风险时，企业应当为员工安排企业医生治疗。企业还要组织紧急救护和消防演练，在工作场所使用安全标识以警示危险和提高安全措施。

（二）雇用外国员工的要求

1. 一般原则

意大利《移民法》适用于非欧盟、冰岛、列支敦士登、挪威、梵蒂冈、圣马力诺共和国、瑞士的自然人以及无国籍自然人（下文所称外国人，是指上述国家以外的有国籍的自然人以及无国籍的自然人）。

欧盟的公民享有不同的身份，因为他们在欧盟之间可以自由来往定居。

意大利移民立法主要有 1998 年 7 月 25 日生效的第 286 号法令（《综合移民法》）和 1999 年 8 月 31 日生效的第 394 号总统令（规定了《综合移民法》的实施规则）。2011 年 5 月 11 日的外交部令规定了不同的签证类型，持有有效签证可以合法进入意大利边境。

意大利于 1990 年 11 月 27 日加入申根协定，意大利移民立法必须遵循 1990 年 6 月 9 日的申根实施协定、1993 年 12 月 14 日的关于签证的一般领事指示、规定申根边界法的 2006 年 3 月 15 日的 562/2006 号 EC 条例、规定国民处境时必须持有签证的第三方国家以及豁免该要求的国家的 2001 年 3 月 15 日的 539/2001 号 EC 条例以及公布《社区签证法案》的 2009 年 7 月 13 日的 810/2009 号的 EC 条例。

2. 以务工身份入境意大利

原则上，在意大利雇用外国人只占很少的人数。

想要在意大利工作，必须首先要取得工作许可，意大利政府每年只会发放少量的工作许可。

工作许可的数量由每三年公布的“计划文件”规定，在其中意大利政府规定了入境管理的主要规则。在制定这些规则时，主要考虑国家的经济和劳动力市场、外国人在意大利的融合程度以及意大利与其他国家签署实施的条约及协定。

所以，工作许可和签证只能在每年的特定时限申请。只要符合申请的最低标准，就不再需要提供其他额外的文件。

3. 申请程序

一般而言，外国人想要在意大利工作，首先需要获得工作签证，然后要申请签证。入境后，应当申请居住许可。

缺少任何一个环节，外国人在意大利停留或者工作均为非法。雇用非法停留或者工作的外国人应当受到刑事处罚。

申请工作许可不能由外国人本人或者其企业代为办理。相反，应当由意大利的机构或者自然人代为办理。

代为申请的机构通常为意大利的有关移民局，其要进行各种检查，如是否符合现有数额的要求以及企业的资质等。当地的警察局也会履行安全检查。如果申请获得许可，企业将会与外国人签订劳动合同，即所谓的居留合同。

一旦获得工作许可，下一步将会转递到意大利外交部门的签证处，这样外国人就可以申请签证。

获得签证后，外国人将能合法地进入意大利工作。在入境的 8 日内，该外国人应当申请居住许可，并签订居留合同。

4. 居住许可期限和续期

居住许可的期限取决于因发放的原因。工作类居住许可的期限为 9 个月（季节性活动）至一年（固定期限合同）或者两年（无固定期限合同）。对于科学研究类的居住许可可以持续至整个科研项目结束，对于跨公司流动的经理及技能型劳动者可以长达三年。

居住许可的续期取决于发放时条件存续的时间，可以续期同样的时间。续期申请应当在居住证届满前至少 60 日前提出申请。

5. 不受任何年度限制可以取得工作许可的工人

意大利实行外国人务工配额制。然而，在一些情况下，雇用外国人工作可以不受每年配额的限制或者超出配额雇佣外国人。这取决于工作的性质，在很大程度上取决于工作的技能和行业。

实际上，经理和高技能人才可以在同一家公司的不同部门流动或者集团的不同公司流动，持有大学学历的工人可以在集团的不同公司流动以便获得专业技能，以及在签订劳动合同的条件下，工人可以暂时入境意大利。

6. 整合协议

超过每年的配额能够入境意大利工作的人员为：大学老师和讲师、笔译和口译人员、海事工作者、艺术家、舞蹈家、职业运动员、护士、科研工作者、取得并经有关部门认证的至少三年高等教育的高技能人才（蓝卡工人）。

16 岁以上的外国人申请意大利居住许可，如果居住期限超过一年，需要同时签订一份整合协议。在协议中，外国人应当承诺在其居住许可有效期内完成特定的目标，比如熟练掌握意大利语、熟知市民文化和知识、保证完成未成年人义务教育、履行税务和财政义务、遵守市民价值整体公约（包含意大利《宪法》主要原则和民主价值观，如男女平等、世俗主义、宗教自由等）。

意大利在国家层面通过提供综合性的措施，支持外国人综合素质的提高。协议采取学分制。外国人在意大利居住期间，其应当完成规定的学分和协议要求额外学分。居住许可届满前，外国人需要证明其已经完成要求的学分，并且还要通过语言测试。未能遵守整合协议的，其居住许可将会被注销或者拒绝续期。

7. 社会安全制度

在意大利工作的外国人应当遵守意大利有关社会安全义务方面的立法。例外的是，暂时到意大利工作的外国人所在国如果和意大利签订有双边或者多边协定，那么劳动合同的双方可以选择不同的社会安全制度。

（三）劳动纠纷

1. 概述

外国人在意大利工作较为普遍。一方面，因为意大利法律不允许随意解雇，因此需要详细及合理的理由来解雇，这在法庭上会受到质疑。另一方面，意大利法律不允许员工放弃法律赋予的权利，也不允许通过协议的方式减损集体谈判协议的约定（如取得工资和经济赔偿金的权利、享有休息的权利和不被降级的权利等）。

因此，员工经常会依法维护自己的权益。

2. 非法解雇的救济

因解雇引起的劳动纠纷，通常情况下，由以下引起的解雇行为无效：口头解雇，种族、性别、背景、语言、宗教信仰、政治观点或工会会员身份，违反保护父母权益规定、任何违反导致无效的法律强制性规定（包括报复性解雇）。

在上述情况下，员工有恢复劳动关系和补缴从解雇之日至恢复劳动关系之日期间的工资和社会保障费用的权利。

在其他情况下，比如解雇行为非法但并非无效，救济方法视解雇的原因和解雇的员工数量的不同而不同。

意大利法律区别多数企业和少数企业，并赋予多数企业相对更多的保护员工的权利。

由于最近立法的修改，解除在 2015 年 3 月 7 日之前雇用的员工需要给予赔偿金，而在这之后（含当日）则不需要给予赔偿金。所以，从可能给予的赔偿金的角度分析，目前意大利有四种不同的解雇制度。

第一，2015 年 3 月 7 日之前大公司雇用的员工解雇制度：对于非法解雇，员工可以要求恢复劳动关系，要求 12 个月工资的赔偿并要求缴纳从解雇之日至恢复劳动关系之日期间的社会保障费用；或者要求 6 ~ 24 个月的工资赔偿。赔偿费用的多少取决于法院认定的非法解雇的原因。

第二，2015 年 3 月 7 日或者之后大公司雇用的员工解雇制度：只有在个别情况下，被非法解雇的员工才可以要求恢复劳动关系（雇员所陈述的理由明显是虚假的；由于商业原因解雇，在任何情况下都不可以恢复劳动关系）

或要求给予劳动合同存续期间 2 倍月工资的赔偿，最低为 4 个月的数额，最高为 24 个月的数额。

第三，2015 年 3 月 7 日之前小公司雇用的员工解雇制度：非法解雇的员工有权要求最后 1 个月工资 2.5 ~ 6 倍的赔偿，在有些情况下，可以要求 10 ~ 14 倍的赔偿，但企业自愿恢复劳动关系的除外。

第四，2015 年 3 月 7 日或之后小公司雇佣的员工解雇制度：非法解雇的员工有权要求劳动关系存续期间月工资 1 倍的赔偿，最低 1 个月最高 6 个月数额的赔偿。

解雇赔偿金适用于行政人员和固定期限合同的员工。

不论企业员工数量有多少，行政人员无权要求恢复劳动关系，除非解雇因歧视或者报复被宣告无效。

如果解雇被认为是不公平或者不公正的，在通知期限届满前或者在给予赔偿金的情况下，员工有权要求 2 ~ 24 倍月工资的赔偿，赔偿的具体数额取决于法院的自由裁量。集体谈判协议规定，每一行业赔偿的数额取决于经理劳动合同的期限。

另外，只有在有合理理由的情况下，才可以提前解除固定期限的劳动合同。如果没有合理理由终止劳动合同，员工有权要求解雇之日至劳动合同届满之日期间的工资赔偿。

3. 争议解决替代方法

在意大利，争议解决替代方法较为常见，立法机构也鼓励这一做法，并出台了友好解决大公司由于商业原因解雇 2015 年 3 月 7 日前和 2015 年 3 月 7 日或之后雇用员工的法定程序。同时，立法机构还给予（部分）税收和社会保障方面的救济措施。

争议解决不仅仅关心解雇行为，在友好解决争议的情况下，员工还需要工会代表或者独立政府官员提供帮助并担任调解员或顾问，以告知员工放弃权利的后果。

劳动关系争议解决协议的达成应当符合上述规定，否则，员工可以（有少数例外情况）在协议签订之日起 6 个月内或劳动合同终止日后的 6 个月内申请撤销（以在后的日期为准）。

通常情况下，争议双方会妥协最终达成协议，员工会放弃自己的权利主张，企业也会支付一定的费用。

4. 争议解决

在意大利，争议可能由以下机构处理：司法机关（普通法院和特别法庭）、仲裁小组、ADR 机构。

（1）意大利的司法机构包括：一是普通法院（审理民事、商事和刑事案件）。包括法庭（意大利全国约有 165 个）、上诉法院（约 26 个；审理对法庭的裁决提出的上诉）和最高上诉法院（在罗马，审理上诉案件和某些法庭一审案件）。另外，还有和平法官（一种非职业法官），他们负责审理小案件，与法庭位于同一地点。二是行政法院（行政区域法庭大约有 20 人，在罗马为国务院）。三是税务法庭。四是其他特别法庭（如审计院、公海最高法庭和对于所有武装部队犯下的所有罪行都有司法管辖权的军事法庭）。

普通法院也可以成立专门的机构处理知识产权、劳动争议和家庭及遗嘱等问题。

《诉讼程序法》规定了相应的审理程序。首要的是公正审理原则，包括由法庭进行审理的权利、接触案卷的权利和积极参与审理的权利。在民事案件的审理中没有陪审员，只是在某些刑事案件中有陪审员。

意大利《宪法》第 111 条规定，任何公民都有向最高上诉法院上诉的权利，不论是普通判决还是特别判决。

民事诉讼程序时限一般较长，尽管各方面已经有所改善，同时取决于受理的法院，高级别的法院相对于低级别的法庭时限会长一些。一般而言，主要的问题是每年新增的大量案件，这给法院增加了巨大的负担。

（2）在民事和商事争议中，可以自由成立仲裁小组，但是争议事项不得涉及双方不能处理的权利，比如家事争议，在此种情况下，只有法官有裁量权。可以设立特别仲裁小组或者常规仲裁小组。特别仲裁规则由双方约定，双方没有约定的，应当遵守意大利民事诉讼法的规定；常规仲裁应当遵守审批机构指定的规则。

（3）除劳资纠纷领域外，ADR 机构在意大利仍然没有太大的发展，原因还不清楚。自 2010 年起，议会已经试图强制民事诉讼的当事人（除个别情形外）首先尝试通过 ADR 机构解决争议，但结果迄今为止并不令人满意。目前，ADR 机构法定的解决方式为调解和协商，其分别于 2010 年和 2014 年推出。

比荷卢投融资法律研究篇

比利时投融资法律研究

Jan Bogaert

一、比利时基本概况

比利时王国是一个自由开放的经济体，位于欧洲中心，享有突出的战略地位。它位于德国、法国、荷兰和卢森堡之间，与英国海峡隔海相望，坐落在欧洲最繁华、人口最密集的地区。

比利时是欧盟和多个国际组织的创始成员，比如经济合作与发展组织和世界贸易组织。比利时首都布鲁塞尔主办了欧盟主要机构的多次会议，如欧盟委员会（欧盟理事机构）、欧洲理事会、欧洲议会以及其他许多委员会和机构，因此布鲁塞尔通常被称为“欧洲的首都”（事实上它的名字认同度也远远超过了比利时的首都）。作为欧盟成员国，比利时的法律监管环境受到欧盟各种法规的影响。

比利时具有高度发达的运输网络和劳动力市场，其经济的开放性发源于其第二次世界大战后初期对欧洲项目的接纳以及向非欧洲市场的转移（包括在转型期与大多数发展中国家和转型国家的双边投资协定），同时任何国内外投资者不受歧视。

作为一个联邦制国家，比利时的政治环境复杂多样，政治权力分布在联邦、地区和社区各级，每个级别都有在一定地域内的立法和行政权力。

佛兰芒语社区、法语社区和德语社区最初处理的事务仅包括面向公民有关语言的事务，如文化、教育和语言的使用。佛兰芒地区、瓦隆地区和布鲁塞尔首都地区处理经济政策、对外贸易、城市发展、环境和就业等问题。然而，有些领域仍处于联邦控制之下，如法律、外交和国防、经济政策的某些部分，以及大部分税收和社会保障支出。

一个相对较小的领土（30528 平方公里）和相对较少的人口（1100 万人），比利时的体制对于初次的投资者显得较为复杂。然而，经验表明，尽管其具有一定的复杂性，外国投资者仍然发现其监管环境相当容易适应。这主要是因为作为一个外向型和开放型的经济体，比利时引以为豪的是对外国投资没有普遍的限制（尽管在欧盟的推动下，这在中期可能会发生变化）。当然，某些行业也要受到监管，这些行业的拟议交易可能需要得到相关监管机构的事先授权或通知。这些受监管的行业具体包括金融服务业、能源、电信、邮政服务业和航空运输业务。此外，比利时竞争管理局或欧洲委员会也会根据交易是否超过一定的营业额来设置门槛。

此外，根据 2007 年 4 月 1 日关于公开收购标准及其执行法令——《收购法》的规定，收购在比利时上市的公司或在比利时上市的外国公司都可能会采取公开收购的形式，因此要受到比利时金融服务和市场管理局（FSMA）的监督。

二、外国投资政策

外国投资在比利时的经济策略中起着举足轻重的作用。比利时的贸易和鼓励政策不会以任何方式歧视国内外公司。一般而言，在进行境外投资之前，不论其性质、金额或法律结构如何，都不得要求向比利时的任何政府机构提交申请或取得批准——在上述管制行业或适用一般合并控制规则的行业，而且据了解，欧盟正在考虑对安全审查机制进行调查。外国投资者可以自由地在比利时建立新的分支机构（如分支机构或子公司）以收购现有的比利时企业，或者与比利时或外国实体建立合资企业。

比利时法律没有具体的规定限制对外国股东的市场准入，对于国有（或国有控股）投资者和私人投资者也没有规定。

比利时法律没有规定在任何投资项目或新企业中外资与国内资本的比例要求。外国投资者可以利用债务融资，并可以自由汇回利润。比利时拥有强大的反贿赂和反洗钱法律，可靠和客观的司法体系，使投资者可以从投资补贴和税收优惠中受益。

三、典型交易结构

投资比利时的人在创立或收购比利时企业时可以选择多种形式。“绿地经营”可以通过设立分支机构、子公司或合资企业来实现。一个外国投资者希望通过收购现有的比利时企业进入市场的“棕地投资”也经常发生。在这种情况下，与大多数其他司法辖区一样，主要关注领域涉及交易类型（资产或股份交易）和目标是否为上市公司。公共交易必须遵守《收购法》，强制透明度要求也可能适用。

（一）公司形式

一家子公司的设立可以根据比利时法律采取几种不同的法律形式，但最常用的公司形式是开放式有限责任公司和私人有限责任公司。这两种公司形式之间的选择将主要取决于投资者的决策：初始股本出资（开放式有限责任公司最低股本为 61500 欧元，私人有限责任公司为 18550 欧元）；治理（一个私人有限责任公司可以由其任何一个或多个管理人员代表，而一个开放式有限责任公司可以有一个更正式的董事会，也可以有一个双层董事会结构和/或更精细的权力分配在各法人团体之间和之内）；股份转让限制（私人有限责任公司中的股份转让在大多数情况下必须获得特别多数股东的批准；原则上，开放式有限责任公司中的股份转让是免费的，但可以根据投资者的意愿进行调整（有先占权、优先权等条款，因此开放式有限责任公司通常更适合于合资企业）；证券权利的定制（开放式有限责任公司允许发行更多种类的证券，包括没有投票权的股票、优先股、利润证书、认股权证和可转换债券）；集团税收的考虑（基于美国税收的考虑，一个私人有限责任公司可以允许“复选框”的待遇，而开放式有限责任公司通常会考虑本身作为美国报税公司）；出口考虑事项（可以列出开放式有限责任公司的证券种类，而私人有限责任公司则不可以）。

其他企业形式（如没有法人资格的企业、合伙企业、非营利性组织等）只在极少数情况下使用，而且是由于非常具体的原因，在本书中不再进一步讨论。

作为设立一个具有法人资格的子公司的替代方案，作为法人实体的投资者可以选择设立比利时分公司。分公司可以由自己管理，但它本身并不是一个独立的法律实体。

就优势而言，子公司的设立将导致新产生一个独立的法律实体。该独立法律实体不会与其母公司分担任何责任（除了某些例外情况，比如比利时子公司在成立之日起三年内破产，以及破产法官认定，从子公司头两年的预期活动来看，子公司的初始股本严重不足），而比利时分公司的外国“母公司”则始终对其分支机构的承诺和责任负全部责任。

比利时《公司法》正在全面更新，其目标是为比利时经济的竞争力作出贡献，并使其对外国企业和公司更有吸引力。新《公司法》将使比利时的公司法律制度更为简单、灵活和连贯。重要的变化包括减少公司表格的数量，废除私人有限责任公司的资本要求，引入多票股份，引入董事责任上限等。预计新《公司法》将于 2018 年获得议会通过。

（二）税收

从比利时税收角度来看，如果一家子公司的注册法定办事处或主要办事处或有效管理机构位于比利时，则该子公司将被视为比利时居民公司。一般而言，比利时子公司按 33.99% 的名义税率缴纳比利时企业所得税（某些低收入小公司的税率较低）。但是，由于多次减免税，子公司通常享受的税率低于名义税率 33.99%。应税基础是以会计利润为基础确定的，但是对于部分或者全部不予扣除的几类费用，若干具体的免除和扣除项目，都有向上的调整。

中小企业和非中小企业持有超过一年的符合资格的股权的资本收益可豁免以 0.412% 的降低税率征税（如果符合条件的股权收益在持有至少一年之前实现，收益税率为 25.75%）。不属于豁免范围的资本利得税是 33.99% 的标准税率。从符合条件的股权获得的股息收入享受 95% 的豁免（收到的股息中只有 5% 须缴纳企业所得税），一般适用名义扣减额（按公司经调整后的股本乘以一次性利息百分比计算）。比利时允许税收损失结转，但不包括税收损失。特许专利的特许权使用费收入也有特定的豁免。

一家外国公司的比利时分公司通常只会缴纳比利时公司所得税（由比利

时分公司赚取或通过比利时分公司赚取的利润）。确定应纳税基数和适用税率的规则在很大程度上与适用于比利时居民公司的规定类似。根据比利时税收协定，根据相关条约的定义，对不符合资格的应纳税常设机构的分支机构可以免除比利时企业所得税。只有为其总部准备或辅助活动的分支机构才有资格获得免税地位（传统上，许多跨国企业的地区总部办公室在这种地位下经营）。

一般来说，位于税收协定国家的常设机构的收入也不在应纳税基础之内。

比利时来源股息原则上须缴纳比利时股息预扣税（普通税率为 30%）。有几个例外以及减少预扣税率适用的情况。由比利时子公司向在欧盟成立的外国母公司或其他符合条件的税收协定国家分配的股息可获得全额免税预扣税，但要求母公司至少持续一年持有 10% 的股权。

比利时分公司对其外国总部的利润分配不视为股息，因此不受比利时预扣税的约束。

作为 2017 年税制改革的一部分，上述税率将作出重大调整。公司税率将从 2017 年的 33.99% 降至 2018 年的 29.58%，又将降至 2020 年的 25%。

（三）并购

外国投资者也可能选择收购现有的比利时企业，而不是建立新的企业。这种交易可以在公共或私人市场上进行。鉴于公共交易受到特定规定的约束，私人交易应遵守比利时《民法典》规定的合同法的一般原则。比利时《公司法典》适用于与公司股本有关的交易，例如合并或者是由比利时《公司法典》严格规定的现金或实物捐助。

非上市实体的并购交易通常以竞争性拍卖的方式进行，尽管单纯以行业逻辑驱动的一对一交易也时常发生。

与许多司法管辖区一样，收购比利时企业的关键是将收购作为股权交易或资产交易进行组织[公司合并，特别是跨境交易是一种不太常用的收购方式，主要是考虑到许多具体（和烦琐）的手续要遵守；但是投资者通过向这些公司增资来获得初创企业和规模企业的股份是相当普遍的]。决定是否选择资产或股票交易的关键驱动因素包括目标公司的风险状况（资产交易通常应允许个别资产的选择，即使社会责任的假设不能被忽略）、税收问题（如上所述，股本资本收益大部分是免除所得税的，而对价与资产账面价值之间的差额将全部缴纳一般所得税；另外，在资产交易的情况下，支付的对价将会形成收购方的可摊销资产）和复杂性（资产交易的时间和成本相当大，因为具体的单个转移制度将不得不遵守有关房地产、知识产权、雇员、合同和政府执照等各类资产类别的相关规定）。

如上所述，收购在比利时上市的公司或在比利时上市的外国公司，根据《收购法》及其实施的皇家法令（这些法律合并执行欧洲收购指令），FSMA将对其进行监督。

只要比利时有收购任何公司证券的公开要约，自愿协商的合同条款就适用。如下情况报价可以被认定为公开：（1）投标人或与其一起行事的人或以其任何形式作出的任何宣传，包含有关投标条件的足够信息，以使证券持有人能够决定转让其证券；（2）投标人或与之共同或以其名义行事的人利用任何广告手段在比利时领土上宣布或宣传此项要约。安全港制度适用于私人配售（向少于 150 名不合格的投资者提供）、对合格投资者独家持有的证券的报价，以及与面值至少 100000 欧元的证券有关的报价。

关于强制性收购的规定适用于单独或与其一致行事的人获得在比利时存在注册办事处的公司中超过 30% 的有表决权的股份，并且至少部分有表决权的股份持有人承认在比利时或另一个欧洲经济区国家的受监管市场进行交易。

比利时《公共收购法》对投标人的国籍、出身或居住地无特殊规定。因此，外国投标不需要预先授权付款（据了解，相当于全部报价的资金必须在比利时设立的银行账户上被冻结，或者必须提供相应数量的不可撤销的无条件信贷额度；如果是交换要约，则投标人必须在规定的时间内持有足够数量的要发行或授权的证券），投资者也可以使用其他货币进行交易。对外国投标人向比利时股东提供的对价形式法律没有具体限制。然而，出于对投资者保护的原因，FSMA 可能会要求投标人在招标说明书中以欧元表示报价。

在发起收购招标之前，潜在收购方可能会积累股份。所谓的利益冲突是受内部交易限制和透明度要求的限制。

第一个例外集中于内幕交易。每当收购方拥有目标公司的非公开内幕信息，收购方就被禁止收购或出售目标证券，直到这些信息被公开或者不再影响相关证券的价格为止。

第二个例外涉及比利时《透明度法》规定的透明度要求，这些要求可能会由于超过某些限值而被触发。根据《透明度法》，所有直接或间接拥有上市比利时公司有表决权的股份的自然人或法人必须向 FSMA 和目标公司的董事会披露此类收购。根据《透明度法》，所谓的透明度通知必须在跨越 5% 的限值（也是 5% 的每个倍数）时提交。此外，公司章程可以提供额外的限值，可以设定为 1%、2%、3%、4% 和 7.5%。对于有表决权的股份转让，自然人或法人下降到上述限值以下时，也需要披露通知。相关门槛值的计算也考虑了子公司和收购方一致行动人士的股权。披露义务也有一些例外，如做市和交易账户豁免。

披露通知的时间规定如下：（1）在引发披露义务的事件发生的四个交易日内，收购方必须通知相关方；（2）在收到通知的三个交易日内，目标公司必须公布通知中包含的信息。不遵守披露义务要承担相应的民事、刑事和行政后果。民事后果可能包括暂停相关股份附带的投票权。此外，收购失败构成刑事犯罪的，FSMA 可以处以罚款。这些罚款的上限为自然人 200 万欧元、法人 1000 万欧元，更高的可达法人年营业额的 5%。然而，违法者获得的利润（或者可避免的损失）可能达到上述金额的两倍。

如果追求利益的话，利益关联方会提出一些典型的问题，例如，投资者自己是否有意发起要约，构成内幕信息，从而禁止根据内幕交易规则获取股份（在比利时缺乏监管指导的情况下，主要是可以在实践中否定了这个问题）；是否股权激励构成发起收购要约的证据，因此本身足以触发开始或关闭的订单；是否采取何种方式实际上触发了透明度披露要求（通常，期权、期货和调期等金融工具本身会触发透明度要求，而以现金结算的衍生合约则不会）。

然而，鉴于大多数比利时公司在很大程度上仍然受到（家族）股东的控制，敌意收购相当罕见，因此，过去的股权构造（特别是保持沉默的情况下）的价值相当有限。比利时直至最近的首选策略仍然是寻求参考股东的不可撤销的承诺，但最近 FSMA 改变了立场，认为在某些条件下，作为一个协议的组成部分（可能触发强制性要约），不可撤销的情况正在变得不太常见。

目标公司在收到要约通知后采取防御措施的能力是有限的（尽管可能会寻求“白色骑士”）。但是，防御性措施仍然可以在嫌疑人存疑的情况下建立，例如，授权董事会发行最多 10% 的新股或者回购最多 10% 的股份。但是，这种针对敌意收购的防御措施可能并不能区分国内和国外的报价。

（四）其他相关的政策

1. 房地产

（1）房地产的利益。比利时的法律区分了房地产的各种权利。物权的数量是法定的，所以不可能通过合同来创造额外的物权。这就是所谓的市场价值理论。

最广泛的物权是完全所有权，即绝对享有和处分资产的权利，但不得以法律禁止或可能危害第三方权利的方式使用权利。

其他权利包括使用权、使用或居住财产权、长期租赁或永佃权、建筑权和地役权。

使用权是最广泛的物权，安全的所有权。它使使用者有权使用他人拥有的财产，并从保留其实质的义务中获益于此类财产的利润或产品。因此，用益物权不能改变财产的目的，必须对财产进行适当的照顾。使用权的期限有限，在使用权终止的时候结束。

使用或居住财产权（使用权或居住权）使该权利的持有人在他们需要的范围内能够为他或她的家庭利益使用他人的财产。

永佃权是一项长期租赁权，赋予承租人土地使用权和建筑权，并从建筑物上收取收入，承租人是业主。作为这种长期租赁的回报，承租人支付所谓的年度地租的报酬。一个永佃权有 27 年的最小期限和 99 年的最长期限。

建筑权赋予在另一人拥有的土地上拥有或建造建筑物的权利。在建筑物权利期限内，受益人是建筑物的所有者，但在终止后，土地的所有者取得建筑物的所有权，而不管受益人是否支付任何款项。

地役权是物权，涉及两个不同所有者拥有的两个财产。它允许一个财产负担，以适应使用另一个财产，被称为主导财产。它可以由合同创造，也可以是主导财产的不可分割的附属权利，也就是说不能单独出售或转让。前者时间有限，后者无限期保持有效。

作为一般规定，外国投资者不得以任何方式限制上述房地产权益。

（2）登记。根据比利时法律，房地产必须在土地登记簿上登记，资产交易、长期租赁、抵押和其他房地产交易，必须在抵押登记处登记。注册后，需要缴纳一定的税款（所谓的注册税）。

（3）所有权购置。如前面所述，收购既可以是股权交易，也可以是资产交易。在房地产领域，所选择的交易结构决定了房地产权益转移的复杂程度。

在股权交易的情况下，没有正式的要求，如公证书。当事人订立股份购买协议，本协议转让持有房地产权益的目标公司的股权。不过，比利时的市场惯例包括对房地产权益的陈述和保证，还包括对失实陈述的补救。

在资产交易的情况下，有两个阶段：资产购买协议和公证书。第一，双方签署资产购买协议。原则上，所有权转让是在签署后进行的。但实际上，通常会延期转让所有权，直到公证书签署。第二，公证书是签署后在抵押登记处登记的。因此，登记职责将履行。

2. 工作

（1）根据比利时法律终止雇佣合同的一般原则。

根据比利时《劳动法》，员工享有相当多的保护。因此，解雇员工需要非常小心和谨慎，因为违规可能会造成民事、刑事或行政后果。

原则上，就业合同可以即时终止，在发生重大不当行为时不管是否有任何通知期限，不需要支付任何补偿金来代替通知。必须遵守严格的手续和时间安排。

在没有重大不当行为的情况下，可以通过发出通知终止劳动合同。在本通知期内，劳动合同仍然有效，劳动者和用人单位必须继续遵守本合同规定的权利和义务。严格的手续必须得到尊重。通知期根据雇员的资历不同而不同，通知期限为两周至十五周及以上。

此外，雇佣合同可以通过支付补偿代替工资和福利（过去12个月的奖金、年终保费、假期工资、雇主供款餐券、雇主缴款住院费、保险、雇主团体保险、健康检查费用、公司车、GSM、笔记本电脑等）。

但是，临时合同是上述终止规则的一个例外。雇主可以随时终止临时合同，无须向临时雇员支付任何赔偿金。如果提前终止临时合同或项目合同，根据与临时就业公司的合同，临时就业公司可能需要支付剩余工作期间的所有费用。

除上面提到的一般原则之外，在比利时解雇一名雇员还有几点需要注意。

① 销售代表。如果这些员工有资格成为销售代表，即主要活动是寻求和

拜访客户的白领雇员，以便谈判或签订商业合同，如果他们能为雇主带来新的客户，这些雇员原则上也有权：代替通知，在正常的补偿金之外的驱逐补偿金（相当于3个月的工资总额和福利，在公司5年内增加1个月的工资和福利，每五年工龄开始）；在雇佣合同终止前带来的订单佣金，但在雇佣合同终止后被接受以及在协议终止后3个月内下达的订单佣金。如果有关雇员的雇佣合约中包含一项禁止竞争条款，则有一个可反驳的推定，即该销售代表已经带来客户，因此有权获得解雇赔偿。

② 防止解雇。根据比利时《劳动法》，某些雇员受到防止解雇的特别保护（如在工会委员会或工会预防和保护委员会中作为工会代表、育儿假、时间信用等）。如果雇主因保护理由不能证明雇员被解雇合法，雇员可以要求保护赔偿。

③ 养老金。原则上，从58岁开始，雇员可享有养老金制度。在这种情况下，雇员有权获得由国家支付的失业津贴（雇主每个月支付65岁以下失业人员的补偿，必须遵守严格的手续）。

④ 解雇的动机。自2014年4月1日起，雇佣期限超过6个月的雇员有权向雇主查询其解雇理由（在通知后6个月内以挂号信方式或在立即终止解雇后2个月内）。如果雇主在雇员要求的2个月内没有通知雇员解雇的理由，雇主必须支付2周的工资处罚。在“明显无理解雇”的情况下——基于与雇员的适宜性或行为无关的理由，或者不以公司的必要为理由而解雇的雇员，而且雇佣合同的雇员通常不会得到正常和合理的雇主的批准的，该雇员可以要求赔偿3 ~ 17周的工资，这取决于被解雇的明显不合理的程度。请注意，如果雇主在雇员要求的2个月内没有通知雇员解雇的理由，雇主可以要求解雇的依据是雇员的适合性或行为或是基于公司的必要。

⑤ 集体解雇。集体解雇的雇主必须遵循严格的程序向雇员代表和某些机关和组织进行通报和咨询。当雇主有意进行集体解雇时，程序开始。

在集体解雇的情况下，在连续60天内受到影响的集体解雇涉及的解雇雇员：在集体解雇之前的日历年度雇用超过20名但不到100名雇员的公司中，至少有10名雇员；在集体解雇之前的日历年，平均雇用至少100名但不到300名雇员的公司中至少有10%的员工；在集体解雇之前的那个日历年，平均雇用至少300名雇员的公司中至少有30名雇员。

⑥ 不竞争条款。不竞争条款规定在不竞争期间支付特定的非竞争性赔偿金，相当于雇员薪金的至少 50%，除非雇主在合同终止后 15 日内通知雇员放弃该条款的适用。

⑦ 和解协议。为了避免有关雇员的进一步索赔，建议与这些雇员达成和解协议，放弃对公司所有进一步的要求，反之亦然。

（2）员工转移。当业务转移发生时，收购方不能简单地挑选员工。所有目标员工原则上自动转移到收购方。他们依据雇佣合同的权利和义务得到保留。这是依据法律规定的。

另外，收购者不能改变目标员工的工作条件，因为这样的改变将被视为是雇员的雇佣合同的终止。

当股份交易发生时，员工在原则上不受交易的影响。事实上，他们的情况仍然是一样的，因为目标在结束时仍然是他们的雇主。解雇合同的一般原则将适用，建议收购者注意集体解雇的严格程序。

3. 司法重组和破产

（1）司法重组。当公司的连续性受到短期、中期或长期的威胁时，比利时公司可以利用三个司法重组程序。这些程序在 2009 年《企业连续性法案》中有规定，并包括破产前暂停债务，以便这些公司解决财务困难。因此，在司法重组过程中不可能启动强制执行程序，所有现行的强制执行程序中止最多 6 个月。法院确定这个初始阶段，可以延长至最多 12 个月，或在特殊情况下延长至 18 个月。

司法重组程序在涉及的债权人数量和董事会是否仍然掌权方面有所不同。它们可以采取协议的形式，也可以包括法院命令，在司法代表的主持下转移公司的业务。

在采取协议形式的程序中，财务困难的公司要么选择友好的解决方案，这涉及最重要的债权人，要么选择一个详细的重组计划，这个计划需要所有受困公司的债权人进行投票。这些重组是相似的，但在细节和债权人方面有所不同，因为董事会在整个过程中始终保持执政权，所以他们与法院命令的业务转移区别开来。

当困难公司处于破产状态，或以协议形式进行重组的尝试失败时，任何利害关系方可以要求法院命令转移业务。然后法庭会决定这样的转移是否有利于维护企业的连续性。在这种情况下，公司的同意是无关紧要的。董事会被剥夺了权力，司法代表（公证人或法庭指定的人员）被任命来监督业务的转移。

（2）破产。根据1997年比利时《破产法》，公司被视为破产的时候，它不再持久地偿还债务，并且它已经用尽了信贷。破产程序可以由破产公司本身，债权人或检察官发起。申请破产的决定属于董事会的职权范围，但法律要求破产公司在停止支付日期的一个月内提出破产申请。

如果所有破产条件都满足，法院将剥夺董事会的权力，指定一个或多个破产受托人作为破产公司资产和负债的管理者，并指定破产法官主管。

债务人的董事必须回应或遵守破产法官发给受托人的传票，并提供所有要求的信息。

从破产令发出之时起，破产受托人将作为债务人的唯一代表，并有权以债务人的名义开立信函。任何债务人收到的与交易有关的付款请求都不得约束债权人。破产受托人将决定是否继续经营或开始出售公司或整个公司的资产。整个企业的收购或其中的一部分，需要得到破产法官的批准。

除有特殊优惠的债权人以外，所有债权的利息也应当被中止，对债务人的资产实行强制执行。限制较少的规则适用于中止与单独担保权益债权人有关的利息和追偿程序，尤其是那些持有一级抵押权的债权人，并应特别注意适用于每种情况的特殊规则。

除非另有约定，现行合同不会由于破产而自动终止。破产受托人必须及时决定是否继续现有合同。交易对手可以要求破产受托人作出决定。如果在两周内没有作出决定，合同将被视为终止。

就雇员而言，他们的合同也不会自动终止。他们享有与合并或收购相同的咨询和获取信息权利。如果在破产程序中发现收购方，收购方有权决定要保留哪些员工以及应该解雇哪些员工。不过，上述关于终止比利时劳动法雇佣合同的一般原则适用。

破产通常在债务人的全部资产变现后按债权人的优先顺序分配到破产受托人所确定的优先顺序之后结束。如果资产不足以支付清算费用，破产可以立即结束，不进行清算。

一旦破产结束，债务人将不复存在。根据比利时《破产法》，公司不能无罪化，应当重新开始。破产对于债务人来说绝不是首选，因为它不可避免地导致债务人的清算和消失。因此被视为债务人被迫终止。

四、审查程序

（一）一般情形

虽然比利时法律没有专门针对限制外国投资的规定，但是在比利时国内、欧洲甚至全球范围内，集中在几个企业之间的任何投资都可能受到国内事先合并控制的批准（独立于注册办事处和相关公司的活动），以下是比利时的累计门槛：两家相关企业必须拥有至少 4000 万欧元的比利时综合营业额，所有相关企业必须在比利时共同营业至少 1 亿欧元。这种兼并控制制度适用于典型的兼并，也适用于收购和某些类型的合资企业。不适用于持股比例不能独立或共同控制的少数股权。调查通常最多 35 个工作日（第一阶段调查）。只有在有限的情况下，才能开展第二阶段的调查工作，可以再延长 60 个工作日。很少有合并最终被阻止，因为在存在竞争问题的情况下，各方可以提交补救措施以减轻竞争问题。

受欧盟兼并控制的合并不再受比利时的兼并控制。

作为欧盟成员国，比利时与欧盟其他国家以及（有一些例外）第三国（参见 TFEU 第 63 条）之间的资本和支付都是自由流动的。此政策的例外情况需经欧盟批准。但是，比利时等欧盟成员国可以根据公共利益要求实施限制（例如，防止违反国家法律和法规，特别是在税收领域和对金融机构的审慎监管方面的法律法规，或防止违反为了行政或统计资料的目的而规定资本流动的申报程序，或防止违反采取基于公共政策或公共安全理由的措施）。

比利时政府依靠能源案件中的合法利益条款来代表比利时国家引入“黄金份额”。比利时政府要求在相关企业占据国家能源供应战略地位的基础上，特别是考虑到比利时依赖国外能源资源，要求获得一个黄金份额。这得到了欧洲法院的批准。

作为欧盟成员国，比利时和其他欧盟国家之间的货物、服务、机构、人员和资本可自由流动。比利时对从第三国进口的商品不征收额外的关税。但是，比利时海关当局确实采用了欧盟通用关税（基于新组合术语的“Taric”法）。例如，比利时海关在此框架下就确认了反倾销措施没有被规避。

（二）主要受监管行业

特定行业的投资还受到特定监管机构的监督。其中包括以下内容。

1. 金融业

自 2011 年 4 月 1 日以来，比利时金融部门所谓的双峰架构，由于实施了体制改革而不再是集中监管模式（在欧洲大部分地区不再被认为是充分的，更不用说是最优的）变成了一个双极金融监管结构。自那时以来，大多数金融机构的审慎监管由比利时国家银行（NBB）掌控，某些类型的金融机构风险较低，但仍受到 FSMA 的审慎监管。

对于在比利时受到监管规定的大多数金融行业参与者而言，要获得相关参与，须经有关监管机构事先评估拟议投资者的适当性。

NBB 主管信贷机构、保险和再保险公司、MiFID 经纪人、结算机构以及电子货币和支付机构。FSMA 保留了这些不受 NBB 监管的金融机构的能力，包括 MiFID 投资组合管理和投资建议公司、基金管理公司、集体投资企业、外汇局、抵押贷款信用事业和消费信贷事业、保险再保险中介机构、银行和投资服务中介机构、职业养老金机构。

2. 能源

能源生产、运输和分配由联邦电力和天然气管理委员会管理。能源行业在外商投资方面没有具体的规定。

然而，第三个“欧洲天然气指令”对天然气或电力运输系统运营商的天然气或电力生产商或供应商的股权（所谓的生产和供应网络的拆分）提供了某些限制。他们的股权可能不是多数股权，不具有投票或任命管理者的权利，只能是财务。天然气或电力输送系统运营商也不会对天然气或电力生产或供应公司感兴趣。在认证程序期间，在比利时国内和欧洲的水平上都要对这种要求的符合性进行了测试。

3. 空运服务

根据欧盟与欧洲经济区的相关规定，欧洲航空公司的外资股份通常被限制在 50% 以下（欧盟和第三国之间的协议可以规定这一规则的例外）。

4. 电信和邮政服务

在欧盟的主持下，电信业和邮政业已经基本实现了自由化。这两个行业都是受监管的行业，但是这些规定主要涉及许可证的转让或转授以及普遍的邮政服务等事宜，而且不会歧视国内外投资者。

5. 安全审查

目前，比利时没有外国的安全审查机制。但是，随着 CFIUS 活动的增加、来自新兴国家的国有企业的投资增加、缺乏互惠（对境外投资的现有限制）及特别是关于中国在战略领域投资的公共辩论的日益增加，欧盟正在就安全审查条例草案进行辩论。如果实施，该条例将允许对外国（非欧盟）投资于欧盟战略行业的安全进行审查。

五、外资保护

如上所述，外国投资一般不受比利时国内的监管或批准。比利时不区分外国投资（不论是否以欧盟为基础）及国内投资。这一基本原则，加上稳定的、大部分是可预测的监管环境，有效的法院系统和法治为比利时第二次世界大战后的经济建立了基本的软基础设施。

对于欧盟内部的投资者，根据欧盟法律，保证与比利时投资者的平等待遇。来自欧盟以外的投资者可以从比利时庞大的双边投资条约网络中受益并享有保护。比利时不仅能够轻松进入广阔的欧洲市场，而且在欧盟之外还拥有发达的投资网络。目前比利时与 100 多个国家签署了投资协议，其中绝大多数是发展中国家或转型期国家。比利时于 1964 年与突尼斯签署了第一个双边投资协定（BIT），不久之后，与其他非洲和亚洲发展中国家有类似的协议。20 世纪 80 年代后期，随着共产主义的崩溃和苏联的倒台，比利时开始与东欧一些国家签订双边投资条约。20 世纪 90 年代，比利时进一步扩大了 BIT 项目，与中南美洲国家达成了协议。

比利时的双边投资条约相当一致：它们以广泛的方式界定投资；禁止东道国政府歧视外国投资，支持国内投资或第三国投资；要求各国政府提供公平、公正的待遇；有义务的东道国政府允许外国投资者转移资金并汇回资本；对征收外国投资者财产要求及时足够的补偿；并允许投资者通过国际仲裁直接向东道国提出索赔，从而寻求所谓的危害救济。

从税法的角度来看，所有比利时纳税人（包括外国公司）都可以要求就特定情况或特定交易进行预先税收裁决。提前决定服务将确认税收法律对税收方面尚未生效的情况或交易的适用性。对于各种交易，包括合并和拆分、出资、转让定价，没有常设机构，参与免税、预扣税、折旧、减税和资本收益，可以获得税务裁决。

六、其他战略决策

比利时在欧洲的购买力中心享有重要的地理位置。首都布鲁塞尔是欧洲总部的所在地，其出色的交通运输基础设施（安特卫普是欧洲第二大港口）将其连接到欧洲腹地，高度密集的知识群体、高水平的教育和高品质的生活，使比利时成为作为东道主的顶级经济体。许多外国公司存在于比利时市场，它们的欧洲总部都设在比利时，其中包括 Euroclear、通用电气和丰田等公司。

荷兰投融资法律研究

Bart Kasteleijn

一、对荷兰外来投资的概述

（一）历史

荷兰东印度公司建立于1602年，它是世界上第一家公共资助和贸易的股份公司，其标志着悠久而丰富的荷兰国际投资和贸易历史的开始。在现今被称为印度尼西亚的这片土地上，除了已经存在的与波罗的海和俄罗斯之间的木材和毛皮贸易（当时称为“汉莎”贸易）之外，荷兰东印度公司还开发了一个基于棉花、香料繁荣的种植园殖民经济。这种经济模式使“荷兰”（正如当时荷兰人所称呼的）成为一个领先的航运国家并且供应着整个欧洲大陆，它在东半球的巨大成功也被西方所仿制并且于1621年建立了荷兰西印度公司。在航空方面，荷兰皇家航空公司是世界上第一家航空公司，成立于1919年。

意大利人（在威尼斯）发明了现代的簿记系统，荷兰人也建立了一个基于资本市场制度化的并且在证券交易所（阿姆斯特丹）进行交易的贸易系统。

这段历史解释了一个小国（33.883平方公里）是如何演变成一个主要贸易国家的，并且随后其也成为一个包含投资银行、金融和商业的中心，在平等对待外来投资者和本国投资者的基础上吸引了大量的外来资金和投资，并且和所有的国家进行自由贸易。

（二）政治

荷兰王国是一个主权国家，具体包括位于加勒比、博内尔岛、圣尤斯特歇斯和萨巴上的三个海外城市，以及三个前荷属安的列斯群岛国家，包括库拉索岛、圣马丁岛和阿鲁巴岛。荷兰分为 12 个省和 390 个市（2016 年数据）。

荷兰王国是属于奥兰杰家族的君主立宪制国家，直到 2013 年，威廉 · 亚历山大国王与马克西马皇后结婚，并且在总理直接负责的情况下主要发挥着仪式和咨询的作用。荷兰王国是一个民主的议会制国家，立法会（第二院和第一院）坐落在海牙。因此，立法机构、司法机构、警察机构以及其他国家基础设施的中央政府、内阁部长以及国务秘书也同样在海牙。阿姆斯特丹是荷兰的首都。新议会的选举每四年举行一次，该选举会形成一个新的内阁。一个多世纪以来，每任内阁都由至少两名成员，但往往会由三名或更多的政党的代表组成。传统上，荷兰拥有一个相对稳定的政治制度，这反映了荷兰社会的协商一致和有效的组织。荷兰著名的“圩田”指的是海平面以下由防洪堤保护着的土地。

荷兰超过三分之一的土地位于海平面以下，并且有三条大河穿过国土。其有着一个很具代表性的机构，称为水资源委员会，主要负责监督管理水和征收税费。

比利时、荷兰和卢森堡一起组成了比荷卢联盟，该联盟具有一定的政治和司法职能。荷兰在 1958 年与其他国家共同创立的欧洲联盟（欧盟）对荷兰社会具有重大的经济和监管作用。但是在政治、军事、司法和税收方面，欧盟成员国基本都保持了自主权。

荷兰是联合国（UN）、北大西洋公约组织（NATO）、“世界人权宣言”（UDHR）以及“欧洲人权公约”（ECHR）的成员国。

所有这些产生的结果便是一个被称为“BV 荷兰”（或“企业 NL”）的稳定的政治环境，也为海外的投资者和富人保证了一个一致的、可预测的、灵活而又可持续的投资环境。

（三）经济

荷兰在欧洲国家的国民生产总值排名第三位（2015 年数据），而国民生产总值是一个国家繁荣和财富的最显著的指标。

荷兰是“通往欧洲的门户”，正服务于 5 亿名消费者，鹿特丹是欧盟最大的集装箱港口，而史基浦机场在欧盟（2015 年数据）排名第四位。

在荷兰有 5000 多家外国公司，其中有 13 家跨国公司属于全球 500 强企业（包括壳牌、联合利华和喜力等）。荷兰在全球人类发展指数排名第四位（2015 年数据）。

荷兰正式被指定的领先工业部门主要有：园艺、农业食品、水、生命科学和健康、化学品、高科技、能源、物流以及创意产业。而其中的重点是服务和知识产业，且政府正在积极推动研发工作，2017 年的研发补贴 / 薪资税额将增加到 1.15 亿欧元。此外，还有很多其他的税务设施、法规的减免、补贴以及融资选择。

在世界排名前 200 位的大学中，有几所荷兰大学具有很高的排名，这也反映在了高水平的技术和经济成就上。高中阶段之前的教育（中等学校）几乎全部由国家资助或补贴，因此实际上是免费的。大学和高等职业教育每年收取 1984 欧元（2016 年数据）的学费（只针对荷兰居民，而外国学生会更高），学习补助也是常见的。

荷兰是经济合作与发展组织（OECD）、世界贸易组织（WTO）的积极成员。它经常被邀请作为观察员参加世界范围内工业化国家的政府间“8 国集团”首脑会议。

荷兰的法定货币曾经是荷兰盾（盾牌，缩写为 f、hfl 或 nlg），但是自从 2002 年欧洲经济与货币联盟（欧盟）成立后，荷兰的货币便为欧元（€）。

除纯粹为了统计目的的超过 25000 欧元的交易通知以外，荷兰中央银行没有外汇管制，也不存在相关的授权或许可。

员工的工作周一般为 38 个小时。雇员的人均产出相较于工资水平（个人生产率）是世界上最高的。23 岁及以上年龄的员工（每周工作满 38 个小时）的最低工资为每月 1551 欧元，相当于每周 358 欧元和每天 71 欧元。基于谈判和协商，员工的工作关系往往是稳定的，这也体现在荷兰员工在欧盟的罢工和停工的排名中接近最低。一个良好的工作与生活平衡被工人和雇主广泛认为是高生产力和良好的精神与身体健康的保证。

在荷兰，目前法定退休年龄是 65 岁，但是将来会阶段性地攀升到 2022 年的 67 岁零 3 个月，并且从 2023 年起，退休年龄将会取决于预期寿命。

自雇人员是一个新的和日益增长的趋势，他们雇用自己而免于缴纳工资税和社会保险费等费用。2016 年，自雇人员规模已经达到 1700 万人左右。

（四）社会

荷兰社会已经发展成为一个具有多元文化和民族的社会，其组成最初来自在第二次世界大战后前殖民地（现在）印度尼西亚的移民，紧接着在 19 世纪 60 年代，来自苏里南和荷属安的列斯的移民也大量涌入，自 70 年代以来，其工人主要来自摩洛哥和土耳其的移民工人。

荷兰的人口密度是世界上最高的，为每平方公里 409.6 人（2016 年数据），绝大多数人生活在被称为兰斯塔德的人口密集的西部。男人和女人享有平等的权利和就业能力，但是妇女群体中的很高比例都要兼职工作，并且与臭名昭著的"玻璃事业上限"相悖。荷兰在联合国人类幸福指数排名第七位（2015 年数据）。

荷兰主要有三个宗教团体，原始的天主教徒和新教徒，以及随着劳动移民而涌入的伊斯兰教徒，宗教被认为是一种个人的而非国家的事情。

荷兰的官方语言是荷兰语，第二语言（非官方的）是英语，并且达到了居民都能说的程度。英语在商业界得到了广泛的使用，并且具有较高的水平，甚至英语还经常成为公司的唯一官方语言。荷兰的第二和第三外语是德语和法语，而法语逐渐被英语所取代。越来越多的荷兰人在学习中文，但是很少有人能够流利地交流，更不用说书写。在阿姆斯特丹、鹿特丹和海牙有三个重要的"中国城镇"，这里的中国人，尤其是低于 45 岁的中国人，能够无缝融入荷兰社会且具有一定的学术学位，同时很多中国传统也没有被忽视。

（五）法律

荷兰采用了在 1689 年出生的法国人查尔斯·德·孟德斯鸠制定的"三权分立学说"，区分了立法、行政和司法三个权力。因此，与中国不同，无论是民事的判决、刑事的判决还是行政的判决，法院均不予执行，而是由执行机构执行，甚至在一些民事案件中是由执政官或者政府指派的私人执行。行政权力往往对待法院的待决事项不做任何评论或行动，影响法院是一种禁忌，法官均为终身任职。

对于在荷兰居住的法律实体以及个人，法律是在全国范围内适用的，不受省级、市级或者城镇级别的法律约束。荷兰的法律属于所谓的民法或者说罗马法法系，依赖于立法（法律和法规），而不是英格兰和英联邦国家的普通法，不主要依赖于判例法（法院先前的判例）。然而，也可以很公平地说，在民法法系中，法院也更倾向于依赖之前法院作出的不同于立法的法院判决，这并不意味着忽略或者谴责立法。

各级法院的主要判决都要在网上和杂志上出版公示，其会被学术人员和其他法律专业人员广泛地解释和评论；而法院却从来没有评论或者解释过它们的决定。

荷兰法院在民事和商事上的诉讼整体上是高效和适宜的，允许原告在早期阶段就提出诉求，被告也必须迅速作出反应，以便法院迅速地作出最终的判决。

二、与中国企业合作的现状和发展方向

中国与荷兰从 1742 年在广东省（现称为广州）成立的一个商业代表团开始便具有了长期的贸易往来，该代表团于 1826 年终止。

如今，荷兰是中国在欧盟的第二大贸易伙伴。根据中国政府报告中的统计数据，2016 年 1–9 月，出口和进口总额（荷兰—中国全部以美元计数）达到 576.8 亿美元。其中，荷兰从中国进口 493.5 亿美元，同比下降 6.9%；荷兰对中国出口 83.3 亿美元，同比增长 12%。贸易逆差为 401 亿元，减少 10%。

荷兰出口到中国的产品主要有电子、食品、饮料、烟草和手表，而从中国进口的则是整个制造范围内的原材料。荷兰在中国的主要竞争对手是德国、美国和日本。中国在劳动密集型行业，如家具、玩具和纺织品等，仍然保持着竞争力。

根据 2015 年欧盟统计局的数据，中国向整个欧盟进口的情况如下（均为欧元）：初级商品总额为 81 亿欧元（其中，食品 / 饮料 48 亿欧元、原材料 29 亿欧元和能源 4 亿欧元），制成品总计 3410 亿欧元（其中，化学品 160 亿欧元、机械和车辆 1760 亿欧元、其他制造商 1490 亿欧元）和其他总计 13 亿欧元，中国对欧盟进口额为 3505 亿欧元。中国向欧盟的出口额是 1700 亿欧元，导致总贸易逆差（欧盟）1805 亿欧元。

欧盟国家从中国的进口额排名分别是德国 690 亿欧元、荷兰 660 亿欧元、

英国550亿欧元、法国280亿欧元和意大利270亿欧元。需要注意的是，荷兰排名第二主要是由于要经过它转口到周边欧盟国家，特别是通过河流、火车和卡车运输到德国腹地。

地址统计显示，有多家领先的中型中国公司在荷兰设立了它们的欧洲总部、营销和销售部门、客户服务中心以及装配/维修基地。中国的汽车和电子工业在荷兰的高科技行业以及环保行业，尤其是水和空气处理（清洁技术）方面的入境投资中占有很大的份额。而最近增长快速的行业是农业和食品加工业。

在荷兰大学的工程学院、经济学院和法律学院有许多中国学生，毕业之后在这里做实习并且留在荷兰工作几年。所有这一切的基本驱动力是技术转让与扩张的出口市场的结合。

最后，中国的“一带一路”倡议将荷兰定位为一个重要的目的地，这也势必会增加中国在荷兰的投资。

（一）投资

1. 市场准入

（1）投资监管部门。在荷兰，其政府部门或国家机构中并不存在对外国入境投资的监管机构，更不用说批准机构。然而，经济部与国防部将会对来自联合国和经合组织黑名单国家（中国未列入名单）的入境投资进行监测。此外，如果有理由怀疑投资者的真正经济意图时，他们将对包括核能、某些海洋和机场基础设施、军事设备以及IT/电信在内的来自国家安全部门的外国直接投资提出异议。此外，司法部会核实与刑事有关的外国直接投资，特别是来自2016年OECD和欧盟发布的反洗钱和恐怖主义金融高风险第三国（中国未列入名单）名单中的国家。

（2）投资法律法规。荷兰立法对所有者和管理者待遇的立场是兼具国家和国籍主义。持有荷兰企业100%股份的外国主体，在任命非居民和非荷兰国民管理或监督董事会、资本出资和还款、跨境债务借贷或分配股利（利润）等方面没有限制，而特许权使用费和管理费，需要考虑跨境税。

跨境转移货币，即外汇，无论是欧元还是其他外币，均不需要经过政府的批准，但超过25000欧元的余额必须通知荷兰中央银行的外汇机构（荷兰银行）。商业银行通过对付款的性质进行分类来将货币进行转入或转出。荷兰银行仅将这些信息用于统计目的，即货币对外贸易余额。根据《防止洗钱和资助恐怖主义法》以及2005年欧盟关于反洗钱的第2005/60/EF号指令，商业银行与其他金融服务提供者如公证人、税务顾问、法律律师、经纪人的转移，都需要向专门机构——金融情报室报告任何所谓的“异常交易”的外汇或其他情况。其间接影响就是加强了政府对私人和企业所得税及增值税逃税的监管。

所有要通过公共采购的货物和服务都要由当地的中央政府在整个欧盟范围内公开招标，公开招标应当具备一定的门槛。向中央政府提供的国防合同，欧盟的门槛（2016年数据）为135000欧元，非国防合同为209000欧元，工程合同的总额为5225000欧元，水、能源、运输和邮政服务的门槛为418000欧元。投标的门槛是基于2012年的《采购法》所制定的。

招标必须及时公布。最低价格通常不是唯一的标准，然而其他的标准必须预先公布，如技术和环境。

（3）投资形式。在荷兰，对于公司和个人而言，根据从低到高的参与程度和资本化排序，主要有以下直接投资方法。

① 公众持股。投资者可以通过股票经纪人在阿姆斯特丹证券交易所（泛欧证交所）购买上市股票。这种被动的金融投资并不需要任何上市公司的积极参与。公司必须向泛欧证交所报告持有5%以上股份的股东的身份，因为这是股价敏感信息。或者，中国投资者可以建立一个新的公司在市场上市（首次公开发行，IPO），当然这种情况迄今为止从未发生过。

② 合同。投资者可以与荷兰方通过签订单独的合同建立合作关系，以便进行开发活动、贸易或投资，而不创造任何形式的法人资格或企业存在。合同各方可以完全自由地在当事人之间划分任何义务、风险和利润分享。

③ 代理。代理是一种特殊的机制，通过合同指定一个代理商（或更多，然后它不再是“独家”代理），允许代理商向批发商或消费者销售中国制造商（委托人）的产品。代理人的报酬，在销售交易中称为佣金，是先前合同约定的百分比。

1986年欧盟关于商业代理机构的指令（1986年12月18日，86/653/EC）尊重欧盟成员国在该机构终止时安置的处理方法，可以在固定赔偿和整体赔偿制度之间进行选择，而且欧盟成员国可以自主确定终止时的最短通知期限。荷兰选择了固定赔偿，即所谓的商誉（自己开发的客户/市场基础），等于代理商在过去五年内所赚取的佣金收入的平均值（更高的商誉赔偿可能要经过事先同意）。法律规定的终止最长期限为6个月，最低不能超过之前合同的相关约定。

代理行为适合出售资本货物或专门服务，这需要广泛的国内指导和密切的援助，不同于直接的销售行为，荷兰代理商在接受代理之后，委托人无须亲自在荷兰或整个欧洲进行投资。

④ 分销（分配、转售）。在这里，中国的主合同允许一个荷兰方在分配地区（荷兰或更多的欧盟成员国）以分销商的名义购买和转售中国制造的产品。分销商的报酬是购价和转售价之间商定的最低保证金。

在没有分销法的情况下，荷兰的《判例法》规定，经销商对于在其领土上允许或容忍的投资有权获得赔偿，包括但不限于建筑和展示室或仓库拆除的非摊销成本、卡车租赁或销售的费用，以及委托人的产品专用人员在法院通知期间的持续工资等。且分销合同中约定的通知期必须与分销商的实际持续时间相称。它的范围可以是3年合同中的6个月到5年合同中的两年不等。如果当事人倾向于跳过通知期，则当事人可以立即支付。如果认为分销商不公平和不合理，通知期和安置费则可由法院进行调整。

《欧盟非竞争法》对于独家代理合同具有强制性的限制，禁止另一家经销商在其境外宣传和销售同一产品，包括运营展厅等。此外，根据欧盟法律，不允许固定垂直价格。

分销商制度通常适用于非市场化的非资本消费品的供应，在这个领域不需要太多的技术知识。

⑤ 特许经营。分销的一种变化是特许经营，由市场各方自行制定行为守则，有关欧洲广泛的某些部门，如快餐，荷兰正在制定它的特许经营法案。

这对密切控制的所谓“系统化运营”是非常适用的，如快餐和汽车租赁行业。

⑥ 分公司。分公司是外国“母公司”的资产和负债的非独立部分，没有法人资格。分公司可以雇用员工、签署合同、发放和收取发票。其收入需要缴纳荷兰企业所得税。

分公司适合于低资本要求和适度操作量的初始阶段企业，以便“试试水”，分公司的注册和注销是简单且不昂贵的。

⑦ 普通合伙（合作关系）。投资者可以通过缔结一项商业协议来建立普通合伙企业，而不用获取法人资格。合伙人对合伙企业承担无限连带责任，其承担的连带责任主要依靠合伙企业的独立资本。这种形式更适合小型、个别企业与合作伙伴的密切合作。

⑧ 合资企业。合资企业由超过一名股东参与，由公司章程或者股东决议控制。公司章程为公司直接执行的权利提供了基础，合资企业协议则增加了公司章程所缺乏的灵活性。如果该合资企业是以企业实体的形式存在，并且是一个由中国母公司控股的荷兰公司，那么该合资企业只能在商会注册。

⑨ 有限合伙企业（有限合伙制）。有限合伙不同于普通合伙的一个变化就是，合伙人可能是未公开的或者是“沉默”的指挥官，它们只能在合伙中表明资本贡献的程度。但是有限合伙必须至少有一个管理合伙人，管理合伙人对有限合伙承担无限责任。但为了限制责任，管理合伙人本身可以是私营公司。

这种形式适合于投资者在分配利润时仍保持未知，并且能够获益于特殊的税收政策，如船只的建造和经营行业。

⑩ 合作。外国投资者可以纳入并成为合作组织的成员，该合作被视为一种所谓的“透明车辆”，出于税收的目的，其有资格获得免税税收协定中股息预扣税给中国的利润返还（见下文税款）。该合作可以将私营公司作为运营公司。

⑪ 基金会。基金会是一个只有董事会的公司实体。基金会既没有成员也没有股东，但可以拥有合同上赋予的内部运营的某些权利。基金会原本是为理想主义目的而保留的，而商业活动也是允许的，但在后一种情况下，基金会将要缴纳公司税。因此，它除了保管一个私营公司的股权，很少用于外国资产的入境投资。

⑫有限责任公司（私营公司）。目前，有限责任公司是荷兰最常用的公司实体（数量超过 80 万家），也被外国直接投资者称为民营企业与有限责任，其字面意思为有限责任的私人公司，这里进一步定义为私营公司。

从 2012 年 10 月 1 日起，为了使私营公司更加灵活、其公司的注册程序更加简便，以及公司章程能够更多地反映出股东的愿望，荷兰的《公司法》被进行了修订。

荷兰《民法》强制性规定应当制定公司章程，无论是法人实体还是自然人，私营公司的章程都反映了公司成员的意图。荷兰法律要求的公司的最低数量为 1 家。要采取的步骤是：名称搜索（通过检索商会和互联网）→制定公司章程（或多或少基于民法规定的模板）→开立银行账户→执行公司章程。实际上，在公证之前，可以通过书面的、合法的授权委托书，并最终提交公司章程和商会的数据。

• 注册资本。法定最低注册资本为 0.01 欧元（包括人民币在内的其他货币），最低股数为 1 股。然而，外国投资者为了证明与荷兰人进行交易的信用价值，同时也为了证明具有与欧洲运营公司的交易意图，在外国直接投资中，特别是来自欧盟以外的国家，如中国，缴纳资本在 1000 ~ 10000 欧元是必要的。已发行的股本可全部或部分缴足。允许对实收股份进行实物出资，不再需要对资产进行认证或进行未经认证的估值，但董事必须验证所提供的实物价值与股份认购额是否价值相当。

• 限制性股票溢价（缓解）。股票的面值和价值在经济角度上来说是等额的，但是从法律的角度来看，它们可以根据需求（除非另有协议）退还，因此从法律角度来看，股票没有资本。对长期的债务或者贷款，税务局没有限制，除非获得的贷款超过已发行资本的 3 倍，内部（税务）税务局便可以拒绝从收入中扣除已付的利息，以便公告其利润，因此荷兰企业的所得税可能会向上调整。

• 股票。在公司章程中，允许规定不同类别的股份，包括普通股、具有特殊权利（尤其是投票权）的优先股（优先股在分配股利方面优先）、其他不同类别的股份（根据字母或者数字的区别用来区别利润分配或者董事会的提名和委任）以及最终全部或部分无投票权或无营利共享（普通）的股份，上述不同的股权分类彼此之间是排除的。

股份被登记（在股东登记册上登记，必须在私营公司办公室保存的小册子）之后，便不得发行股票证书，不得持有不记名股份。

对于已发行的股份，投资者在公司章程（禁止条款）中可以规定其转让性而不必须排除或者限制其转让性。

可以创建股份（证书）的存托凭证，用来分离投票权和获得股息的权利，例如在一个家族控股的公司，通常是通过一个基金“基金会管理处”（SAK），一个具有特殊目的的私营公司股东介入管理，并转而向最终受益人发放存权凭证。

• 股东大会（股东大会，AVA）。除非公司章程规定了较高的百分比或者将法定人数设置为高于 50% 以外，股东大会上的表决通常是按照简单多数票（51%）进行。股东大会每年至少召开一次，本人或者通过授权代理参加，可以在私营公司的注册地址或办公地址或荷兰其他地方甚至在国外进行。当然，如果所有的股东以书面形式（也可以通过电子邮件）达成一致，也可以在股东大会之外达成决议。

私营公司年度财务账目的签署和通过，就意味着管理委员会在上一个财政年度期间的行为的结束。此外，除非这家有限责任公司是一家所谓的大的由监督委员会直接任命的私营公司结构，否则，股东大会都可以任命，暂停和解除管理和监督委员会成员。需要注意的是，这种类型的私营公司并不适合大多数的对外直接投资。

股东大会可以完全决定公司股份的回赎、股本的减少，与另一公司的合并，发行新股，出售私营公司的资产和其他主要经营事宜，以及将私营公司转换成另一种形式的公司实体，解散（清算）或者自行申请破产等。此外，通过公司章程或者全体股东的决议，也可以实施关于某些交易或其他活动的董事会决议，当然这需要股东大会的事先批准。这也增强了股东在董事会和股东出现分歧时候的控制能力。只要不会从根本上限制董事会的活动，也允许股东大会就私营公司的运作向董事会作出有约束力的指示。

• 董事会（管理）。执行董事、常务董事或者管理委员会，由至少一名独立董事或者与经过授权可以代表私营公司的董事共同组成（与一名或多名其他董事一起）。董事会成员的名称为董事，但是一些非董事会的成员，如一个非法定的财务总监和运营总监也可以担任董事。董事会也有经营公司、保持良好企业形态的责任，如果不这样做，应当承担责任。然而，股东大会依然是公司结构的最高权力机构。董事可以是外国公民，也不必在荷兰居住，而且一个荷兰或外国的法人实体也可以担任董事。

在私营公司破产之前的 3 年期间，如果管理人对私营公司明显疏忽管理从而导致破产，管理委员会和每位董事，根据法律的相关规定，都能要求其对私营公司的破产负责。如果年度财务账户没有及时存入商会，以及私营公司的账簿和管理文件没有妥善保存，并且不能真正了解财务状况时，董事被认为是有责任的（除非他们能够证明该责任是可以免除的）。

负债等于私营公司的全额赤字（剩余的未偿还债务）。保险政策涵盖这种责任并不罕见，但是在一个较小的外国直接投资中，从母公司中借调一名董事的情况并不常见。根据法律的规定，董事责任的一种形式可以是税务局内部记载的私营公司未支付的税款余额（工资税、社会保障保险费和增值税）。如果他及时通知国税局的纳税申请失败了，这名董事也将会被告知这一情况。

如果破产管理人决定不提出损害赔偿请求，或者私营公司已进入自行破产清算时，董事会也可能因管理不善而向私营公司的债权人（或股东）承担责任。在向部分债权人偿付债务之后，董事会和控股股东依然要对未支付的债权人承担责任，这被称为“揭开公司的面纱”。如果股东不能通过所谓的“支付测试”（或分布测试），即破产以后的债务以及预期的债务证明向股东分配股息是不正当时，董事会也有责任重新分配股利（或分担损失）。

除此之外，根据公司自治的原则，正确执行事务的董事和股东都是免责的，甚至私营公司将被允许继续运营，继续负债，这将为公司负债的改善提供一个合理的预期。

• 监事会。公司章程可以规定设立一名或多名监事，监事可以作为管理委员会的一部分，联合执行董事和非执行董事构成“一元制”的董事会，也可以作为监事会的组成部分与董事会构成“二元制”。监事成员必须是自然人。非执行董事及监事的任务是监察及向执行董事提供意见，他们不参与私营公司的日常管理，因此，他们不承担管理责任（但缺乏监督承担责任例外）。在密切持有外国直接投资的合资企业中，董事会中应该有足够的代表，而监事会则几乎没有附加的要求。

• 代理持有人。管理委员会可以任命一名或多名普通代理人，通常是公司的工作人员，代理人员具有有限的权限，比如合同价值（如 20000 欧元）以内或者有限的交易权限。如果代理情况被提交到商会，在代理权利范围内以及超过范围的情况下，代理将会被第三方运用。

• 年度存款账目。管理委员会签署年度账目，并且股东大会在此后两个月内批准年度账目，批准的时间应当在 8 日以内，（在内部记录的延期之后）最终年度账目必须在 12 个月内存入商会（2016 年新增规定）。为了防止董事承担相应的责任，应密切注意这一最后期限。

如果私营公司的股东与公司的董事、总经理一致，那么年度账目的签署被视为股东的批准（忽略所谓的微型公司类别）。根据私营公司的收入和资产负债总额，主要存在三种年度账户：一是最小的类别，即总资产低于 600 万欧元，净收入高达 1200 万欧元，员工人数低于 50 名，只有缩减的资产负债表没有损益表。二是中间类别（资产 2000 万欧元、净收入 4000 万欧元和 250 名以下员工），规定了一套更具体和分层的资产负债表和损益表。三是最高类别（超过中间类别的数据），完整而详细的资产负债表和损益表是强制性的，必须由荷兰特许会计师（注册会计师）审计。集团公司可以储存位于荷兰或欧盟的母公司与子公司的年度账户，从而减少全部数据的公布。

⑬ 公众有限责任公司（有限责任公司）。最重要的一种企业类型是公众有限责任公司。不同于私营公司，公众有限责任公司允许不记名股份，并且对股份的转让没有限制，因此被称为“无名公司”。公众有限责任公司用于并主要用于证券交易所上市。公众有限责任公司的内部运作与私营公司的内部运作类似，但具有不同的股东权利和资本保护。因此，它通常只适用于超大型的对外直接投资。

（4）市场准入和审查标准。除了特殊的国家安全和欧盟洗钱国家黑名单，荷兰法律对于外国投资者是完全中立的，这样他们会承担同等的义务，被赋予与国内荷兰投资者同等的权利。同样，荷兰法律也没有保留单独形式的外国持有或投资的法人实体，如中国外商独资企业和中外合资企业。此外，也没有像外国投资产业指导目录那样区分鼓励、限制和禁止的三个类别的工业部门。

董事和股东可以是非荷兰人，也可以是荷兰非居民，私营公司的通信地址甚至可以在国外。除了在 OECD 金融行动特别工作组（FATF）“国家黑名单”上列出的国家（不包括中国）外，荷兰的国家补贴和银行融资也是中立的。然而，在部分荷兰公司或前荷兰国有的公司中，对外直接投资可能遭到州政府的审查或事实抵制。

2. 融资

（1）融资的简介和主要金融机构。荷兰作为一个开放的社会，以其著名的银行和金融业务而闻名。以下是关于某些财务活动的监管制度和财务主题的简要而非详尽的概述。

① 监管环境——一般情形。

荷兰《金融监管法》（AFS）包括荷兰金融机构的详细制度，具体包括市场准入（许可）、审慎规则、市场行为规则和市场行为监督等规定。基于欧洲经济区内的协调统一，荷兰可以为各种金融机构获得欧洲金融“护照”，包括商业银行、投资公司、保险公司和投资基金，从而使金融机构能够在整个欧洲经济区国家范围内基于本国的监管基础追求企业的目的。

在荷兰金融监督部门存在两个监管机构进行合作。其中，荷兰中央银行行使审慎监管的职能，具体包括流动性监管和荷兰金融机构的财务稳健监管。荷兰中央银行具体监管银行、保险公司（包括养老基金）、支付机构和结算机构。荷兰金融市场管理局对金融市场进行监督，其监督的目的在于规范金融机构和上市公司的经营行为。荷兰金融市场管理局监督所有有关金融经营的市场行为（包括那些由荷兰中央银行审慎监管的事项），并负责向金融机构发牌，特别是投资基金、投资公司（证券经纪）、信贷提供者和金融顾问。

进一步讲，欧洲中央银行和荷兰中央银行进行合作，并负责向荷兰银行授予许可证。因此，金融机构通常受到荷兰中央银行和荷兰金融市场管理局（如果适用，也包括欧洲中央银行）的监管，监管和合作之间的任务与责任分工也都规定在规则之中。

② 银行和金融机构——股票交易。荷兰主要有四大银行，即荷兰银行（在股票交易所上市）、荷兰合作银行（与成员合作）、荷兰国际银行（股票上市）和荷兰储蓄合作银行（现为国有），它们都向零售和批发客户提供一般的银行服务。除此之外，荷兰的各种小银行和外国银行，由于在欧洲经济区内存在席位，受益于欧洲护照制度，在荷兰市场上十分活跃。此外，来自欧洲经济区以外的各种银行通过设立子公司的形式，在荷兰获取银行牌照的基础上提供服务。阿姆斯特丹证券交易所属于世界上最古老的金融市场，成立于1606年。目前，阿姆斯特丹的证券交易所是泛欧交易所集团的一部分，在布鲁塞尔、巴黎、里斯本和伦敦都经营着交易市场。

③ 银行——金融公司。荷兰金融市场管理局对于没有银行牌照，却作为

银行从事从专业市场参与方以外（“专业市场参与方”，包括银行、养老基金和金融机构）的其他方收拢资金，并将这些资金用于自己账户的行为加以禁止。此外，也禁止在没有这些资金的情况下宣传偿还资金的能力。

在各种例外和豁免的条款中，最重要的是集团财务公司的适用例外，主要适用于专业从事吸引公众资金并将这些资金借给集团公司的实体。只要满足以下条件，这些金融公司就无须具备获得银行牌照的法定要求：一是根据荷兰金融市场管理局第 5 章（包括招股说明书要求）的要求，发行证券吸引可偿还资金；二是该财务公司的母公司对和可偿还资金有关的所有义务作出了无条件的担保（或者存在一个无条件的担保，由一家在欧洲经济区内获得许可的银行作出）；三是通过发行证券获得的可偿还资金，应当在财务公司和集团公司之间的借贷中达到最少 95% 的比例。

据估计，在荷兰存在 7000 多家这样的金融公司实体，而不受到荷兰中央银行的监管。如果这是通过发行证券进行的，并且所有这些都符合荷兰金融市场管理局第 5 章的规定，那么吸引无偿借贷是允许的。

④ 投资基金。自 2013 年 6 月 22 日起，荷兰金融市场管理局将投资基金区分为两类：一是集团投资可转让证券的承诺（UCITS），对其的监管基于荷兰金融市场管理局实施的 UCITS 指令；二是替代投资基金（AIFs），对其的监管基于荷兰金融市场管理局实施的替代投资基金管理人指令（2011/61/EU）。基于荷兰的 UCITS 或 AIFs 的基金管理人在荷兰提供和营销投资基金，需要遵守许可证的要求。有关 UCITS 和 AIFs 的所有规定一般是针对基金管理人的，而不是基金本身，同时，也适用欧洲护照制度。对于基于 AIFs 管理的小型荷兰投资基金，缓解注册制度在没有取得欧洲护照时也是适用的。

⑤ 信托管理办公室。许多从事公司服务（信托管理）的公司遵循对公司有利的税收制度，都设立在荷兰。信托机构的监管主要依赖信托办公室作出的《荷兰法案》（《信托局监管法案》），盎格鲁撒克逊信托概念不是荷兰法律中的概念，荷兰的信托办公室是旨在追求其业务而提供信托服务的法律实体（或自然人，或合伙）。信托服务通常包括管理服务（提供董事）或提供定居服务与法律或税务咨询。信托机构应从荷兰中央银行处获得许可证。由于信托机构通常服务于“铜板公司”，因此它们被认为是一个涉及洗钱和恐怖主义融资的风险因素。目前，荷兰中央银行正在持续监督信托部门，而

且议会也正在准备一项关于信托局监管法案修正案的立法提案。特别地，这些立法建议向立法者提出了禁止根据信托局监管法案颁布的法令，向某些公司结构提供信托服务的可能性。

（2）外国企业融资条件。一般来说，外国公司在荷兰获得融资是没有障碍的。荷兰对于货币的转移没有限制，荷兰银行对本地和外国实体的融资也是持开放的态度。主要的荷兰银行通常是根据贷款市场协会（LMA）的格式给它们准备融资文件，并且根据具体的荷兰法律进行调整。对于基于 LMA 文件的外国公司的主要融资，通常选择英国法律（当 BREXIT 生效时，这可能会改变）与英国法院管辖。这类财务文件通常用英语起草。安全包规则通常因抵押品的不同受到不同的法律管辖，荷兰房地产的抵押权或荷兰公司的股份质押是根据荷兰《民法》在公证人主持下订立契据而强制建立的。抵押契据必须用荷兰语编制，民法公证人将准备一份官方翻译。定期安全包制度通常还包括（取决于借款人的业务）贸易和公司间应收款的质押、银行应收账款质押、保险应收账款质押、知识产权和动产的质押。

《金融监管法案》在第 5 章中规定了在荷兰应当如何发行证券。在荷兰，发行人只有提交招股说明书，并经过主管监管当局批准时，方可向公众发行证券。也就是说，在此种情况下，受监管市场才接受证券上市。招股说明书应根据“欧盟招股说明书”规定的规则编制。对于一般的荷兰证券发行公司，荷兰金融市场管理局是批准招股说明书的主管监管机构。如果在欧洲经济区的另一成员国提供证券，荷兰金融市场管理局根据发行人的请求向提供证券的国家的主管监管机构发出批准证书。

就发行证券而言，招股章程规定有若干例外及豁免条例。只要向少于 150 名自然人或法人发行，或者证券在价值至少为 10 万欧元（或者证券的名义价值至少 10 万欧元），在这种情况下，向公众发行的证券不受招股说明书要求的限制。向合格的投资者提供产品，包括银行、金融机构和养老基金，以及向公众提供。在 12 个月内价值不超过 250 万欧元的，不含招股说明书的要求。在同一类别的证券已经在受监管市场上市并且延期少于已上市资本的 10% 的情况下，在市场上进行证券交易是免费的。对于某些证券，需要插入一个明确的说明，表明该证券不受荷兰金融市场管理局的监管，不受招股说明书要求或许可证的约束，而是对所有发行材料都具有一定的强制性要求。

（3）并购。中国投资者在荷兰进行投资的一种选择是收购后持续经营，或者是荷兰或欧盟两家现有公司的股份或资产的法定或合法合并，而中国投资者作为合并和收购的一方，简称并购。荷兰法律不允许与非欧盟公司进行跨境合并，因此，除非中国公司首先创建一家荷兰子公司作为合并实体，否则该公司不符合合并条件。

股份收购法律程序的缺点便是时间较长，这也是其成本和新业务运营风险的一种不利因素。成功收购的关键是适当的尽职调查和意愿，以弥合商业文化差距。

典型的并购股份流程如下：

公司财务顾问和律师事务所紧密合作，根据潜在买家签署的“预告文本”或投资备忘录（IM），确定并接触荷兰“目标”（将被收购的公司），与其签订非披露协议（NDA）承诺保密。寻找目标公司的费用，收购成功后相关的费用可安排在任意一方。然后，潜在买方和卖方签订意向书（LOI），其中包含主要交易项目，并规定对目标的法律、税务、财务、技术和商业文件尽职调查以及将目标的管理信息在“数据室”透漏给采购公司的顾问，无论是以文本还是数字格式。

尽职调查后的报告可以提示买方中止交易或重新协商交易的价格和条件，这又可以激励卖方放弃交易。然而，根据双方都有诚意谈判的法律原则，并且以适当的公平和合理性行事，任何一方都不能预先放弃。如果目标公司满足涉及劳动力的某些实质标准，则买方必须首先告知海牙中央监管委员会和工会即将开展收购的意图（《决定合并守则》，2015 年规定）。然后，买方律师在交易后 6 ~ 12 个月内起草买卖合同，约定买方的陈述和保证，并附有赔偿保证等买方应该披露的信息。

另外，在签订销售合同之后或同时，买方将指定一个荷兰民法公证人见证股份所有权转让契据的签订（强制性规定）。公证人将作为新的所有人进入买方成为目标公司的股东登记册上的一员。公证人将向商会提交新的管理和监督董事、代理人和新股东的名称（只有当有一个股东时）。整个并购流程将需要 2 ~ 8 周或更长的时间，这取决于交易的规模和复杂程度。在资产交易（非房地产）的情况下，所有权的转让是通过非公证契约进行的，但是律师的专业援助仍然是需要的。

（4）竞争条款。

① 监管部门的竞争规定。

欧洲的竞争政策是欧盟内部市场的重要组成部分，其目标是以更低的价格为欧洲每个人提供更优质的商品和服务。欧盟竞争政策的意义在于提供规则以确保公司彼此公平竞争。这能鼓励企业和提高效率，为消费者创造更广泛的选择，并有助于降低价格和提高质量。这就是欧盟打击反竞争行为、审查合并行为和国家援助并鼓励自由化的原因。欧盟竞争政策主要基于《欧洲联盟运作条约》（TFEU）第101条（旧第81条）和第102条（旧第82条）。

TFEU 赋予欧盟委员会适用欧盟竞争条款的权力，并为此拥有一些调查权力（如在商业和非商业场所进行检查、提供书面信息请求等）。委员会还可以对违反欧盟反托拉斯条款的企业实行罚款。通过授权，国家竞争管理机构（NCA）也有权充分适用 TFEU 第 101 条和第 102 条的规定，以确保竞争不被扭曲或限制。国家法院也可以适用这些规定，以保护 TFEU 赋予公民的个人权利。

为了落实欧盟竞争政策，1998年新荷兰《竞争法》（*Mededingingswet*）生效。从那时起，荷兰的反垄断和反垄断监管符合TFEU第101条和第102条的规定。

荷兰竞争管理局（ACM）执行荷兰《竞争法》，在荷兰受到影响的情况下，国家当局也有权强制执行 TFEU 第 101 条和第 102 条的规定。荷兰法院也必须适用这些条款。

② 《竞争法》的简介。

欧盟《竞争法》适用于限制竞争并作用于欧盟成员国之间贸易的协议、决定或协同行为以及兼并和反竞争行为。荷兰《竞争法》只适用于荷兰境内，如果荷兰境内的竞争受到限制，不影响欧盟成员国之间的贸易。

TFEU 第 101 条（卡特尔禁令）禁止在内部市场上以防止、限制或扭曲竞争为目的（或效果）的企业之间的协议、企业协会的决定或协调一致的做法。限制竞争的合同条款和 / 或协议无效，这种无效可以在自然人当事人之间的民事法庭诉讼中确立。荷兰《竞争法》第 6 条对禁止或扭曲荷兰市场竞争的合同条款和 / 或协议也有类似禁令。

卡特尔禁令不适用于：根据欧盟区块豁免条款达成的协议（如垂直协议

的欧盟区块豁免条款或技术转移协议的欧盟区块豁免条款）；受益于荷兰政府法令确定的区块豁免的协议；有关公共服务公司（承担提供一般经济利益服务的承诺）的某些协议或做法；行业中的集体就业协议和集体养老金协议；不太重要的协议。欧盟委员会认为，可能影响成员国之间贸易并可能产生预防，限制或扭曲内部市场竞争的企业之间的协议不会明显限制第 101 条所指的竞争条约：如果协议双方所持有的总市场份额对受协议影响的任何相关市场不超过 10%，而该协议是在其中任何一个实际或潜在竞争者的企业之间达成的市场（竞争者之间的协议）；如果协议各方持有的市场份额对受该协议影响的任何相关市场不超过 15%，而该协议是在任何非实际或潜在竞争者的承诺这些市场（非竞争对手之间的协议）。根据荷兰《竞争法》，这种所谓的免税豁免适用于限制竞争的协议，涉及不超过 8 家年营业额不超过 550 万欧元的公司（如果有关公司主要在货物供应方面活跃），或 110 万欧元（在所有其他情况下）。

此外，在下列情况下，可以宣布 TFEU 第 101 条不适用：任何协议或类别之间的协议；企业协会的任何决定或类别的决定；任何协调一致的做法或类别的协调做法。这有助于改善产品的生产、分销、促进技术或经济进步，同时允许消费者公平分享所产生的利益，并且不对有关承诺施加对实现这些目标并非不可或缺的限制；使这类企业有可能消除有关产品的大部分的竞争。

TFEU 第 102 条规定禁止在某一特定市场上占主导地位的公司滥用该地位，例如通过收取不公平的价格，限制生产，或拒绝为消费者创新的行为。荷兰《竞争法》第 24 条也包括类似的禁令，该条还指出，可以根据要求向受托提供一般经济利益服务的企业授予豁免。

欧盟委员会还对合并进行控制。欧盟控制合并的法律基础是欧盟委员会条例（EC）139/2004，即欧盟合并条例。该法规禁止兼并和收购，这将大大降低单一市场的竞争。例如，如果它们将创建垄断公司，可能提高消费者的价格。

委员会原则上只审查与欧盟范围的较大合并，意味着合并公司达到一定的营业额门槛。有两种替代方法来达到欧盟维度的营业额限制。

第一种选择需要：一是所有并购公司的全球营业额合计超过 5 亿欧元；二是欧盟范围内至少两家公司中的每家公司的营业额超过 2.5 亿欧元。

第二种选择要求：一是所有合并公司的全球营业额超过 25 亿欧元；二是所有合并公司在至少 3 个成员国中的每个合并营业额超过 1 亿欧元；在第二点中所包括的 3 个成员国中至少两个企业的每个企业的营业额超过 2500 万欧元；欧盟范围内至少两家公司每家的营业额超过 1 亿欧元。

在两个备选方案中，如果每个企业在同一成员国内将其欧盟范围的营业额的三分之二以上归档，则不能满足欧盟的要求。通常每年向委员会通报约 300 个合并项目。

在实施之前，必须通知欧盟委员会与欧盟相关的任何合并项目。公司可以事先联系委员会，了解如何最好地准备它们的通知。根据案例的复杂性，有预先准备的模板用于通知它们的合并：如果合并公司没有在相同或相关的市场运营，或者如果它们只有非常小的市场份额没有达到指定的市场份额限制，合并通常不会引起重大的竞争问题：合并审查因此由简化程序涉及例行检查；市场份额门槛是：在任何两个竞争的市场上的市场份额为 15%，在垂直相关市场上的市场份额为 25%；在这些市场份额限制之上，委员会进行全面调查。

任何新通知的详情均在竞争委员会的网站和欧盟官方公报上公布，以便任何有关单位可以与委员会联系并提交关于合并的意见。

不在欧盟范围的较小合并可能会在成员国竞争管理机构的职权范围内。有一个转介机制，允许成员国和委员会根据有关公司的要求和成员国的请求，在它们之间转移案件。这允许公司从一站式审查中受益，并将案例分配给最适当的权威机构。

荷兰《竞争法》第 29 条规定了进行集中的企业何时需要事先通知 ACM。部分须经通知和事先批准，其中：上一个日历年内提出的集中所涉各方的总营业额超过 1.5 亿欧元；与此同时，至少两个拟议集中的缔约方在上一个日历年单独实现了荷兰 3000 万欧元或更多的营业额。

对于荷兰医疗保健行业的部分，适用不同（较低）的流动率门槛：上一个日历年中提议集中所涉各方的合并营业额超过 5500 万欧元；与此同时，拟集中的至少两方分别在上一个日历年实现了 1000 万欧元以上的荷兰营业额。

公司合并的部分要求其中一个或多个公司获得对另一公司的控制，并且两个或更多公司建立了一个完整的（独立运营）合资企业。

③ 调节竞争的措施。

欧盟委员会和 ACM 对违反欧盟或荷兰《竞争法》规定的罚款限制在公司总年营业额的 10% 以内。如果该集团的母公司在侵权期间对子公司的运营产生决定性影响，10% 的限额可以基于公司所属集团的营业额。从侵权行为结束到委员会调查开始为止，有五年的有限期。

欧盟委员会鼓励参与卡特尔的公司提出证据，帮助委员会检测卡特尔并建立案例。第一家提供足够的卡特尔证据从而使委员会能够追究这一案件的公司可以获得罚款的完全豁免；后续公司可以减少最多 50% 的罚款，否则将被征收全额罚款。

作为欧盟《竞争法》全面执行的一部分，委员会还制定并实施了一项关于欧盟《竞争法》适用于国内法院损害赔偿诉讼的政策。它还与国家法院合作，以确保欧盟竞争条款在整个欧盟的一致适用。

欧洲的竞争政策是欧盟内部市场的重要组成部分，其目标是以更低的价格为欧洲每个人提供更优质的商品和服务。欧盟竞争政策是通过应用规则，以确保公司彼此公平竞争。这不仅可以鼓励企业和提高效率，还可以为消费者创造更广泛的选择，并有助于降低价格和提高质量。这些是欧盟打击反竞争行为、审查合并和国家援助并鼓励自由化的原因。

3. 土地及房地产相关法律法规简介

（1）私人权利与人权。荷兰《民法》区分仅提供强制效力的法律行为（只能在协议各方之间强制执行的权利）和具有专有效力的法律行为（对每个人可强制执行的权利）。荷兰《民法典》中规定了所有权、其他权利（如租赁权、地役权和抵押权）和人身权利（如买方或承租人的权利）。

所有权是指拥有充分享受商品和以绝对方式自由使用的权利，前提是这不与第三方权利和法律限制或不成文法的规定相冲突。因此，人们在实际财产中可能获得的最高利益及其他权利都来自所有权。为了创造除所有权之外的权利，相同的规则适用于所有权本身的转让。

（2）荷兰不动产。荷兰的房地产通常分三个阶段出售和转让：

阶段 1：购买协议。一旦卖方和买方就买卖不动产达成协议，他们就受该协议的条款约束。协议不需要书面形式：协议可以口头订立，在特殊情况下甚至可以从其他情况推断。然而，一般来说，广告不被视为要约，而仅仅是提出要约的邀请。因此，买方对广告的积极响应本身不会束缚所有者。

与英国不同的是，购买协议的订立并不会导致某种形式的所有权的成立。订立购买协议只会产生两项主要义务：卖方将不动产的所有权转让给买方的义务以及买方支付购买款项和接受不动产所有权的义务。

阶段 2 和阶段 3：不动产的转让是通过在荷兰民事公证人之前签署转让契据，并在土地注册处的公共登记处登记该契据。公证人确保契约的注册在其签署后尽快完成，其不受国家保证。所以，注册不会去除所有权的任何缺陷，理论上，即使谨慎的买家也有一定的风险，虽然该风险相当小。

一般来说，不动产买方的安全取决于公证人的诚实、知识和技能，他受到严格的职业道德守则的约束，并且有失职保险。公证人是一名转让律师，他有责任确保转让是有序的，并代表卖方和买方行事。荷兰对不动产所有权的问题很少出现，因为自1956年以来，立法者强制要求转让不动产的公证契约。

（3）不动产买家。不动产的买卖协议不需要满足任何形式的要求，所有权在转让不动产之前不会转移给买方。除非相关各方另有约定（在一定限度内可以达成一致），不动产必须转让给买方明确接受的任何其他特殊收费和限制的方式。因此，除非根据一般公认的原则，应该由买方发现的以外，卖方有义务披露所有特殊的收费和限制。

由于在荷兰的所有权仅通过转让契据的登记而转让给买方，不动产实际上可能会不止一次地出售给不同的买方，从而导致了哪个买方拥有最终权利的冲突。按照这种方式，购买的选择权或优先权也可能会达不到目的。

直到不动产被转让，具有最大权利的买方（第一顺位买方）被认为具有更强的权利。然而，如果不动产转移给具有更新的权利的买方（第二顺位买方），则该转让本身是合法的。然后，第一顺位买方可以对卖方因违反合同而造成的任何损失承担责任。第一顺位买方还可以要求第二顺位买方将不动产转让给他，但是只有当第二顺位买方知道第一顺位买方的权利时才能实现。这项索赔是基于非法行为或侵权原则。为了防止后来的买家以及其后的所有权人（如抵押权人或债权人的附属物）提出的索赔，买方可能已将他的采购协议进行公证。该公证有效期为公证日后 6 个月，之后可能不再公证 6 个月。

（4）经济所有权。一般来说，经济（或“实益所有权”）是指在协议的基础上，一个人向卖方支付价格来购买，并表现出他好像是不动产的所有者。

虽然买方不是合法的拥有者，但他承担与房地产相关的所有利益和费用以及它的风险。鉴于上述意见，买方 / 经济所有人承担相当大的风险，无须作出进一步安排，并应自我防范诸如卖方死亡、破产或拒绝转让不动产之类的危险。为了防范这些风险，买方通常会要求对方抵押不动产，以确保卖方履行购买协议下的义务，以及不可撤销的委托代理转让不动产。出售经济所有权过去由于其财政收益而受欢迎。然而，在 1995 年之后，经济所有权的转让与转让合法所有权时所缴纳的转让税相同，这种现象已变得不太常见。

（5）公寓。水平细分的基本问题是，单位业主的权利和义务如何与建筑物所在的土地所有权有关。在业主以及在整个建筑物的法律程序中，代表业主如果受到邻近建筑物的威胁，谁会采取行动？

为了解决这些问题，《民法典》载有规定，在转让公寓时，买方应成为整栋建筑物和地块的共同拥有人；获得他的单位的专用权；成为业主协会的成员。这三个要素在任何情况下都不能分开，由荷兰民事公证人协会的标准章程组织与法律一起提供对上述所有问题的答案。

公司权利本身的分立和业主协会的成立，是通过在土地注册处的公共登记册注册一份在公证人签立的分契契据的核证副本而进行的。

如今在荷兰，这种法律建设被广泛使用，不仅用于一幢单位，而且用于商业和混合商业 / 住宅开发。

（6）出租和租赁。租赁权（erfpacht）是一种物权，它授予在特定时期或无限期内使用和占用另一方享有不动产的专有权。该项权利是在土地注册处的公共登记册上登记在公证人执行的契据副本的核证副本而制成的，该权利可以转让或抵押，有时需要得到不动产所有人的事先同意。通常情况下，承租人将支付年租金（canon），但也可能双方同意单独支付资本金。

租赁权并不常由私人或公司授予。相反，租赁权通常由荷兰较大城市的城市委员会授予，如阿姆斯特丹、鹿特丹、海牙和乌得勒支。城市地面租赁是城市发展和扩展的一个方面，因此与历史上城市的发展不可分割地联系在一起。自 20 世纪初以来，在阿姆斯特丹几乎所有的市政府都以租赁形式出租给城市。

租赁权是一种出租人的权利，它授予在一段时间或无限期内使用和占用另一方不动产的专有权。虽然租赁不是一种物权（因此不能抵押），但它确实有一些与《财产法》有关的要素，其中最重要的是在出售和转让不动产的情况下，租赁权不会因此消灭，买方仍然受到现有租赁合同的约束。荷兰法律通常区分租赁无限期的住宅物业和租赁最初五年的零售物业，这些物业除非承租人终止租赁，否则将根据法律延长五年。工业或办公楼物业通常租赁期为五年，承租人可选择续约五年。

（7）《国际民法》。就荷兰《国际民法》而言，《不动产法》受到财产所在国可强制执行的法律规定的约束。出售财产的转让是通过登记公证书的方式进行的。因此，英格兰买家不可能要求他们的英国律师在荷兰拟定不动产转让合同。荷兰的不动产买卖协议不需要满足形式上的任何要求。因此，如果荷兰人向荷兰人口头出售其财产给英国人，在荷兰方面并不会出现任何问题：除非双方事先同意出售和购买（而不是所有权的转让）受英国法律管辖，否则荷兰人将不会出现问题。

根据荷兰法律，当事人不能同意财产的转让受英国法律的管辖，因为根据法律原则，只有荷兰法律可以适用于转让。由于对形式没有要求，双方可以用任何他们想要的语言（只要他们理解所选择的语言）制定和执行销售和购买合同。然而，转让契据只能以荷兰语执行。当因果系统盛行时，关于潜在买卖协议的有效性的问题则按照《国际民法》的规则来回答。

（8）公共法。对于使用不动产的公共来源的法规有很多限制。下面将简要说明规划和建筑规章以及环境法规。

① 规划和建筑规章。《城乡规划法案》（TCPA）和《住房法案》规范了不动产的开发和使用。根据TCPA，市议会有义务准备和采用地方分区计划。分区计划须经省政府批准。地方分区计划必须详细列出允许的使用和发展方式，并且不得干扰上级的区域分区计划或国家计划。只有根据在分区计划的特定部分内允许的开发和使用，才允许施工。

根据一些免税、住房法案的要求，对新建筑的任何改变或翻新现有的建筑工程都需要建筑工程施工许可证。只有在建筑活动和使用符合分区计划的情况下才允许许可。除此之外，建筑许可证还需要根据《中央建筑法令》和当地的建筑规章（Bouwverordening）进行开发、处理建筑物的设计和建造以及提供服务、配件和设备。

② 环境法规。《土壤保护法》规定了对污染土地的清理方法。重点在于

污染者和污染土地所有者或承租人需承担清理的财务负担。根据《土壤保护法》，不动产的所有者或持有者负责清理受污染的土地，除非本人能证明其与污染没有法律上的利害关系，没有其他责任，也不知道或不可能知道污染在其收购的土地。因此，不需要首先找到实际污染者，也不需要污染者无力偿债。在实践中，通常难以避免责任，买方也将进行土壤调查。根据《土壤保护法》，省级当局可以给予清理令，该命令将在土地登记处登记。

（9）抵押。住宅物业融资最常用的方法是抵押贷款，该项权利是在土地注册处的公共登记册内登记在公证人签立的契据的核证副本而制成的。抵押对后续第三方有效。在不动产转让后，如果没有解除由卖方取得的抵押贷款，抵押持有人将保留其权利。理论上，买方可能面临一种令人不愉快的情况：获得了一个受卖方授予的抵押权的不动产，但是由于上述公共登记和公证人的强制干涉，如果买方不知情，就不可能发生。

荷兰法律对抵押贷款的一个特点是抵押贷款对其确保的贷款的依赖：没有债务就不可能转让抵押贷款。在荷兰法律中，抵押不是独立存在的。如果债务完全偿还，抵押就会解散，即使它仍然在公共登记册登记，直到通过在公证人执行的取消契据的注册副本的注册取消。当贷款人指定其索赔时，该索赔的抵押权自动转移给受让人。

荷兰抵押贷款法律的另一个重要之处是抵押权人在不受法院干预的情况下执行抵押权下的合法权利的能力。第一抵押贷款一般是最优惠的债务（除了内部收入服务和社会保障部门的索赔）。此外，如果债务人破产，抵押权人可以在没有任何进一步授权的情况下取消其抵押。在荷兰，抵押贷款融资非常发达，有很多商业银行、商家和储蓄银行都使用抵押贷款融资，而且无论是荷兰人还是外国人，他们都开发了成熟的金融抵押产品。

（10）具体税。根据某些免税政策，转让税（overdrachtsbelasting）是由于在荷兰购置不动产（所有权或租赁权），根据转让契据征收，或在授予租赁权的情况下征收适用的。相对于正常的租赁，在免税政策下的租赁或转租赁不需要缴纳转让税。转让税应由买方支付，除非双方另有约定。转让税是根据购买价格（或物业的实际价值）计算的，目前的转让税率为住宅物业的2%，其他不动产的为6%。《法律交易税法》（*Wet op Belastingen van Rechtsverkeer*）也针对股权转让：对象或其实际活动包括获取、转让或者开发房地产的公司，并且这些资产包括不动产的 70% 以上。

不动产的转让和租赁免征增值税。但是，以下情况征收增值税：新开发的房产在第一次占用之前或之内的两年内的转让，即新建的房产，或已经准备发展的土地；卖方和买方选择使其缴纳增值税的财产转让，只有在财产用于增值税相关供应服务或货物至少 90% 受制于征收增值税，或根据增值税应纳税租金租给提供服务或货物的承租人，其中至少 90% 需要缴纳增值税。

这里需要说明的是，增值税目前的征税率为 21%。

4. 税

（1）税制和规则。荷兰有一个统一的全国税制，除了 i.a. 次级地方城市税外，还有水利税和省道税。欧盟税务规则和法规对荷兰《税法》具有重大影响，但荷兰《税法》保留了其主权。

（2）税的分类和税率。

① 公司所得税。一般来说，荷兰居民公司根据其全球收入须缴纳企业所得税（CIT）。但是，某些收入可以免税。非居民公司有有限的纳税义务。只有荷兰来源收入纳入外国公司应税企业的 CIT 基础。标准的企业所得税税率为 25%（2017 年），在某些情况下，减税税率为 20%（2017 年）。

荷兰公司纳税人对与合格股权相关的所有利益免交荷兰税，如现金股利、实物红利、红股、隐性利润分配、资本利得和货币兑换等。但是，为了应用参与豁免，应满足以下要求：（控股）公司拥有被投资公司至少 5% 的股份；不是有价证券投资；如果持有利息的子公司的利润受到至少 10% 的有效利润税或者如果子公司的大部分资产不符合被征收低税率的自由证券投资的资格，参与豁免也适用。

特殊制度适用于自行开发的无形资产的收入。在创新框中，应税公司可以在某些条件下选择对这些无形资产产生的应税利润实行较低的有效利率。通过减少税基，创新箱的有效税率为 5%（2017 年）。荷兰创新箱制度按照经济合作与发展组织的指导，与所谓的“联系分数”一致。此外，应税公司必须有荷兰政府发布的研发声明和所谓的“入场券”（如专利或软件）。

如果荷兰公司纳税人迁移，退出税是由于隐藏储备和商誉的实现和未实现利润。税收时刻是在迁移时计算和形式化的。当荷兰仍然可以征税时，不需要退税，如在荷兰继续设立常设机构。如果新居住地位于欧盟 / 欧洲经济区成员国内，则应缴纳的税款可能会延期。

执行特定研发活动的公司可能受益于第一笔 35 万欧元研发工资成本和其他研发费用及投资的 32%（2017 年）税收抵免（最多达 40% 的创业公司），16%（2017 年）的费率适用于超过 35 万欧元的成本和投资。

② 增值税。荷兰增值税（VAT）是由纳税者在商业过程中在荷兰提供的货物和服务收取的，除非供应品为 0 额定或豁免。荷兰增值税制度是统一的欧洲制度（欧盟增值税指令）的一部分。增值税纳税者是指在荷兰从事商业活动的任何个人（个人或公司）。如果企业对在荷兰的交易需要缴纳增值税，则必须注册增值税。无论进口商是否是增值税纳税人，进口货物进入荷兰的增值税也应缴纳。荷兰的标准增值税率为 21%（2017 年），某些商品和服务税率降低 6%（2017 年）。此外，在荷兰，0 税率用于欧盟成员国之间的交易，即所谓的货物内部交易。

③ 预扣税。荷兰不征收向荷兰境内外的各方支付的利息、特许权使用费和资本收益的预扣税。在没有税收协定的情况下，荷兰公司的股息分配须缴纳 15%（2017 年）的预扣税。

④ 个人所得税。个人居民纳税人对他的全球收入征税。如果一个人与荷兰有很大的联系，例如，在荷兰生活、工作，他就被视为居民纳税人。非居民一般仅对其荷兰来源收入纳税。然而，非居民也可以申请被视为居民为税务目的，所谓的 30% 的设施。

简而言之，根据荷兰个人所得税，可以区分三种不同类型的应税收入，每类都有自己的税率：

• 第 1 类：利润、就业和自置居所收入。这包括工资、养老金、社会福利、公司车和自用物业的 WOZ 价值，累进率最高为 52%（2017 年）。

• 第 2 类：以 25% 的比率（2017 年）大量股权收入（至少 5% 的股份）。

• 第3类：来自储蓄和/或投资的收入按照2.87% ~ 5.39%的当量收益征税。这类收入按30%的统一税率征税。

（3）税务申报和优惠。所有纳税申报都可以由税务机关完成，但对于公司及其职员来说，通常是会计师以他们的名义报税，而在更复杂的情况下则是税务律师。

预缴税制度对税务机关具有约束力。与税务机关之前和税后回报的谈判是常见的。

（二）贸易

1. 部门监督贸易

作为世界上最大的出口和进口经济体之一，同时拥有在世界十大国际贸易中较前的排名，荷兰有一个非常开放的经济，没有什么贸易限制，除了军事和两用领域（通常用于民用目的但可能有军事用途的产品和技术），还加入了联合国和欧盟贸易禁运。

贸易由经济部监督，该部可促进荷兰成为一个具有强大的国际竞争地位和可持续发展眼光的经济体。此外，海关在执行对军用和两用货物贸易的限制、执行适用的贸易禁运和打击假冒产品方面也起到非常重要的作用。

2. 贸易法律和法规简介

荷兰与107个国家，包括中国（1987年2月1日起生效）签署了双边投资条约。此外，荷兰是世界贸易组织（WTO）的成员，也是在WTO主持下执行的大量条约的缔约国。荷兰还是世界知识产权组织（WIPO）《保护文学和艺术作品伯尔尼公约》《巴黎公约》《欧洲专利公约》等对促进贸易和保护知识产权至关重要的条约的缔约国。

3. 贸易管理

在学校系统中，从高中、大学和高等职业教育（HBO）开始，荷兰对国际贸易给予了极大的关注，从而产生了一个适用国际贸易和工作人员必备的语言英语及其他外语。

4. 进出口商品检验检疫

当从欧盟外部进口货物到荷兰时，通常需要进口关税。此外，还可能需要增值税，所有欧盟成员国适用相同的共同关税（CCT）。荷兰海关当局征收和收取税款，并将收集的款项转移到欧盟。海关当局不对欧盟成员国之间交易的产品征收进口关税。但是，将支付增值税。

增值税税率适用于荷兰的商品和服务供应品。在某些情况下，增值税可以在反向收费机制下宣布。这意味着进口商支付增值税，而不是非欧盟供应商。这适用于进口商是在荷兰建立的或有常设机构的企业家或法人实体。

消费税是基于消费行为而支付的，包括酒精饮料（如啤酒和葡萄酒）、烟草制品（如香烟和雪茄）和矿物油（如柴油或汽油）。消费税应用于烟草制品及非酒精饮料的进口。

在某些情况下，对进口货物征收其他征税，如对农产品征收农业税或对工业产品征收反倾销税。这些税收旨在防止产品（如中国钢铁）以非常低的价格进入欧洲市场。

荷兰的包装法规完全符合欧盟法律。使用CE标志认证的要求因产品而异。对于一些低风险Ⅰ类产品，制造商（或进口商，如果产品在欧盟以外生产）可以自己证明是否符合欧盟的要求，并附上CE标志；而对于有些产品，则需要由指定机构（认可的认证机构有KIWA）进行认证。CE标志要求用户界面软件、用户手册、警告标签和技术手册应采用本国语言，即荷兰语。对于Ⅰ类和Ⅱa类医疗设备，说明手册是可选的，但如果提供，则必须使用荷兰语。对于类别Ⅱb和Ⅲ，必须始终提供手册，并且必须以荷兰语提供。

《欧盟反盗版法规》（APR）为欧盟知识产权所有者提供了一种有用的和具有成本效益的武器，用于打击（被怀疑）侵犯知识产权的贸易。它允许海关当局在它们进入欧盟市场之前在边境地区扣押甚至销毁假冒商品，而无须法院命令。荷兰海关当局非常积极地执行APR。与许多其他欧洲国家不同，荷兰海关当局还针对专利侵权行为采取行动，但由于复杂性，只有在权利所有者的请求下才能行动。

5. 海关管理

许多公司选择荷兰作为其欧洲物流的地点，因为荷兰海关当局以促进国际贸易和海关程序的实用和积极主动的方式而闻名。鉴于荷兰作为欧洲门户的地位，荷兰海关有着丰富的物流流程经验。海关当局愿意在初步阶段与希望通过荷兰进口和出口的企业讨论现实状况与实际情况，来允许公司介绍/解释它们的具体情况，并确定这种情况是否为荷兰海关可以接受的，如果不能被接受，这些公司就会在稍后阶段被昂贵的评估所惩罚。

（三）劳动

1. 有关劳动的规定

（1）就业合同。当满足以下条件时，在荷兰存在雇佣协议：雇员有义务在雇主的监督下进行工作；雇主有义务为雇员支付工资。

荷兰雇佣协议可以书面或口头缔结。根据雇员的要求，雇主根据荷兰《民法典》的规定，有法定义务向雇员提供书面就业协议，提供条款和条件的证据。某些条件如试用期和不竞争条款只能以书面形式商定，并应由双方签署，否则无效。

（2）集体劳动协议。除强制性法律以及雇主和雇员在就业协议中相互同意的规定外，雇主协会和工会之间的集体劳动协议（CAO）也可以影响就业条款。这些 CAO 的规定推翻了一般劳动法。

（3）试用期。缔约方可以并通常同意初始试用期，且必须以书面形式约定才有效。最长试用期为两个月，而无限期的劳动协议，试用期应在 6 个月至两年之间。因此，对于少于 6 个月的固定期间，试用期是无效的。在试用期内，雇主和雇员均可随时终止雇佣协议，而无须终止雇佣期，并且没有支付遣散费的义务。规避方式在 CAO 中是可能的。

（4）期限和基于项目的雇佣协议。雇佣协议可以在一定期限（固定期限合同）、无限期限、特定任务或项目期间达成一致。

固定期限在商定的确定期限届满时自动结束。然而，自 2015 年 1 月 1 日起，雇主有义务在定期合同至少 1 个月前通知雇员。合同延期后，雇主必须通知雇员适用的条件。无限期的合同在雇主或雇员发出通知后结束。本通知受制于严格的法律条款。

（5）从固定期限到无限期。自动适用无限期的合同：当同一雇主每隔不超过 6 个月商定一个固定期限的 3 个以上连续雇佣合同时；当劳动合同的总期限不超过 6 个月时，超过两年或更长。

（6）假日和假日津贴。全职雇员除法定假日外，每年最多可享有 20 个工作日（全薪）的假期。假期津贴是年薪总额的 8%，并在 5 月每年支付一次或每月分期付款连同薪金支付。

（7）疾病。如果雇员因病而无法工作，雇主必须继续支付工资的至少 70%，最长期限为两年。大多数公司将在疾病的第一年支付 100%。除非在特殊情况下，否则不允许在疾病期间解雇。

（8）终止。终止雇佣协议有四种方法：即时解雇；通过向大区法院（Cantonal Court）提出解散劳动协议的请求；通过在公共就业服务局（UWV）提交有此目的的请求；在双方同意的基础上达成协议。

即时解雇。在紧急事故的情况下，雇主可以立即解雇雇员。紧急原因是一种事件或事件的组合，其中雇主不能合理地期望继续保持工作关系，例如，雇员殴打、严重侮辱或严重威胁雇主、他的家人或其他雇员，发生盗窃、贪污、欺骗、欺诈或其他可公诉的罪行等不值得雇主信任。此外，当劳动协议立即终止时，存在非常严格的正式法律条件，因此强烈建议及时与律师进行协商。

通过判决终止。为了有通过法院手段终止的就业协议，可以基于合理的理由向法院提出请求，如缺乏履行或不满意的工作关系。如果法院解散合同，将授予所谓的“过渡费”，并将考虑通知期。

UWV 许可证。基于经济原因的终止受限于可从公共就业服务局（UWV）获得的许可。当许可证被授予时，雇主可以终止劳动协议，但必须遵守通知期减去 UWV 程序的持续时间。员工有权获得转移支付。

相互同意。雇主和雇员可以通过双方同意自由谈判终止协议。为此，雇主通常向雇员提供赔偿。作为雇主，最重要的是确保雇员的同意是明确的。签署书面和解协议是至关重要的，雇员应被给予两个星期来考虑，雇员可以在此期间撤销协议，而不必给出任何理由。

（9）过渡性补偿。自从 2015 年中期引入新的劳动法立法以来，所谓的“州法院公式”以前习惯的计算方法不再有效，而是引入了过渡性补偿。根据这一新的赔偿制度，每当离职雇员在合同持续至少两年并且不是由于紧急原因或退休而终止时，有权获得过渡性补偿。

过渡性补偿大致计算如下：补偿金额等于前 10 年服务期最后一次获得的平均月薪的 1/6，以及每增加半年服务期最后一次获得的平均月薪的 1/4。年龄在 50 岁或以上且服务超过 10 年的雇员，直到 2020 年，有权享受半个月的 50 岁以下服务半年的工资。

过渡性补偿的最大值为：76.000 欧元（2017 年）。

雇主在最后 5 年的雇用期间支付费用，目的是增加雇员的就业能力，可以从过渡性补偿中扣除。

除过渡性补偿外，雇员还可以向法院要求合理的补偿。但是，这种合理的补偿只针对特殊情况，很少授予。

（10）集体解雇。根据《集体解雇通知法》（*Wet Melding Collectief Ontslag*）的规定，如果荷兰的雇主在3个月内要求解雇20多名雇员，必须将这一意向通知UWV和相关工会。

此外，雇主必须积极咨询工会，了解如何避免或减少集体冗余，以及如何减轻集体冗余的后果。这次磋商的结果可能影响 UWV 的决定。雇主有权在收到 UWV 的许可并完成所有手续后终止雇佣协议。

（11）工会

《工会法案》（WOR）要求所有雇用 50 名或更多人员的企业创建和维护工会。工会有权获知所有相关的公司信息，管理层必须每年至少举行两次会议，讨论有关公司的一般问题。

管理层有义务向工会提供就任何有关(甄选)的预期决定提出意见的机会:

① 转移对整个企业或其一部分的控制；

② 建立、接管或放弃对另一企业的控制，或对另一企业进行重大修改或切断与另一企业的永久合作企业，包括进行、实施重大变更或切断由于这种企业或为其利益的重要财务控制；

③ 终止企业或其主要部分的运营；

④ 企业活动的显着减少、扩张或其他变化；

⑤ 组织或权力分配的重大变化；

⑥ 公司运营的新位置；

⑦ 以团体形式招聘或借用劳动；

⑧ 重大投资；

⑨ 引入或改变重要的技术系统；

⑩ 委托外部专家提供上述建议。

建议请求必须尽早提交给工会，以便对拟议的决定产生重大影响。咨询请求必须附有对拟议决定的理由，公司员工的预期后果以及对这些后果采取的拟议措施的相当详细的总结。在工会提交意见后，公司可以作出决定，如果它们的意见没有或只有部分遵循，则必须给出理由。如果此请求未提交或建议被忽略，工会可在管理层书面通知该决定后一个月内向阿姆斯特丹上诉法院的企业商会提出上诉。在这一个月期间，公司必须暂停执行该决定。

唯一可以提出上诉的理由是，如果公司权衡所涉及的利益，公司不能合理地达成决定。由于审查范围有限，在实质性问题上不容易提出上诉。然而，公司的程序错误往往导致对工会有利的判决。企业商会认为，如果公司没有征求工会的意见，就会产生一个无可辩驳的推定，即如果它权衡了所涉及的利益，它不能合理地达到其决定。如果企业分庭认为公司不能合理地决定是否权衡这种利益，公司可能需要全部或部分撤回该决定，并撤销该决定的具体后果。

另外，拥有 10 ~ 50 名员工的公司必须设立人员代表，即 PVT。其规则和条例参考大型工作委员会，但其功能要轻得多，并且除非有规定，否则决定不得向企业商会申诉。低于 10 名员工的公司在这方面没有义务。

2. 聘用外国雇员的要求

（1）工作许可证。非欧盟外国人出于商业目的（出席商务会议、谈判、研讨会或进行实况调查），可以通过特别签证促进计划“橙色地毯”申请荷兰商业签证。中国居民可前往在荷兰驻北京大使馆或荷兰驻上海和广州领事馆以及中国各地的各个机构申请，处理时间为 48 个小时，且节省了复杂性。该签证在整个欧盟申根地区有效。如果入境的目的是工作，每个非欧盟外国人都需要工作许可证。

（2）申请程序。对于工作和停留时间超过 3 个月的居留许可（MVV）必须从上述荷兰大使馆、领事馆和中国机构申请。没有工作的居留许可证只能用于重要的个人目的，如家庭团聚。

对于工作，获得 MVV 的最流行的路线是所谓的高技能或知识移民（KM）过程。为此，外国居民必须在荷兰有一个无限期的就业，30 岁以下的工作人员最低月薪为 3170 欧元，30 岁以上的工作人员月薪为 4342 欧元，如果工作人员在荷兰的大学毕业，所有的最低月薪为 2272 欧元（2016 年所有金额）。

雇主必须被荷兰移民局（IND）认定为赞助者。申请 IND 的一次性申请费为 5276 欧元或 2638 欧元。存在不足 18 个月的公司需要一个商业计划，除非它们雇用超过 50 名员工。KM 无限期有效，无限数量的 KM 工作者有效。

获得 MVV 的替代途径是遵循证明空缺不能由任何欧盟公民或任何具有合法居住权的非欧盟公民填补的程序。这是一个耗时的并且昂贵的方案，没有确定的结果。

IND 的 2013 年《现代移民政策法规》（MoMi）旨在通过将以前单独的 MVV 和随后的居留许可申请合并为一个单一程序来加速和简化程序。

违反移民规定将受到最高 12000 欧元的处罚。

在使用 MVV 进入荷兰后，可以在向当地市政当局注册并且在 Rijswijk 的 IND 获得居留许可后立即开始工作。有效期与荷兰劳动协议的期限相关，不超过 5 年。

经过 5 年的就业和通过荷兰语言和文化融合考试，KM 许可证持有人有资格获得永久居留许可，独立于工作状态。

最后，MoMi 适用于所谓的富有移民（WM）或黄金签证途径的居留许可给外国人，个人资本超过 125 万欧元。资本必须由（外国）银行对账单证明，由荷兰驻华大使馆或领事馆合法化。资本上的（利息）收入必须并且仍然在荷兰。WM 不需要工作许可，也没有指定它的停留目的，也没有在申请之前通过整合考试。居留许可有效期为 5 年。WM 富有移民不需要工作许可证。

（3）社会保险。原则上，外国雇员享有平等的权利，并与家庭雇员享有平等的义务，因此有资格获得所有现有的公共社会证券保险，具有非歧视性的基础。然而，2016 年 9 月 12 日，中国和荷兰签署了一项双边条约，如果在本国保有投资，中国和荷兰将在接收国相继推迟对借调人员的保险，保险期最长为 5 年。新条约限于老年养恤金、失业和疾病。

3. 劳资纠纷

除非仲裁得到明确和适当的同意，否则大区法院（Cantonal Court）专门授权所有劳资纠纷。雇主和雇员被允许在法庭上出庭，但相当习惯的是，他们（两者）由法律上的律师或至少由专业律师和来自工会或司法协助保险人的非律师协助。

对于上面所述的终止合同纠纷，如果立即解雇，员工可以在即期终止之日起两个月内向法院提出申诉，提出异议；雇主将有机会提交辩护陈述书，而通常在短期内进行聆讯。法院可以拒绝或拒绝解雇，并命令雇员继续工作。

如果法院要求解散，法院将允许员工有公平的时间提交辩护陈述。法庭听证会将在大约 4 周内进行。在此后 3 个星期内，法官将作出决定，批准或拒绝解除劳动合同。

（四）争议解决

1. 争议解决的方法和机构

四种解决争端的方法为法院、仲裁（机构或特别）、有约束力的意见和调解。

（1）法院。法院的正式层次结构首先从下到上是对（民事和商业）案件的一审法院或大区法院，索赔价值高达 25000 欧元；其次是 11 个地区的中级法院或地区；再次是 4 个上诉法院；最后是海牙的一个最高法院。

最高法院和行政法院在欧盟法律涉及的情况下提出上诉，对卢森堡的欧洲法院开放。关于人权问题，向法国斯特拉斯堡的欧洲人权法院提出上诉。

（2）仲裁。仲裁在一系列仲裁法庭中制度化，包括从荷兰鹿特丹国家总法庭荷兰仲裁研究院（NAI）到专门的行业法庭，包括 Raad van Arbitrage voor de Bouw、建筑业仲裁委员会、热带水果仲裁法庭。

荷兰是 1958 年《纽约公约》关于承认外国仲裁裁决的缔约国，这有利于迅速促进在所有工业化国家和许多发展中国家的所有《纽约公约》国家颁布的外国仲裁裁决的执行。中国是《纽约公约》的签署国。

（3）有约束力的意见。如果仲裁取代并排除正常法院，私人争议解决方案是有约束力的意见。虽然在民事诉讼法中也有规定，但对诉讼当事人仅具有约束力，除非一方适用于法院，将有约束力的意见搁置一边，因为它对该当事人不公平。

（4）调解。调解在荷兰调解研究所或特设机构中被制度化，是法院普遍和鼓励的，但法院只会拒绝（即使这是合同约定的）处理没有通过调解的案件，因为调解显然对结果的达成是有益的。在实践中，任何一方的律师之间在诉讼前的惯常的谈判将被认为是诉讼前阶段的充分调解。

2. 法律适用

法院应适用由法律文本及其立法历史组成的法律。它们不被允许将法律与宪法相匹配，因为这是立法者的特权。然而，法律可以与取代的欧盟法律相匹配，只要它直接适用于成员国。欧洲人权公约也是如此。

行政案件的诉讼费（griffierecht）与许多周边国家相比较低。例如，在 2017 年针对原告和被告的州案中，如果案件价值高于 12500 欧元，关税法律实体的诉讼费用为 939 欧元，自然人的诉讼费用为 470 欧元。对于法律实体，如果案件价值低于 10 万欧元，法律实体的诉讼费用为 1924 欧元，自然人的诉讼费用为 883 欧元；如果案件价值高于 10 万欧元，法律实体的诉讼费用则为 3894 欧元，自然人的诉讼费用为 1545 欧元。上诉法院和最高法院的关税水平较高，法律实体的最高关税和 10 万欧元以上的索赔价值为 5200 欧元。

失败案件的当事人通常被命令向胜诉方偿还全部费用。此外，所有法院通常根据已公布的关税结构给予代理律师费用的偿还，尽管很少是实际的成本费用。

律师代表当事人（原告或被告）进行诉讼在地区法院和高级法院的民事和商业案件是强制性的。

证人听证主要由法官进行，没有普通法中习惯的交叉询问，当事人的律师通过主审法官提出问题，可以推翻审讯。

地方法院院长之前的禁令救济（kort geding）的简要程序以其简短而著称（在 14 日内，1 ~ 1.5 个小时内听证，在 10 日内进行书面判决并不少见）；主审法官是倾向于解决争议的；法院费用和法律费用很低，通常在 1200 欧元的水平。

一方面，在民事和商业案件中扣押资产，包括冻结银行账户、限制工资或扣押债务人或扣押第三方债务人，这些资产很容易申请，并被广泛使用且收取相对较低的法院费用，而且不必向法院缴纳保证金。另一方面，被扣押的债务人方很容易地向法院申请，在明显没有根据或有罪的扣押情况下取得解除扣押。此外，根据法律规定扣押的一方必须在被扣押方提出适当的（荷兰）银行担保以抵偿索赔价值时立即解除扣押。不适当的扣押造成损失的情况很罕见。

2017 年，阿姆斯特丹地区法院计划在一个称为荷兰商业法院（NCC）的新商会开始一个以英语（口头和书面）进行的特别诉讼选择，同样在上诉中，荷兰商业上诉法院（NCCA）主要处理商业案件。预计这种专用工具可以用于外国缔约方和跨境交易。诉讼当事人必须在合同中选择 NCC/NCCA，或在发起诉讼之前就此具体达成协议。

2001 年欧盟条例关于承认和执行民事和商业判决的管辖权，通过要求快速通道，向一个欧盟成员国法院作出判决，可在另一个资产所在的成员国的法院承认执行。

卢森堡投融资法律研究

GéraldOriger　Sarah-NadaArfa[①]

一、卢森堡基本概况

作为欧盟成员国，卢森堡的法律和监管环境受到欧盟层面通过的各种法规和指令的影响。然而，卢森堡这些标准的转换一直是在卢森堡坚持建设成为世界主要金融中心之一的理想目标的情况下实现的。卢森堡立法机关巧妙地利用欧洲法规和指令中可用的活动空间来保障稳固的投资者保护性、金融部门的稳定性和有力的反洗钱行动。因此，金融公司可以从各种复杂而灵活的投资工具和特殊用途工具中享受益处，其中大部分益处来自有利的行政和税收待遇。[②]

此外，严格地说在卢森堡没有关于受控外国企业的立法。作为企业融资的主要中心，许多全球性公司选择卢森堡作为其全球总部的所在地，[③] 中国投资者和企业对卢森堡的吸引力也作出了积极回应。

卢森堡是中国境外投资的前 20 个国家之一。如果在欧洲进行投资，卢森堡是投资者最常选择的国家。同样，所有建立欧洲企业的中资银行都选择了

---

① GéraldOriger 和 Sarah-NadaArfa 分别是 StibbeAvocats 的合伙人和律师。

② 资料来源：www.luxembourg.public.lu/catalogue/economie/lfb-conquer-world-lux-headquarter/lfb-conquer-world-2011-EN.pdf。

③ 例如，GuardianIndustriesCorp、Amazon、Millicom、Paypal、AppleiTunes、Rakuten、DuPont-TeijinFilms、FanucRobotics、Skype 和 Delphi 都选择了卢森堡作为其欧洲业务总部所在地，载 www.luxe mbourgforinance.lu/entrepreneurs-corporate/domiciliation-corporate-headquarters。

卢森堡。卢森堡现在或即将成为8家中资银行的住所地。[①] 因此，多年来中国与卢森堡的商业关系日益强大。

卢森堡金融行业的主要参与者是卢森堡证券交易所（the Boursede Luxembourg），该证券交易所管理着超过102个国家的2700多家债券上市交易。卢森堡证券交易所对中国公司特别有吸引力，因为它是唯一允许人民币债券上市而不征收任何印花税的欧洲国家。伊斯兰金融和小额信贷在卢森堡也越来越发达。

务实的税收和法律框架，加上充满活力和商业友好的政治环境，使卢森堡对跨境和跨行业的投资者有很大的吸引力。

规范卢森堡公司成立和运作的主要法律是1915年8月10日（经修订）的《商业公司法》，该法经2016年8月10日的《公司法改革法案》（第5730号法案）全面改革。

金融或保险部门的所有专业活动都必须经过事先的部长级协议。同样，所有在金融领域从事专业工作的公司都受到卢森堡金融监督机构卢森堡金融监管委员会（CSSF）或小额信贷保险机构（CAA）的审慎监管，该机构负责监督卢森堡的保险和再保险业务。

规范银行业的基本法律是1993年4月5日经修正的《金融部门法》。卢森堡关于保险业务的立法主要是1991年12月6日关于保险业的法律，以及1997年7月27日经保险合同（统称《保险法》）修订的法律。

特定的法律框架也随着时间的推移而转变，具体表现为为小众产品和提供服务的公司提供服务，如涵盖债券发行银行和金融科技行业。

另外，卢森堡金融部门的代表一方面必须尊重打击洗钱和资助恐怖主义的措施，[②] 另一方面要遵守有关金融隐私的严格规定。

二、外商投资政策

卢森堡金融部门在稳定的社会和政治环境中运作，并得到稳健且合理的

① 8家中资银行为交通银行、招商银行、中国农业银行、中国银行、中国工商银行、中国建设银行、中国光大银行、上海浦东发展银行。

② 资料来源：www.luxembourgforinance.lu/inancial-institutions/banks/legal-environment。

适用规则的支持。卢森堡的立法经常在与特定行业和部门协商后通过。

信贷机构和投资公司受到特定的批准和通知要求的规范。《金融部门法》包含了金融行业参与者的基本规则，它设置了进入金融服务业的规定、专业义务、其他审慎的规则和行为规则、审慎监督、金融业专业人士的重组和清盘程序、存款担保和投资者赔偿计划；它也创造了适用于所有提供金融服务的受监管实体的金融业专业人士身份。这些实体必须获得 CSSF 的许可证（CSSF 的书面授权），才能申请金融业专业人士身份并进行其财务活动。

金融业专业人士们获得许可证后，将受CSSF的监管。金融业专业人士被分为三个小组：投资公司、专业金融业专业人士（投资公司除外）和辅助的金融业专业人士（PSFsdesupport）（开展辅助的或辅助金融部门活动的活动）。

根据《保险法》的规定，保险公司适用同样的要求。民航局除了监督卢森堡的保险和再保险业务以外，还颁发许可证并监督保险业务、再保险业务以及保险和再保险中介机构。

此外，相关规制还涉及上市公司的交易大多数情况下可能采取收购的形式。卢森堡的收购要约受2006年5月19日关于公开收购招标的法律(《收购法》)管辖《收购法》贯彻了 2004 年 4 月 21 日欧洲议会和理事会指令 2004/25/EC 号的要求。收购招标是公众向公司证券持有人[①] 作出的收购全部或部分以强制或自愿为目的的证券收购的要约（《收购法》规定每股收益的 33.33% 作为控制的门槛）。

《收购法》适用于在一个或多个欧盟成员国的受监管市场上获准进行证券交易的卢森堡公司，以及在卢森堡受监管的市场上进行证券交易的另一成员国的公司。

如果受要约公司在卢森堡的注册办事处和 / 或如果该公司的证券在卢森堡受监管的市场上进行交易，CSSF 将对投标进行监督。

《收购法》规定了一个强制性的出价结构来保护小股东。在强制投标制度下，如果一个自然人或法人因购买股票而等于或超过合资格企业 33.33% 的股份控制界限，则该人必须提出购买小股东的股份。这样的要约必须以公平、

① 根据《收购法》的规定，证券被定义为附有公司投票权的证券。

公正的价格进行。

《收购法》引入了挤出和抛售的概念（也称为强制回购）：强制挤出程序是要约人的权利——进一步进行一个允许要约人持有至少 95% 的股本和目标公司的投票权的证券的强制收购，——要求剩余的证券持有人以合理的价格将这些证券出售给要约人；出售程序是目标公司证券持有人的权利——进一步强制性收购——要求持有至少 90% 的目标公司股本和投票权的要约人以合理的价格购买证券。

此外，2012 年 7 月 21 日颁布的法律[①] 为在一个或多个成员国受监管的市场上交易的证券引入了一些权利和义务；[②] 其规定相关证券不允许在一个或多个成员国受监管的市场上进行交易。同时，根据欧洲议会和理事会 2003 年 11 月 4 日指令 2003/71/EC 号第 3 条所规定的公布招股说明书的义务的公开发行的对象，其在此基础上又规定了某些条件。这些权利和义务是：

（1）对大股东有利的挤出权，可以要求剩余证券的持有人在为他们出价后出售这些证券。大多数股东必须首先通知 CSSF 他们打算行使挤出权的意图，并且必须承诺进行交易直至完成。大股东也必须确保他们能够以现金形式提供全部的对价。挤出权必须根据独立专家撰写的报告以合理的价格行使。其余证券持有人可以在拟议价格公布之日起 1 个月内提出异议。

（2）对少数股东有利的出售权，即有权强制大股东购买其股份的权利，条件是在一个关于在履行出售权的条件得以实现的该天履行出售权的通知被送达 CSSF；在过去 3 个月内应公布大股东收购证券的通知；且最迟的出售程序至少在 CSSF 决定公布价格的两年前发布。建议的公平价格和异议程序的确定与上述挤出程序相似。

（3）在卢森堡注册办事处的公司有通知和公布信息的义务。

另一项管理外国投资的重要法律是 2008 年 1 月 11 日发布的关于证券发行人透明度要求的法律，这些证券在经过修订的《透明度法》规定的市场上进行交易。《透明度法》将欧洲议会的指令 2004/109/EC 和理事会 2004 年 12 月 15 日的指令(《透明度指令》)转化为卢森堡法律，最近指令 2013/50/EU(《透明度修正指令》)转变为 2016 年 5 月 10 日的卢森堡法律(《透明度修正法》)。

---

① 该法于 2012 年 10 月 1 日生效，并在 2012 年 7 月 27 日的第 152 期卢森堡官方公报上公布。

② 法律是指附有投票权的公司的证券，包括代表发行投票指令的可能性的股票的证书。

《透明度指令》对适用于投资者保护和市场效率的目标的信息施加了一定程度的披露要求。《透明度法》意义上的唯一的规范市场是卢森堡证券交易所。

《透明度法》的规定适用于根据该法卢森堡是其本国成员国的发行人。例如，如果发行的证券在卢森堡被允许进行交易，第三国发行人可以选择卢森堡作为其本国成员国；如果还没有选择他们的本国成员国的发行人进行证券交易，卢森堡可以被视为本国成员国。相关发行人需要提供持续的定期信息（在《透明度法》中定义为“受监管信息”），其中主要包括定期财务报告及与主要持股和内部信息有关的信息。

《透明度修正法》在卢森堡这一块的主要变化：对于卢森堡是本国成员国的发行人，通过取消某些透明度要求来减轻行政负担；对于卢森堡是本国成员国的外国发行人，以及与采掘业或原生林采伐有关的活动：发布关于向政府付款的报告的新要求；对于投资者来说，现在对通过更广泛的金融工具进行股票投资的投资者施加通知义务；CSSF获得明显的新的禁令和制裁权力；对于本国成员国的披露也进行了重大修改。

新市场滥用规则包括关于市场滥用的第596/2014号条例和关于市场滥用刑事制裁的第2014/57/EU号指令，于2016年7月3日在卢森堡生效，废止了的依照2006年5月9日的法律已在卢森堡转化为第2003/6/EC号指令。

虽然自2006年以来，针对在卢森堡证券交易所管制市场上市的证券发行人，管理市场滥用的规则已经生效，现在这套新规则已扩展到在卢森堡证券交易所欧元MTF市场上市的证券发行人。

卢森堡是第一批采用反洗钱法的国家之一，其应用领域不断扩大。根据经济合作与发展组织金融行动工作组的建议，卢森堡于2010年10月27日通过了三项新法律，并于2010年10月29日通过了《大公国条例》，从而对该领域的立法进行了根本的改革。

2010年10月27日的法律扩大了洗钱的定义以及主要侵权名单，目标是将所有犯罪（包括恐怖主义融资）的收入作为目标。相关的犯罪将被处以6个月以上的监禁。

此外，防止洗钱的措施适用于金融业的所有专业人士，包括保险公司、公证人、房地产经纪人、审计师、赌场、律师、税务和财务顾问，以及高价值商品的销售人员。

2010 年 10 月 27 日的法律对专业义务也进行了加强，主要是预防性质的适用制度要求金融行为者在建立业务关系或交易之前检查其客户身份或资产的受益所有人。财务人员在整个业务关系期间，特别是针对交易资金来源，必须继续监督客户的交易，并向检察机关的财务信息单位报告任何洗钱迹象。

应该指出的是，《银行保密法》在个人或公司因洗钱而被起诉时不适用。①

除此之外，其他法律法规来源也适用于外国投资。其中，包括《劳动法》、2005 年 7 月 10 日关于证券招股说明书的法律以及实施经修订的《招股说明书指令》（招股书）的交易许可。

卢森堡立法正在不断发展，以跟上海事部门各种活动，以及金融、保险和物流部门的活动的发展。根据 1994 年修订的《1990 年海事法》，海事事务专员负责给卢森堡海事事业的监管者以及参与组织和组建公共海事登记的人提供指导。

三、典型的交易结构

（一）概述

由于卢森堡和中国的税收优惠政策，中国投资者多选择卢森堡公共有限责任公司（SA）或私人有限责任公司（Sarl）作为投资工具，因此经修订的《公司法》除欧洲公司外还认可以下 8 种具有法人资格的商业公司。

1. 公众有限责任公司（SA）

SA 的公司形式通常用于以进行一项或多项融资证券化或重新包装交易提议发行股票、债券、票据或其他证券的公司。这是由一个或多个对公司和第三方的责任仅限于其投入资本的人员构成的。

SA 的资本必须至少为 3 万欧元② 或等值的外币，并分成股份。

---

① 资料来源：www.luxembourgforinance.lu/why-luxembourg/legal-environment/anti-money-laundering-legislation。

② 向公众有限责任公司提供股份或应收款项等投资，原则上需由外聘审计员估价。

一个 SA 通常由一个董事会来管理，除非是唯一的股东，该董事会必须至少有三个成员，而该实体可以由一个唯一的董事管理。董事可以自由撤职，他们的任期（原则上可以更新）不得超过 6 年。董事没有强制性资格；[①] 此外，没有国籍或居住要求适用于董事。公共有限责任公司也可以选择两层董事会结构（由监事会监督的管理层）。

公众有限责任公司有义务委任法定审计师，负责公司业务的控制和公司年度审计的审计工作。符合某些资产负债表，营业额和就业标准的大型卢森堡公司必须委任在卢森堡特许的外部独立审计师。

2. 简化股份公司（SAS）

这种新的公司形式是基于法国的 SAS 模式。所有适用于 SA 的条款将适用于 SAS，除了公司治理结构以及股东可以自由决定 SAS 股份所附的权利和义务。

3. 私营有限责任公司（Sàrl）

Sàrl 在没有公开发行证券的情况下经常被使用，但是根据《公司改革法案》，Sàrls 现在可以在某些条件下发行债券和可转换债券，并遵守法定的有关非股东在 S.àrl 的批准的规定。Sàrl 由一个或多个成员组成，最多不超过 100 人，其责任仅限于他们的投入资本。Sàrl 的股本必须至少为 12000 欧元或等值外币。Sàrl 可能有一个或几个董事，在卢森堡的做法中通常被称为经理人。他们没有强制性的资质要求，也没有国籍或居住要求。不超过 60 名股东的私人有限责任公司不需要任命法定审计师。

股份可以在股东之间自由转让，但如果事先获得占公司四分之三股本的股东的书面同意，则只能转让给第三方。但是，公司章程现在可以将这个大多数要求降低到 50%。此外，《公司法改革法案》现规定了一个框架组织有序退出（通过股份回购或出售给另一个股东 / 善意的第三方），时间不得超过 6 个月。

4. 普通合伙（SNC）

在 SNC 中，所有成员对公司的所有义务承担连带责任。

5. 普通有限合伙（SCS）

① 除非公司追求受特定许可的商业或受管制的活动。

SCS 具有法人资格，由一名或数名承担连带责任的合伙人（活跃合伙人）以及一名或一名以上责任范围仅限于其投入资本的有限责任股东（有限责任合伙人）组成。

6. 特殊有限合伙（SCSp）

SCSp 的制度与 SCS 相似，但 SCSp 没有法人资格，给合伙协议中的创始人 / 合伙人留下更大的契约自由，以规范 SCSp 的运作和组织。

在执行 2011 年 6 月 8 日欧洲议会和理事会关于另类投资基金管理人（AIFMD）的 2011/61/EU 号指令的情况下，SCS 和 SCSp 的制度已经完全改革。SCS 和 SCSp 用于构建受监管的（SIF 和 SICAR，这些条款将在下面部分中定义）以及不受监管的投资工具。

7. 股份有限公司（SCA）

SCA 具有法人资格，由一名或数名共同负责的合伙人（活跃合伙人）和有限责任股东，其责任仅限于其对资本（有限责任合伙人）的缴款数额；与 SCS 相比，SCA 的资本通常会被分成股份。

8. 合作公司（SC）

SC 具有法人资格，必须至少有两名成员的股份数目和出资额可变，并且其股份不可用于第三方。

（二）投资基金的结构范围

卢森堡是投资基金形成和分配的主要地点，是世界第二大基金管辖区。由于历史原因，在卢森堡设立的大部分基金都是根据《UCI 法案》（UCITS）第一部分对可转让证券进行中的集体投资进行的。UCITS 是主要为散户投资者设计的流动性基金，受益于欧洲的营销护照，允许他们通过一个简单有效的监管机构向所有欧盟成员国推销其单位和股票，以便监管机构知悉。

关于另类投资基金部门，根据经修订的 AIFM 法，2013 年 7 月 12 日关于另类投资基金管理人（AIFM）的法案将 AIFMD 转变为卢森堡法律，以便提供统一和全面的为另类投资基金（AIF）的管理者创建一个单一的市场。AIFMD 的应用为卢森堡另类投资基金行业带来了诸多挑战，同时也为卢森堡提供了一个在另类投资市场创造新品牌的机会，类似于卢森堡 UCITS 的全球成功品牌。AIFMD 为 AIFM 引入了一个欧洲护照，希望在欧盟范围内销售和分销其 AIFs。

卢森堡大公国已经发展成为替代性投资基金的“去”岸，特别是近十年来卢森堡合伙形式的封闭式基金。卢森堡正在战胜其竞争对手并获得竞争力，特别是该行业的离岸金融中心。多年来，在英国、苏格兰、英属维尔京群岛、百慕大、开曼群岛或特拉华州建立的“盎格鲁—撒克逊”有限合伙制结构是基金发起人和投资者在替代性或私人基金部门中投资工具的选择。卢森堡大公国的外部因素和内部改革的结合使卢森堡的伙伴关系结构成为焦点。在另类投资基金领域，卢森堡已经开发并提供了广泛的可用工具，这些工具包括受监管较多的基于零售投资者的基金；受管制较少的投资工具 SIF 或 SICAR）；无管制的工具（RAIF 或有限合伙）。由于这种变化，卢森堡基金业为任何基金赞助商提供了找到合适的投资工具以适应其需求和期望的机会，并且可以根据目标投资者和目标投资进行量身定制，包括但不限于符合伊斯兰教法的投资工具、小额信贷投资工具或社会责任投资工具。

卢森堡基金通常分为两类：一是产品管制基金，即受卢森堡监管机构监管并获得金融部门监管的基金；二是作为产品不直接受制于不受监管的资金——由 CSSF 监督和批准，但可以通过其管理者间接受到监管（如通过在 AIFMD 下的外部的 AIFM）。受监管和不受监管的基金通常都会受益于具有吸引力的和完善的税收制度，无论是通过完全的税收透明度和中立性，还是通过免税（不包括名义上的订购税）或准免税。

根据《证券化法》的规定，私募股权结构也可以通过受监管[①] 或不受监管的证券化工具来建立。

此外，家族财富管理公司[②]（SPF）是代表个人为管理私人财富而设立的工具。其独家目的是收购、持有、管理和出售金融资产，他们不得从事任何商业活动。[③] SPFs 是被动投资工具。

以下是通过股东协议在卢森堡法律下成立合资企业的可能性。卢森堡投资基金通常采用以下法律结构之一：

---

① 一些不受监管的证券化公司可能会在个案的基础上落入 AIFMD 的范围。

② 家庭财富一词是指私人财富。法律并不要求各个股东之间有家庭联系。

③ 例如，SPF 可以作为一系列投资者或由员工或经理人获得公司股份的公司结构，载 http://www.luxembourgforfinance.com/en/family-wealth-management-company-spf-0。

（1）一个契约结构——一个共同基金 FCP 等。FCP 是共同所有制，共同所有者仅在相关的 FCP 中承担其贡献。FCP 不具有法人资格，因此必须由卢森堡管理公司代表共同所有人进行管理。然而，自卢森堡有限合伙制度改革以来，FCP 失去了市场份额，但在某些情况下 FCP 可能仍然是有吸引力的工具（如某些目标投资者管辖区）。

（2）企业 / 公司结构——SICAV（社会资本变量）或 SICAF（社会资本与固定资产投资）。SICAV 是一家投资公司，其资本永远等于其净资产，即资本自动增加和减少，特别是由于认购和赎回，没有任何进一步的手续。SICAV 可以以不同的法律形式来构建，如 SA、SCA、Sàrl、SCS 或 SCSp。SICAF 是拥有固定资本的投资公司。SICAF 中的投资者每次赎回或认购股份将导致修复资本的增加或减少，导致 SICAF 的公司章程的修改或被授权资本覆盖，视情况按照有关 SICAF 的组织章程规定而定。SICAF 由于其灵活性有限而不是最受欢迎的结构，然而由于税务方面的考量其仍然经常被选择。

（3）合伙结构——有限合伙可以有法人资格（SCS），也可以没有自己的法人资格（SCSp）。至少有一个无限的普通合伙人和至少有一个有限合伙人之间形成有限的合伙关系。SCS 和 SCSp 制度为投资者提供了与“盎格鲁—撒克逊”有限合伙模式相媲美的广泛的契约结构灵活性。

（三）调节基金

1. UCITS

《UCI 法案》在其第一部分与 UCIs 的第二部分（UCI 法案第二部分）中区分了 UCITS。

UCITS 通常是为散户投资者设计的，可以在 UCITS 下使用欧洲市场执照，在 EEA[①] 中自由销售和分销。UCITS 受到严格的投资限制。UCITS 只能投资于流动性投资（如可转让证券、货币市场工具、存款、金融衍生工具和 UCITS 等），并受到严格的风险分散要求和交易对手风险限制。UCITS 必须指定一个当地的保管人，该保管人也须符合资格要求和严格的责任制度，并与《UCI 法案》和欧盟 2014 年 7 月 23 日关于 UCITS 的 2014 年 91 号指令

① EEA 包括欧盟成员国以及冰岛、列支敦士登和挪威。

（UCITSV 指令）一致。

2. UCIII

UCIs Ⅱ是 UCI 被授权的第二部分。第二部分的 UCIs 虽不属于 UCITS 指令的范围，但可以向卢森堡的散户投资者使用。第二部分 UCIs 的法律制度不像 UCITS 那样严格，但仍然受到 CSSF 的严密审查。[①] 它们可以投资于其他类型的资产，以符合风险多样化要求的 UCITS。第二部分 UCI 必须指定一个当地的存款机构，它也必须符合资格要求、具有严格的责任制度和合格的外部审计员。

（四）SICAR

2004 年，《SICAR 法案》的通过标志着卢森堡发展成为国际公认的私人股本和风险投资中心。SICAR 被认为是一种监管宽松、灵活、财政中立的投资工具，旨在解决私人股本和风险资本投资者的具体结构性需求。SICAR 是一家风险资本投资公司（法国兴业银行投资公司）。因此，它必须只进行符合风险资本的投资（在证券交易所上市、发展或上市时，基金对实体的直接或间接贡献）。CSSF 已经发布了关于这一概念的指导，并阐明了《SICAR 法案》下的风险资本的特点：一种高于普通投资风险的风险和发展目标实体的意图。

SICAR 不受任何风险分散要求的约束，并且受到“较轻”的监管制度的约束，而非 UCIs 的第二部分。在此基础上，它们被“消息灵通的投资者”保留投资。[②]

SICAR 可以采取公司形式（财政不透明）或有限合伙制的法律形式。《SICAR 法案》包含了许多公司法要求的减损，使 SICAR 从结构化的角度变得灵活，PE/VC 基金条款很容易在 SICAR 文档中注册。

一个 SICAR 也可以被组织成一个“伞”状结构，有几个分隔的隔间。这

---

① 第二部分 UCIs 在《AIFM 法案》的意义上通常被认为是 AIFs，并被要求指定一个 AIFM，除非他们受益于《AIFM 法案》提供的任何豁免。第二部分 UCIs 由一个授权的 AIFM 管理，从护照允许 AIFMs 进入市场，并通过一个监管的通知程序，将 UCI 的股份、单位或合伙利益分配给欧盟内部的专业投资者。

② 根据《SICAR 法案》，知情投资者应是机构投资者、专业投资者或其他符合以下条件的投资者：以书面形式表示见多识广的投资者的地位；在公司至少投资 12.5 万欧元；他的专长、他的经历和他的知识充分评价投资风险资本（消息灵通的投资者）。

让一个 SICAR 可以有数个不同的投资策略，并在一个相同的法律结构中满足不同类型投资者的需求。

一个有吸引力的税收制度所带来的好处，根据其在法律形式上的不同而有所不同，但一般来说，它是对投资者的税收中性或准税收中性。一个 SICAR 必须任命一个符合资格要求的外部审计员和地方保管人。

（五）专业投资基金

专业投资基金（SIF）是由《SIF 法案》创立的，是一个监管宽松、操作灵活、财政高效的多用途投资基金制度，为国际机构和合格投资者基础设计。对于任何类型的战略（如风险投资房地产、私人股本、基础设施基金、基金基金、对冲基金和有形资产基金）而言，SIF 都是非常成功的工具。

SIF 必须符合风险分散原则，原则上不能在单一资产上投资超过 30%。SIF 只有在《SIF 法案》下才为消息灵通的投资者保留。[①]

SIF 可以采取公司法律形式（财政不透明）或有限合伙的法律形式。《SIF 法案》包含了一些公司法律要求的减损，使 SIF 从结构化的角度变得灵活（开放式基金和封闭式基金和半开放式基金在 SIF 制度下都是可能的）。

SIF 也可以被组织为“伞”状结构，有几个独立的子基金。这使 SIF 具有不同的投资策略，能够在同一法律结构内满足不同类型投资者的需求。

SIF 从一个有吸引力的税收制度中获益，该制度因其已被纳入的法律形式而有所不同，但一般来说，它可以构建一个类似于税收中性的 SICAR。

SIF 必须任命一个符合资格要求的外部审计师和地方保管人。

（六）不受监管的基金

1. 有限合伙（SCS 或 SCSp）

卢森堡引入 SCSp 是为了培育卢森堡其他类投资基金业。SCS 机制的特征是增强结构的可能性和灵活性，这是 SCS 机制的关键优势。

SCS 和 SCSp 可能是一个不受监管的实体，但也可以受管制（第二部分 UCI、SIF 或 SICAR）。SCS 或 SCSp 是通过合伙协议（LPA）在有限或无限

① 进一步的详细资料载于 2007 年 8 月 3 日，在基金的背景下，CSSF 循环 07/309 风险扩散。

的条件下，由一个或多个具有无限责任的普通合伙人和一个或多个有限合伙人（其责任通常限于其合伙利益的数量）之间达成的。

SCS 和 SCSp 的税收和企业待遇相似。SCSp 有许多特定的特性。与其他司法管辖区（如英国）的合伙制结构不同，普通合伙人不需要披露合伙企业中每个有限合伙人的身份。

LPA 可以自由地组织 SCS/SCSp 的特征，如合伙人的权利和 SCS/SCSp 的损益，关于转让合伙企业利益的规定、合伙利益的问题和补偿，合作伙伴的表决权，经济利益的分配等。

2. RAIF

RAIF 是由《RAIF 法案》引入的，它是在成熟的 SIF 机制的基础上建立的，但是 RAIF 无须经过 CSSF 的批准或受监督。

RAIF 可以非常迅速地建立，并提供所有资产配置和灵活的结构，这是全球其他类资产管理公司所期望的。

RAIF 不受 CSSF 的监督，不需要任何事先授权。但 RAIF 必须符合 AIF 标准，原则上应由外部完全许可的 AIFM 管理。

然而，RAIF 的间接监督是保证通过 AIFM 确保监督主管部门有关 RAIF 符合适用 AIFMD 产品规则（例如，往下的信托和审计师，RAIF 的年度报告的内容和 RAIF 资产的估值等）。因此，根据 AIFM 的欧盟营销护照，RAIF 可以向欧盟的专业投资者销售和分销。

只有“消息灵通的投资者”才可以使用这些融资平台。在公司制或合伙企业的形式下，RAIF 可以以 SICAV、SICAF 或 FCP 的形式构建。此外，还可以设置一个 RAIF 作为保护伞结构和保护环。

在符合条件的资产或投资政策方面，融资不受任何特殊限制，这就允许在资产投资方面具有明显的灵活性。原则上，RAIF 仍将遵循风险分散原则（除非 RAIF 选择仅投资于符合资格的风险资本投资）。

RAIF 将需要提供一个文件，该文件必须在其封面页上包含一个清晰可见的声明，该文件不受 CSSF 的监督。

《RAIF 法案》使现有的卢森堡投资结构（无论是否受到监管）在一定条件下（投资者和实体必须符合 AIFMD 的要求）可以进行融资转化。投资工具如第二部分 UCI、SIF 或 SICAR 且包括提供文件必须获得 CSSF 的批准，并修改该基金的本章程文件。一个非卢森堡的实体也可以转换成 RAIF。

（七）不受监管的组织形式

1990 年，卢森堡执行了欧盟对完全征税的卢森堡公民的公司的附属指令。因此，在卢森堡法律中引入了大量从股份中获得的股息和资本收益的“参与豁免”，并创建了一种新型控股公司——SOPARFI。

卢森堡通过这些不受监管的特殊目的公司，在私人股本和风险资本基金方面积累了专业知识。SOPARFI 是指在一般企业税收制度下进行控股或融资活动的金融参与公司。

SOPARFI 的时间效率、隐私问题和成本使它们非常适合私人股本投资。通常情况下，私人股本基金将投资于 SOPARFI，该基金又反过来投资于一个目标。

SOPARFI 不受某一特定法律的管辖，而是由公司法的一般条款管辖。SOPARFI 通常采用 SA、Sarl、SCA、SC 或欧洲公司的形式。

一个 SOPARFI 可能且尤其可能是：

（1）卢森堡或外国公有或私有公司持有、购买、出售和管理股权；

（2）持有、购买、出售和管理卢森堡或外国公司发行的债券、债券、证书和其他债务工具；

（3）持有、购买、销售、管理专利或其他知识产权，并授予相关许可证；

（4）财务及向关联公司提供财务援助；

（5）发行债务工具（如可转换优先股）；

（6）授予担保，或质押，为担保其债务或其他公司的债务而对其资产进行担保和授予证券。

（八）证券化工具

证券化工具由《证券化法案》管理。《证券化法案》对于结构化的可能性和可以证券化的资产是特别灵活的。它允许证券化多种类型的资产（股票、贷款、次级债券或非次级债券）、风险、收益和活动，并使机构投资者和个人投资者都能获得证券化。因此，证券化可以优化公司的融资，或个人或家庭财富的管理，同时也能给投资者带来良好的回报。

证券化工具可以建立被商业公司或管理公司管理的证券化基金，可以设置一个“伞形”结构，可以设置独立的隔间，允许使用同一个工具进行不同的证券化交易。

法律对一些标准的证券化技术给予法定保护，如真正的销售、圈护、非请愿和有限的追索权。

卢森堡法律保证了证券化工具的税收中性。证券化基金被视为投资基金，投资者按照其所在国的规则征税。证券化公司完全应纳税，但向投资者支付的款项是完全免税的。它们可以从欧洲的指令和双重税收条约中获益。

连续向公众发行证券的证券化工具必须由 CSSF 监督，必须批准它们的公司章程或管理条例，并且应当视情况授权其管理公司。①

（九）合资企业——卢森堡的股东协议

在卢森堡，股东之间的协议通常以大纲来保证双方各自的权利和义务（如在合资企业或私人股本交易的背景），此外，视情况可能已经包含在相关的公司的章程内。

强制性和公共政策规则，以及《合同法》的一般规则（如契约自由和诚信原则）管理着这些协议的有效性和可执行性。

四、审查程序

（一）概述

虽然卢森堡的《竞争法》于 2004 年 5 月 17 日通过，但它没有国内的合并控制制度。然而，欧洲关于合并控制的规则② 适用于卢森堡，因此在满足欧盟合并控制规定的门槛时，从事合并、收购或在卢森堡或来自卢森堡的合资企业必须将其合并行为通知欧盟委员会合并专责小组。

卢森堡关于资本和支付自由流动以及关税制度的情况与比利时的情况

① 根据 CSSF 在 2013 年 10 月 23 日关于证券化的常见问题，证券化工具如果每年向公众发行超过 3 个问题，就被视为连续发行证券。

② 资料来源：2004 年 1 月 20 日，理事会第 139/2004 号决议关于控制各项事业之间的浓度。

相同。[①]

（二）监管行业

在卢森堡，各种各样的活动都没有受到监管，金融部门的监管是金融市场力量和稳定的关键。根据《金融部门法》，任何人都必须在CSSF书面授权的情况下从事信贷机构的业务或金融部门的活动或金融部门的联系或补充活动。

在提交书面申请并进行调查后，授权被授予无限的时间。

2011年9月2日的法律明确提出了在欧洲内部市场内免费提供服务的概念。因此，在瑞士联邦或在欧洲经济区的国家设立的企业可在卢森堡进行临时的商业活动、制造或自由活动，而不需要在那里设立永久的机构[②]，不需要获得营业执照和事先通知。[③]

（三）外国投资者保护

卢森堡拥有非常强大的投资者保护文化，并在全球范围内保持着最大的双边投资保护条约。[④]2012年10月24日的CSSF通告审查了卢森堡UCITS管理公司和自营投资公司的授权和组织，除此之外，还规定了适用于其理事机构的要求。它阐明了适用的物质要求，并明确规定了内部控制职能和授权，其中包括行政管理。

（四）其他战略决策

由于最近的全球性变化，卢森堡对当地物质的需求有了相当大的重视，这意味着投资者最好避开那些与卢森堡没什么关系的架构；相反，它们更倾向于那些实力更强大的本地机构。我们可以通过在卢森堡设立办事处、在当地雇用工作人员，以及在卢森堡执行一些管理和业务职能来实现。尤其在中国，

① 有关进一步资料，请参阅比利时章节。

② 资料来源：www.guichet.public.lu/entreprises/en/creation-developpement/autorisation-etablissement/prestation-transfrontaliere-services/prestation-occasionnelle/index.html。

③ 资料来源：prestation-transfrontaliere-services/prestation-occasionnelle/index.html。

④ 资料来源：http://eur-lex.europa.eu/LexUriServ/LexUriServ.do?uri=OJ:C:2013:131:0002:0098:EN:PDF。

我们可以看到特定的规则和通告，规定了所需的物质水平。这一趋势与基金领域的发展情况相比较，特别是在执行 AIFMD 的情况下，对当地物质的重视将继续增加。

卢森堡在过去几年里一直在增加其避免双重征税的条约系统，特别是与中国香港签订的条约是最好的条约之一。与中国签订的条约对中国和中国的出境者都是非常有利的。

需要注意的是，从中国进口货物到卢森堡时，卢森堡有一个很好的基础设施——卢森堡机场，它在欧洲的货物量排名第五位。此外，进口关税和进口增值税可能会被推迟，直到货物实际上被卖给欧盟的客户，这将给现金流带来巨大的好处。在这方面，卢森堡是为我们提供这些利益最有利的司法管辖区。

在资金方面，卢森堡的 UCITS 是亚洲分布最广的基金之一。也就是说，亚洲个人通常持有卢森堡的基金，这是由于卢森堡基金在发行时以一种亚洲身份获益。

就在香港证券交易所上市的卢森堡公司而言，卢森堡公司在申请入会时，也从同样的便利和简化规则中受益。因此，在香港证券交易所上市的公司是可以被考虑的，例如，投资将从亚洲获益，同时从优良的条约网络和有利的税收待遇中获益。

虽然卢森堡的名称在英语中的本意有大的国家的含义，但是与中国香港类似，卢森堡这个国家的规模有限，它的一个巨大优势是允许采取快速而灵活的决策。因此，卢森堡通常被认为是首先影响商业发展趋势的国家之一，为改善商业环境提供新的法律服务。

新西兰投融资法律研究篇

新西兰投融资法律研究

James Jung　Hak Jun Lee

一、新西兰基本概况

新西兰是一个独特的国家,它的地理和经济状况,加上其法律和金融制度,使它在南太平洋脱颖而出。新西兰的经济是以市场为中心的。新西兰不仅通过其法律，而且通过政府政策和外汇及金融市场间接鼓励外国投资。外国对新西兰证券交易所和财产的大量投资证明了这一点。

新西兰位于西南太平洋，由两个大岛和一些较小的岛屿组成，总面积为268000平方公里，与不列颠群岛或日本相似，目前的人口约为470万人。

新西兰是一个议会制民主国家，集中的一院议会位于首都惠灵顿。新西兰大选每三年举行一次。自1996年以来，新西兰一直实行混合成员比例代表制选举制度。议会席位的最高数目为120席，并规定了“悬空”席位。这一制度与目前在德国实行的制度相似。

新西兰议会颁布了与新西兰境内公司的经营有关的所有立法，并由政府机构管理。

新西兰的法律制度是以普通法为基础的，类似于英国和其他许多西方国家的法律制度。大多数刑事和较小规模的民事案件由地方法院处理。高等法院主要审理民事案件和更严重的罪行。有两个用于上诉的法院，即上诉法院，在某些情况下，还有最高法院。

二、设立公司

海外公司或公司可通过下列方式在新西兰设立办事处：在新西兰注册海外公司的分支机构；在新西兰成立本地附属公司；收购一家新西兰注册公司，该公司随后即可成为该海外公司的子公司。

（一）在新西兰注册一家海外公司

海外公司如欲在新西兰注册分行，必须先向公司注册处处长申请保留其名称。然后必须于开始在新西兰开展业务的10个工作日内提出注册申请，说明海外公司的名称、注册国家、海外公司董事的全名和住址、海外公司在新西兰的营业地点的地址、在新西兰居住或注册的至少一个人的全名和实际地址，他们有权代表海外公司在新西兰接受文件服务，并提供海外公司成立的证据。注册申请必须附有海外公司的任何组织文件的副本。

（二）合并子公司

在新西兰成立的子公司必须至少有一名股东和一名董事。附属公司必须有送达地址和在新西兰实际地址的注册办事处。在新西兰注册的公司必须至少有一名董事居住在新西兰或执行国。在执行国居住的董事也必须是该国注册公司（不包括海外公司的分支机构）的董事。执行国将由条例决定。目前，唯一的执行国是澳大利亚。

新西兰公司的股票没有票面价值或名义价值。公司的股本价值没有最低要求。根据1993年《公司法》，公司董事必须确定他们认为对公司及其股东都是公平和合理的新股发行价格。

与分公司一样，申请必须以名称设定请求开始。一旦获得名称批准，必须提交以下公司注册文件：

（1）每个董事同意担任董事的同意书；

（2）每个股东同意担任股东的同意书；

（3）公司章程的副本，如果建议有一份（1993年《公司法》的默认条款将在没有章程的情况下适用）；

（4）服务文件和注册办事处地址的详细资料（两者都必须是位于新西兰

的实际地址）以及公司注册处处长可能发送通信的邮政地址详情；

（5）股东和董事的姓名和地址详情，每位董事的出生日期和地点的详情；

（6）如果董事居住在执行国，则该董事也是执行国的董事；

（7）公司的最终母公司信息，这些资料包括姓名、登记号码、注册国家及任何其他规定信息；

（8）新西兰公司办公室要求的任何额外文件，包括对董事和股东的身份和地址的核实文件。

（三）在新西兰注册海外公司或注册 / 收购子公司

是否以在新西兰注册海外公司的方式设立海外公司的分公司，或是否成立或收购一家新西兰子公司，将取决于法律结构（新西兰和海外）、税收后果以及其他商业考虑因素。还应该考虑以下内容：财务报告要求；与分支机构相比，附属机构涉及更多的行政工作，因为必须在新西兰保存记录和法定登记册，还需要遵守 1993 年《公司法》所载的新西兰公司法律；有限责任子公司对其新西兰业务负有有限责任，分公司之所以不这样做，是因为它没有与海外公司分开的法律身份。

（四）财务报表

新西兰的公司不需要编制全面的、通用的财务报表，除非它们属于某些类别。这些类别包括：大公司；上市公司；在新西兰开展业务的大型海外公司；股东超过 10 人的公司，除非公司选择不遵守规定；如果公司选择了遵守法规，则少于 10 个股东的公司。

有关公司必须向新西兰公司办事处提交财务报表的要求也发生了变化。一家大型海外公司一般仍需向公司办公室提交报表。

（五）批文

除非触及新西兰的海外投资限额，否则通常唯一需要政府同意的是公司注册处处长同意使用公司名称（对于子公司和分支机构而言）。除非在登记册上已经有相同或几乎相同的名称，否则名称许可一般随时可用。

虽然对外国公司在新西兰允许的商业经营类型限制甚少，但外国投资受新西兰 2005 年《海外投资法》（《OI 法案》）和根据《海外投资法》制定的 2005 年《海外投资条例》的控制。

海外人士的定义在《OI 法案》第 7 条中有详细的规定，包括非新西兰公民和通常不在新西兰居住的个人；在新西兰境外成立的法人团体或新西兰任何附属公司拥有任何此种法人团体 25% 或以上的股份；法人团体，其中任何类别股份的 25% 或以上由一名海外人士持有；法人团体，其控制该法人团体 25% 或以上的组成的权力是由一名海外人士持有的；法人团体，其在法人团体的任何会议上行使或控制行使 25% 或 25% 以上投票权的权利，由海外人士持有或拥有 25% 或以上。

一些商业交易，例如，捕鱼配额的投资或购买某些敏感的房地产，将永远需要同意。否则，如果超过 1 亿新西兰元的上限（或澳大利亚非政府投资者为 5.01 亿美元），则只有海外人士才需要同意。

三、收购企业

根据《OI法案》，在海外人士进行某些投资的情况下，需要得到新西兰海外投资办公室（OIO）的同意。需要同意的非土地投资包括在任何一年中创立一项超过90天的新业务（单独或与另一人合伙），预计在创办企业时预计会产生的总开支超过1亿新西兰元；在新西兰目标公司或目标公司及其25%或更多子公司的证券价值、转让代价或资产价值超过1亿新西兰元的情况下，获得新西兰公司证券的25%或更多的所有权或控制权；增加海外人士已拥有或控制25%或以上比例的公司证券的拥有权或控制权；收购用于在新西兰开展业务的财产（包括商誉和其他无形资产），其中收购的对价超过1亿新西兰元。

如果海外人士获得拥有土地的公司的股份，并且该收购需要根据《OI 法案》进行审查。

非土地收购的 1 亿新西兰元同意限额不适用于某些澳大利亚投资者。2017 年 1 月 1 日，澳大利亚非政府投资者的限额增加至 5.01 亿美元［澳大利亚个人或澳大利亚实体在澳大利亚或与一个或多个指定投资者（一个或多个澳大利亚或新西兰个人）进行实质性业务活动时拥有超过 75% 的所有权或控制权益，且不是澳大利亚或外国政府投资者］，这一数额每年按通货膨胀率调整。澳大利亚政府投资者的限额提高到 1.05 亿美元（是澳大利亚政府或设在澳大利亚的实体或分支机构，占澳大利亚政府拥有或控制的 25% 以上），但也每年因通货膨胀而调整。

如果投资需要同意，则只有在申请人满足某些标准时才给予。这些人包括海外人，或者，如果该人不是个人，控制相关海外人士的人必须：有与投资相关的业务经验和敏锐的头脑；对投资有明确的财务承诺；性格良好；不属于 2009 年《移民法》第 15 条或第 16 条所述类型的个人（其中列出的人不符合该法的豁免或许可，通常是因为犯罪或恐怖主义记录）。

与海外人士有关的 25% 的限额不是新西兰政府打算限制外国投资的优先级别。这仅仅是官方参与的一个数额。

虽然一个海外人士 100% 的所有权可以在所有工业部门得到批准，但一些设在新西兰的公司对外国所有权有限制，特别是在新西兰的捕鱼配额领域。

财政部部长负责有关控制新西兰境内外国投资的政策，但在某些土地申请方面与土地信息部长分享，就获得新西兰捕捞配额的某些申请与渔业部部长分享。

《其他投资规例》也就批准申请的申请、收费、申报及金钱规定制定程序。

四、购置不动产

（一）批准购买

OIO还负责管理新西兰某些类型的土地的购买。《OI法案》规定了需要OIO同意的特殊类型的土地和权益，包括超过5公顷的非城市土地；大部分离岸岛屿上的陆地；超过0.4公顷的土地，包括或毗邻敏感土地，如某些岛屿、保护区、历史或遗产地区或湖泊；包括或毗邻前滨的超过0.2公顷的土地。

在新西兰购买商业或工业用地，如果不是或毗邻敏感的土地，通常不会受到很多限制。

关于土地问题需要注意的是：《OI 法案》涵盖农村和城市土地；取得土地的目的与此无关；如果境外人士（或与境外人士有关联的人）购买境外人

士已经拥有的毗邻土地，需要另行同意。

除了申请人在购买企业方面要达到的标准（相关商业经验和敏锐度、财务承诺、良好品格以及不属于2009年《移民法》第15条或第16条所指的个人），以下也是必要的：该海外人士，或如该人并非个人，则指控制该有关海外人士的个人，通常在新西兰居住或拟无限期在新西兰居住；建议的土地投资（任何申请的主体）将会或可能会使新西兰受益，而且如果土地属于非城市土地，这种收益将会或可能是实质性的和可识别的；如果相关土地是农场土地，该农场土地或与该境外投资有关的证券已经在公开市场上提供给非海外人士。

相关的政府部长必须考虑投资是否会对新西兰产生实质性的和可获得的利益。只考虑：

（1）海外投资是否会或可能导致：在新西兰创造新的就业机会，或保留本来或可能丧失的现有就业机会；在新西兰引进新技术或商业技能；新西兰出口商的出口收入增加；在新西兰增加市场竞争、提高效率或生产率，或加强国内服务；为发展目的向新西兰引进额外投资；在新西兰增加对新西兰初级产品的加工。

（2）是否有或是否将建立适当的机制，以便：保护或加强现有的重要土著植被和土著动物群的重要生态；保护或加强鳟鱼、鲑鱼和其他受保护野生动物的重要生境的现有地区，并为公众提供、保护或改善步行进入这类生境的机会；保护或加强有关土地内的历史遗产；提供、保护或改善相关土地（或该土地的任何部分）的步行通道。

（3）如有关土地是或包括前滨、海床、河床或湖泊的河床，则无论该前滨、海床、河床或湖床是否已按照有关规例向官方提供。

（4）任何其他在《投资规例》中订明的事宜。

《OI 法案》列出了部长们在评估敏感土地的海外投资是否会或有可能惠及新西兰时必须考虑的若干因素。例如，部长们必须考虑投资是否会或可能给新西兰带来其他相应的好处；海外人士此前是否曾在新西兰进行过投资，以及投资是否有可能实现或推动新西兰政府的重大政策或战略。2008 年 3 月修订了《OI 法案》，规定部长们还必须考虑海外投资是否会或可能协助新西兰在敏感的土地上维持新西兰对战略重要基础设施的控制。其他考虑因素还包括新西兰的经济利益是否将得到海外投资的充分推动，以及新西兰人将会或可能监督或参与海外投资的程度。

2012 年 2 月高等法院对 TiroaE 和 THapeB 信托基金和另一个诉土地信息及其他行政长官的判决为 OIO 和相关政府部长在确定海外投资敏感土地是否会或将会有利于新西兰时必须采用的评估方法提供了指导。在作出决定之前，OIO 和相关政府部长一直在评估一个拟议的海外投资对现状的好处——海外投资前的状况与海外投资后的可能情况相比。高等法院认为，OIO 和有关的政府部长采纳了这一评估方法，相反指示 OIO 和相关的政府部长评估拟议的海外投资的好处，如果没有对海外投资作出同意，将会发生什么情况。

这种解释要求海外投资者考虑到其他潜在投资者（无论是新西兰居民还是海外投资者）的存在以及其他潜在投资者提议的投资可能带来的好处，并向投资组织和有关政府部长表明，他们提议的投资将给新西兰带来的好处大于其他潜在投资者所带来的好处。在没有其他潜在投资者存在的情况下，对现状的评估仍然适用。

（二）注册要求

有关土地转让的要求是：房产买卖双方必须提供其新西兰税务局编号（税号）及其他详细资料［除主房外（此例外情况不适用于海外人士或信托）］；在另一个国家居住的税务居民也必须提供与该国家相同的 IRD 号码；海外人士（尚未拥有税号的）需要有新西兰银行账户才能申请税号。

（三）托伦斯土地登记制度

新西兰在托伦斯土地登记制度下运作，每一块土地通常都有自己的所有权。新西兰政府保证标题的准确性，公众可以通过搜索获得少量费用。登记系统是一个电子系统，不再有书面凭证。

（四）土地买卖合约

根据新西兰的法律，出售任何土地的合同必须以书面形式由有关各方签署，以便依法执行。

（五）1991年《资源管理法》

1991年的《资源管理法》将有关使用新西兰自然资源（如土地、水、矿物、海岸线和空气）的法律合并在一起。该法案的序言指出，它是为了促进自然和物质资源的可持续管理。因此，任何与工业产权有关的新的重大发展，如有关工业产权的新发展，都必须审慎考虑，并可能需要多项批准才可进行。因此，每一项投资建议都需要根据这项立法、适用的区域和地区计划以及专家法律和相关专家咨询意见分别加以审议。政府目前正在考虑对该法进行改革，以便通过更有效的资源管理制度促进经济增长，从而减少对批准和相关要求的需求。

（六）2004年《建筑法》

所有建筑物均受2004年《建筑法》的管制和控制。每一座新建筑都必须遵守必要的建筑规范，以确保安全和无障碍居住。

（七）土地债权

除了根据《海外投资法》和《其他投资条例》要求征得同意外，应当指出的是，新西兰境内的某些土地可以归还给王室，以满足新西兰土著毛利人根据1975年《怀唐伊条约法》提出的要求。私人拥有的土地不属于官方所有，除非有标记。任何这类标记都将显示在土地本身的所有权上，并将在必要的检索后向任何可能的购买者清楚地说明。政府若要归还任何土地，便须缴付现时的市价。

五、税收

（一）所得税

一般来说，新西兰居民在世界范围内的收入被征税，而非居民只对来自新西兰来源的收入征税。

个人被视为新西兰税务居民，如果他们：在新西兰拥有永久居留地，无论他们在新西兰境外有没有这样的居所；任意12个月内在新西兰实际居住超过 183 天。

公司被视为新西兰税务居民，如果：他们在新西兰注册；他们的总部位于新西兰；他们在新西兰拥有自己的管理中心；董事会对公司的控制权在新西兰行使，无论其董事的决策是否限于新西兰。

收入将被视为源自新西兰，如果：它来自完全或部分在新西兰开展的任何业务；它来自位于新西兰的财产处置；它是根据在新西兰订立或全部或部分履行的合同而产生的。

截至 2011 年 4 月 1 日，新西兰居民支付税率如下：

（1）适用于个人（根据与低收入家庭有关的某些规定）：收入高达 14000 新西兰元，税率为 10.5%；收入为 14001 ~ 48000 新西兰元，税率为 17.5%；收入为 48001 ~ 70000 新西兰元，税率为 30%；收入为 70001 新西兰元或以上，税率为 33%。

（2）对于所有公司，适用 28% 的统一税率。

（3）预扣税适用于从新西兰获得某些类型的非居民代扣代缴收入的非居民，即利息、股息和特许权使用费。

非居民代扣税应注意下列例外情况：新西兰加入的所有双重税收协议规定，新西兰可以对股息收入征收的最高预扣税率为 15%；新西兰加入的大多数双重税收协议对利息和特许权使用费的最高预扣税率为 10%；在某些情况下，可以支付 2% 的任何利息支付而不是支付非居民扣缴税款；向有关海外当事人支付款项的，适用特别规则。

新西兰已与包括澳大利亚、奥地利、比利时、加拿大、中国、智利、捷克共和国、丹麦、斐济、芬兰、法国、德国、中国香港、印度、印度尼西亚、爱尔兰、意大利、日本、韩国（大韩民国）、马来西亚、墨西哥、荷兰、挪威、巴布亚新几内亚、菲律宾、波兰、俄罗斯、萨摩亚、新加坡、南非、西班牙、瑞典、瑞士、泰国、中国台湾、土耳其、阿拉伯联合酋长国、美利坚合众国、英国和越南的一些国家或地区达成双重税收协定。

如果资金是由新西兰居民公司从非新西兰居民公司的非居民借款，非居民放贷人在新西兰没有固定的机构，支付给非居民贷款人的利息可免缴非居民预扣税，但须由新西兰居民公司缴付 2% 的应缴利息。但是，新西兰居民公司必须获得税务局局长批准的发行人身份。如果获得批准的发行人身份，新西兰居民公司可以选择支付征收或非居民预扣税，这取决于非居民贷款人的情况和偏好。如果核准的发行人税款未支付任何利息支付，则应支付非居民预扣税。

转让定价和资本弱化规则也适用。这两个主要特点是：转让定价制度要求对任何进出新西兰的货物和服务的供应，均适用于相关缔约方之间的任何长期价格；在资本弱化制度下，由单一的非居民或共同拥有或控制公司 50% 或以上股份的非居民共同控制的企业，只有在债务总额不超过总资产的 60% 的情况下，才有权扣除借款的利息支出。

（二）商品和服务税

商品和服务税（GST）按商品及服务税注册人在新西兰提供的任何商品或服务的价值 15% 的比率支付，这是基于增值原则的间接消费税。

商品和服务税是对从事应税活动的人提供的货物和服务征收的。进口商品也征收消费税。注册 GST 的人必须对其所有应税供应品（或销售）收取 GST，并可要求 GST 支付其应纳税活动所产生的费用。净差额的结果是向新西兰税务局支付或退款。

下列用品不受商品和服务税的限制：金融服务、住宅租金、出口船舶（船只）、外国游乐船、家庭用品、进口服务、互联网销售、贸易管制、在新西兰境外提供的服务、临时进口、货物或人员进出新西兰、由非营利机构提供的捐赠货物和服务、精细金属。

下列用品按零税率征收商品和消费税：出口货物；位于海外的货物；作为“持续经营”的应税活动；新提炼的贵金属；“出口”服务；某些须缴纳消费税和石油税的供应品；某些电信服务的供应；作为资源同意条件或作为发展出资的土地的出资；企业对企业的金融服务供给；一个商品税注册人向另一个商品税注册人提供的物品，其中包括土地，如果获得该土地的人打算使用该土地作应税用品，而且该土地将不被用作该人或有关人员的主要住所。

有限范围的货物将以附加销售税的形式进一步征收间接税，如机动车辆、燃料、酒精和烟草等。

（三）海关和消费税

政府还通过海关和消费税对特定的进口货物征税。根据货物来源国和进口货物的种类，费率差别很大。涉及进口货物，出口在海外组装的部件或再次进口制成品的任何商业企业都应与新西兰海关部门仔细核对。

（四）附加福利税

雇主向雇员提供附带福利的价值（FBT），包括私人使用汽车（包括其可用性）、补贴或贴现商品及服务，以及向雇员提供低息贷款，均须缴付附带福利税。

（五）印花税

新西兰的交易不需要支付印花税，特别是土地转让、租赁、股份转让和证券交易免收印花税。

（六）资本收益

某些土地交易的一些资本收益可能应纳税，例如，土地是由从事土地交易业务的人获得的。如果取得收益的人被视为股票交易者，或为转售目的而获得股份，则股票交易收益也应纳税。

根据 2015 年《税收法》（《住宅用地亮线测试法》）的规定，购买后两年内出售住宅物业产生的收益将被征税。这方面的例外情况包括财产是卖方的主要住所，是作为关系财产结算的一部分转让的，或者是从已故遗产继承的。

（七）赠与税

新西兰从 2011 年 10 月 1 日起取消赠与税，所以不缴纳赠与税。

（八）遗产税

新西兰无须支付遗产或死亡税。

六、货币监管、资本和利润转移、投资激励

（一）汇率制度

新西兰的货币兑换制度基本不受限制。几乎所有的外汇管制都在 1984 年底取消。自 1985 年 3 月以来，被称为“奇异果”的新西兰元被允许自由浮动。

外汇管制的缺乏对新西兰经济产生了重大影响，其中包括所有汇款都可以通过注册银行办理（受联合国制裁、新西兰金融交易报告规则和反恐融资规则规定的披露）；在新西兰赚取的利息，利润和股息可以免费汇给非居民；在非居民资本返还方面不需要批准，包括财务收益或资本化利润。

然而，新西兰根据《投资组织法》和《其他投资条例》拥有外国投资控制权。虽然新西兰没有明确的经济激励机制，但由于新西兰对自由贸易的明确政策，外资在新西兰等地区投资，如旅游业或出口本地制成品（直接有助于外汇收入），尤其受到欢迎，新西兰政府通过新西兰旅游局和新西兰贸易和企业等机构在这些领域提供援助。一些地区当局也对其特定地区的投资者提供有限的援助。

（二）银行和金融服务

大部分商业银行服务由主要的注册交易银行提供，即 ANZ 新西兰银行有限公司、ASB 银行有限公司、新西兰银行、Kiwibank 有限公司、香港上海汇丰银行有限公司和 Westpac 银行公司，这些银行提供各种服务。大多数财务调节通过对公司资产的担保方式进行担保，并且通常需要大股东的个人担保。

还有其他多种金融借贷或相关金融服务机构，如建筑协会、商业银行、财务公司、受托人公司、保险公司、信用合作社以及股票和代理商等。政府最近已制定法律，促进投资者和机构对金融市场的信心和参与，以及促进健全和有效率的非银行金融体系。该立法为金融服务提供者建立了登记制度。立法的主要目的是：查明金融服务提供者；允许对金融服务提供者进行更有效的监测和评价；提供有关金融服务提供者的信息；协助履行新西兰的反洗钱义务；确保金融服务提供者的控制所有人、董事和高级管理人员不具有某些刑事定罪，不破产，并且不受公司、证券或消费者立法管理的禁止；建立

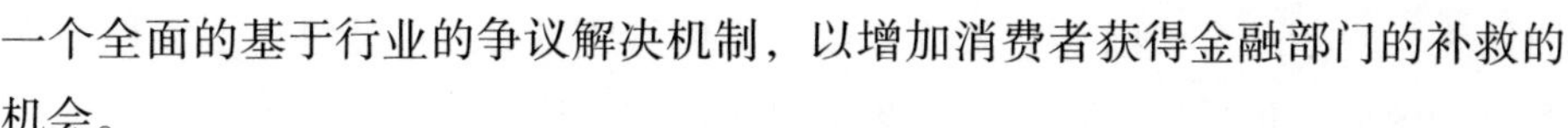

一个全面的基于行业的争议解决机制，以增加消费者获得金融部门的补救的机会。

主要商业银行还提供其他普通商业服务，包括信用证、汇票、商业票据设施、定期贷款和外汇。

（三）储备银行

新西兰储备银行是新西兰的中央银行，根据 1989 年《新西兰储备银行法案》和其他附属法律运作。

该行的三大主要职能：一是为保持价格稳定而制定货币政策。法律规定，财政部部长和储备银行行长必须另行签署具体目标。目前的政策目标要求将基础年度通货膨胀率保持在 1% ~ 3% 的范围内，但也必须适当考虑到政府整体更广泛的经济目标。二是促进健全和有效的金融体系。这主要是通过注册和监管银行，并监控每家银行的行为和持续状况来实现的。三是满足公众的货币需求，并提供一系列支付和清算服务。

（四）金融市场

一般来说，新西兰的金融市场（股票、债券、期货和期权）主要由行业监管机构通过一系列政府部门规定来监管。证券交易所必须进行注册并受金融市场管理局（FMA）监管。目前，新西兰有一个注册交易所 NZXLimited，该交易所经营主要证券交易所（NZSX）、债券市场（NZDX）和替代交易所（NZAX），适用于较少数的发行人。FMA 管理新西兰的金融市场。FMA 负责监管与金融服务和证券市场有关的公司法、证券和财务报告。

FMA 授权期货经销商。除非 FMA 授权，否则任何人均不得交易期货（广泛定义，包括期权）。NZX 有限公司的 NZX 期货和期权规则允许它授权被赎回者为期货和期权参与者。

七、竞争法规和竞争条例

1986 年《商业法》为促进消费者长期利益的市场竞争提供了框架。《商业法》由商务委员会（Commission）管理。《商业法》禁止某些反竞争行为或做法，包括两个或以上个人或企业的集体行为具有或可能具有实质性减少竞争的效果，包括采取行动排除竞争对手或固定价格；单一个人或企业利用企业的市场力量（定义为相当程度）或导致供应商的货物可由其他企业出售的最低价格的规范的单方面行为。

有一些例外情况，包括其他法规授权的行为；合伙企业中没有任何合伙人是法人的商业伙伴之间的协议；非竞争条款，如关于出售企业中供应商的股份或雇员根据雇用合同限制贸易的规定；知识产权。

《商业法》还禁止任何可能会大幅减少市场竞争的合并或收购。市场一词的定义是指新西兰的商品和服务以及其他商品和服务的市场，事实上，这些商品和服务从商业常识上而言是可以替代的。因此，如果一项收购的结果是单方面或不协调或协调的市场力量的行使范围有所扩大，则该收购很可能被视为大大减少了一个市场的竞争。

《商业法》规定了向委员会（在执行任何协议之前）寻求许可的机制，即拟议的收购不会导致竞争大幅减少，因此不会构成违反《商业法》的行为。即使某项交易被认为大大减少了市场竞争，但其对公众的好处大于其造成的危害时，也可寻求授权。

根据新西兰的标准，对违规行为的处罚力度很大，对个人处罚是 50 万新西兰元，对公司处罚是 1000 万新西兰元，或是违约造成的商业收益的 3 倍，或是公司及其子公司营业额的 10%，以较大额为准。委员会还有权撤销之后被认定违反《商业法》的交易。《商业法》还专门对电力行业进行了规定。

八、知识产权保护

（一）版权、商标、外观设计及专利

新西兰的知识产权立法主要源自英国立法和普通法。然而，随着新的数字和电子世界的到来，政府越来越多地对版权立法进行审查。

（二）版权

1994 年《著作权法》（《版权法》）为文学、戏剧、音乐或艺术作品、

录音、电影、传播作品和印刷版本的原创作品提供版权保护。版权存在于劳动、技能或独立判断已被使用的任何作品中，而不要求以原创或新颖的形式表达思想。

这项权利属于作品本身，并属于作者或创作者，除非作者已被委托创作该作品或在就业中创作该作品。根据新西兰签署的《伯尔尼公约》，作品一经创作就拥有版权——不需要登记。

作品的版权所有人有权在新西兰从事下列行为：复制作品；向公众发布作品；在公共场所表演、播放或展示作品；将作品传达给公众；对作品进行改编；授权他人进行这些行为。

文学、戏剧、音乐和艺术作品的版权通常持续到作者的一生，再加上死后 50 年。虽然新西兰不要求有版权通知，但最好是公示该通知，以便根据国际公约提供更好的国际保护。

（三）商标

2002 年《商标法》提供了商标保护制度。《商标法》确定商标保护的权利范围；概述了注册商标的过程；定义可以注册为商标的内容；为注册商标提供执法机制；包含遏制盗版版权作品和假冒商标的措施；包含众所周知的商标的保护。

《商标法》规定的商标注册自注册之日起生效，为期 10 年。商标可以延期 10 年，同时商标的申请人或所有人有责任在到期日前更新商标。

（四）设计

1953 年《外观设计法》下的注册设计保护规定了从产品的视觉设计中创造市场优势的独家权利。注册外观设计禁止他人未经同意使用该设计。

注册设计必须是新颖的，并具有一定的视觉吸引力，而不是完全与产品的使用或功能有关。通过工业工艺应用于物品的形状、配置、图案或装饰物以及具有视觉吸引力的设计都是允许进行注册的设计。

根据《外观设计法》，保护期限为最初 5 年，加续期 5 年。国际保护要求在每个使用国家注册设计。

（五）专利

专利保护新发明。一项发明必须是原创的、有用的，并且对于试图达到相同目的并且在主题领域具有知识的任何人都不是显而易见的。

新产品、制造工艺、化合物和生物技术都可以获得专利。药品和机器属于可以获得专利的其他发明。

申请一项新的专利注册是一项有效的策略，其中一项发明具有重大意义并可能带来长期商业收益。该专利赋予了 20 年内制造、销售、进口和使用专利发明的专有权。此后，任何人都可以自由使用本发明。

国际保护要求在每个使用国家注册发明。

（六）商业和公司名称——假冒

新西兰目前没有企业名称登记册。虽然公司名称可以根据 1993 年《公司法》注册，但这并没有赋予将该名称作为商标专用的权利。然而，如果一家公司以品牌名称或商标，也是注册公司名称进行交易，可能会出现假冒问题。

防止假冒行为通常与保护商誉有关，其目的是防止当一个企业试图通过篡夺他人的声誉或商誉而导致企业之间的不正当竞争。虽然 1986 年《公平交易法》同样禁止贸易中的误导和欺骗行为，但它主要集中在消费者保护上。另外，假冒则更多地涉及不公平的商业竞争，并侧重于商业或贸易保护。这两个动作经常被一起调用。

（七）网络或域名

域名作为商标注册申请的对象并不常见。当接受商标注册的域名时，关注的重点是与标准地址代码相关的任何标识符，如 www、com 和新西兰境内的 .co.nz。

新西兰的法院考虑了域名问题，特别是保护企业免遭域名抢注。

（八）平行进口

《1998 年版权修正法》放宽了新西兰的《平行进口法》，并根据 1994 年《版权法》修改了“侵权”的定义。

在制造的时间和地点为不侵犯版权的物品，在进口到新西兰时不属于侵权复制品。然而，非正版或盗版货物仍然被禁止进口，根据经修订的立法，处罚也有所增加。平行进口的商品有时会与盗版和冒牌商品混淆。平行进口货物是合法制造的商品，来自授权或许可的海外供应商，而不是进口国知识产权的所有者。盗版或冒牌货品是未经知识产权所有人授权而生产的侵权制成品。

九、劳动和就业

（一）最低要求

新西兰立法为雇员提供了一些最低限度的法定权利：

（1）2000 年《就业关系法》（ER 法）为就业期间无理解雇和无理行为提供补救措施。

（2）2003 年《假期法》规定了病假、丧假、每年四周的假期，并承认圣诞节和复活节等公共假期。

（3）1987 年《育儿假和就业保护法》规定育儿假可达 52 周，这一期间包括 18 周的带薪假。带薪育儿假期间由新西兰政府供资。在大多数情况下，雇主必须保持雇员的职位空缺，并可使用临时替代者。

（4）1993 年《人权法》禁止基于各种理由的歧视，包括性别、种族和残疾歧视。新西兰没有退休年龄。1993 年《人权法》禁止性骚扰和种族骚扰。

（5）1983 年《最低工资法》规定了工人的最低工资标准。

（6）1972 年《同工同酬法案》禁止男女同工不同酬。

（7）1983 年《工资保护法》规定了必须如何支付工资，并防止在没有雇员书面同意的情况下从雇员工资中扣除工资，但在有限情况下除外。

（8）1993 年《隐私法》规定如何收集、储存、获取、使用和披露个人信息。

（9）2015 年《工作场所健康和安全法》规定了确保工作场所安全的要求。

（二）2000 年《就业关系法》

《就业关系法》是新西兰劳动和就业法中的一项关键立法。它承认工会，并侧重于就业关系，而不是就业协议。《就业关系法》包括一项关键原则，即就业关系各方必须真诚地相互处理。这适用于雇主、雇员和工会之间的所有交易。

虽然有某些最低法定条件，但大多数雇用条款和条件可继续由雇主与雇员或雇主以及代表雇员的注册工会直接谈判。

《就业关系法》促进工会和雇主之间的集体谈判，并要求“本着诚意”进行谈判。集体协议是雇主和工会之间的合同。作为工会成员的个人可以就额外的个人条款进行谈判，条件是这些条款不违反集体协议。

《就业关系法》要求签订书面就业协议。雇主须备存一份经签署（或有意签署）的雇佣协议或构成雇员个别雇佣条款及条件的现行雇佣条款及条件。在雇佣协议中必须包括有最低限度的要求。

（三）雇员类型

大多数雇员将签订长期雇用协议，雇员的就业将无限期地继续，直至根据就业协议和就业立法终止雇用为止。

固定期限的雇员和就业协议是允许的，但受到管制。在订立协议时，雇主必须根据合理理由，在某一指定日期或期间结束时、在某一特定事件发生时或在某一特定项目结束时，有真正的理由使该协议终止。终止就业的原因和方式必须记录在协议中，在需要时也可以用临时雇员。

（四）试用期

允许有试用期，但受到严格管制。试用期不超过 90 天，必须记录在雇佣协议中，并由雇员签署。如果雇主在试用期内解雇雇员，雇员无权就解雇提出个人申诉或其他法律程序。

（五）问题解决

劳资纠纷包括在雇佣关系过程中出现的问题。这些争议中的大多数是通过 ER 法中的机制处理的，这些机制将这些机制定义为“雇佣关系问题”，员工可以就这些问题（包括无理解雇）提出“个人申诉”，这可能引起诉讼程序。

ER 法支持并促进成功的雇佣关系，雇佣关系的当事人通常需要通过政府资助的调解程序解决雇佣关系问题，然后再前往就业关系管理局（调查并确定雇佣关系问题）。

（六）健康和安全

2015 年《健康与安全法》的主要目的是鼓励企业界人员对工作中的健康和安全管理负责，主要责任在于开展业务或承诺的个人 / 实体（PCBU），以在合理可行的范围内确保其工人在工作时的健康和安全和 / 或任何其他可能存在风险的人的安全。PCBU 包括公司、合伙人、其他实体、个人。

《健康与安全法》要求公司的官员（包括董事、合伙人或担任其职务，允许他们对 PCBU 管理产生重大影响的人）进行尽职调查，以确保 PCBU 符合其《健康与安全法》范围内的职责。

PCBU 的职责包括提供和维护不危及健康和安全的工作环境、安全的工作制度、物资的安全使用，以及提供必要的培训、指导和监督，以保护所有人免受其工作带来的健康和安全风险的影响。PCBU 还必须与对同一工作或工作场所负有责任的其他 PCBU 进行磋商、合作和协调。PCBU 有义务与工人在健康和安全方面进行商议，并允许工人参与改善工作健康和安全的机会。

违反《健康与安全法》可能导致重大处罚，包括罚款、赔偿和监禁。根据违反职责的情况，可以对 PCBU 和 / 或其官员进行处罚。

（七）裁员

真正的裁员是终止新西兰就业的正当理由。当员工的职位对企业的需要而言是多余的，就会出现裁员。裁员必须有真正的商业理由，才能依法证明是合理的。雇主不得因表现不佳、不相容或不当行为等其他原因宣布雇员被解雇。

雇主通常会在作出任何决定之前，与任何可能受影响的雇员协商。必须发出终止通知。没有法定的裁员补偿。不过，如果有关的雇佣协议规定雇员有权获得裁员补偿，则必须支付。有时，雇佣协议规定，在技术裁员的情况下，不支付补偿金，如雇主（或在买卖交易中购买该业务的人）提供的雇员条件与其目前的角色不相上下。如果雇佣协议中没有裁员补偿权利，雇主就没有义务支付裁员补偿。

在出售或转让业务时可能会出现裁员情况。如果企业是通过不同的实体作为持续经营企业收购的，那么从技术上讲，这意味着雇主已经改变了，因此出现了裁员现象。当发生这种情况时，卖方业务的雇员在技术上是多余的，买方通常可以选择是否雇用他们（除以下所述受 ER 法保护的某些类别的雇员外）。如果只购买一家公司的股票（而不是资产），则不会出现裁员情况，因为员工仍然受雇于同一家公司。

ER 法案专门处理雇员的转职。受影响的员工根据 ER 法分为两类：一是弱势雇员（通常是从事清洁或餐饮服务的人员）；二是其他员工。

弱势雇员有权按照同样的雇用条款和条件转职到新雇主。请注意，雇员人数在 19 人或以下的雇主可获豁免遵守这项规定。

对于不属于弱势的雇员而言，雇主必须与新购买者协商，如果企业被另一实体收购为持续经营的话，其雇用雇员的前景如何。在每个雇佣协议中都需要雇员保护条款，并涉及雇主和新雇主对受影响雇员的谈判和处理。

（八）2001 年《事故赔偿法》

新西兰的人身伤害赔偿制度是独一无二的。2001 年《事故赔偿法》是新西兰自 1974 年起实施的一项无过失事故计划。新西兰政府通过事故赔偿公司提供工伤赔偿和非工伤赔偿。这一制度的效果是，除在非常有限的情况下，任何人都无权对在新西兰遭受的人身伤害提起诉讼。

（九）KiwiSaver

KiwiSaver 是一项涉及雇主、计划提供者和几个政府机构的政府倡议。这是根据 2006 年《KiwiSaver 法》制定的。这项自愿的长期储蓄倡议旨在帮助新西兰人增加财政独立和为退休储蓄。

KiwiSaver 成员通过定期缴纳总工资或报酬来建立储蓄账户。为他们的账户作出贡献的 KiwiSaver 成员也有权获得相当于雇员工资 3% 的强制性雇主供款。

（十）包工

包工对雇员而言的法律地位不同。定义一个人是否是雇员的法定测试不仅涉及协议的审查，而且涉及关系的“真实性质”。因此，无论书面协议如

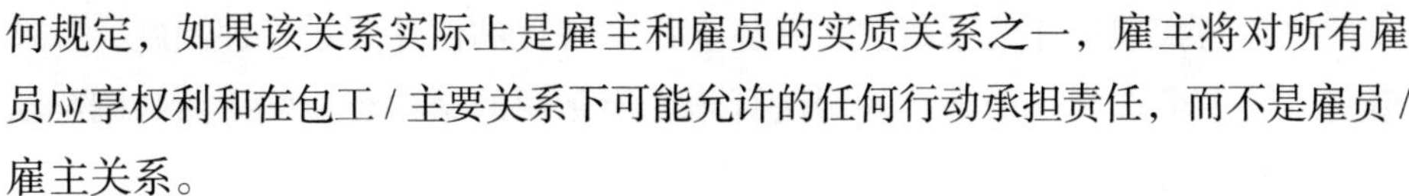
何规定，如果该关系实际上是雇主和雇员的实质关系之一，雇主将对所有雇员应享权利和在包工 / 主要关系下可能允许的任何行动承担责任，而不是雇员 / 雇主关系。

十、其他适用的商业立法

（一）1993 年《公司法》

新西兰的公司法规主要包括：

1993 年的《公司法》，管理新西兰公司的组建和运作；2013 年的《财务报告法》，其中规定了公司和其他实体的财务报告要求。

《公司法》与以前的法律和大多数联邦司法管辖区不同，有以下区别：

（1）公营和私营公司之间没有区别。

（2）公司只需要一个股东，没有票面价值、名义价值或维持股本的概念。

（3）公司不需要有章程（类似组织章程大纲及章程细则），但章程确实使公司能够根据《公司法》采取某些允许性的规定，也为公司提供了更大的明确性和确定性。因此，制定章程通常是可取的。

（4）在公司可以向股东分配和进行某些其他交易之前，公司必须满足《公司法》中详述的“偿付能力检测”。

（5）在股东和债权人保护的前提下，公司可以购买自己的股份，为收购自己的股份提供资金。

（6）在公司进行一项重大交易（通常是一项涉及公司资产价值一半以上的交易）之前，需要 75% 的股东批准。

（7）投票反对获得 75% 或以上多数批准的重大交易的股东在某些情况下可能要求公司回购其股份。

《公司法》还规定了诸如公司及其高级人员的权力、董事的职责、会议的进行和清算等事项。

（二）2008 年《有限责任合伙法》

《有限责任合伙法》于 2008 年 5 月生效，其目的是废除 1908 年《合伙关系法》的特别伙伴关系条款，并建立一个现代的伙伴关系管理制度，以便新西兰商界可选择一个与海外司法管辖区所采用的结构相似的灵活和国际认可的商业架构；促进新西兰风险投资业的发展。

（三）2013 年《金融市场行为法》

2013年《金融市场行为法》(FMC法案)管理金融产品的建立、推广和销售，它还具体规定了提供、交易和交易金融产品以及监管某些金融服务的金融业人士的现行要求。

FMC 法案包含披露要求，并规定在大多数情况下，为散户投资者量身定制产品披露声明，并准备和提供给潜在投资者。

FMC 法案涉及内幕交易、市场操纵和披露大量证券持有人的相关利益，以及董事和高级管理人员的披露要求。

（四）1993 年《收购法》

新西兰有一个规范守则公司控制权变更的收购制度，即在注册证券交易所上市的公司、在前 12 个月上市的公司以及超过 50 名股东的实体。

根据 1993 年《收购法》和《收购守则》，任何人不得成为收购公司 20% 或 2 个以上投票权的持有人或控制人。收购委员会对《收购守则》作出规定，并有权给予豁免。

当一个人试图超过或超过 20% 的限额时，可以通过以下方式做到：对收购公司所有证券的全部报价；向所有持有人提供部分要约，以便获得超过 50% 的投票权（或与提供人无关的股东批准的较小百分比）；非关联股东的授权。

《收购守则》要求所有股东得到平等对待，包括价格方面的待遇。如果股东持有或控制的比例超过 50%，则每年可能会增加 5%。超过 90%，则适用强制收购条款。《收购守则》还禁止防守战术。对违反《收购守则》的处罚是对个人 50 万新西兰元以及对法人公司 500 万新西兰元的罚款。

（五）电子交易

2017 年《合同与商法》（CCL 法）第 4 部分包括与电子交易有关的规定，

并以联合国国际贸易法委员会模式为基础。CCL 法第 4 部分旨在促进或便利电子商务技术的使用，并平等对待基于纸张的文件和基于计算机的信息。

最近取代 2002 年《电子交易法》的 CCL 法第 4 部分旨在使新西兰的立法适应通信技术的发展，而不需要大规模取消纸面要求或干扰这些要求所依据的法律概念和方法。也就是说，《刑事诉讼法》所载的电子交易条款并没有改变法律义务的性质，而是允许在交易和信息管理中使用电子技术。它以两种方式实现了这一点。第一，这些规定减少了围绕电子信息的法律效力、发送时间和地点以及电子通信的接收方面的不确定性。第二，它们允许某些纸面法律要求，例如，要求以书面形式，包括签名或保留文件，通过使用等同于电子技术的功能来满足。

CCL 法并不试图定义一种与任何纸质法律要求等同的基于计算机的方法，而是将重点放在功能以及如何通过电子技术来实现这些功能。CCL 法涵盖的技术并非严格的电子技术，包括电子、数字、磁性、光学、电磁、生物识别和光子通信手段。

（六）1986 年《公平交易法》

1986 年《公平交易法》适用于货物和服务的推广和销售的所有方面。其目的是确保向客户提供关于货物和服务的全面和准确的信息。它禁止某些不公平的做法，并规定了消费者信息和产品安全标准。它禁止从事贸易的人进行误导或欺骗性行为。《公平交易法》提供了很大程度的消费者保护。违反《公平交易法》可导致巨额罚款。

（七）1993 年《消费者保障法》

1993 年《消费者保障法》为购买商品和服务时保护消费者提供法定保障。《消费者保障法》适用于贸易人员（包括制造商、进口商和分销商）向消费者提供的商品或服务。

消费者是指购买通常为个人或家庭用途而购买的商品或服务，但不用于转售、生产中使用，或在货物情况下修理土地上的货物或固定装置的人。

《消费者保障法》确定包括维修、更换和退款在内的法定保证或补救措施。此外，消费者可因货物或服务未能达到法定担保而对可预见的合理损失寻求损害赔偿。在贸易者和消费者之间订立违反《消费者保障法》的合同是被禁止的，并可能导致巨额罚款。

（八）1993 年《隐私法》

1993 年《隐私法》旨在保护个人的隐私，与个人信息的收集、使用、访问、更正和披露有关。《隐私法》确立了保护个人信息的 12 项隐私原则。在商业中，《隐私法》的应用出现在销售和市场、信用控制和就业等领域。

（九）1999 年《个人财产证券法》

1999 年《个人财产证券法》（PPSA）规定了个人财产担保权益的确认和监管制度。担保权益是一项交易所产生或规定的个人财产权益，以保证付款或履行一项义务。例如，这包括在供应方面保留所有权条款，以及一年以上的租赁或委托。

所有担保权益均按照法定优先权规则排列。一般原则是在个人财产证券登记册（www.ppsr.govt.nz）上登记的担保权益优先于未登记的利益。在登记的利益之间，一般而言，首先登记的担保权益将具有优先权。在公司进入破产管理或清算的情况下，公司的资产将根据注册权益的优先级进行分配。但是，这条规则有一些例外。如果提供货物，而且担保权益完全是为了保证支付担保品全部或部分购买价款的义务，则这是一种“购买款担保权益”，对特定货物给予“超级优先权”。

（十）2009 年《反洗钱和打击资助恐怖主义法》

《反洗钱和打击资助恐怖主义法》规定包括金融服务提供者和赌场在内的“报告实体”有义务侦查和制止洗钱和资助恐怖主义行为，其要求包括进行风险评估和客户尽职调查（包括客户身份验证）。它为处理洗钱和资助恐怖主义行为提供了一种基于风险的办法，包括一种监督、监测和执行制度。该法还介绍了新的民事和刑事犯罪。

（十一）2008 年《金融服务提供商法》

《金融服务提供商法》要求所有金融服务提供者都必须登记。它建立了

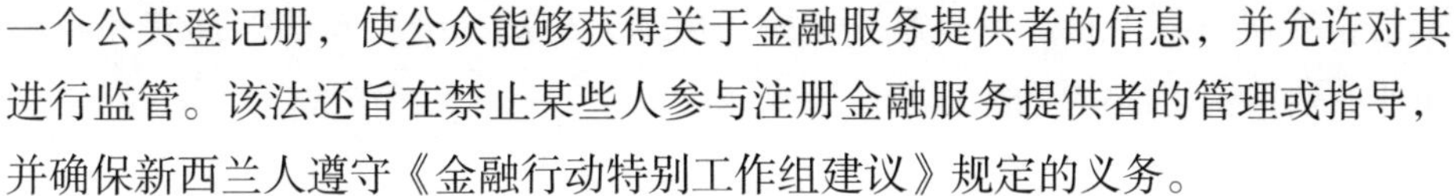

一个公共登记册，使公众能够获得关于金融服务提供者的信息，并允许对其进行监管。该法还旨在禁止某些人参与注册金融服务提供者的管理或指导，并确保新西兰人遵守《金融行动特别工作组建议》规定的义务。

十一、移民

新西兰政府通过新西兰移民局对移民到新西兰进行控制。适用的条例会有相对频繁的变化。有执照的移民顾问可以提供最新的建议。

（一）入境要求

一般来说，到新西兰的外国游客（澳大利亚人除外）在进入新西兰之前必须安排现行签证。某些国家的国民可以在没有签证的情况下访问至多3个月。

可能适用于移民的签证类型包括：居留签证——对希望在新西兰永久居留的人；企业家工作签证——为希望在新西兰拥有和经营自己企业的人签发的工作签证（最长可达3年，能够在6个月或两年后申请居留权）；工作签证——为希望在新西兰临时工作的人提供的工作签证（最多3年，可以进一步延期）；访客签证——仅限临时访问而非工作（最多9个月，并可能再延长3个月）；学生签证——用于临时学习（可在任何超过3个月的学习课程期间使用）。

（二）新西兰居留权

新西兰移民政策的目标是促进具有社会凝聚力的经济增长。这一目标的基本原则是：加强新西兰的人力资本；加强国际联系；鼓励企业和创新；维持社会凝聚力。

同时，该政策的目的是保持对移民出于社会原因和人道主义原因进入新西兰的规定。

希望在新西兰永久定居的潜在移民必须获得居留证和签证。潜在移民可通过下列类别获得新西兰居留权：“技术移民”类别（申请人可根据积分制度获得居留资格）；“家庭”类别（申请人可根据其与新西兰居民或公民的关系获得资格）；“投资者”类别（申请人可根据在新西兰进行的投资而有资格获得居留权）；“企业家”类别（申请人可以根据在新西兰拥有和经营企业的资格获得居留资格）。

（三）更详细的移民政策

有两种不同的投资者类别如表 1 所示：

表 1 两种不同的投资者类别

	投资者 +	投资者
投资资金	3 年在新西兰投资 1000 万新西兰元	4 年在新西兰投资 300 万新西兰元
最大年龄限值	无	65 岁
最低英语水平限值	无	雅思综合成绩为 3 分或 3 分以上的有英语背景或熟练的英语使用者
在新西兰的最少逗留时间	3 年投资期的最后两年，每年 44 天；如果投资者在增长投资中至少投资了 250 万新西兰元，则在 3 年投资期间的任何时间，每段时间为 80 天（第二年和第三年后提交证据）	在新西兰每年 146 天，如果投资者在增长投资中至少投资了 75 万新西兰元，则在 4 年投资期间的任何时候都有 438 天（第二年和第四年后提交证据）
商业经验	无	最少三年

（四）居留获批后

如果居留申请获得批准，申请人必须将投资资金保留在可接受的投资中，期限为 3 年或 4 年，视类别而定。主要申请人必须符合表 1 所列在新西兰所需最少时间的要求。

技术移民类别也是一个基于积分的系统，重点是具有高学历和工作经验并在新西兰有工作机会的申请人。申请人首先必须提交一份“利益表达”，其中针对各种因素要求积分。分数最高的申请人将被邀请申请居留。

家庭类别侧重于新西兰居民或公民与海外人之间的现有家庭关系。如果申请由新西兰亲属担保，配偶 / 事实上的伴侣、父母、受抚养子女或新西兰居民或公民的兄弟姐妹可以申请居留。

企业家类别侧重于申请人成功经营以某种方式使新西兰受益的业务的能力。在申请此类别的居留之前，申请人必须有下列任何一项：（1）在新西兰自己的企业成立并受雇至少两年；（2）持有长期营业执照，在新西兰成功创办了一家自营业务的企业，投资了 50 万新西兰元，并为新西兰公民或居民创造了至少三个新的全职工作岗位。

所有类别均须符合健康和品格要求，而除家庭类别外，所有类别均须具备最低的英语语言能力标准。

十二、法律制度与争端解决

健全和可预测的法律制度是在外国进行任何重大投资的基本要求。新西兰的法律历史上基于英国的法律，并且与英国一样，新西兰仍然是普通法司法管辖区，其民法包括“共同”或法官制定的法律和新西兰一院议会的规约。

最近，新西兰已经利用其他国家，特别是澳大利亚和加拿大等英联邦国家的法律制定其章程。例如，新西兰的 1993 年《公司法》和 1999 年《个人财产证券法》具有鲜明的北美风格，1986 年的《公平交易法》和 1986 年的《商业法》严格遵循澳大利亚的《贸易惯例法》（自 2010 年更名为《竞争和消费者法》）。

新西兰《商业法》的核心是健全的合同法结构，与其他发达国家的制度密切相关。从本质上讲，商业承诺将得到执行，或者未履行商业承诺将得到补偿。目前存在着一系列被广泛接受的抗辩，但总的来说，这些都遵循商业常识。

一个完善的法律体系是重要的，但这些法律会不会得到执行？新西兰的法院运作良好，与许多其他国家的法院相比，效率高、效果好。任何法院的法官都没有已知的腐败案件。法官由总检察长任命，而不是由选举任命。他们通常来自一群受过尊重的经验丰富的律师，他们表达了对司法任命的兴趣。

新西兰有四个主要的法院：第一级是拥有管辖权的地区法院，使其能够处理争议金额高达 20 万新西兰元的案件；第二级是高等法院，它有管辖权处理任何有价值的商业纠纷；第三级是上诉法院；第四级是最高法院。地方法院有权向高等法院提出上诉，并有权在高等法院或上诉法院允许的情况下向上诉法院提出上诉，只有在法院给予许可的情况下，才可向最高法院提出上诉。高等法院的裁决可以向上诉法院提出上诉，并可以向最高法院提出上诉。

高等法院具有全面的监督作用，能够以偏见、缺乏管辖权或不合理为由审查任何行政或司法法庭的裁决。

在一些领域有单独的专门法院和法庭。值得注意的是，可将轻微争端提交争议法庭；就业问题由就业法庭处理；规划和环境事项由环境庭处理；新西兰土著人民毛利人与土地有关（或涉及其他传统毛利人权利）的传统权利的争端由怀唐伊法庭一审处理。某些建筑纠纷由“防风雨房屋解决服务处”审理。

通常情况下，案件在 12 ~ 18 个月内由初审法院处理。由于所有法院都有简易判决和罢免司法管辖区，因此可以更快地处理明确案件。法院现在有广泛的权利来管理它们面前的案件，并规定文件发现和其他程序步骤的范围和性质。法院不能要求当事方使用调解等其他解决办法，但它们确实有能力举行旨在法官监督和协助下解决争端的司法解决会议。

新西兰是 1958 年《联合国承认和执行外国仲裁裁决公约》的签约国，并制定了仲裁立法，使国际仲裁与国内仲裁保持一致。法院将坚持提及仲裁，并假设减少司法干预仲裁。新西兰拥有大量国际和国内仲裁员，能够提供合理、高质量的决策。

新西兰也是 ICSID 关于解决国际投资争端以及《国际货物销售公约》的公约签署国，因此，它有意遵守这些领域的国际标准。法官们赞赏新西兰是全球经济的一部分，并越来越多地参考国际法律公约和协议，如《统一合同法原则》。

总的来说，新西兰商业环境的新进入者不太可能遇到有关基本合同法、合同可执行性或法院程序的任何意外。

印度投融资法律研究篇

投资目的地——印度

Majmudar & Partners

一、印度基本概况

印度是世界上最大的民主国家，拥有全球约六分之一的人口，也是世界上增长最快的经济体之一。按名义国内生产总值（GDP）排名，印度居世界第六位；按购买力平价计算，印度在 2017 年[①] 排名第三位。印度经济因其人口和强劲的消费模式而得到加强，其经济基本保持稳定。印度政府（GOI）也在 1991 年后实施经济自由化改革，将印度转变为投资友好的目的地，印度的外国投资流入量在 2016 年增长了 18%，达到了创纪录的 464 亿美元。

媒体报道显示，外国投资者对印度的信息技术、电信和建筑行业更感兴趣，最近还把重点放在媒体、银行、非金融服务和保险领域。过去 20 年来，印度的平均增长率约为 7%，成为最稳定、最重要的 G20 国家之一。印度的国内生产总值增长确实下滑，受 2016 年 11 月的去货币化影响，从 2015—2016 年的 7.9% 下降至 2016—2017 年的 6.8%，但此后加速增长，预计未来两年将分别上升至 7.2% 和 7.7%，并最终升至 8% 左右[②]。印度的制造业是 GOI 雄心勃勃的增长计划中的关键角色，据报道，GOI 计划将该部门对该国国内生产总

① 资料来源于国际货币基金组织（IMF）世界经济展望数据库，载 https://www.imf.org/external/pubs/ft/weo/2017/01/weodata/weorept.aspx?pr.x=31&pr.y=13&sy=2016&ey=2020&scsm=1&ssd=1&sort=country&ds=.&br=1&c=534&s=NGDPD%2CNGDPDPC%2CPPPGDP%2CPPPPC&grp=0&a=。

② 资料来源于国际货币基金组织（IMF）世界经济展望数据库，载 https://www.imf.org/external/pubs/ft/weo/2017/01/weodata/weorept.aspx?pr.x=31&pr.y=13&sy=2016&ey=2020&scsm=1&ssd=1&sort=country&ds=.&br=1&c=534&s=NGDPD%2CNGDPDPC%2CPPPGDP%2CPPPPC&grp=0&a=。

值的贡献从目前 15% ~ 18% 的贡献率提高到 25%[①]。

GOI 为实现这一目标所采取的主要举措是“印度制造”和“印度技能”[②]。前者旨在使印度成为全球制造业中心并创造就业机会，后者侧重于培养非熟练劳动力并提高其就业能力。

此外，印度的服务业占其国内生产总值的 60% 以上。它为外国投资，特别是在信息技术、银行和通信服务领域，提供了一个非常有吸引力和强有力的目标。印度独特的人口结构和受过教育、成本低廉、技术熟练的劳动力的存在，使印度在服务业领域获得了更多的投资。

GOI 还把重点放在“营商便利”上，并将其视为印度制造、印度创业、数字印度等举措取得成功的关键因素，它旨在减少商业活动中的繁文缛节和多种业务流程，同时澄清并提高政府政策对投资者吸引资金的政策透明度。政府为方便营商而带来的一些重要改变如下。

（一）促进投资

一是建立了投资者便利小组，为投资查询和向外国投资者提供手把手服务提供主要支持；二是印度与中国、韩国、日本、加拿大和美国建立了一个专门的服务台，以促进和加快投资建议，并加强经济联系；三是一个单一窗口的在线门户网站，任何希望开办新企业的投资者都可以利用核心服务获得必要的清关、许可证、完成强制性税务登记和所需的监管备案；四是为处理由外国投资者提交的有关零售 / 出口导向单位案件的申请，制定了一份具体时间表的清单；五是有限责任合伙企业的投资已经开放给特定行业的外国投资者。[③]

（二）简化劳动法的管理

印度的劳动法已成为工业发展的障碍。为了简化劳动法的管理，一个在线门户网站“ShramSuvidha”已经启动，这将有利于：便于在一个地方报告各种劳动法；合并劳动监察信息及其执行情况；向单位分配劳工识别号码以

---

① 资料来源于财政部网站，载 http://indiabudget.nic.in/ub2017-18/bag/bag1.pdf。

② http://www.makeinindia.com/goi-initiatives。

③ http://www.makeinindia.com/goi-initiatives。

便于网上注册和提交报税表；向雇员国家保险公司及员工公积金组织等实时登记。[①]

（三）简化印度业务运作

GOI 已经进行了以下改变：限制新的电力连接获得同意 / 或无异议证书的需要；启动环境和森林清理的在线申请和监督程序；简化取得工业执照；简化取得工业执照的表格；内政部在 12 周内批准工业执照申请的安全许可；双重用途物品（防务和民用物品），除非列为防务物品，否则不需要工业许可证；工业许可证的初始有效期从两年增加到三年，以便采购土地并获得必要的审查许可 / 批准；制定了常见问题并将其上载于产业政策和促进部的网站；将进出口货物所需的强制性文件数从 11 件减至 3 件。[②]

另外，印度司法体系高度发达，遵循法院的等级模式。新德里最高法院是最高法院。紧随其后的是邦高等法院和下属地区法院。上诉是从下级机构到上级机构的，决定是根据大量已确立的案例法和立法本身发布的。

（四）与中国企业合作的现状和方向

最近，印度与中国的关系引起了全球的广泛关注，尤其是因为它们是亚洲人口占主导地位的主要发展中经济体，正努力解决减贫和发展等共同问题。新闻报道显示，在世纪之交，印度和中国的贸易总额约合 30 亿美元，其中印度和中国的商品贸易总额约为 1000 亿美元。

2016—2017 年两年期首脑级会谈进一步加强了两邻的关系，印度总理纳伦德拉莫迪和习近平主席多次会面，讨论经济增长计划并商定制定印中关系和增长战略的联合倡议。印度总理最近还在上海举行的两国商界人士聚会上发表了讲话。应当指出，两国企业在贸易、投资和融资等领域共签订了 26 项协议，投资价值 220 亿美元。

这些会议还推动设立了一个专门工作组来处理印度公司在中国市场准入条件方面遇到的问题。两国还在讨论在铁路、智慧城市和技能开发领域的合作。据报道，中国政府对印度的高铁项目感兴趣，并将帮助印度火车站升级。

① GOI 劳工和就业统一门户，载 https://shramsuvidha.gov.in/。

② http://www.makeinindia.com/goi-initiatives。

还有一项建议，即在印度建立一所拥有中国专业知识的大学，以推进印度技能倡议。

另外，两国就共同制作电影问题签署协议，将开创两国合作的辉煌时代。印度的媒体和电影业是一支全球性的力量，但由于中国对外国电影的内部政策，印度一直未能确保在邻国中国站稳脚跟。这一合作制作协议很可能会促使多家电影公司签约，并为更多的印度电影增加大量观众。

二、投资

（一）市场准入

1. 部门监督投资

印度工业政策与促进局（DIPP）工商部负责监管印度投资。DIPP 印发了外国直接投资政策（FDI 政策），近年来一直在提供越来越广泛的印度市场投资渠道。

2. 投资行业的法律法规

（1）外汇管制法。印度的外汇管制受到1999年《外汇管理法案》（FEMA）的管理，以及根据FEMA颁布的通告、通知和新闻说明（TISPRO 法规）进行管制。

（2）部门特定法律。除上述一般性法律外，还有与金融服务（银行业务、非银行金融服务、保险，如 1949 年《银行业监管法案》、1938 年《保险法案》等）、基础设施（机场，如 1994 年《印度机场管理局法令》等），以及其他部门有关的具体法律也可以适用。

3. 投资形式

（1）外商直接投资路线。为了在印度建立业务或投资，非居民必须遵守印度的外汇管制条例。外国公司对印度公司的投资受 TISPRO 法规和 DIPP 颁布的工业政策规定的约束。

此外，外国直接投资政策将 DIPP 和印度储备银行（RBI）投资相关的新闻稿和通知稿合并为一份文件，使外国投资者更容易检查外国直接投资进入印度的适用法律和程序。外国直接投资政策每年更新一次，目前的外国直接投资政策自 2017 年 8 月 28 日起生效。

（2）国外风险投资路线。允许在印度证券交易所（SEBI）项下注册的外国投资者（SEBI）根据 2000 年 SEBI（外国风险资本投资者）条例①，作为外国风险投资者（FVCI）投资于某些公司，如开办公司、基础设施部门、基础设施金融公司和资产金融公司的核心投资公司。为鼓励通过 FVCI 路线进行投资，SEBI 和 RBI 特别为 FVCI 提供了以下优势：

① 免费定价：FVCI 不需要遵守定价要求，并且可以以任何价格认购，购买或出售证券。②

② 锁定：2009 年 SEBI（发行资本和封闭要求）法规规定，进行首次公开发行的公司的整个发行前股本（除长期锁定的某些发起人的资金外③）自公开发行之日起 1 年内锁定。④SEBI 已豁免 FVCI 不受这一锁定要求的约束，只要 FVCI 在向 SEBI 提交招股说明书草稿之日起至少持有了 1 年所涉股份。⑤因此，FVCI 如果愿意，可以在上市后退出其投资。⑥

（3）外国证券投资路径。2014 年《SEBI（外国投资组合投资者）条例》（FPI 规则）规定了通过外国证券投资路线进入印度的投资。通过 FPI 规则进行证券交易不需要 SEBI 的批准。基于风险的方法，FPI 可分为三种类型，以了解客户。

此外，FPI 规则允许第Ⅰ类 FPI 和第Ⅱ类 FPI（由适当的外国监管机构直接监管的 FPI）发行、认购和以其他方式处理境外衍生工具。⑦但是，那些没有直接管制的 II 类 FPI（由于其投资管理人受到适当管理而被归类为Ⅱ类

---

① SEBI（2000 年《外国风险投资者条例》）第 2 章：管理 FVCI 与 SEBI 的注册。

② NishithDesaiAssociates，私募股权和房地产债务，http://www.nishithdesai.com/fileadmin/user_upload/pdfs/Research20Papers/Private_Equity_and_Debt_in_Real_Estate.pdf。

③ 2009 年《SEBI（资本和披露要求的发布）条例》第 36 条。

④ 2009 年《SEBI（资本和披露要求的发布）条例》第 37 条。

⑤ 通过2012年5月21日生效的2012年《SEBI（替代投资基金）条例》，将该豁免插入2009年《SEBI（资本与披露要求发布）条例》的第37条。

⑥ Nishith Desai Assoliates，私募股权和房地产债务，http://www.nishithdesai.com/fileadmin/user_upload/pdfs/Research20Papers/Private_Equity_and_Debt_in_Real_Estate.pdf。

⑦ 2014 年《SEBI（外国投资组合投资者）条例》第 22 条。

FPI）以及所有Ⅲ类 FPI 不得发行、认购或处理境外衍生工具。[①]

4. 市场准入和检验标准

（1）部门政策。目前大多数行业都允许 100% 的外商直接投资，如农业、种植园、采矿、广播、民用机场、工业园区、电子商务等。然而，少数部门仍然不允许外国投资，即原子能、铁路运营（铁路基础设施除外）、彩票业务、赌博和投注、银会、Nidhi 公司、可转让发展权交易、房地产业务或建造农场房屋，以及雪茄、雪果、小雪茄和烟草香烟或烟草替代品制造。在其他一些部门，GOI 限制了外国投资上限。例如，保险公司的外国投资不能超过 49%，私人银行不得超过 74%。[②]

（2）间接外商投资。印度公司没有被居民实体拥有（超过 50% 的资本并非由印度公司 / 印度居民实际拥有）和 / 或控制（印度公司 / 居住在印度的公民无权任命多数董事或控制管理和政策决定）的任何下游投资都被视为间接外国投资，并受下游投资所在行业的部门政策约束。

（3）自动批准。符合自动投资条件的公司在投资前不需要获得任何政府部门的批准。[③] 在这种情况下，被投资公司必须在收到投资资金后的 30 日内，并在配发证券后的 30 日内，通过银行向 RBI 报告。因此，在自动路径下投资的外国公司在开始运营之前，必须将公司或有限责任合伙公司合并。

（4）审批路径。对于不属于自动路径的外商直接投资项目或活动，政府部门根据 DIPP 颁布的标准操作程序，通过其各部门的行政部门批准，如提案：

① 需要根据 1951 年《工业（发展和管理）法》获得工业许可证；

② 关于收购一家现有印度公司的股份，该公司不经营任何业务，只是持有对其他公司的投资，并提议从事不属于外国直接投资自动路线的活动；

③ 超过公示的部门限制或强制要求政府批准的提案，如外国直接投资超过 49% 的单品牌零售；

④ 对于外商投资不属于外商直接投资自动路径的行业，且超过 50% 的被投资公司股份由非居民持有或非居民有权任命超过一半的被投资公司董事

① Nishith Desai Assoliates，私募股权和房地产债务，http://www.nishithdesai.com/fileadmin/user_upload/pdfs/Research20Papers/Private_Equity_and_Debt_in_Real_Estate.pdf。

② 《外国直接投资政策》第 5 章规定了外国直接投资的具体行业条件。

③ 《外国直接投资政策》第 3.4.1 条。

会或控制管理和政策决定的；

⑤ 由印度公司就资本货物、机械、设备的进口或营运前或公司成立前的开支发行股本；

⑥ 外资总额超过500亿印度卢比需要内阁经济事务委员会批准的。

（二）财政

1. 主要金融机构

印度的主要金融机构如下：

（1）印度基础设施金融有限公司。印度基础设施金融有限公司（IIFCL）是2006年成立的全资GOI公司，为可行的基础设施项目提供长期融资。有资格从国际金融合作组织获得财政援助的部门要遵守政府和印度共和国政府批准并不时修订的基础设施分部门统一清单，主要包括交通、能源、水、卫生、通信、社会和商业基础设施。[①]

（2）印度进出口银行。印度进出口银行（EXIM银行）是由GOI全资拥有并于1982年成立的专门金融机构，用于融资、推动和促进对外贸易。进出口银行将信贷额度扩展到海外金融机构、地区开发银行、主权政府和海外其他实体，以使这些国家的买家能够按照递延信贷条件从印度进口发展和基础设施项目、设备、商品和服务。它专注于加强项目出口，并通过推出“买家信用——国家出口保险账户”计划提供了更多的资金选择。该行通过向印度引进技术，以及印度公司在海外设立合资企业、子公司或进行海外收购等业务，促进双向技术转让。为促进印度的出口，该行继续实施贷款计划，为出口型公司的研发活动提供资金。[②]

（3）印度小型工业发展银行。印度小型工业发展银行（SIDBI）是根据印度议会的一项法案于1990年4月2日成立的。它是一个促进、资助和发展微型、小型和中型企业部门的金融机构。它还承担协调从事类似活动的其他

---

① 印度基础设施金融有限公司（IIFCL）资料来源于GOI财政部金融服务部官方网站，http://financialservices.gov.in/banking-divisions/Financial-Institutions-and-others/India-Infrastructure-Finance-Company-Ltd-%28IIFCL%29?page=1。

② 印度进出口银行（EXIMBank）资料来源于GOI金融部财务部官方网站，http://financialservices.gov.in/banking-divisions/Financial-Institutions-and-others/Export-Import-Bank-of-India-(EXIM-Bank)。

机构的职能。SIDBI 还以贷款、赠款、股本和准股本的形式向非政府组织和微型金融机构提供财政援助，用于向微型企业和社会经济较弱阶层提供贷款，使它们能够在可持续的基础上从事创收活动。①

（4）国家住房银行。国家住房银行（NHB）是根据1987年议会法案设立的。国家住房管理局是住房方面的一个顶级金融机构，是促进住房融资机构以及为此类机构和类似事项提供财政和其他资助的主要机构。NHB登记、监管和监督住房融资公司，通过现场和非现场机制监督其活动，并与其他监管机构协调。②

（5）印度工业金融公司。印度工业金融公司（IFCI）成立于 1948 年，为印度工业提供中长期资金。IFCI 主要向制造业、服务业和基础设施部门提供中长期财政援助。通过其子公司和联系组织，IFCI 已多元化进入一系列其他业务，包括经纪、风险资本、金融咨询、存款服务、保理等。作为其发展任务的一部分，IFCI 是国家证券交易所、印度股份有限公司、技术咨询机构等的发起人之一。③

2. 外国企业融资条件

外国企业可以选择进入印度，在国内设立分支机构、项目或联络处。外国企业也可以选择与其他印度实体建立合资企业，或者以公司或有限责任合伙的形式设立自己的子公司，这些公司在印度法律下都被注册为印度实体。

如果外国实体选择建立印度的法人团体，它们可以选择通过外部母公司或外国银行（或其他允许的外国贷款人），按照 RBI 关于外来商业借款、贸易信贷、授权经销商和非授权经销商以外的外币借入和放款（ECB Master Direction）的规定，通过外部商业借贷（ECB）获得贷款来为该印度法人团体提供融资。ECB Master Direction 按照 FEMA 下三份与 ECB 相关的规定整合 ECB 框架。

---

① 印度小型工业发展银行（SIDBI）资料来源于金融部金融服务部官方网站，http://financialservices.gov.in/banking-divisions/Financial-Institutions-and-others/Small-Industries-Development-Bank-of-India%28SIDBI%29?page=2。

② 国家住房银行（NHB）资料来源于 GOI 财政部金融服务部官方网站，http://financialservices.gov.in/banking-divisions/Financial-Institutions-and-others/National-Housing-Bank-%28NHB%29?page=2。

③ 印度工业金融公司（IFCI）资料来源于 GOI 财政部金融服务部官方网站，http://financialservices.gov.in/banking-divisions/Financial-Institutions-and-others/Industrial-Finance-Corporation-of-India-(IFCI)。

①

ECB 是由合格居民实体从认可的非居民实体筹集的商业贷款，并应符合诸如最低期限、最终用途是否准许的规定、最高全额费用上限等参数。通过 ECB 融资的框架最近已被 RBI[②] 修订，并显著放宽了允许的放款人、以印度卢比计价的借款（RDB）和长期外币标价的借款（LTB）的规则。

根据修订框架，RBI 根据贷款期限、货币和最低平均期限（到期期限）创建了三类 ECB。这与《外汇管理（借贷或外汇借贷）条例》（ECB 条例）的先前规定完全不同，根据该条例，可根据期限、贷款人的类型、借款人的类型和资金的使用情况，按照自动途径或批准途径，利用 ECB。

（1）中期外币计价的 ECB，到期日为 3 ~ 5 年（轨道Ⅰ）。

① 金额：高达 5000 万美元的欧洲中央银行可以有 3 年的到期期限，超过 5000 万美元的 ECB 可以有 5 年的到期期限。以前，高达 2000 万美元的 ECB 可能只有 3 年的到期期限。

② 符合条件的借款人：轨道Ⅰ下的 ECB 符合条件的借款人名单有所缩小。根据轨道Ⅰ，合格的借款人是制造业和软件开发部门、航运和航空公司、SIDBI、特殊经济区（SEZ）中的公司或经营单位以及获得 RBI 许可的 EXIM 银行。

③ 认可的贷方：国际银行，多边、地区和政府所有的金融机构，出口信贷机构，设备供应商，外国股东（包括在借款实体中持有至少25%直接股权的外国直接股东，或在借款实体中至少持有51%间接股权的间接股权持有人，或拥有共同海外母公司的集团公司），印度银行的海外分支机构或附属机构（遵守适用的审慎准则），国际资本市场投资者，海外长期投资者，如审慎监管的金融实体、养老基金、保险公司、主权财富基金、位于印度国际金融服务中心的金融机构，是轨道Ⅰ认可的贷款人。修订后的框架除养老基金和保险公司等长期贷款机构外，还引入了ECB条例中列出的贷款机构，从而增加了轨道Ⅰ下的认可贷款机构。

① 《欧洲央行条例》、2000 年《外汇管理（转让或发行任何外国证券）条例》和 2000 年《外汇管理（担保）条例》。

② 外部商业借贷（ECB）政策——经修订的框架，RBI，［A.P.（DIR 系列）通函 32 号］2015 年 11 月 30 日。

④ 全成本上限：所有成本上限（印度借款人根据 ECB 向外国贷款人支付的总成本），其到期日为 3 ~ 5 年，在 6 个月伦敦银行同业拆借利率（LIBOR）或适用于某一特定货币的基准上，每年为 300 个基点。对于到期日超过 5 年的 ECB，在 6 个月伦敦银行同业拆借利率或适用于特定货币的基准上，每年为 450 个基点。在违约的情况下，应支付的罚金利息不得超过合同利息率的 2% 以上。全成本上限已经降低。此前，对于到期日为 3 ~ 5 年的 ECB，6 个月伦敦银行同业拆借利率为 350 个基点，对于到期日超过 5 年的 ECB，6 个月伦敦银行同业拆借利率上限为 500 个基点。

⑤ ECB 允许的最终用途：在修订框架下允许的最终用途基本上与 ECB 条例下的相同。除了现有允许的最终用途，航运公司和航空公司还可分别用于进口船只和飞机，以及支付已发运或进口但未付款的资本货物的费用。但是，进口规定的二手货物和 EXIM 银行贷款的 ECB 必须事先获得 RBI 批准才能允许。

此外，如果 ECB 由外国股东持有，而 ECB 的到期期限为 5 年，则 ECB 可用于一般企业目的，包括作为营运资金使用（包括在借款实体中持有至少 25% 直接股权的外国直接股东，或在借款实体中至少持有 51% 间接股权的间接股权持有人，或拥有共同海外母公司的集团公司）。这与以前的情况相比发生了重大变化，只有在到期期限为 7 年并且满足其他某些条件的情况下才可以为一般公司目的筹集 ECB。

但是，ECB 不允许用于在民用航空领域的营运资金，根据 100 亿美元计划获得持续外汇收入的企业偿还印度卢比贷款 / 新增资本支出，或修改框架下的低成本经济适用住房部分。

如果在 ECB 条例修订框架生效之前就贷款签署协议并获得贷款登记号码，则实体可根据 ECB 条例为上述最终用途募集 ECB，直至 2016 年 3 月 31 日。

（2）10 年 AM 的 LTB（轨道Ⅱ）。

① 金额和到期日：在轨道Ⅱ下，无论 ECB 的金额如何，ECB 的到期日将为 10 年。因此，符合条件的借款人（以下列出）只有在 ECB 有 10 年的到期期限时才符合轨道Ⅱ的资格。

② 合格借款人：轨道Ⅱ的合格借款人包括第一轨道合格借款人、基础设施行业公司、控股公司、核心投资公司、房地产基建信托基金（REITs）和基

础设施投资信托基金（INVITs）。这将为房地产投资信托基金和基础设施投资信托基金募集资金敞开大门，鉴于该领域的资金缺乏，这是非常必要的。

③ 认可的贷方：所有符合轨道 I（海外分支机构和印度银行子公司除外）的合格贷款机构均能够支付轨道Ⅱ的 ECB。

④ 全成本上限：伦敦银行同业拆借利率的最高息差可为每年 500 个基点，其余条件应符合轨道 I 的规定。预计长期 ECB 具有较高的全额成本上限将导致长期资金的可用性对印度的基础设施需求而言非常重要。

⑤ 允许的最终用途：第二轨道下的 ECB 可用于所有目的，但以下情况除外：房地产活动；在资本市场上的投资；将所得款项用于国内股权投资；以上述任何目标转贷给其他实体；购买土地。此外，控股公司可以使用 ECB 收益为其基础设施专用车辆提供贷款。经修订的框架仅规定了 LTB 许可最终用途的负面清单，这将使借款人（尤其是基础设施公司）能够筹集长期资金。

（3）成熟期为 3 ~ 5 年的 RDB（轨道Ⅲ）。

① 金额和到期日：轨道Ⅲ下的 ECB 金额和到期日与轨道 I 相同。

② 符合条件的借款人：根据 1956 年和 / 或 2013 年《公司法》注册的所有符合条件的借款人、非银行金融公司（NBFCs）和符合条件的 NBFC- 微型金融机构（MFIs），在中央或邦法规下注册的信托和合作社，从事小额贷款活动的非政府组织，从事支持基础设施的公司，提供物流服务和杂项服务的公司（包括研究开发和培训）以及经济特区和国家制造业和投资区的开发商（NMIZ）将有资格在轨道Ⅲ下进行借贷。经修订的轨道 III 下的新框架明确列入了符合条件的借款人，如物流服务公司等新类别。

③ 认可的贷方：所有符合轨道 I（海外分支机构和印度银行子公司除外）列出的合格贷款机构均可根据轨道Ⅲ授予 ECB。此外，NBFCs-MFIs，其他符合条件的小额信贷机构（非营利公司和非政府组织）能够利用规定的合格境外机构和个人的 ECB。

④ 全成本上限：全成本上限将符合市场条件，并且不会施加人为限制。

⑤ 允许的最终用途：ECB 可用于所有目的，但以下情况除外：房地产活动；在资本市场上的投资；将所得款项用于国内股权投资；以上述任何目标转贷给其他实体；购买土地。但是，对于 NBFCs、SEZs 和 NMIZs 的开发商，NBFCs-MFIs，其他合格的 MFIs，非政府组织以及根据 1956 年或 2013 年《公

司法》注册的非营利公司，ECB 所允许的最终用途有一定的限制。

此外，符合资格的机构可在每一财政年度的自动路线下，在三条轨道下，提高不超过以下所列限额的 ECB：基础设施和制造行业的公司最高 7.5 亿美元；软件开发部门的公司最高 2 亿美元；为从事小额信贷活动的实体提供最高 1 亿美元的资金；其他实体最高 5 亿美元或同等价值。

（三）兼并和收购

2013 年《公司法》、1961 年《所得税法》（ITA）以及任何其他印度立法中都没有界定“兼并”一词。“兼并”一词通常是指两家或两家以上的公司组合成一个联合实体。《公司法》规定了一种安排或折中方案的等价概念，该方案由一个公司、其股东和/或其债权人根据计划的性质而订立。[①]《公司法》还规定了“合并”[②]，通常指两家或两家以上公司合并成立新公司，合并后的公司不再存在的交易。

另外，收购或接管涉及一家公司收购另一家公司的股本或资产和负债的控股股份。根据程序不同，收购可能属于友好或敌对类别。收购人可以选择通过与目标公司签订协议，从公开市场购买目标公司的股份，或者直接向其股东要约收购目标公司的股份。这些交易通常通过股份收购或资产购买交易进行。以下立法主要管理印度的兼并和合并：

1. 2013 年《公司法》

有关印度非上市公司的兼并与收购受 2013 年《公司法》的规定约束，以确保投资者的利益不受影响。《公司法》第 230 条至第 240 条，与 2016 年《公司（折中、安排和合并）规则》一起形成了管理这些交易的代码，并规定了启用这些交易的程序。

如果一家公司决定与另一家公司合并，它必须通过其董事会的决议，然后向国家公司法庭（NCLT）（由其自己或与其他公司联合）提出合并申请，除此之外，还应附上形式为 NCLT-2 和 NCLT-6 的妥协或安排方案的副本，并附上所有必要的披露和费用。申请公司还必须披露每一类成员或债权人已被批准为 NCLT 批准该计划的依据。在收到 NCLT 的命令后，公司必须召开一

① 《公司法》第 230 条至第 232 条。

② 《公司法》第 232 条。

次全体债权人或类别债权人的会议，并向公司的所有成员或类别成员和债权证持有人发出一份按《公司法》的要求，以规定格式发出的通知，其中必须载有该计划的所有细节和其他细节。

然后，公司必须召开通知会议，批准该安排。该计划据说是在代表债权人价值四分之三的多数人或类别债权人或成员类别（视属何情况而定）亲自投票、以委托书或邮递投票方式投票同意的情况下，在会议上获得批准的。本次会议的主席必须在固定的时间表内向 NCLT 报告投票结果，然后以指定的形式向 NCLT 呈交请愿书，以批准该计划。[①]NCLT 将在审查文件后批准该计划。

《公司法》还规定了快速兼并、合并或分拆，在这种情况下，已付股本为 500 万印度卢比或营业额低于 2000 万印度卢比的私营公司不需要 NCLT 批准就能启动这些程序。

另外，GOI 早些时候只允许国内合并和收购，即合并后继续运营的合并公司是一家印度公司。然而，通过从 2017 年 4 月 13 日起生效的公告，GOI 公布了《公司法》第 234 条，允许印度公司与外国公司兼并或合并。[②] 第 234 条设想了两种合并——一家外国公司与一家印度公司合并，由此产生的实体是一家印度公司；一家印度公司与一家外国公司合并，由此产生的实体是一家外国公司。

根据《公司法》第 234 条申请与印度公司合并的外国公司必须满足某些要求，包括：

（1）属于管辖范围：① 其证券市场监管机构是国际证券监督委员会多边谅解备忘录的签署方或印度双边证券交易谅解备忘录的签署方；② 其中央银行是国际清算银行的成员；③ 在金融行动特别工作组的公开声明中没有将其列为具有战略性反洗钱或打击恐怖主义融资缺陷的管辖权，而对这些缺陷适用对策措施，或在解决这些缺陷方面没有取得足够进展，或未承诺与金融行动特别工作组共同制订一项行动计划，以解决这些缺陷。

（2）获得 RBI 的事先批准。

---

① 2016 年《公司（妥协，安排及合并）规则》。

② GOI 资料来源于公司事务部，http://www.mca.gov.in/Ministry/pdf/section234Notification_14042017.pdf。

（3）遵守《公司法》第 230 条至第 232 条及其规定的要求。

另外，如果一家在印度境外注册的外国公司正在合并为一家印度公司，则只需遵循上述步骤（2）和步骤（3）。

如上所述，一旦这些步骤得到遵守，妥协或安排计划连同寻求其批准的申请一并提交 NCLT。一旦获得 NCLT 的批准，各方就可以推进妥协或安排。

2. 2011 年《收购守则》

在印度上市公司的股份收购中，即上市公司在其股票上进行公开交易的情况下，还需要牢记 2011 年《SEBI（实质性收购股份和接管）规则》（《收购守则》）的规定。《收购守则》规定了一系列关于披露的严格要求，并规定了在这种股票收购超过收购守则门槛的情况下，公共股东可以选择退出。

《收购守则》规定，当收购者有权获得公司总股份或公司总表决权的 5% 以上时，收购人有义务在获得这些股份或表决权之前向目标公司和相关证券交易所披露其总持股。收购者需要根据收购人的持股门槛来满足额外的披露要求。此外，如果收购者获得超过 26% 的投票权和 / 或目标公司的控制权，则要求其向公司的公众股东提供强制退出公司的要约。为了实现这一强制退出要约，收购方必须提出至少收购目标公司 26% 的股份。《收购守则》还规定了确定此强制退出要约的要约价格的参数。

3. 《上市规则》

2015 年《SEBI（上市义务和披露要求）法规》（《上市规则》）适用于在印度证券交易所上市的印度公司。上市公司要继续上市，必须遵守《上市规则》规定的条件，包括以公平、迅速的方式向股东披露上市公司的所有重要信息。上市公司还与本次股票报价前的股票交易所签订了上市协议。本协议包括上市条款，并规定公司须遵守《上市规则》及上市协议的任何附加条款。

4. 《内幕交易法规》

另一个关于印度兼并和收购的相关立法是限制公司内部人士获取内幕信息（UPSI，即未公布的价格敏感信息）的一套 2015 年《内幕交易法规》，并通过交易公司证券从它们对 UPSI 的了解中获利。

就《内幕交易法规》而言，任何人如属于有关联的人、拥有或可使用任何 UPSI 的人，均为内幕人士。此外，根据《内幕交易法规》，每一个有关联的人都是内部人。另外，如果局外人访问或拥有任何 UPSI，外部人员即不是关联人员的人也将成为内部人员。实际上，任何 UPSI 的通信、UPSI 的采购和持有 UPSI 时的证券交易都不受内幕交易法规的许可。

（四）竞争规则

1. 部门监督竞争规定

印度竞争委员会（CCI）审查包括涉及外国实体的组合在内的组合，并检查是否存在对印度相关市场（由 CCI 确定）的竞争产生可观的不利影响的可能性。CCI 还拥有 CCI 总干事的调查权。

2. 《竞争法》简介

GOI 于 2009 年 8 月 28 日颁布了《竞争法》，取代了 1969 年《垄断和限制性贸易惯例法》（MRTP 法），自 2009 年 9 月 1 日起生效。这部《竞争法》将印度竞争执法的重点从限制垄断转向通过禁止反竞争协议、滥用支配地位和管制联合来促进公平竞争。

CCI 于 2003 年通过成立《竞争法》，并于 2009 年开始审理案件。CCI 规范反竞争行为，并有权下达命令纠正任何损害竞争的情况。此外，竞争上诉法庭（CAT）于 2009 年 5 月 15 日成立，是一个准司法机构，CAT 现在审理对 CCI 通过的命令提出的上诉。《竞争法》还将民事法院的管辖权排除在竞争委员会有权决定的所有事项之外。

GOI 授权 CCI 审查对竞争有明显不利影响的大型联合。《竞争法》规定了将一项交易视为“联合”的最低门槛，超过某个门槛的联合必须在生效或结束前通知 CCI。《竞争法》第 5 条规定了资产和营业额的界限，在此基础上各方可以评估特定交易是否需要事先通过 CCI 批准。

表 1　收购方和目标（联合）的门槛

资　　产	
在印度	200 亿印度卢比（2.985 亿美元）
全球	10 亿美元［包括印度至少 100 亿印度卢比（1.4925 亿美元）］
周　　转	
在印度	600 亿印度卢比（89.552 亿美元）
全球	30 亿美元（包括印度至少 300 亿印度卢比，即 44.776 亿美元）

表 2　收购方集团交易完成后的限额（包括目标）

资产	
在印度	800 亿印度卢比（11.9 亿美元）
全球	40 亿美元（包括印度至少 100 亿印度卢比，即 1.4925 亿美元）
周转	
在印度	2400 亿印度卢比（35.8 亿美元）
全球	120 亿美元（包括印度至少 300 亿印度卢比，即 44.776 亿美元）

最近，政府豁免了在印度资产价值不超过 35 亿印度卢比或在印度营业额不超过 100 亿印度卢比的企业的控制权、股份、表决权或资产的收购从 CCI 获得并购前批准（目标测试）的需要。此外，GOI 豁免了兼并和合并（包括《公司法》下的兼并和合并），不需要 CCI 批准，并修订了目标测试以计算企业用于此豁免目的的价值。现在，为了计算印度资产的价值和被收购、控制、兼并或合并的企业的营业额，只考虑实际被收购、兼并或合并的部门或特定业务的资产和营业额。因此，如果某项收购涉及剥离企业的一个业务部门，则只会考虑该业务部门的资产和营业额（而不是整个企业的资产和营业额），以检查目标测试是否满足。这项豁免有效期至 2021 年 3 月 4 日。

此外，《竞争法》规定，在交易通知送达 CCI 或 CCI 批准之日起 210 天之前，联合不能生效，以较早的日期为准。但是，这些要求不适用于风险投资基金，在 SEBI 注册的外国机构投资者和公共金融机构的投资，而且这些投资只需在收购日后 7 天内通知 CCI。

3. 管制竞争的措施

除了上面讨论的《竞争法》的程序，下列条例对于通知联合也是必不可少的：

（1）2011 年《印度竞争委员会（与组合有关的业务交易程序）条例》。

（2）2009 年《印度竞争委员会（一般）条例》。

（五）土地和房地产

1. 土地及房地产相关法律法规简介

印度有大量法律规范土地和房地产相关交易。房地产一般包括土地、建筑物、基本权利等。房地产可以按永久占有或者租赁的方式持有。在永久占有中，所有权人对财产拥有绝对权利，并可自由转让财产。动产所有权的证明是根据 1908 年《登记法》登记的转让文件，通常是一份转让契据。

在印度，邦政府对工业区的房地产拥有所有权。邦政府通常会与投资者签订长期租约，并为他们提供进入土地的途径。印度当局根据土地用途的意图将土地划分为不同的区域，即住宅区、商业区、工业区、经济特区等。经济特区向其单位提供各种奖励和优惠。住宅和商业处所，如公司的办事处，往往是以休假许可的方式提供的，而持牌人只有权占用和使用该处所，但无权取得对该处所的任何所有权。

从外国投资者的角度来看，管理印度不动产买卖的主要法规是2000年《外汇管理（印度不动产取得和转让）条例》（《不动产法规》），与 FEMA 一起解读。在印度境外居住的外国公司在印度设立了分支机构、办事处或其他业务地点，在印度进行任何允许的活动，可以在印度获得不动产以进行其业务。根据《不动产法规》取得不动产，外国实体必须遵守适用的土地法和房地产法，并须在取得任何财产后90日内，以规定的形式向印度储备银行提交申报。另外，一旦一家公司在印度注册，它就可以其名义购买、持有和处置财产。

2. 中央立法

（1）1872 年《印度合同法》：该法具体规定了当事方之间协议的基础，并规定了合同能力、协议的有效性、对协议的考虑、订立合同的意图以及任何此类协议条款的可行性等问题。

（2）1882 年《财产转让法》：1882 年《财产转让法》是印度财产转移的主要立法。关于不动产，它规定了转让人和受让人的资格标准、限制财产转让的条件、欺诈性转让、出售、交换、抵押和不动产押记、租赁、留置权、赠与等。

（3）1882 年《印度地役法》：1882 年《印度地役法》规定了个人的基本权利，即财产所有人必须迫使另一财产的所有人允许做某事，或为了占支配地位的物业单位的利益而不做某些事的权利。这项法案规定了道路权、照明权、航空权等权利。主张基本通行权的人，可以就强制令提出诉讼——限制妨碍通行或获得损害赔偿。

（4）1908 年《注册法》：该法案提供了一种公开登记管理印度任何不

动产的销售、抵押、赠与、租赁（1 年或更长时间）的文件的方法。它还管辖非遗嘱性文书的登记，这些文书的目的是创造、宣布、转让、限制或消灭不动产超过某一特定价值的任何权利、所有权或权益。[①] 根据本法登记与不动产有关的文件时，文件必须包括足以识别该文件的描述。[②]

（5）2013 年《获得公平补偿的权利和土地获取、恢复和重新安置透明度法》：该法已废除并取代 1894 年《土地征用法》，它规范了土地的获取，并规定了向印度受影响的人提供赔偿、恢复和重新安置的程序和规则。该法规定向被剥夺土地的人提供公平的赔偿，使购置土地的过程具有透明度，以建立工厂或建筑物、基础设施项目，并确保受影响者得到恢复。

（6）1899 年《印度印花税法》：1899 年《印度印花税法》和《国家特定印花税法》管理与印度不动产有关的文件的印花税。

（7）2016 年《房地产（监管和发展）法案》：该法旨在规范发起人与消费者之间的房地产交易，并引入了房地产项目注册等概念；发起人为房地产项目收到的资金存入单独的指定账户；在发起人的网站上显示与项目有关的细节以确保透明度；并强制发起人获得足够的保险以涵盖项目中的所有权和成本上升风险。该法旨在为加快房地产消费者与房地产开发商之间的纠纷解决铺平道路。该法的规定是对印度现有不动产法律的补充；但是，如果发生冲突，本法的规定将优先适用。

请注意，这些核心法案可能已被各邦部分修订，因此，在遵守其规定时必须谨慎。

3. 邦立法

除上述中央法律外，印度各邦在各自邦的领土内都有自己的管辖房地产的法令。主要的邦法案如下。

（1）《土地收入法案》：国家特定的土地收入法律规定了土地、公共道路等不属于其他人的国家的所有权。它们还规定了有关侵占公共土地、收入征收、维护土地权利记录等的规定。

（2）《国家租金管制法案》：国家特定的租金管制法律规定了除了某些明确的原因和规定的条件之外，保护承租人免遭租赁资产驱逐的条款；并保

① 1908 年《注册法》第 17 条。

② 1908 年《注册法》第 21 条。

护租客不必支付超过公平 / 标准的租金。此外，它们还规定房东有权驱逐犯有某些特定行为的房客，如转租、拖欠租金等，以及当房东要求房屋供他自己居住时。由于办公室往往是租用的财产，这些立法也对商业企业有意义。

（3）其他法案：此外，某些法令，如 1974 年《孟买大都会区域发展管理局法》，对孟买大都市区、马哈拉施特拉邦的发展和规划作出了规定。各邦的公寓和公寓的所有权也由某些法令管辖。

（六）税收

1. 税收政策和规则

在印度，征税的权力通常由中央政府和邦政府来分配。根据 1962 年《所得税规则》，中央政府负责所得税等直接税；而邦政府则负责增值税、印花税和入境税等间接税。自 2017 年 7 月 1 日起，印度实施了自独立以来最大的税制改革，制定了全面、双重的商品和服务税，取代了过去复杂、多层次的间接税制。

2. 主要类别和税率

（1）所得税。

① 公司应税收入的范围：居住在印度的公司应对其全球收入征税。居住在印度以外的公司仅在印度就以下收入征税：在印度累积或产生；在印度收到或视为已收到；非居民公司从印度的资产或收入来源（薪金、利息、版税和技术服务费）；来自印度境内的商业联系或因转移位于印度的资本资产而产生。商业联系一词通常用于印度税法中，而不是税务条约中提到的常设机构（PE），用于对企业产生的利润征税。业务联系一词在其范围上被认为比 PE 更广泛。

② 公司的居住地位：如果公司是印度企业，即该公司在印度注册，或其有效管理地点在该国，则该公司被视为印度居民。

③ 条约的压倒效应：根据《税务条例》，适用的避免双重征税协定（DTAA）的规定，只要对纳税人更有利，即凌驾于该协定的规定之上。因此，如果 DTAA 规定降低税率，或限制征税范围，则纳税人的责任将相应地受到限制。

④ 常设机构：通常，根据 DTAA（涉及企业利润征税）的规定，除非企业通过位于印度的 PE 在印度开展业务，否则缔约国不得对其他缔约国的企业

的利润征税。在某些情况下，外国客户可被视为在印度拥有 PE，在这种情况下，外国客户的某些可归因利润将在印度按约 44% 的税率纳税。另外，如果外国企业将雇员或其他人员派往印度，而这些人员在印度停留的时间超过 DTAA 中规定的提供包括的服务以外的服务，则可视为在印度提供服务。因此，从非常驻企业的角度看，外包合同的构建、对 PE 风险的审查以及采取措施缓解风险显得尤为重要。

⑤ 税务居留证：为了利用 DTAA 的优势，外国公司需要提供居住国税务机关出具的居留证副本以及 ITA 表格 10F 中的其他规定文件。

⑥ 技术服务的使用费和费用：根据 ITA，印度企业向非居民支付的任何此类款项都应在印度征税，税率为 10%（不包括附加费和教育费用），印度企业有义务对此类付款预扣税款。

⑦ 股息分配税：印度公司应按 15% 的税率缴纳股息分配税，并对支付的股息支付适用的附加费和教育税，实际税率为 20.36%。但须缴纳股息分配税的股息，不应由受助人征税。如果居民个人、印度教不分家庭或印度境内的商户收到的股息超过 100 万印度卢比，则按 10% 的税率征收附加税。

⑧ 最低替代税：只有在根据正常所得税规定应缴的税款低于调整后账面利润的 18.5%（不包括适用附加费和教育费用）的情况下，最低替代税才适用于调整后的公司账面利润。根据税收法规的正常规定，最低替代税额的税收抵免将被允许免除任何未来的纳税义务。

⑨ 公司以外实体的替代最低税率：如果备选最低税额超过所得税规定的应付款，则对这些实体（公司除外）按调整后总收入的 18.5%（不包括适用的附加费和教育程度）适用备用最低税率。根据 ITA 的规定，已支付的替代最低税额的税收抵免将被允许抵免任何未来的纳税义务。

⑩ 预扣税规定：任何人向印度境内的非居民或居民支付应课税的税款，均应根据 ITA 的有关规定，从此类付款中扣缴税款。如果没有永久账户号码，则可适用较高的预扣税率。但是，如果满足某些条件，这项规定就会放宽。

⑪ 利息支付减让性税率：对借入的外币的利息部分，可以实行 5% 的减让性扣缴税率。但是，这一福利须符合特定条件。

⑫ 股票回购：向股东回购股份的非上市公司应缴纳 20% 的附加税（不包括适用的附加费和教育费用）。本税由公司按回购金额与股票发行价之间

的差额支付（不可扣减的业务支出）。收到的回购金额免征收款人手中的税款。

⑬ 一般的反避税规则：一般的反避税规则规定授权印度税务当局宣布纳税人输入的“安排”是不允许的回避安排。其后果包括根据 ITA 的规定或适用的税收协定否认税收优惠。可对所输入的任何步骤或安排的一部分援引这些规定，并可宣布该安排或步骤为不允许的回避安排。不过，这些条文只适用于有关安排或步骤的主要目的是取得税项利益的情况。在下列情况下，反避税规则的规定不适用：相关纳税年度安排的税收优惠（所有各方）不超过 3000 万印度卢比；在 SEBI 注册的 FII 没有在非居民投资者的税收协定或 FII 投资项下享受任何利益；截至 2017 年 3 月 31 日的 FII 投资。

⑭ 间接转让条款：根据 ITA 的规定，非居民收入将被视为在印度直接或间接地通过或从任何业务联系、财产、资产或收入来源或从位于印度的资本资产（股份或其他利息）的转移中积累或产生。2012 年《金融法》引入了间接转移规定，明确指出，如果离岸资本资产的价值（直接或间接）实质上来自位于印度的资产，它将被视为位于印度境内。一般来说，对一家外国公司而言，只有当位于印度的资产价值超过 1 亿印度卢比，而且在印度的资产至少占离岸转让人公司拥有的所有资产价值的 50% 时，间接转让规定才适用。间接转让条款不适用于在 SEBI 注册的Ⅰ类和Ⅱ类 FPI。

⑮ 资本收益收入：资本资产转让所得收入按照资本利得收益征税。资本资产被定义为除纳税人为个人使用而持有的个人财产之外的任何财产。税率取决于收益是短期的还是长期的资本收益。此外，短期资本资产是指被在转让日期之前，评估人持有不超过 24 个月（除股票或优先股，在认可证券交易所上市的证券，共同基金单位等）持有的资本资产。除短期资本资产以外的资产被视为长期资本资产。长期资本利得税的税率为 20%（不包括附加费和教育费），短期资本利得税的税率为 30%（不包括附加费和教育费的居民）和 40%（不包括附加费和教育费的非居民）。

⑯ 其他来源的收入：任何特定收入项目未涵盖的任何收入，均应在其他来源的收入总目项下征税。为赚取这类收入而产生的全部和专门支出将允许扣减。

⑰ 赠与税：ITA 包含关于收受人（亲属除外）收受包括股份在内的金钱或财产的馈赠的征税规定，这些馈赠是纳税人在没有考虑的情况下，或超过

考虑范围 50000 印度卢比的情况下收取的。这类赠与将以居民 30% 的税率和非居民 40% 的税率在“其他来源”项下的受赠者手中征税。

⑱ 配发股份的溢价：私人公司将按照超过公平市场价格的居民股票发行金额的 30% 税率（不包括附加费和教育费）缴税。

⑲ 资本弱化规则：公司通常通过债务和股权的混合进行资本化。各国的税法通常允许扣除已支付的利息，从而允许公司确定其报告的利润数额。如果一家公司的债务融资较高，它可以申请更多的利息扣减，并报告较低的应纳税利润。因此，与股权相比，债务通常是一种税收效率高的融资方法。经合组织 BEPS 倡议之后，ITA 规定，支付给关联企业并由实体索赔的利息费用应限于利息、税收、折旧和摊销前收益的 30%，或以支付给关联企业的实际利息数额为限，以较少者为准。这一限制适用于印度公司，或作为借款人的外国公司的常设机构，该公司就向非居民或非居民的永久机构发行的任何形式的债务支付利息，并且是借款人的联营企业。

⑳ 转让定价：印度的转让定价规则规定，来自关联企业之间的国际交易或特定国内交易的任何收入均为公平交易价格。作为关联企业，除其他外，一个实体必须拥有超过规定限制的另一个实体的投票权；而且它必须有权在另一方的董事会中任命超过一半的董事。规则还规定了适用于公司和家族企业的具体关系。转让定价规则规定了以下五种确定任何交易的公平交易价格的方法：可比较的非控制价格法；成本加法法；转售价格法；利润分配法；交易净保证金法；任何其他方法，考虑到非关联方在不受控制的情况下在类似交易中收取的价格。如果在印度负有纳税义务的实体与其关联企业进行国际交易或指定的国内交易，则必须在提交纳税申报表之日或之前通知所得税主管部门此类交易。

㉑ 预先定价协议：ITA 支持纳税人和中央直接税局之间的预先定价协议（APA）。APA 规则提供了有关流程的详细指南以及信息、数据、费用详情，需要提交的表格等。纳税人可以在提交正式的 APA 申请之前，先进行预先备案咨询，这可以匿名方式完成。在双边 / 多边 APA 的情况下，纳税人的关联企业可以向另一个国家的主管当局启动 APA 程序。纳税人必须在 APA 适用期间提交年度合规报告。随着跨国公司努力应对经合组织基础侵蚀和利润转移项目的影响，以及国内立法改革，转让定价正变得越来越具有挑战性。通

过 APA 采取先发制人的方法来管理全球转移定价争端，既可以提高效率，也可以提高效率。ITA 还公布了 APA 回滚规则，这些规则为纳税人提供了一个选项，以便在前 4 年内将 APA 回滚到同一国际交易中，但需满足特定条件。

㉒ 平衡征税：随着信息和通信技术的扩大，数字化商品和服务的供应和采购在印度经历了指数式扩张。这些新的商业模式已经产生了新的税收挑战，即难以确定支付性质的特征，并建立税收交易或活动与税收管辖区之间的联系；以及寻找交易或活动以及确定纳税人的所得税目的困难。因此，在 ITA 中引入了一个名为“平衡征税”的新章节，规定对在印度没有常设机构的非居民在提供网上广告、数字广告或 GOI 可能规定的任何其他在线广告设施或服务时收取或应收的总报酬征收 6% 的均衡税。

㉓ 外国人的税收：因工作目的进入印度的外国人有责任缴纳税款，具体取决于他们在有关财政年度的居住状况。这是根据他们在国内实际存在的天数来计算的。印度的财政年度从任何一年的 4 月 1 日开始，到次年的 3 月 31 日结束。根据 ITA 的规定，如果符合下列条件之一，个人被认为是印度居民：在有关课税年度，他们在印度逗留了 182 日或以上；在相关纳税年度内，他们在印度已经工作了 60 日或更长时间，以及在前四个纳税年度内已经在印度工作了 365 天或更长时间。外国个人不符合上述条件的，在有关财政年度内，作为非居民缴税。

（2）所得税下的纳税申报和优惠。根据 ITA 的纳税申报是通过在 GOI 所得税部门的网站上提交所得税申报表（ITR）来进行的。这个过程是完全自动化的，并且有指导性计算器帮助纳税人计算对他的纳税责任。申报是根据上一年作出的。IT 制度中的税收优惠适用于个人纳税人和应纳税所得低于 25 万印度卢比和 30 万印度卢比的老年公民。①

（3）商品和服务税。从 2017 年 7 月 1 日起实行的商品和服务税（GST）是印度间接税改革领域的重要一步。

① 代替税收：商品及服务税已取代下列税种：由中央政府征收和收集的税，如中央消费税、消费税的特殊附加税、海关附加税、海关特殊附加税、服务税、中央附加税，以及与中央政府提供的货物与服务有关的税收；邦政

① 资料来源：http://www.incometaxindia.gov.in/charts%20%20tables/tax%20rates.htm。

府征收的增值税、中央销售税、奢侈品税、入境税、消费税、娱乐税（地方机构除外）、广告税、购置税、彩票税、博彩和赌博税，以及与商品和服务供应有关的邦附加税。目前，人类消费的酒精、石油产品，即石油原油、汽车用油（汽油）、高速柴油、天然气、航空涡轮燃料和电力，都被排除在商品和服务税范围之外。

② GST 的适用性：GST 适用于货物或服务的供应，而不适用于货物的制造、货物的销售或服务的提供，这是早先的概念。消费税是以目的消费税为基础的，而不是以原产地征税为基础的。换句话说，GST 将是在供应链所有点征收的增值税，并允许对用于供应的投入所支付的任何税收进行抵免。

③ CGST、SGST 和 IGST：GST 是以双重方式实施的，中央政府和邦政府在一个共同的税基上同时征收 GST。中央政府对国家内部货物或服务供应征收的商品或服务税称为中央商品和服务税（CGST），邦政府征收的商品或服务税称为邦商品和服务税（SGST）。同样，综合商品及服务税（IGST）由中央政府征收和管理出口（被认为是零额供应）和国家间商品和服务供应。根据被征税货物的种类，GST 税率目前固定在 0、5%、12%、18% 和 28%。

④ GST 下的税务申报和优惠。为减轻纳税人的负担，税务申报已全面电子化。货物和服务税网（GSTN）是 GOI 根据 1956 年《公司法》第 25 条作为一家私营公司设立的。GSTN 为纳税人提供三项前端服务，即协助开展 GST 注册，缴纳税款和申报纳税申报表。GSTN 还将为 31 个邦和选择此类模块的联盟区域开发后端 IT 模块。

目前，GST 制度允许向小规模纳税人提供税收优惠。普通门槛豁免适用于 CGST 和 SGST。年营业额为 200 万印度卢比的纳税人免缴商品及服务税。此外，年营业额高达 500 万印度卢比小规模纳税人（包括特定类别的制造商和服务提供商）可以使用复合办法（以不带进项税额的统一税率缴纳税款）。

三、贸易

（一）部门监督贸易

GOI 商业和工业部是管理印度内部和与其他国家贸易的首要机构。商务部与外贸总局和反倾销总局等有关部门合作，促进和保护进出印度的贸易。中央税务和海关委员会（CBEC）在国税部的工作中，也监督货物和服务进出口的关税、消费税和消费税的税率。

这些部门共同管理和监督印度贸易的各个方面，并在法律、规则、规章、通知、框架、方案等的广泛框架下发挥作用。

（二）贸易法规简介

1. 1975 年《海关关税法》

1962 年《海关关税法》规定对所有进口到印度的货物收取基本关税。1975 年《海关关税法》中提到了货物税的税率（源自国际统一制度命名法）以及关于关税的一般解释规则。

如果认为存在需要立即采取行动在突然增加进口某些类别商品时保护某些特定行业的利益的情况，则 GOI 也有权提供保障责任。在关键情况下，即使在不发现出口国倾销或补贴等不公平贸易做法的情况下，也允许征收临时保障税，但不得违反最惠国条款。临时保障税的有效期不得超过 200 天。[①]

GOI 可以对进口到本国的进口物品进一步征收反倾销税，价格低于类似司法管辖区中这些进口物品的价格。[②] 印度的反倾销条款是以 1994 年《GATT 第六条实施协定》（俗称《反倾销协定》）为基础的。

2. 2017 年 IGST 法

随着印度实行 GST 制度，反补贴税（为抵消优惠或补贴的影响而征收的额外进口税）和特别附加税（对进口货物支付的一种特殊关税）已归入 IGST。我们总结了商品及服务税对贸易的整体影响如下：

（1）货物进口：进入印度的每一个进口都将被视为邦际供应，并将与海关的基本关税一起接受 IGST。根据进口货物的价值和对货物征收的关税，将对任何进口物品征收 IGST。

（2）服务进口：商品及服务税制度规定服务接受者以非居民提供的服务按逆向收费缴纳税款。

（3）货物和服务出口：印度的出口属于零税率供应范围，并且在满足某

① 1975 年《海关关税法》第 8B 条。

② 1975 年《海关关税法》第 9A 条。

些条件的情况下不会对其收取消费税。

3. 1992 年《对外贸易（发展和管理）法》

鉴于对外贸易和对印度的投资自由化，GOI 已根据对外贸易政策（FTP）实施了各种计划，以激励对特定部门或地区的投资。印度的进出口受1992年《对外贸易（发展和管理）法》（FTA）管辖。中央政府成立了 FTA 下的对外贸易总局，负责制定和执行每五年修订一次的 FTP。

为鼓励出口，FTP 采用了各种计划，如出口促进资本货物计划，出口导向单位、电子硬件技术园区、软件技术园区、生物技术园区和经济特区。在电子硬件技术园区计划或 GOI 的软件技术园区计划下注册的单位在未经任何监管机构批准的情况下，允许自动路线下的外资参与率达到 100%。通过自动路线允许 100% 的出口导向型单位和经济特区的直接投资。

4. 2005 年《经济特区法案》

印度通过制定 2005 年《经济特区法案》，向 2021 年 4 月 1 日前经济特区的单位提供税收和其他福利，促进了经济特区的建立。经济特区单位必须为出口目的制造或生产货物或物品，或提供服务，应当按规定的生产百分比生产，或者达到规定的最低外汇利润。除制造业外，为出口目的，这些单位还可从事维修、再造、改造、再设计和提供专业服务等活动。

就经济特区单位而言，从商业生产开始之日起 15 年内，出口所得的利润可以免除。在印度，财政年度从 4 月 1 日延续到下一年的 3 月 31 日。其他税收优惠包括免税进口资本货物和原材料，免除中央消费税。经济特区的开发商还可以在 15 个连续的评估年度中的任何 10 年内获得免税期。但是，自 2012 年 4 月 1 日起，经济特区单位和开发商有义务支付最低的备用税以及自 2011 年 6 月 1 日起的股息分配税。

任何有兴趣设立单位的人都必须向有关当局申请。申请必须采用规定的格式，并且必须包括规定的附件和项目报告，详细说明项目的拟议地点、基础设施、财务预测和可行性。在大多数行业中，允许 100% 的外国直接投资在特区设立一个单位。

5. 邦和 MEIS 方案

印度政府推出了“印度服务出口计划”，从 2015 年 4 月 1 日起，根据现行 FTP（自 2015 年 4 月 1 日起运作），取代先前 2009—2015 年 FTP 下的“从印度提供服务”计划。根据“印度服务出口计划”，通知服务的服务提供者可按其外汇净收益的 3% 或 5% 的比率以可转让关税信用凭证作为奖励，这些收入可用于支付一些中央关税 / 税收，如基本关税。此外，现行 FTP 中的印度商品出口计划（MEIS）也奖励出口通过关税信用凭证在印度生产或制造的货物。[①]

6. 2000 年《外汇管理法》

FEMA 促进对进口商和出口商的外部贸易和支付，并监督印度的外汇市场。根据联邦紧急事务管理局的各种法规，例如，2015 年《外汇管理（商品和服务出口）条例》和 2000 年《外汇管理（许可资本账户交易）条例》，通过为印度的外国实体提供简化程序来促进贸易。

2015 年《外汇管理（商品和服务出口）条例》特别规定了出口申报程序和事先获得印度或 RBI 的贸易管制当局批准的情况、出口商可以提供的豁免申报、指定的申报机构等。

2000 年《外汇管理（许可资本账户交易）条例》管理在印度和印度以外的外币账户的维护、印度境内居民在印度和海外提高外币贷款等，从而协助出口商在海外交易。

（三）海关管理

为了简化从印度进口和出口，FTA 规定为每个进口商或出口商分配一个进口商—出口商代码[②]，该进口商—出口商代码将在进口商或出口商向任何指定机构、授权经销商银行或 RBI（视情况而定）提交的申报表的所有副本中标明。

为协助进口商和出口商，海关代理商或清算机构的服务可在国际港口和机场提供。海关代理人是由海关关长根据规定进行筛选后获得正式许可的专业专家团体。[③] 此外，CBEC 还任命了经 CBEC 批准发挥各种作用的经授权的经济经营者，如进口商、出口商、仓库所有人、海关代理人、货运代理和承

---

① 印度服务出口计划资料来源于 http://pib.nic.in/newsite/PrintReleasc.aspx?relid=155323。

② FTA 第 7 条。

③ 2004 年《海关代理许可条例》。

运人。[①]

各种公共和私营缔约方还提供综合海关管理系统，以支持和便利进出口流程，并降低相关成本。此外，它们还协助遵守与贸易有关的规定，并使海关处理、货物过境和向有关当局提交有关文件、货物和服务的适当分类、所需的一切形式的电子通信和文件印刷等过程顺利进行。

（四）进出口商品检验检疫

1. 印度出口检验委员会

印度出口检验委员会（EIC）由 GOI[②] 成立，旨在通过质量控制和装运前检验为发展出口贸易提供支持。EIC 公布商品及其最低出口标准，并建立合适的检验和质量控制机构。

除了其咨询作用外，EIC 还对五个出口检查机构进行技术和行政控制，这些机构分别设在钦奈、德里、科奇、加尔各答和孟买，这些机构是由商务部、GOI[③] 和与这些机构合作的 38 个分部和实验室为执行 EIC 的措施而设立的。

2. SPS 措施和在印度的实施

印度遵循世界贸易组织的《卫生和植物检疫措施协议》[④]（SPS 措施），其中规定了最终产品标准；工艺和生产方法；测试、检查、认证和批准程序；检疫处理，包括与运输动物或植物有关的相关要求，或与运输过程中生存所需的材料有关的要求；有关统计方法的规定，抽样程序和风险评估方法；以及与食品安全直接相关的包装和标签要求[⑤]。因此，GOI 已修改印度关于进出口商品检验检疫的法律法规以符合世界贸易组织的要求。

3. 植物和动物检疫

在与植物和植物有关的进出口方面，农业和农民福利部农业、合作和农

---

① CBEC 资料来源于税务局、GOI、授权经济运营商（AEO）实施计划——2012 年 11 月 16 日修订指南（2012 年第 28 号通告——海关）。

② 1963 年《出口（质量控制和检验）法》第 3 条。

③ 1963 年《出口（质量控制和检验）法》第 7 条。

④ 世界贸易组织《关于实施卫生和植物检疫措施的协定》，载 https://www.wto.org/english/tratop_e/sps_e/spsund_e.htm。

⑤ 世界贸易组织《关于实施卫生和植物检疫措施的协定》，载 https://www.wto.org/english/tratop_e/sps_e/spsund_e.htm。

民福利部下属的植物保护、检疫和储存局是管理当局。动物（尤其是畜牧业和相关产品）的相关进口和出口同样由 GOI 农业部的畜牧业、乳业和渔业部负责。各部门制定规章和程序，管理植物和动物以及所有相关产品进口到印度并制定检疫要求。

植物和植物产品出口前的检查和植物检疫证明是[①]以《国际植物保护公约》规定的方式进行的，也符合《濒危野生动植物物种国际贸易公约》关于禁止或限制植物物种详细清单的要求。[②]所有植物和植物产品及其他受管制物品只能通过政府不时为此公布的、属于有关国家或区域植物检疫站管辖范围内的特定入境港进口到印度。入境时，应当实行检疫，并经有关主管部门妥善检验、取样和实验室检验后，方可放行。[③]

在印度，所有畜产品只通过动物检疫和认证服务（AQCS）站进口，在那里动物和动物产品在放行前进行检疫和检验。AQCS 除其他外按照 1898 年《家畜进口法》的规定防止畜禽疾病的进入；执行关于牲畜和畜产品进出口的中央政府命令和通知；提供国际公认的扩大出口的认证服务；以及以调节、限制、禁止畜禽产品进口为目的，防范兽类重要外来病的传入。它还颁发了用于进口伴侣动物（仅限宠物狗和宠物猫）、动物（鸟类、哺乳动物、鱼类和爬行动物）、动物产品和成品皮革的无异议证书以及健康证明 / 出口健康证书，以促进活动物出口。[④]

一旦对进口 / 出口物品进行检查，并获得合格证书，这些物品将被发放给贸易商，供其采取进一步行动。

四、劳动

（一）劳动法规简介

在印度投资的公司需要了解印度的《劳动法》和《就业法》。许多邦政

① 《国际植物保护公约》第 4 条。

② 资料来源：http://plantquarantineindia.nic.in/pqispub/html/ExpCert%20Req.htm。

③ 2003 年《植物检疫令》（进口印度管理条例）。

④ 动物检疫和认证服务部，农业和农民福利部，畜牧业、乳业和渔业部，GOI，http://aqcsindia.gov.in/。

府都对中央政府通过的《劳动法》进行了修订。各邦政府也颁布了各自邦特有的《劳动法》。下文概述了一些关键的就业法规。一些邦政府也开始允许在自我认证的基础上遵守这些法律。

1. 1847 年《工业纠纷法》

1847 年《工业纠纷法》（IDA）是一项中央立法，规定了雇主与其工人之间的劳资纠纷的调查和解决。IDA 确定了对工业纠纷具有管辖权的各个当局以及需要遵守其规定的当事方。此外，IDA 规定了雇主在解雇、裁员、关闭、罢工、停工和其他雇用纠纷方面的法律义务。根据企业雇用的工人人数不同，规定了不同的程序。IDA 进一步规定了工作委员会[①] 和调解官员[②] 等各种机构来解决工业企业中工人、雇员和官员之间的纠纷。争议可能会升级到劳动法院[③]、劳动法庭[④] 或国家法庭[⑤]。

2. 1948 年《工厂法》

1948 年《工厂法》规定了与工厂劳动有关的法律，它规定了哪些场所可能被称为工厂，并且还包含有关健康、安全、成人工作时间、青年人就业等方面的条款。与《工厂法》规定的罪行有关的争端和申诉可向法院不低于院长会议治安法官或一级治安法官的法官提出。[⑥]

3. 1970 年《合同劳工（管理和废除）法》

1970 年《合同劳工（管理和废除）法》（CLA）适用于在前 12 个月内任何时间雇用 20 名或更多合同工的企业，或在前 12 个月内任何雇用 20 名或更多工人的承包商。企业是指从事工业、贸易、商业、制造业或职业的任何场所。《民事责任法》界定了承包商和主要雇主，并详细说明了他们各自与合同工人有关的责任。如果承包商不支付工资和法定福利，主要雇主有最终责任。此外，《劳资协议》载有多项改善合约劳工工作条件的条文。与《刑事诉讼法》下的罪行有关的争端可提交法院审理，任何法院低于院长会议治安法官或一级治安法官的法官都无权审判根据《刑事诉讼法》应受惩罚的任

① IDA 第 3 条。
② IDA 第 4 条和第 5 条。
③ IDA 第 7 条。
④ IDA 第 7A 条。
⑤ IDA 第 7B 条。
⑥ 1948 年《工厂法》第 105 条。

何罪行。[①]

4. 1972 年《酬金支付法案》

根据 1972 年《酬金支付法案》，任何在过去 12 个月内任何时间雇用 10 人或以上人员的商店或机构，任何工厂都必须向已连续服务超过 5 年的员工支付酬金。应酬金额按该雇员最后提取的工资计算，按每连续服务年度应支付的 15 日工资计算。这笔款项是在员工退休、辞职、退休或死亡时支付的。不过，雇主无须向因行为不当、道德败坏等情况而终止服务的雇员支付酬金。有关本法所述罪行的申诉可向法院不低于大都会治安法官或一级司法治安法官的法官提出。[②]

5. 1952 年《雇员公积金和杂项规定法案》

根据 1952 年《雇员公积金和杂项规定法案》（《公积金法》），雇主及其雇员须向公积金供款，而公积金的福利则由雇员享受。此外，这项立法还包括任何国际工作人员，即持有非印度护照的雇员。唯一的例外是印度已经进入社会保障均衡协议（SSA）的国家的国民，如比利时、德国、法国等。根据国际开发协会设立的法庭也有权根据《公积金法》审判犯罪和投诉。[③]

6. 1965 年《支付奖金法》

1965 年《支付奖金法》规定，在一个会计年度的任何一天，每一家工厂和每一家雇用 20 人以上的机构都要支付奖金。《支付奖金法》于 2015 年进行了修订，每月领取工资或工资不超过 21000 印度卢比的雇员有资格领取奖金，适用于支付奖金的员工范围有所扩大。修正案还将奖金计算上限提高至每月 7000 印度卢比或政府确定的预定就业最低工资，以较高者为准。《支付奖金法》规定的罪行可由法院不低于主席裁判官级别或第一级裁判官的法官审理。[④]

7. 《商店和企业法》

每个邦都有自己的《商店和企业法》（SEA）。SEA 涵盖雇员和雇主的法定义务和权利。根据 SEA 对商店或企业的定义，任何商业办公室都必须注册。SEA 还规定了与工作环境、每天和每周工作时间、休息时间间隔、开门

---

① CLA 第 26 条。

② 1972 年《报酬支付法》第 11 条。

③ 《公积金法》第 7D 条。

④ 《奖金支付法》第 30 条。

和关门时间、假期、就业和终止规则有关的其他要求和准则。通常情况下，管理人员不属于SEA的范畴。此外，工厂通常被排除在SEA的管辖范围内，因为它们受到《工厂法》的管辖。另外，每个国家在SEA中制定自己的规则。各邦政府规定的争端可由治安法官解决。

8. 1961年《学徒法》

1961年《学徒法》规定了对工业界学徒的培训，并规定了被任命为学徒的规则和条件，以及签订学徒合同的强制性要求。最近，《学徒法》已经修订，包括：危险行业雇用的学徒的最低年龄要求，以及学徒的工作时间和休假权利［根据雇主的判断（早先由1992年《学徒规则》确定）］。根据《学徒法》，没有具体审理案件的规定。[①] 案件可向任何有足够管辖权审判该法所述罪行的地方法官或法院提出。

（二）聘用外籍员工的要求

1. 工作许可证

对希望在印度开展业务或在印度就业的外国人提供两种主要类型的签证：工作签证和商务签证。外国人事务部、内政部与外国人地区注册办事处（FRRO）在印度的某些邦一起为希望进入印度的外国人办理签证手续。

（1）就业签证。工作签证是颁发给在印度注册的组织中在印度工作的外国人的。有关国家的大使馆或领事馆可向申请人发放工作签证，签证有效期通常为自签发之日起1年，无论合同如何，但高技能人员除外，该类人的签证可延长至3年。在印度有关邦，可从内政部或FRRO获得进一步的延期。

要获得工作签证的资格，该员工必须属于某些类别[②]，其中包括：

① 外国公民来印度担任印度公司支付固定报酬的合同顾问；

② 自谋职业的外国国民来印度提供工程、医疗、会计、法律或以独立顾问身份提供的其他高技能服务，但法律允许提供这种服务；

③ 印度公司向外国公司支付费用/特许权使用费中，外国公民向其提供技术支持/服务转让技术/服务；

④ 被外派公司聘用的高级管理人员和/或专家，他们被调往印度从事具

① 《学徒法》第33条。

② 工作签证（E）资料来源于移民局、GOI内政部、http://boi.gov.in/content/employment-visa-e。

体的项目 / 管理任务。

申请人还必须符合以下条件才有资格获得工作签证[①]：

① 申请人应是一名高技能和 / 或合格的专业人员，由印度的一家公司 / 组织 / 工业 / 企业根据合同或在高级职位、技术专家、高级行政人员或管理职位等的雇用基础上聘用或任命；

② 日常、普通或秘书 / 文职工作不会获得工作签证；

③ 员工的工资每年必须超过 25000 美元。

（2）商务签证。商务签证被严格地授予那些想与印度进行商务往来的人，如代表印度以外的公司进行销售或建立联系。商务签证自签发之日起，有效期可达 5 年，但可在这方面提出申请时予以延长。每次访问在印度停留的时间限于 6 个月。[②]

要获得商务签证：

① 申请人应是有保证的财务地位的人，并应具备拟从事的业务领域的专门知识；

② 申请人不得为货币借贷或小额贸易或全职工作，包括在印度支付工资而访问印度。申请人必须遵守所有其他要求，如缴纳税款等。

2. 申请流程

① 申请程序及费用。申请签证时，申请人应在网上填写签证申请，并将网上填写的申请和所需文件打印出来，前往最近的大使馆。这两种签证的费用取决于申请人所在国家的大使馆或领事馆。

② 所需文件。申请工作签证，申请人将需要下列适用于他的一些文件：有效期 6 个月的护照、护照大小照片、护照照片副本、网上填写的表格副本、委任书、合同书、申请人简历、组织登记、税务责任信、项目细节、印度组织的保证人信、雇主的证明信等。[③]

申请商务签证时，申请人需要下列文件：一本有效期为 6 个月的护照、护照大小照片、护照照片副本、网上填写的表格副本、印度组织的保荐信、

---

① 工作签证（E）资料来源于移民局、GOI 内政部、http://boi.gov.in/content/employment-visa-e。

② 商务签证（B）资料来源于移民局、GOI 内政部、http://boi.gov.in/content/business-visa-b。

③ 商务签证（B）资料来源于移民局、GOI 内政部、http://boi.gov.in/content/business-visa-b。

海外母公司的保证人信、证明其财务状况和在预定业务领域的专长等。[①]

3. 社会保险

《公积金法案》是印度的平等社会保障立法，它涵盖了母国尚未与印度签订 SSA 协议的在印度的国际雇员或工人。如果印度与申请者的母国之间存在 SSA，则 SSA 的规定将优先于《公积金法案》适用。对于不在 SSA 保障范围内的雇员或工人，其公积金缴费受《公积金法案》和 1952 年《雇员公积金计划》的管辖。国际雇员或工人必须根据《节约储金法》向有关当局登记，从其在印度就业的第一天起生效，而不论该雇员计划在印度逗留多长时间或他从任何就业中获得的收入。国际工人或雇员可根据《特别服务协定》的规定（如适用）或在其工作结束时，申领其公积金福利。

（三）劳动纠纷

不同的《劳工法》（可能由有关邦政府修订）规定了管理和裁决雇主和雇员之间争端的各种不同的当局。

为了减轻日后发生劳资纠纷的风险，雇主可采取若干步骤，消除雇员雇佣条款的含糊之处。通常的做法是向员工发出要约函和详细的雇佣合同，其中包括薪酬结构、利益冲突条款、保密和不公开要求、争议解决条款等，以确保员工充分了解自己关于工作机会的权利和责任。尽管印度的《劳动法》没有强制规定要约函或就业协议，但如果双方之间有任何争议，这些法律有助于保持双方之间的协议记录。

五、争议解决

（一）纠纷解决方法和机构

印度的争端解决方法可分为两大部分：诉讼（在印度法院系统中）和替代争议解决（包括斡旋、仲裁和调解程序）。

1. 诉讼

新德里最高法院是印度最高法院，其次是邦高等法院。司法机构的最低

① 商务签证（B）资料来源于移民局、GOI 内政部、http://boi.gov.in/content/business-visa-b。

级别包括遍布全国的各地区法院和小型法院。此外，还设立了所得税上诉法庭（税务案件）和 NCLT（2016 年 6 月 1 日起取代公司法委员会审理公司法争端）等法庭，就特定问题作出裁决。根据适用的法律规定，上诉可能涉及上诉委员会或高等法院（或者在 NCLT 决定上诉的情况下，上诉法院）。在某些情况下，如果被上诉的裁决来自一个法庭或一个与高等法院同等地位的委员会，上诉可以直接向最高法院提出。

除非在印度法院对判决提起新诉讼，否则大多数外国判决在印度是不可强制执行的。但是，印度承认某些国家的上级法院通过的法令，并且这些国家的上级法院通过的法令是可强制执行的，只要这些法令不违反印度的公共政策。

2. 替代争议解决

经修正的 1996 年《仲裁与调解法》是印度仲裁与调解的管辖法。印度也是《纽约公约》和《日内瓦公约》的签署国。印度的仲裁协议可以由外国法律管辖，只要该协议的一方是外国公民或实体。此外，在政府公布的领土内，根据上述两项公约中的任何一项公约，在商业法律关系引起的争端中作出的裁决被视为外国裁决。因此，外国裁决可在印度强制执行，许多外国公司与印度公司签订合并条款，规定仲裁应根据其国家的法律进行管辖。然而，一项外国裁决可能会受到质疑，理由是它违反了印度的公共政策，尽管印度法院已经限制了这一例外。

此外，法院和仲裁员鼓励各方通过调解解决争端。只有在双方进行磋商和讨论之后才能达成调解协议。这样的协议对当事人具有约束力，不具有上诉性。但是，当事人有权随时放弃调解程序，并在协议中援引仲裁条款（如有），或在任何具有管辖权的法院提起诉讼（在没有仲裁条款的情况下）。

调解是替代性争议解决的另一个重要的自愿方法。一名中立的、技术熟练的调解员通过试图达成妥协来帮助争议各方讨论和解决争议。各方可以自由选择不解决，或者决定解决方案的条款依据。根据 1908 年《民事诉讼法》第 89 条的规定，调解可以通过法院附设的程序或法院授权的程序进行，也可以通过争端各方之间的完全私人程序进行。法院附设或授权的程序对当事方具有约束力，不像私人调解的结果。调解使各方能够确定解决争端的时间、地点、条件和费用，从而成为解决争端的一种普遍选择。

（二）法律适用

如上所述，1996 年《仲裁和调解法》管辖印度的仲裁和调解程序。此外，诸如 1908 年《民事诉讼法》和 1973 年《刑事诉讼法》等某些法规通过规定在印度法院提起诉讼时应遵循的程序来协助印度的争端解决程序。

1908 年《民事诉讼法》规定了提起诉讼的文件和归档要求、某些特别诉讼的程序、向高级法院提出上诉的程序等。1973 年《刑事诉讼法》规定了调查任何罪行的方法、收集与犯罪有关的证据、审判期间和被定罪者的待遇、某些案件的惩罚数额等。

此外，1872 年《印度证据法》规定了印度法院对民事和刑事诉讼不同类型证据的可采性规定。1872 年《印度合同法》和 1897 年《通用条款法》也是印度法院经常提到的确定争议存在的基础或解决争端的文书。

2015 年，GOI 颁布了《高等法院商事法院、商事庭和商事上诉庭法》，该法规定在地区一级设立商业法院，并在高等法院和高等法院上诉庭设立审判庭，审理超过某一特定价值的商业纠纷。商业纠纷，包括与商人、银行家、金融家和贸易商的普通交易有关的争端，例如，与商业文件有关的争端，包括对此类文件的执行和解释；商品或服务的进出口；货物运输；基础设施合同，包括投标；以及其他特定类型的协议，现在将完全由根据本法设立的法院审理。这将减轻印度法院系统的过重负担，并能更快地解决争端。

印度投融资环境

Prof.Dr.N.L.Mitra,Partner
Fox Mandal & Associates

一、综述

（一）工作环境

印度在政治上是一个民主共和国，其经济目标是社会主义（就福利国家而言——以最广泛的形式建设市场社会主义），并在社会上致力于世俗主义，它必须确保正义、言论自由、机会平等和友爱。[①]

1. 政治环境

国家拥有中央强大的联邦结构，由 29 个邦省和两个联盟领土组成。印度议会和各邦立法机构选举代表的依据是五年任期，以成年人选举权为基础。议会实行两院制，LokSabha（下议院，545 名议员）、RajyaSabha（邦议会，245 名成员）由各邦立法成员选出，其中三分之一的议员任期满六年退休两年，而众议院选举则在五年的全部任期结束时举行。本届议会包括第十六届 LokSabha。政府是由一个或多个政党组成的联合政府。以现任总理纳伦德拉莫迪先生为首的部长会议是由全国民主联盟产生的，这个联盟是由 27 个主要政党和小党派组成的右翼合作组织。尽管印度人民党在议会中占绝对多数，

① 印度《宪法》序言如下：“我们印度人民决心将印度建设成为主权社会主义民主国家，并为所有公民争取：良好的法治、社会、经济和政治环境；自由的思想、表达、信仰和崇拜；平等的地位和机会；促使其中的所有法维尼亚人确保个人的尊严和国家的统一和完整；在 1949 年 11 月 26 日我们的组织大会这一天，在此采取行动，制定并产生我们自己的《宪法》。”

但是在保护奶牛等问题清单上确实引起了政治争议，特别是在食物权方面。

2. 经济环境

印度自独立以来，一直是一个国家驱动的经济体，直到1991年，发达的印度资本主义发展得非常不平衡。规划委员会运作了60年，已经结束并由NITIAAYOG取而代之。NITIAAYOG主要编写部门政策文件。首相请经济顾问委员会回来，在严格的“财政纪律”内，就10个经济参数向首相提供咨询意见。印度从计划经济向市场经济的发展步伐相对缓慢。印度从1919年开始实行可调整的外国直接投资政策，部门基础为初始国内需求驱动型增长，直到2001年，然后是计划委员会和财政部以国内需求为主导的增长政策。印度政府工业政策部有一项关于外国投资的窗口清理政策。DIPP现在被废除并实行自由化制度。除了少数被确定为“没有外国投资”政策的部门外，所有工业部门，包括矿山和矿产部门，都必须向外国直接投资开放，包括服务部门。有两个重要的经济运作方式，一是以淡化腐败和收回因腐败行为而产生的黑钱为目的的非货币化，二是将商品和服务税（GST）作为综合税征收。这两项经济措施都会立即产生反弹效应，也会对经济提振产生长期影响。

3. 社会环境

ManmohanSingh 博士在上届政府的三项重大议会法案中提出，将食物权和受教育权纳入令人印象深刻的基本权利清单，具有深远的社会和经济影响。最高法院最近的两项裁决也将对宗教和社会生活产生非常重大的影响，一项是关于穆斯林丈夫单方面宣布妻子离婚的三重标准，宣布这种做法违反印度《宪法》规定，侵犯了穆斯林妇女的平等权利；另一项是关于隐私权，宣布这是生命权的一个综合部分，是所有人的一项基本权利。

4. 法律环境

印度法律体系（ILS）以普通法体系为基础，主要基于书面和编纂的法律，通过司法解释的方式适用于每一案件的实际情况。由于国家是联邦制国家，根据印度《宪法》第 246 条的规定，国家和联邦政府之间的权力分配有三个清单。清单一规定了议会制定法律的权力以及高层管理人员按照联盟政府规定的项目进行管理的权力；清单二列举了邦立法机关立法的权力和国家行政机构管理列在表上项目的权力；清单三包含邦和联盟可以行使的权力清单。有关政府各部制定政策，必要时向议会提出有关法律和规则的建议。行政和监管权力属于有关政府的行政人员，而规定的监管权则分配给适当的监管机构。大多数调查领域属于联邦政府（印度政府）清单一，具体如表 1 所示：

表 1　国家和联邦政府之间的权力分配清单一

任务中提到的主题	权力（联盟 / 邦）	有关部门
1. 投资	联盟	工业部
（1）市场准入	联盟	财政部
（2）财政	联盟	财政部
（3）兼并与收购	联盟	公司事务部
（4）竞争管理	联盟	公司事务部
（5）土地和房地产	邦	土地和土地收入部
（6）税务	联盟	财政部
2. 贸易	联盟	商务部
（1）部门	联盟	商务部—进出口部
（2）贸易法	联盟	Do
（3）贸易管理	联盟	Do
（4）检查	联盟	Do——运输和运输部
（5）海关	联盟	财政部
3. 劳工		
（1）法律	邦和联盟	法律和司法部
（2）处理外国雇员	联盟	外交部
（3）劳工纠纷	邦	司法部
4. 争议解决		
（1）方法和机构	邦	高等法院及法律和司法部
（2）法律适用	邦	高等法院

印度正在迅速发展形成一种混合法律文化，在大多数民事和商业及投资活动中纳入监管制度，然后由印度最高法院的司法复审权对其进行裁判。表 2 显示了分配的任务、管理权力机构和有权对监管机构的命令作出决定的法庭的名称。大多数法庭都没有权利向有关高等法院提出上诉。监管上诉法庭通

过民事法院和高等法院的管辖权，加快了对商业纠纷的裁决。

表 2 分配的任务、管理权力机构和有权对监管机构的命令作出决定的法庭名称

任务中提到的主题	有关部门	监管者	法庭
1. 投资	联盟财政部	印度证券交易委员会	SEBI 上诉法庭
（1）市场准入	Do	Do	Do
（2）财政	Do	印度储备银行 / 公司事务部 /SEBI	Do
（3）兼并与收购	联盟公司事务部	SEBI/ 竞争委员会	SEBI 上诉委员会 / 竞争委员会上诉会
（4）竞争管理	Do	竞争委员会	竞争委员会上诉法庭
（5）土地和不动产	邦土地和土地收入部	收入委员会	民事法庭
（6）税务	联盟财政部	收入部门	部门和上诉官员 / 上诉委员会
2. 贸易	联盟对外贸易部		
（1）部门	Do	对外贸易部	上诉机构，SLP 下的 HC 和 SCI
（2）贸易法	联盟法律和司法部		
（3）贸易管理		Do	
（4）检查		Do	
（5）海关	联盟财政部	海关和货物税司	部门上诉机构，HC 和 SCI 上诉处
3. 劳工	联盟 / 邦劳动与就业部	根据各种劳工和工业法进行检查	劳动上诉法庭，HC 和 SCI 特别请愿书（SLP）
（1）法律			
（2）处理外国雇员	联盟外交部	护照和签证办公室	HCandSCI 的 SLP
（3）劳工纠纷	联盟 / 邦部门	部门调解和调停的官员	劳工上诉法庭，HC 上诉处和 SCI 上诉处
4. 争议解决			
（1）方法和机构	联盟 / 邦法律和司法部	方法：调解、调停、仲裁	HC 上诉处，SCI 的 SLP
（2）法律适用	Do	检察员	劳工上诉法庭；HC 上诉处，SCI 的 SLP

最近，议会颁布了《破产法》，作为退出的法律手段之一。任何问题都有以下的法律规定：（1）议会 / 立法机构通过的法案和法规；（2）由监管机

构根据该条款的规定制定的条例；（3）监管机构根据该法的规定制定的法规；（4）部门 / 监管机构的授权下的指示、命令通知；（5）该法赋予的指导方针和咨询说明；（6）内政部的新闻稿。政策文件仅仅是没有法律效力的指令。监管当局拥有完整的权力来规范该系统的运作，并提供命令、指示和指导方针。违反监管秩序或方针，应向监管上诉法庭提出上诉。

所有与外国当事人的协议都必须有仲裁条款来处理商业和公司纠纷。印度的仲裁遵循印度仲裁委员会制定的规则。不过，当事各方可自由选择国际商会所规定的仲裁中心、程序和仲裁规则。仲裁裁决必须通过法院命令来执行，因此，裁决须由拥有管辖权的执行令的最高法院作出。

印度的司法制度如下：所有商业、民事和刑事案件都在地区一级由地区法院审理。从地区法院向具有管辖权的高等法院提出上诉，然后再向最高法院提出特别请愿书（SLP）。法律专业人士可分为两种：一是邦方面包括地区层面上公共起诉人 / 政府请愿者的法律专家和高等法院层面上的法律总顾问 / 总检察长（在一些邦的刑事案件中）的法律专家；二是私人法律从业人员（称为律师），主要为私人当事人提供服务，一般由律师事务所处理一般的公司和商业案件，包括银行和金融、兼并和收购以及外国投资，这些律师事务所（如英国律师事务所）处理公司和企业的一切事务。

（二）中印关系

从历史上看，印度和中国是相互关联的，而中国游客实际上也给印度文明带来了丰富的遗产。年轻的中国佛教僧人玄宗大约在 1500 年前来到印度，并写了关于印度历史和文化的文章。在中国共产党革命运动初期，当日本占领中国时，五名年轻的印度医生与柯棣华医生一起，被印度国民大会派遣到医疗服务小组中，在争取共产主义运动的激烈斗争中为中国人民服务。柯棣华医生至今仍受到中国政府的尊重。印度与中国两大文明古国，目前在政治和经济上都是两个最大、最强的力量，两者之间有文化联系也有政治摩擦，尤其与两国之间的喜马拉雅边界有关的政治摩擦。但是，许多通过文化、贸易、商务和人民之间的关系而产生的良好关系比在边界问题上的某些利益冲突更为有力。

印度的贸易关系由来已久，虽然在 20 世纪 90 年代初，印度的贸易篮子很小，当印度和中国这两个国家在1991年开始全面的经济改革时，双边贸易关系自然地被忽略不计。到2008年，中国成为印度最大的贸易伙伴。到2012年，印度对中国的贸易逆差达到391亿美元（国际货币基金组织，2013）。贸易失衡主要是由于国内需求拉动经济增长的DDLG政策、外国投资和中国的出口带动经济增长（ELG）的间接性特性所导致的印度国内消费增加。印度目前的“印度制造”政策强调制造业，现在可能会进行投资，以增加对ELG的重视，并通过降低DDLG进行投资调整。2008年中国加大对DDLG投资力度的政策调整——10次ELG的调整，这可能会扩大中国在印度各部门投资的机会，特别是钢铁、替代能源、基础结构发展等领域，增加从印度扩大商品和服务进口的机会。印度通过亚洲和南盟区域协会与东亚和南亚国家不断发生贸易关系，也为中印贸易关系开辟了一个新的机遇。中国很有可能通过投资制造/组装硬件、电信和电子产品来利用“印度制造”政策，中国也可能会安排技术转让以增加与印度公司的合资企业。由于在这两个国家中，国家在经济运作中起着领导作用，因此许多事情都取决于双边谈判。中国在“一带一路”倡议中，将中国、巴基斯坦、阿富汗、俄罗斯、伊朗、孟加拉国、缅甸、印度、印度尼西亚、马来西亚等国家，通过丝绸之路经济带和21世纪海上丝绸之路连接起来，该倡议旨在在欧亚大陆建立一条综合的经济走廊，包括公路、铁路、交通公路、经济开发区。中国在积极发展的政策下设立了一个400亿美元的基金，但在最近召开的金砖国家北京会议上，成员国还未能就“一带一路”达成协议，尤其是出于政治方面的考虑。

印度反倾销局隶属于商务部和印度联合秘书部，并利用中国加入世界贸易组织和取得最惠国地位的条件，向中国提出了最多的反倾销指控。经济学家认为，这是一个初期问题，两大发展中经济体未来必须有更好的经贸合作和贸易关系，这样才能实现TRIMs协议。

二、投资

印度从1991开始就从指挥经济转向全球经济，以适应经济全球化的进程。印度采用了国内需求拉动增长（DDLR）计划，打算用拖沓的校准方法，调整其开放投资大门的经济计划。不过，印度的农业部门不对任何外国投资开放，除了缓慢限制部门覆盖面，在该部门规定的受管制条件下允许外部投资于商农领域，如园艺、养蚕、畜牧业、畜牧、花卉养殖、养蜂业、种籽和蔬菜种植。在过去的十五年经济改革中，印度资本家大量地涌现，印度工业企业现在越来越多地在印度以外的地区投资。但是，农业和农场的资本流动远远不能满足需求。

（一）国内投资

直到 1991 年，印度都遵循一个非常僵硬的经济结构形式，即由国家驱动指挥经济，通过一个计划委员会来管理根本规划并以自上而下的方式进行规划和发展。然而，自 1991 年以后至今，只有农业和相关部门一直保持原有的状态，完全保持小规模的独立运作方式，仍然无法通过公司组织结构加以规范。

（二）在印度的外国直接投资（FDI）

寻求外国直接投资的主要目标是吸引和促进投资，以补充国内资本、技术和技能，促进经济增长。为此，印度政府制定了一个称为外国直接投资政策的政策框架。政府密切关注印度的投资情况，并因此不断更新和修改外国直接投资政策。最近的修订发生在 2017 年 8 月 28 日，当时工业政策和促进部（DIPP）发布了 2017—2018 年更新和修订的外国直接投资政策（FDI 政策，2017 年）。

（三）可以通过 FDI 投资的实体

在印度成立的公司：可以是私人或公共有限公司，允许全资和合资企业，私人有限公司要求最少有 2 名股东。

有限责任合伙：允许根据政府途径，在自动路径下无条件允许 100% 外国直接投资的部门。

独资或合伙公司：在印度储备银行批准下，印度储备银行与印度政府协商决定申请。

联络处，分局（BO）或项目办（PO）：这些办事处只能开展印度储备银行指定的活动，政府和印度储备银行授予批准书。满足特定条件的 BO/PO 可以适用自动路径。

其他结构：外国投资或对非营利公司等其他机构的出资也须遵守《外国捐款管理法》（FCRA）的规定。

（四）外商投资

经济投资规范在部门上被划分为几条对外投资的定标线，这样“亚洲虎”的现象就不会再发生。过去 20 年左右，经济对外国投资的开放程度已经得到了校准。该政策由外国投资促进委员会（FIPB）监督，且最近关闭了一个窗口清算系统，因为该问题已经直接由财政部和总理办公室（PMO）处理。框架如下：

（1）投资高达 100% 的完全没有任何监管要求的行业，通常被称为“自动和 100% 外国直接投资”，包括建筑和发展以及基础设施等核心部门在内的制造业工业部门的大部分经济活动属于这一类。

（2）自动化程度达到一定投资水平并高于所需总投资比例，且高于先期许可所需的部门。国防材料生产、银行和保险业、零售业等一些行业属于这一类。

（3）有些行业不是自动化的，而是走有条件的批准路线。目前这份清单非常短，如在可控制条件下生产种子和蔬菜可能被允许吸收高达 100% 的外国投资。

（4）现在有些部门还被允许吸引外国投资，如核能、赌博、农业，除上述以外，还包括房地产。

在对部门具体说明的一些详细分析中有一些讨论。有关法律制度载于 2000 年《外汇管理法》和关于外国投资的两项条例，即 2000 年《外汇管理（印度以外居民收购和转让安全）条例》以及 2004 年《FEMA（任何外国证券的转让或发行）条例》。此外，每年印度储备银行都会通知 MasterCirculars，来回提供最新的外商投资框架。

（五）根据外国直接投资政策发布的证券类型

股票：根据《公司法》规定发行的股权（如适用），应当包括已部分支付的股权。

优先股：优先股必须全额支付，并且应强制并完全转换为股票。

企业债券：债券应要求全额支付，并应强制和完全转换为股票。

认股权证：完全强制性和强制性可转换认股权证。此外，认股权证包括由印度公司根据公司法条款（如适用）发行的股份认股权证。

（六）2017 年外国直接投资政策

2017 年外国直接投资政策对以前的 2016 年外国直接投资政策进行了以下重要修订。主要修订内容如下：

取消外国投资促进委员会（FIPB）：对外国直接投资制度最重大的修改是由经济事务部发布的 2017 年 6 月 5 日公布的通知所带来的制度变化，确认取消 FIPB（以前的政府机构，授权批准需要政府批准的外国直接投资提案）；并引入了"外商投资便利化门户"（FIFP）这一行政机构来惠及外国直接投资申请人。

"2017 年外国直接投资政策"将行业特定的行政部委 / 部门定义和列为"主管部门"，其被授权准予政府批准外国直接投资。"2017 年外国直接投资政策"中列出的主管部门包括在单一品牌、多品牌和食品零售贸易方面的外国直接投资申请的 DIPP，以及印度经济事务部在金融服务部门的外国直接投资申请的 DIPP。

DIPP 还发布了"标准作业程序"（SOP），其中规定了申请的详细程序和时间表，以及处理政府批准印度外国直接投资的"主管当局"名单。

根据 SOP，投资者需要在 FIFP 网站上提出申请，并提交指定文件，包括相关的特许文件、董事会决议等。然后在两天内，将申请提交给有关主管部门和印度储备银行（根据《外汇法》的角度发表意见）。需要安全许可的提案（如国防和电信等领域）也应提交给内政部。主管当局应按照 SOP 规定的格式处理完整的提案并将该提案的批准 / 拒绝转交给申请人。

（七）禁止的行业

以下行业禁止吸收外资：彩票业务，包括政府 / 私人彩票、网上彩票等；赌博和赌钱，包括赌场等；银会；Nidhi 公司；可转让发展权贸易（TDRs）；房地产业务或农庄建设；制造烟草或烟草替代品的雪茄、方头雪茄烟、小雪茄和香烟；不对私营部门投资开放的活动 / 部门，如原子能和铁路运营。

（八）许可的行业

1. 农牧业

在以下活动中，通过自动路径允许该部门的外商直接投资达到100%：

（1）受控条件下的花卉栽培、园艺和蔬菜及蘑菇栽培；

（2）种子和种植材料的开发和生产；

（3）畜牧业（包括养殖狗）、养鱼业、水产养殖业、养蜂业；

（4）与农业和相关行业有关的服务。

除此之外，任何其他农业部门 / 活动都不允许外国直接投资。

2. 种植园行业

在以下活动中，允许自动路径下的100%外商直接投资：

（1）茶叶行业，包括茶园；

（2）咖啡种植园；

（3）橡胶种植园；

（4）小豆蔻种植园；

（5）棕榈油树种植园；

（6）橄榄油树种植园。

除此之外，任何其他种植园部门 / 活动都不允许外国直接投资。此外，如果将来出现土地使用变化，需要事先获得有关邦政府的批准。

3. 采矿、石油和天然气

（1）矿业。以下活动允许100%的外国直接投资：

① 采矿和勘探金属和非金属矿石，包括钻石、金、银和贵重矿石，但不包括含钛矿物及其矿石；受制于1957年《通过自动路径的矿山和矿物（发展和管理）法案》。

② 通过自动路线进行的煤炭和褐煤开采，供电力项目、钢铁和水泥单位以及1973年《煤矿（国有化）法》规定允许的其他符合条件的煤炭和褐煤开采活动。

③ 通过自动路线建设洗煤厂等煤炭加工厂，但条件是公司不得开采煤炭，不得在公开市场上销售其选煤厂的洗煤或煤粒，并应向那些提供原煤给煤炭加工厂进行洗煤和分选的各方供应经过洗煤和分选的煤炭。

④ 含钛矿石和矿石通过政府途径的采矿和矿物分离，其增值和综合活动符合部门规章和 1957 年《矿山和矿物（开发和法规）法》。

⑤ 用于分离含钛矿物和矿石的外国直接投资将受到下列附加条件的制约:

• 在印度境内设立增值设施，同时进行技术转让；

• 在矿物分离过程中处理尾矿应按照原子能监管委员会框架的规定执行，如2004年《原子能（辐射防护）规则》和1987年《原子能（安全处置放射性废物）规则》；

• 对于 2006 年 1 月 18 日由原子能部发布的通报 No.S.O.61（E）中列出的采掘“指定物质”时，不允许外国直接投资。

（2）石油和天然气。石油和天然气领域的勘探活动、与石油产品和天然气销售相关的基础设施、天然气和石油产品的销售、石油产品管线、天然气 / 管道、LNG 再气化基础设施、市场研究和制定以及私营部门的炼油业务允许 100% 外国直接投资，但须遵守石油销售部门现有的部门政策和监管框架以及政府关于私人参与勘探石油和国有石油公司发现油田的政策。

然而，公共部门承诺（PSU）在石油炼制过程中允许通过自动路径进行 49% 的外商直接投资，而不会对现有事业单位的国内股权进行任何撤资或摊薄。

4. 制造业

根据外国直接投资政策的规定，制造部门的外国投资处于自动化路径之下。此外，制造商被允许不经过政府批准而通过批发和 / 或零售（包括通过电子商务）销售其在印度制造的产品。

尽管有关于贸易部门的外国直接投资政策规定，但对于涉及印度制造和 / 或生产的食品的零售交易，允许进行政府批准路线下的 100% 外商直接投资，包括通过电子商务的零售。

5. 国防工业

根据 1951 年的《工业（发展和管理）法》，国防工业允许外商直接投资，但须获得工业许可；根据 1959 年《武器法》制造小型武器和弹药。国防工业部门允许 100% 的外国直接投资，但只有 49% 通过自动路径，超过 49% 的，凡投资可能导致获得现代技术，或因由有关当局记录的其他原因的，均须经政府批准。

有关外国直接投资的其他条件如下：

（1）在允许的自动路线水平内注入新的外国投资，如果公司不寻求取得工业许可证，导致现有投资者改变所有权模式或将股份转让给新的外国投资者，则需要政府批准。

（2）商业和工业部产业政策与推广部会同国防部和外交部进行磋商，并考虑许可证申请和颁发许可证。

（3）该部门的外国投资受到国防部的安全审查和指导。

（4）被投资公司应在产品设计和开发方面做到自给自足，被投资公司/合资公司以及制造工厂也应该有对在印度制造的产品的维护和全生命周期的支持设施。

6. 服务业

（1）广播。电子传输［（建立上行枢纽/传输）、直播电视、有线网络（多系统运营商（MSOs），用于实现数字化和寻址能力的网络升级］、移动电视、天空头端（HITs）以及由其他不用于实现数字化和寻址能力的网络升级的 MSO 组成的有线网络和本地有线运营商，允许高达 100% 的外国直接投资。

在地面广播调频（调频广播）情况下的广播内容服务和上行“新闻与时事”电视频道中，允许通过政府路径的高达 49% 的外国直接投资。

在上行“非新闻和时事”电视频道中，允许自动路径下的外国直接投资达到 100%。

但是，如果公司已经有许可证，且投资是用于导致所有权模式发生变化的外国投资，或现有投资者将股份转让给新的外国投资者的情况，也需要政府批准。

（2）印刷媒体。目前的政策允许处理新闻和时事的报纸和期刊通过政府路线吸收 26% 的外国直接投资。这类投资须遵守 2008 年 4 月 12 日由信息和广播部发布的印度版外国杂志处理新闻和时事指南。

7. 民用航空业

民航部门的外国直接投资政策可分为以下几部分：机场、航空运输服务、民用航空领域的其他服务。

（1）机场。在绿色地块项目中，允许自动路径下 100% 的外商直接投资。在棕色地块项目中，允许 100% 的外国直接投资。其中，通过自动路径允许最多 74% 的外商直接投资，而超过 74% 的外商直接投资需要政府批准。

（2）航空运输服务。对于定期航空运输服务和区域航空运输服务，外国直接投资可达 100%。其中，通过自动路径的允许最多 49% 的外国直接投资，而超过 49% 的外国直接投资则需要政府批准。但是，NRI 投资者允许通过自动路径进行高达 100% 的外国直接投资。对于非定期航空运输服务，允许通过自动路径进行高达 100% 的外国直接投资。对于直升机和水上飞机服务，通过自动路径允许进行高达 100% 的外国直接投资。

（3）民用航空领域的其他服务。在地勤服务、MROs、飞行培训机构和技术培训机构中，允许通过自动路径进行最高 100% 的外国直接投资。此外，投资上述三个方面的一些附带条件如下：

① 航空运输服务将包括国内定期客运航空公司；非定期航空运输服务、直升机和水上飞机服务。

② 根据上述限制和入境路线，允许外国航空公司参与经营货运航线、直升机和水上飞机服务的公司的股权。

③ 外国航空公司也允许向运营定期和不定期的航空运输服务的印度公司投资资本，最多允许投资达到其实收资本的 49%。这种投资将受到一些条件的限制，例如，要根据 GOI 批准路线进行；49% 的限制将包含 FDI 和 FII/FPI 投资；如此进行的投资将需要遵守相关的 SEBI 法规以及其他适用的规则和条例；只有在印度注册营业地点的公司才能授予预定经营许可证，主席和至少三分之二的董事是印度公民，印度国民等拥有实质性所有权和控制权。

8. 建设发展：乡镇、住房、建成基础设施

在发展部门，允许自动路径下的外国直接投资达到 100%。但此类投资要受到以下条件限制：

（1）每个项目下要开发的最小面积为：

① 在发展公用地块时，没有最低的土地限制要求。

② 在建设开发项目的情况下，最低建筑面积为 20000 平方米。

③ 如果是组合项目，则需要同时遵守上述两个条件。

（2）被投资公司必须在项目启动后 6 个月内吸收最低限额为 500 万美元的外国直接投资，该项目的启动日期是相关法定机构批准建筑计划 / 布局计划的日期。随后的外国直接投资可从项目开始起至 10 年期间内或在项目完成之前进行，两者以较早的期限为准。

（3）投资者将获准在项目完成后或自最后投资之日起3年后退出，但须发展干线基础设施。

（4）根据事实和情况，政府可在项目完成前允许一名非居民投资者将外国直接投资或股权转让给另一非居民投资者。这些方案将由FIPB根据具体情况进行审议。

（5）该项目应符合适用的建筑物管理条例、邦政府 / 市政府 / 地方政府的规则和其他条例中规定的规范和标准。

（6）该项目应符合由有关邦政府 / 市政府 / 地方政府制定的可适用的建筑物管制规例、附例、规则及其他规例所规定的规范和标准，包括土地使用要求以及社区设施和公共设施的规定。

（7）被投资的印度公司只允许获准出售已开发的地块。就本政策而言，所开发的地块意味着提供包括道路、供水、街道照明、排水和排污等主干基础设施的地块。

（8）被投资的印度公司应负责取得所有必要的审批，包括建筑/布局规划、开发内部和周边地区及其他基础设施、开发支付、外部开发和其他费用的审批，并遵守邦政府/市政/当地有关机构的适用规则/规章/条例所规定的所有其他要求。

（9）有关邦政府 / 市政 / 地方机构批准建筑 / 开发计划，将监测开发商是否遵守上述条件。

9. 工业园区

新的和现有的工业园区允许通过自动路径实现最高100%的直接投资。根据外国直接投资政策，工业园是一个项目，在该项目中，为工业活动的目的，开发并向所有分配单位提供以已开发土地或已建空间为形式的优质基础设施，或与公共设施相结合的基础设施。

外商直接投资政策明确，如果工业园满足以下条件，工业园区内的外商直接投资将不受适用于建设发展项目的条件的限制：包括至少10个单位，单个单位不得占用可分配区域的50%以上；用于工业活动的面积的最小百分比不得低于总可分配面积的66%。

10. 卫星——建立和运行

通过政府路线的外国直接投资，投资于遵守空间部或印度空间和研究组

织（ISRO）部门准则指导的卫星项目的建立和运行的，允许达到 100%。

11. 私营保安机构

私人保安是指由非公职人员提供的保安，以保护或保障任何人或财产，或两者兼备，包括提供装甲车服务。私营保安机构是指从事提供私人保安服务的政府机构、部门或组织以外的个人或团体，包括私人保安人员或其主管培训，或为任何工业或商业经营、公司或任何其他人或财产提供私人保安。

私营保安机构允许外商直接投资达到 74%，但只有 49% 允许通过自动路径获得，超过 49% 的投资需要得到政府的批准。另外，外国直接投资要符合 2005 年《私营安保机构（监管）（PSAR）法》。

12. 电信服务

所有电信业务都允许 100% 的外国直接投资，包括 I 类电信基础设施提供商，即基础、统一接入服务、统一许可（接入服务）、联合许可、国家 / 国际长途、商用 V-Sat、公共移动无线中继服务（PMRTS）、全球移动个人通信服务（GMPCS）ISP 许可证、语音邮件 /Audiotex/UMS、IPLC 转售、移动号码便携服务，以及其他服务提供商除外的 I 类基础设施提供商（提供暗光纤、通道权、管道空间、塔）。

但是外国直接投资超过 49% 的需要政府批准。另外，电信业的外国直接投资中，被许可人和投资者须遵守有电信部（DoT）随时通知的许可和安全条件，但允许“其他服务提供者”在自动路径下进行 100% 的外国直接投资。

13. 取货批发贸易 / 批发贸易

允许参与现款取货批发贸易 / 批发贸易活动的贸易公司在自动路径下吸收 100% 的外国直接投资，该政策把“现款取货批发贸易”下允许的活动范围定义为面向零售商、工业、商业、机构或其他专业业务用户，或面向其他批发商和相关附属服务提供商的货物 / 商品销售。

14. 电子商务活动

电子商务活动允许自动路径下 100% 外国直接投资，但外国直接投资政策只允许电子商务实体参与企业对企业（B2B）的电子商务，而不能参与企业对消费者（B2C）的电子商务。

此外，在基于库存的电子商务模式中，外国直接投资是不被允许的，其仅允许在基于市场的模式中。电子商务的市场模式被定义为“由电子商务实体在数字和电子网络上提供信息技术平台，作为买方和卖方之间的促进者”。

另外，电子商务实体销售额不允许超过从一个供应商或其集团公司通过其市场实现的销售额的 25%，且提供市场的电子商务实体不会直接或间接影响商品或服务的销售价格，并且其应保持一个公平的竞争环境。

15. 单品牌产品零售交易（SBRT）

SBRT 的外国投资旨在吸引生产和销售方面的投资，增加消费者获得这类货物的机会，鼓励增加从印度采购商品，并通过获得全球设计、技术和管理实践来提高印度企业的竞争力。因此，SBRT 中的外国直接投资可以达到 100%，其中通过自动路径的最高为 49%，超过标准的需要政府批准。

单品牌产品零售交易的外国直接投资应符合以下条件：

（1）要销售的产品只能是“单品牌”。

（2）产品应在国际上以同一品牌销售，即产品应在除印度以外的一个或多个国家以同一品牌销售。

（3）SBRT 只涵盖在制造过程中被打上烙印的产品。

（4）非居民企业或实体（无论是品牌所有者还是其他实体）应被允许直接或通过与品牌所有者达成的进行单一品牌产品零售交易的合法协议，在国内为该特定品牌进行“单一品牌”产品零售贸易。

（5）在涉及外国投资达到 51% 以上的提案中，30% 商品价值的采购由印度完成，且最好来自所有部门的微型和中小型企业、乡村和家庭工业、工匠和手工业者。这些采购规范不适用于自开业，即从事单一品牌零售贸易的实体开设第一家门店之日起至 3 年的时间内，这些实体拥有“最先进”和“尖端”技术，而且不可能在当地采购。

（6）通过实体店经营的 SBRT 实体可以通过电子商务进行零售交易。

16. 多品牌零售交易

多品牌零售贸易中，各种产品在政府路径下的外国直接投资允许达到 51%，其需要符合以下条件：

（1）新鲜农产品，包括水果、蔬菜、花卉、谷物、豆类、新鲜家禽、渔业和肉类产品，可能无品牌。

（2）外国投资者引进的外国直接投资的数额最低是 1 亿美元。

（3）第一批 1 亿美元的外国直接投资中，至少有 50% 应在 3 年内投资于“后端基础设施”，其中“后端基础设施”将包括所有活动的资本支出，不包括前端单位，例如，后端基础设施包括在加工、制造、分销、设计改进、质量控制、包装、物流、仓储、仓库、农业市场生产基础设施等方面的投资。

（4）所购买的制成品 / 加工产品的采购价值至少有 30% 来源于总工厂和设备投资额不超过 200 万美元的印度微型和中小型工业。

（5）零售销售点只能在以 2011 年人口普查为依据，人口超过 10 万的城市设立，也可以根据各邦政府的决定在任何其他城市设立，其也可能覆盖这些城市 / 城市群界限周围 10 公里的区域；零售地点限于符合有关城市总体 / 区域计划的地区，并为交通连接和停车等必要设施提供相应的服务。

• 政府有权第一个采购农产品。

• 对于从事多品牌零售贸易活动的外国直接投资公司来说，任何形式的电子商务都是不允许的。

17. 制药业

制药行业中，在自动路径下，允许绿色地块的外国直接投资达到 100%，而在政府路径下，允许棕色地块的外国直接投资达到 100%（对现有公司的投资）。然而，不得在自动路径或政府批准路径下使用“不竞争”条款，除非在特殊情况下经过政府的批准。

（九）金融行业的外国直接投资

资产重组公司。允许在自动路径下对资产重建公司进行 100% 的外国直接投资。但也有一些条件，包括外国机构投资者 / 外国证券投资者的总持股比例必须低于实收资本总额的 10% 的规定。同时，此外，金融情报机构 / 外国证券投资机构已获准将每批证券最高 100% 投资于 ARCs 发出的证券收据，但须遵守印度储备银行的指示或指引。

银行业（私营部门）。私营部门允许外商直接投资达到 74%，其中 49% 的外国直接投资可以通过自动路径进行，但超过 49% 限制的，需要政府批准。这一限制包括外国机构投资者 / 外国证券投资者的证券组合投资方案（PIS）、非证券投资机构的投资，前 OCBs 在 2003 年 9 月 16 日之前收购的股票，且将继续包括 IPO、私募、全球存托凭证 / 美国存托凭证和从现有股东手中收购股票。此外，一家私人银行从所有来源获得的外国投资总额最多可达银行实收资本的 74%。无论何时，实收资本中至少有 26% 必须由居民持有，外国银行的全资子公司除外。

银行业（公共部门）。该部门只允许在政府路径下最多 20% 的外国直接投资，且外国直接投资制于 1970/80《银行业公司（收购和转让企业）法案》。这个上限（20%）也适用于印度国家银行及其联营银行。

信用信息公司（CIC）。CIC 允许外国直接投资在自动路径下达到 100%。然而，投资于 CIC 须遵守 2005 年《信贷信息公司（监管）法案》，并从印度储备银行获得许可。此外，外国机构投资者 / 外国证券投资者投资要符合以下条件：单一实体应直接或间接持有低于 10% 的股权；任何超过 1% 的收购都必须作为强制性要求报告给印度储备银行；向 CIC 投资的外国机构投资者 / 外国证券投资者不得根据其所持股份在董事会寻求代表权。

证券市场中的基础设施公司。符合 SEBI 法规的证券市场中的基础设施公司，即证券交易所、存托机构和清算公司，外国直接投资最高可达 49%。在证券交易所、存托机构和清算公司中，49% 的外资持股将受到外商直接投资（FDI）最高 26% 和外国机构投资（FIIs）最高 23% 比例的限制。只有获得外商投资促进委员会的批准，才允许对这些基础设施公司进行外国直接投资。

FII 在这些基础设施公司 23% 的投资只允许通过二级市场购买，且 FII 无权被任命为任何董事会代表，包括一致行动人在内的任何外国投资者都有权持有该基础设施公司超过 5% 的股权。

根据《证券合同（监管）（公开发行证券交易所增持股份管理办法）规定》，任何人直接或间接持有股票交易所的外商投资的额度为 5%。

资产管理公司和资产重组公司允许外商直接投资达到 100%。

保险。在这个行业允许通过自动批准路线的外国直接投资达到 49%。但是，需要事先获得 IRDAI 的批准。包括外国投资在内的所有投资超过公司已缴股本的 1% 的印度保险公司，需要事先获得 IRDAI 的批准。所有外国投资必须遵守适用的 IRDAI 规定，其中规定了保险公司计算外资股权的方式。在印度保险公司单独的外国投资者没有单设的投资上限——49% 的限额适用于所有外国投资。

所有印度保险公司必须按照 IRDAI 关于印度拥有和控制的准则（“控制

准则”）中规定的方式“由印度人拥有和控制”。非居民投资者的权利通常需要根据“控制准则”和 IRDAI 关于保险公司公司治理的规范进行谈判。从监管的角度来看，必须在考虑到上述授权的情况下进行投资。从印度保险公司退出的外国投资者在退出之日起两个财政年度结束之前，不得投资于新的合资保险公司。

白标 ATM 业务。在白标 ATM（WLA）操作中允许外国直接投资达 100%，但需满足以下条件：

任何有意设立 WLA 的非银行实体都应具有根据最近财政年度经审计的资产负债表所示的最低净值 100 亿印度卢比，并且随时维持这一水平；如果该实体还从事任何其他非银行金融公司（NBFC）活动，则设立 WLA 的公司的外国投资也应遵守 NBFC 活动中外国投资的最低资本金规范。

其他金融服务。其他金融服务是指受金融监管机构监管的金融服务活动，即 RBI、SEBI、IRDA、PFRDA、NHB 或任何其他金融部门监管机构。根据有关监管机构 / 政府机构的规定，允许规定条件，包括最低资本金规范下的外国直接投资达到 100%。

在所有那些不受金融部门监管机构监管，或者只有部分金融服务活动受到监管，或对监管监督存在疑问时的金融服务活动中，允许政府批准路径下的外商投资达到 100%，但须遵守条件，包括政府可能做的最低资本要求等决定。

1. 市场准入

一般公司通过直接和间接投资进入主要资本市场。

进入孟买证券交易所或国家证券交易所进行间接投资等二级市场准入可以通过两种方式完成：

（1）通过设立银行机构成为经纪人、承销商、做市商等，可以成为市场中介机构。这个在行业自动路径下可进行 100% 外商投资。

（2）通过和SEBI境外机构投资者（FII）一起注册设立外国金融机构（FII），可以通过经认可的中介机构对市场工具进行投资，但须符合规定的投资限制条件。设立作为市场中介的金融机构可以吸收100%外国直接投资。在这种情况下，机构也可以成为做市商，并以自己的名义买卖证券。其可以为自己和客户获取投机和套期工具，如衍生品和期权。如果其是和SEBI一起注册的FII，其可以在原始国发行“参与性票据”，通过发行该票据，其可以在注册P.Notes的条件下获得证券。

2. 融资

如有100%的外商直接投资可用，直接融资通过建立全资子公司（WOS）来实现的；不允许100%外商直接投资的合资企业（与印度实体合资），设立分支机构或其他营业场所［根据2000年《FEMA（设立分支机构或其他业务办公室）条例》］，可以通过股权或债务工具融资。

间接投资是通过建立在印度SEBI注册的FII来完成的。FII随后可以通过市场中介机构在中等和一级市场上购买和出售证券，但如果有外国直接投资，则限制总量。

3. 兼并和收购

（1）简介。2013年《公司法》（CA）第230条至第240条和2016年《公司（妥协、安排和合并）规则》规定了与安排、妥协、合并和合并计划有关的规定。这些规定与并购规则一起于2016年12月15日生效。除这些规定外，还通知了2016年《公司（未决诉讼移交）规则》，因此，向印度各高等法院提出的所有诉讼均移交给国家公司法律法庭（NCLT）各自的法官席，包括与合并和合并申请有关的诉讼。

（2）与债权人和成员的妥协和安排。根据CA第230条第13款，安排包括重组公司的股本。公司或其债权人/成员或清算人（如果公司正在清盘）可向NCLT申请公司与其债权人/成员或其任何类别（如适用）之间的妥协或安排。NCLT根据此类申请，可酌情命令召开债权人/成员或其任何一类会议。如果在这样的会议上，代表债权人或债权人或成员或类别成员（视情况而定）的价值四分之三的多数人可以亲自或通过代理或邮寄投票方式表决、妥协或安排，如果这种妥协或安排得到NCLT的批准，那么它对公司、所有债权人或债权人或成员或类别成员（视情况而定）具有约束力，或者清盘人及公司的分担人（如属公司清盘）。

CA也授权NCLT执行其作出妥协或安排的命令，其中包括监督妥协/安排的实施和公司清盘的权力，如果NCLT认为命令不可能执行得令人满意或公司无力偿还债务。

（3）兼并和公司合并。CA第13条第232款规定，如果根据CA第13

条第230款向NCLT提出制裁妥协或安排的申请，并且此类妥协或安排涉及重建、合并或分拆计划，那么NCLT可按照CA第13条第230款的程序和上述规定，命令召开债权人/成员的会议（视情况而定）。如果必要的多数人同意该计划，并且如果遵守了CA第13条第232款规定的程序，则NCLT可以通过一项同样的制裁措施。

（4）小公司合并或控股公司与其全资子公司（WOS）合并。CA的第233条第13节包含了简化程序，用于小型公司，即非上市公司和其实收资本的公司不超过500万印度卢比或可能规定的不超过5亿印度卢比的较高数额，营业额不超过20亿印度卢比的规定数额和控股公司与其WOS合并和合并时的简化程序。

该计划应由中央书记官长而非NCLT提交并批准。

（5）有关安排或合并计划的程序。

① 向NCLT提交申请。第一步是要求公司向NCLT提交以下文件：

• 以表格NCLT-1提交NCLT的申请（涉及多个实体的合并/安排的联合申请可由合并或安排一方酌情提交）；

• 以NCLT-2表格提供的录取通知书；

• 以NCLT-6表格提供的誓章；

• 妥协、合并或安排方案（计划）副本一份，连同CA并购规则规定的有关披露。

② NCLT申请听证。NCLT可酌情召开成员/债权人会议或免除转让方和受让方公司的债权人会议。

③ 通知成员和债权人。下一步是通过法庭任命的主席，以法庭指定的主席的身份，将CAA2表格中的成员/债权人通知在会议日期确定前至少一个月，发送到所有债权人、成员、债券持有人及其任何一类的登记地址。此外，并购规则还规定，通知应随附妥协方案或安排副本以及根据并购规则提供的详细情况说明。

④ 在报纸上刊登广告。按照NCLT的指示召开会议的通知应以CAA2表格的形式在至少一份英文报纸和至少一本在公司注册办事处所在国的广泛发行的白话报纸，或可能由NCLT指导的报纸上刊登广告。该通知也应在印度证券交易委员会网站上公布。

⑤ 通知监管机构和主管部门。在向会员 / 债权人发送通知后，公司向中央政府、公司注册处处长、所得税主管部门（所有情况下）、印度储备银行、印度竞争委员会、证券交易所（适用情况下）等监管机构，以及 NCLT 指示的其他部门监管机构发出会议通知。

⑥ 服务宣誓书。在会议规定的日期前不少于 7 天提交主席宣誓声明，说明所有关于通知发出的指示以及召开会议的广告。

⑦ 会员 / 债权人会议。会议结果应由会议主席在会议结束后 3 日内或在 NCLT 可能规定的时间内，以 NCAT 表格形式向 NCLT 报告。

⑧ 在 NCLT 之前提交申请。公司应当在多数成员 / 债权人确认计划后向 NCLT 以 CAA5 表格确认该计划，数额占出席会议和投票的债权人 / 成员总数的四分之三在主席提交报告后 7 天内以电子方式投票。

NCLT 须定出聆讯呈请的日期，而聆讯通知则须在会议通知刊登广告的同一报章或 NCLT 所指示的其他报章刊登广告，而该公告须在所定的聆讯日期不少于 10 日前刊登。

⑨ NCLT 对方案实施制裁时发出的指示。NCLT 在制订计划时也可能会提供其认为适当的指示，以便正确实施该计划。

⑩ 向公司注册处处长提交命令。公司应在收到 NCLT 命令的 30 日内，向公司注册官提交 NCLT 订单的核证真实副本。

4. 竞争规定

在印度开放其经济政策并于 1969 年 5 月 20 日生效后，《竞争法》于 1969 年生效，1969 年的《垄断和限制性贸易惯例法》（MRTP 法）被废除，因为它被认定为恶法，而当下需要的是促进公平竞争，而不是限制竞争。

（1）《竞争法》的目标。《竞争法》的目标如下：

① 考虑到该国的经济发展，设立印度竞争委员会（CCI）；

② 防止对竞争有不利影响的做法（AAEC）；

③ 促进和维持市场竞争；

④ 保护消费者的利益；

⑤ 确保印度其他市场参与者进行的贸易自由。

因此，《竞争法》的主要目的是通过禁止反竞争协议、滥用支配地位和通过监管竞争来确保市场上的自由和公平竞争。

（2）印度竞争委员会（CCI）。根据《竞争法》第 7 条，组建了一个称为 CCI 的权力机构，该机构由一名主席和至少两名成员组成，最多由 6 名成员组成。CCI 是一家法人团体，拥有永久继承权和法定公章，可以动产和不动产取得、持有和处置财产，并签订合同并能够起诉和被起诉。

（3）CCI 的职能和权力。为了实现《竞争法》的目标，CCI 拥有以下职能和权力：

① 查询企业的某些协议和优势地位；

② 进行这种调查；

③ 下达某些命令，这些命令必须符合行政法规的合理性、公正性、相称性和与母公司法规相一致的标准。

（4）竞争委员会总干事的调查（DGCC）。《竞争法》第 19 条授权 CCI 对收到的任何信息或参考或诉讼进行调查。如果 CCI 发现表面证据确凿的案件，它将指示 DGCC 调查此事。DGCC 的报告将由 CCI 审议，CCI 将听取有关各方的意见，然后通过它认为合适的必要命令。

（5）向国家公司法上诉法庭提出上诉（NCLAT）。自2017年5月26日起，NCLAT被指定为上诉当局，审理和处理针对CCI根据与合并通知、委员会的调查和处罚有关的特定条款发出的任何指示或作出的决定或命令提出的上诉。这种上诉必须在收到CCI的命令/指示/决定后的60天内提出。早些时候，指定的上诉当局是竞争上诉法庭。

对 NCLAT 的指示、决定或命令感到不满的人可以在指示、决定或命令之日起 60 天内向印度最高法院提出上诉。

（6）反竞争协议

《竞争法》第 3 条规定，企业、个人或企业或个人的组织，包括卡特尔在内，不得就生产、供应、分销、储存、购买或控制货物或提供服务达成协议，这些协议可能会在印度造成 AAEC。《竞争法》第 19（3）条规定，在确定协议是否具有 AAEC 的同时，CCI 应适当考虑所有或任何下列因素：

① 在市场上创造新进入者的障碍；

② 将现有的竞争对手赶出市场；

③ 通过阻碍进入市场取消竞争；

④ 给消费者带来利益的累积；

⑤ 生产或分配货物或提供服务方面的改进；

⑥ 通过生产或分配货物或提供服务促进技术、科学和经济发展。

以下协议将被视为在印度拥有 AAEC：

① 直接或间接确定销售或采购价格的协议，如搭配安排；

② 限制或控制生产、供应、市场、技术开发、投资或提供服务的协议，如独家供应协议；

③ 通过分配市场地区、货物性质或客户数量或任何其他类似方式（如独家分销协议）来分配市场或生产来源或提供服务的协议；

④直接或间接导致招标或共谋招标的协议。

在此，被指控放纵反竞争行为的当事人必须证明上述协议不会在印度造成 AAEC。

（7）滥用优势地位

《竞争法》第 4 条规定，企业不得滥用其主导地位。优势地位是企业在相关市场中享有的优势地位，使其能够独立于市场竞争力而运作，或影响其竞争对手或消费者或有利于其的相关市场。企业从事下列活动的，应当认定为滥用支配地位：

① 直接或间接地在购买或销售商品或服务中设定歧视性条件，或在商品或服务的购买或销售（包括掠夺性定价）中设定价格；

② 限制商品的生产或服务提供或市场，或限制与货物或服务有关的技术或科学发展损害顾客的利益；

③ 滥用导致拒绝进入市场的行为；

④ 订立与其他方接受的与合同标的无关的附加义务合同；

⑤ 利用一个相关市场的主导地位进入或保护另一个相关市场。

（8）组合规则

组合规则包括：

① 一个或多个人获得一个或多个企业的控制权、股份、投票权或资产；

② 当一个人已经直接或间接控制另一个从事相似、相同或可替代商品或服务的生产、分销或交易的企业时，由一个人控制企业；

③ 企业合并与并购。

5. 土地和房地产

印度拥有世界第二大人口，到 2035 年可能会成为世界上人口数量超过中国的人口第一大国，但印度总面积只有 3287000 平方公里。土地是印度的一个国家主体。印度土地分类如下：林地主要是密林，没有耕种，这些森林被细分为保留林、保护林和未分类森林；牧场或牧场仅用于放牧的目的；农业和农田用地用于农业、种植农作物和其他形式的传统农业，印度有着不同的农业用地特征，如灌溉、未灌溉、宅基地，农业为国家农村居民的生活提供支持；商业用地是用于商场、广场和法律规定的所有其他商业场所的土地，由于印度主要有农地，许多商业用地现在由于城市化和这些土地周围的其他形式的发展而转变为农地；工业用地用于各种类型的工业，如果它们失去农业地的地位，甚至可能由各邦政府机构分配给想要建立任何行业的人，那么这些土地也会从农业土地上转换为工业用地；居住用地在城市和村庄周围，主要用于居住住房、公寓楼和经济适用住房聚居区。

（1）财产的含义。

财产一词与可移动或不可移动的东西的所有权有关。动产和不动产由不同的法律和程序处理。移动财产由 1930 年《货物销售法》处理，不动产由 1882 年《财产转让法》处理。为了解财产何时是动产或不动产，必须理解这种财产的真实性质。1882 年《财产转让法》没有对不动产这个词作出任何定义。第 3 条只规定，“不动产不包括立木，种植庄稼和草地”，必须研究 1897 年《通用条款法》和 1908 年《注册法》，以理解不动产的含义。

1908 年《登记法》规定：“不动产包括土地、建筑物、世袭津贴、道路权、照明和渡船权、渔业权或任何其他利益，这些权利来自于土地或其他附在地球上的东西，或永久系于任何附着在地球上但不存在木材、种植作物或草的东西上。”

1897 年《总则法》第 3（26）条规定：“不动产应包括土地、土地产生的利益或永久固定在地球上的东西。”

然而，土地通常被定义为不动产、房地产（及其上生长的一切）、地下矿业权和空域（政府根据这些土地的位置作出合理限）。

（2）与土地有关的权利。

联合国大会于 1948 年 12 月 10 日在法国巴黎 DeChaillot 宫中通过的《世

界人权宣言》第17条（拥有财产权）规定：“每个人都有权单独拥有财产，也有权与他人联合拥有财产”，并进一步规定“不得任意剥夺他人的财产”。印度是“世界人权宣言”的签署国之一。

印度《宪法》于1950年1月26日生效，财产权是第19条（1）款（f）和第31条的基本权利。第19条第（1）款（f）与《宪法》第31条一起，禁止政府在没有“法律授权”的情况下剥夺它的财产，并且进一步规定“该法律必须为被占有或取得的财产提供赔偿或明确确定赔偿给予的原则和方式”。

但是，有人注意到这些条款阻碍了国有化和土地改革。因此，1978年加纳塔党通过了印度《宪法第44次修正案》，删除了第19条（1）款（f），其中规定每个人都有权通过合法途径获得任何财产，将其作为自己的财产并自由处分，但仅限于公共福利的紧急情况或国家为保护预定部落的利益而实施的任何其他限制，并且删除了第31条第（1）款，其中规定任何人的财产权不得被剥夺，除非法律授权。

《宪法第44次修正案》的目的和理由说明规定：“鉴于争取赋予基本权利的特殊地位，财产权——曾经多次为此修订《宪法》——将不再是一项基本权利，而只是一项法律权利。为此目的，正在对第19条作出必要的修正，并删除第31条。然而，将确保将财产从基本权利清单中删除不会影响少数群体建立和管理自己选择的教育机构的权利。同样，拥有土地供个人耕种和在最高限额内获得按市场价值计算的赔偿的人的权利也不会受到影响。虽然财产不再是一项基本权利，但它将被明确承认为一项法律权利，规定除非依法，否则不得剥夺任何人的财产。”

（3）征用权原则。

与世界上许多国家一样，印度的征用权原则是主权国家在未经个人同意的情况下获得私人财产供公共使用的权力。作为行使这项权力的一部分，收购之后将支付足够的报酬。这一学说是建立在两条格言的基础上的，即人民的福利是至高无上的法律，公共需要是最高的，这意味着公共必要性大于私人必要性。根据印度《宪法》附录7第42号清单第4项，工会和邦政府有权制定有关收购财产的法律。

征用权原则被政府滥用，当局滥用权力，将土地授予政治关系良好的高收入私人参与者。征用权是一种后来被用于商业盈利活动的东西。2013年，国会领导政府通过旨在平衡业主利益及为工业和城市扩张提供土地的需求的立法，从而保护土地所有者特别是农民的利益。

（4）2013 年《获得公平补偿的权利和土地获取、恢复和重新安置透明度法》。

2013 年《获得公平补偿的权利和土地获取、恢复和重新安置透明度法》自 2014 年 1 月 1 日起生效，是印度议会制定的一项土地征用法，规定了补偿、恢复和安置的程序和规则。该法取代了 1894 年的《土地征用法》。2013 年《获得公平补偿的权利和土地获取、恢复和重新安置透明度法》要求进行强制性社会影响评估（SIA），并征得私人公司征地时 80% 受影响家庭和公私合作项目征地时 70% 受影响家庭的同意。接收同意的过程是与 SIA 研究一起进行的。该法的问题如下：

① 某些家庭试图提取额外补偿，从而拖延了项目并影响了受益家庭；

② 为了公共目的而进行的收购似乎过于模糊，而且没有明确界定，让政治有机会发挥作用并引起各种纠纷；

③ 该法偏袒土地所有者，不满足穷人的需求，也不为他们提供医院、学校和其他就业机会。

由于实施该法时遇到许多困难，因此必须进行某些修改，同时在征地时保护农民和受影响家庭的利益。2014 年 5 月，印度人民党（Bharatiya Janata Party）领导全国民主联盟（NDA）席卷全国，并力求立即改革征地程序。

NDA 政府希望把重点放在基础设施建设上，以促进其经济议程，因此它必须在 2014 年 12 月颁布征地修正案条例，以期在议会预算会议上提出新的立法。

根据拟议的 2015 年法案，将有五类豁免，不受前一项法案的某些规定的限制，包括同意取得。这些项目包括：国家安全和国防生产；农村基础设施，包括电气化；为穷人提供的经济适用住房；工业走廊；公私伙伴关系项目，在这些项目中，土地继续归中央政府所有。

根据 2013 年法案的规定，这些类别也免除 SIA 条款。

（5）国家和中央立法。

印度《宪法》第 7 条提到三个名单：工会名单上列出了 100 个项目，议会拥有专权立法；国家清单中有 61 个项目，各邦有权就这些问题制定法律；

并行清单列出了 52 个项目，其中各邦和联盟政府可以立法。

收购和申购财产属于并行清单。由于 2015 年法案尚未通过，因此许多邦根据印度《宪法》第 245 条第（2）款对 2013 年法案提出申诉，其中规定："如果一国立法机关就并行清单中列举的事项之一提出的任何规定与议会或现行法律就此事提出的早先法律的规定相抵触，那么，该国立法机关制定的法律，如果已保留给总统审议，并已得到总统的同意，应在该国优先执行；但本条中任何条款均不应阻止议会在任何时候就同一事项制定任何法律，包括增加、修改、变更或废除邦立法机关制定的法律。"许多邦如 TamilNadu、Gujarat 和 Telangana 已经根据第 245 条第（2）款实行追索权。据估计，由于土地收购问题，90 亿美元的资金被搁置。Gujarat、Rajasthan、Maharashtra、Jharkhand 和 Telangana 通过寻求总统同意，利用《宪法》第 254 条第（2）款颁布了新的法律。

① 中央立法。议会通过了这些中央立法，以管理全国各地的所有土地。印度负责管理土地的主要立法如下。

• 1882 年《财产移转法》规定了通过出售、赠与、交换、释放、退回、遗嘱和抵押等方式转让财产，并规定了哪些财产可以转让，哪些财产不能转让；它还界定了动产和不动产是什么，并讨论了谁可以转让，谁不能转让。

• 1872 年《印度合同法》谈到了当事人的合同能力、有效合同的必要要素、具有约束力的合同的法律和责任、合同的类型和救济等问题。

• 1908 年《登记法》规定了与不动产转让有关的文件向指定登记当局登记的程序。该法确保记录和保存关于出售和购买土地的所有文件，确保所有权明确，防止欺诈交易。该法还提到了强制登记的文件。

• 1872 年《印度证据法》适用于民事和刑事诉讼程序以及印度法院的整个证据受理制度。

• 1899 年《印度印花税法》规定了印花税的指导原则，需要在所有登记的文件上支付印花税，并且税率因国家而异（由国家立法决定）。印花税是对各种产生、转移、限制、延长、消灭或记录任何金融义务的法律文书支付的，但不包括汇票、支票、本票、信用证和保险单。

• 1963 年《时效法》规定了不同诉讼的时限，受害者可向法院寻求补救或正义。

• 1925 年《印度继承法》是涉及有关无遗嘱继承的法律。

• 1963 年《具体救济法》以英国给予或拒绝救济的原则为基础，这是原告通过民事法院寻求司法补救的一种形式。该法案涉及具体履行方式、各种公平补救办法以及可在不同情况下提出的不同类型的诉讼。

• 1881 年《票据法》是与本票、汇票和支票有关的法律，它旨在防止欺诈性交易，并且如果不遵守该法案的某些部分，则将追究刑事责任。

• 2002 年《金融资产证券化和重建及证券利息执行法》(SARFAESIACT)，该法允许银行和金融机构在借款人无法偿还贷款时拍卖房产（住宅和商业），它使贷款人能够通过采取恢复或重建措施来减少其不良资产。

• 1948 年《工厂法》规定了有关在印度各地建立工厂的有关操作安全、劳动力福利的法律，并规定了不遵守该法规定的程序的惩罚措施。

• 2016 年《房地产（监管和发展）法》旨在监管和促进房地产部门，以确保和保护消费者，并规定了有效的补救机制。

上述法律相当于印度颁布的适用于整个印度的大部分主要立法。然而，每个邦都有制定自己的法律和规则的自由，而这些法律和规则是次要于主要立法的。以下是印度一些邦在土地及其发展方面的一些重要法案。

② 邦立法。

卡纳塔克邦

• 1964 年《卡纳塔克邦土地收入法》规定了税收官员的权力、土地管理和土地收入征收、土地出让和调查数字的分歧。

• 1961 年《卡纳塔克邦土地改革法》规定了租户的权利、全国土地所有权上限、对农地转让的限制以及对土地有关案件的法院管辖权。

• 1957 年《卡纳塔克邦印花税法案》规定了征收印花税的文书，提及不同文书的印花税税率及未适当印章的票据的效力。

• 1969 年《卡纳塔克邦工厂规则》是在主要中央立法的监督下制定的一套规则，规定卡纳塔克邦整个工厂的建立和福利。

• 1961 年《卡纳塔克邦商店和企业法》规定了卡纳塔克邦商店和商业机构的工作条件和就业条件。

• 2002 年《卡纳塔克邦工业（促进）法》旨在通过简化监管框架和程序投资来促进工业发展和促进新投资，为投资者提供一个友好的环境。

• 1987 年《卡纳塔克邦城市发展管理局法》旨在规定设立城市发展当局，负责计划在邦和邻近地区发展主要和重要的城市地区。

• 1966 年《卡纳塔克邦工业区发展法案》旨在制定特别规定，确保在卡纳塔克邦建立工业区，并普遍促进工业的建立和有序发展，并为此目的设立工业区发展委员会。

泰米尔纳德邦

• 1961 年《泰米尔纳德土地改革（土地上限固定）法》规定了可由个人拥有的农业用地数量，并为他们规定了土地上限。这一行为防止某些土地集中在少数人手中。

• 2013 年《泰米尔纳德邦印花税法》提供了吸引关税的工具，提到了不同票据上印花税的税率以及这些票据未被适当印章的效力。

• 2007 年《泰米尔纳德邦工厂法》是在主要中央立法的监督下制定的一套规则，该立法规定了泰米尔纳德邦各地工厂的设立和福利。

• 2012 年《泰米尔纳德邦基础设施发展法案》，泰米尔纳德邦基础设施发展委员会是根据这一法案设立的，负责监督和制定 21 个部门的政策，包括供水、下水道和社会基础设施。

• 1876 年《泰米尔纳德邦土地收入评估法》旨在对永久居住地产的被转让部分进行单独评估。

• 2005 年《泰米尔纳德邦经济特区特别条款法》规定了建立经济特区的指导方针以及我们与这些机构有关或附带的其他事项。

• 1997 年《泰米尔纳德邦工业用地征用法》对加快购置工业用地和其他与此有关的事项作出了特别规定。

• 1994 年《泰米尔纳德公寓所有权法案》规定了个人公寓的所有权，并规定这种公寓是可以继承和转让的不动产。

喀拉拉邦

• 1971 年《喀拉拉邦土地改革（修正）法案》涉及租户的权利、某些土地所有权的限制、税收、土地上限和全邦各地土地法庭的组成。

• 1959 年《喀拉拉印花税法案》提供了吸引关税的工具，提到了不同票据上印花税的税率以及这些票据未被适当印章的效力。

• 1999 年《喀拉拉邦基础设施投资基金法》规定了投资国家基础设施项

目的基金和与之相关的事项。

• 1993 年《喀拉拉邦工业基础设施发展法》规定了在喀拉拉邦建立工业区和组织工业发展中心，并为工业设立基础设施并为此构成工业基建发展公司。

• 1983 年《喀拉拉公寓所有权法》规定了个人公寓的所有权，并规定这种公寓是可以继承和转让的不动产。

• 1981 年《喀拉拉邦征用和购置财产法》是一项为公共目的征用和购置财产的法律，而非联盟的目的。

马哈拉施特拉邦

• 2015 年《工厂（马哈拉施特拉修正案）法》管辖与在全邦建立工厂有关的法律和其他附带事宜。

• 1976 年《马哈拉施特拉邦住房和地区发展法案》是关于统一、巩固和修订有关住房、修缮和重建危险建筑，并进行贫民区改善工程的法律。

• 1976 年《马哈拉施特拉邦移民项目移民安置法》规定了从公共事业项目中获得的土地上无居所的人的重新安置以及与此有关的事项。

• 1970 年《马哈拉施特拉公寓所有权法》规定了个人公寓的所有权，并规定这种公寓是可以继承和转让的不动产。

• 1966 年《马哈拉施特拉邦土地收入法》是关于统一和修改马哈拉施特拉邦土地和土地收入法的法案。

• 1961 年《马哈拉施特拉邦工业发展法案》是为保证马哈拉施特拉邦工业区有序建立，并为整个工业组织提供协助而制定的特别规定。

上述法案是各邦就当地的经济、社会需求和基础设施状况而制定的少数法案。每一个邦都有自己的法案来规定对登记票据支付的印花税。

（6）现在的印度房地产。

印度房地产开发的问题是，国家不认证土地所有权。一般而言，收入记录不作为所有权文件进行核算，所有权仅基于先前转让的顺序确定，这就是造成大量诉讼的原因。《财产转让法》《印度登记法》和《印度证据法》是影响印度全国土地所有权的三项立法，该种制度规定买家在购买前须仔细审查某一地块的业权，这是一项很大的责任。

根据《2016 年世界投资报告》，印度在发展中亚洲的外国直接投资排名第四，并已吸引了 320 亿美元的私募股权。房地产投资信托基金（REIT）使印度对全球和印度投资者都具有吸引力，并已获得印度证券交易委员会（SEBI）的批准。房地产投资信托基金是一种创造资金的过程，用于投资商业空间、住宅单元、酒店和其他有利可图的房地产。REIT 提供高收益红利、透明度和低风险投资，因为它们通常的目标是将大量资源投资于已完成的项目。就像网上交易的普通股票一样，REIT 股票也用于交易，从而增加了进入 REIT 的现金流量。

在印度引入商品和服务税（GST）旨在通过提高税收透明度来消除困扰该国的复杂税收结构。在这种新结构下，建设项目将征收 9% 的邦消费税和 9% 的中央消费税。GST 促进了投入税抵免的实行，即在生产或服务的每一阶段所支付的投入税抵免可以在随后的增值阶段得到利用。因此，最终消费者只需承担供应链上最后一家经销商所征收的税款，并在较早的阶段就会产生效益。

《贝纳米物业法》也对全国房地产业产生了重大影响，它旨在减少经济中不明身份的资金。该法禁止一切非法的贝纳米交易，并规定对违反该法规的行为处以最高七年监禁和罚款（相当于财产公平市场价值的 25%）。新法律规定当局对任何贝纳米交易进行查询。上诉法庭将审理对裁决当局下达的命令提出的上诉，而针对审裁处命令的上诉，则会由高等法院聆讯。

经济适用房的外部商业借款（欧洲中央银行）和国家住房银行（NHB）的融资增加。由总理担任主席的联盟内阁批准推出“2022 年全民住房”，目标如下：贫民窟居民的贫民窟改造，由私人开发商参与，以土地为资源；通过信贷挂钩补贴，推动建设弱势群体的经济适用房；与公共和私营部门合作的经济适用房；受益人主导的个人住房建设或装修补贴。

这些房屋通常位于地铁和一线城市的外围，并且是首次面向中低收入阶层的购房者。

莫迪政府在 2016—2017 年联盟预算中采用的土地转型管理制度、土地记录的数字化已在国家土地档案现代化计划下重新启动。这种土地记录管理现代化制度旨在减少土地纠纷，提高土地记录维护系统的透明度。该计划的主要组成部分是：包括突变在内的所有土地记录的计算机化；地图的数字化、文本和空间数据的整合；调查 / 重新调查和更新所有调查和解决记录；创建原始地籍记录；电子化登记及其与土地记录维护系统的整合；开发核心地理空间信息系统（GIS）。

最近，在基础设施法方面的发展是2016年《房地产（监管和发展）法》，这是印度议会的一项法案，旨在保护购房者，并帮助促进对房地产行业的投资。该法案规定必须对正在进行的项目进行登记，并强制要求每个邦制定自己的一套规则，并建立监管机构以监督整个邦的所有基础设施建设。

（7）结论。随着2014年新政府上台，许多政策变化使印度成为对投资者友好的环境，促进了大量的外国直接投资。2017年8月28日，工业政策和产业政策部（DIPP）发布了2017—2018年最新修订的外国直接投资政策（2017年外国直接投资政策）。纳入了印度政府2017年发布的各种通知，旨在消除多层次的官僚主义，并积极促进外国直接投资。过去两年房地产市场的外国直接投资流入量很大，预计近期外国直接投资将大幅增加。

6. 税收

（1）印度税收体系。

虽然印度是联邦制国家，但印度并不像美国那样遵循税收联邦制。印度遵循古老的税收原则，即“除法律授权外，不得征收税款”。[①] 成文法中精简了两个法律分支，一个是对个人和机构的收入征收直接税，另一个是对货物和服务征收间接税。在某些特定的行业中，诸如消费税这样的税收是分开征收的。依据《宪法》，收税权力（立法）已被列入联邦清单一中第82项至第97项，供议会根据附表7制定规则；清单二是各邦对第46项至第63项的入围产品的征税；清单三是同期产业清单，其中联盟和国家都可以在第35项、第44项入围名单上征收税款。然而，在《宪法修正案》通过后，由于GST的引入，所有这些税种除了特定的行业清单之外，所有商品和服务税都被纳入商品和服务税，最终目标是保持征收两种税收，一种征收个人收入，另一种征收商品和服务税。有些税由联邦和各邦征收、收集和占用[②]；有些由联邦征收，但分配给各邦[③]；有些税由联邦征收，但由国家征收和占用[④]。

鉴于上述情况，在直接税的框架下，1961年《所得税法》（ITA）规定

① 为印度《宪法》第265条的规定，这一普通法原则征税的年龄与大宪章一样古老。

② 印度《宪法》第268A条、第270条规定，除第168条、第168条（2）和第269条所述之外，联邦清单一所列的所有税收和关税均在联邦和各邦之间征收和分配。《宪法》以财务委员会的名义设立了一个宪法机构，不时分配这些财政资源。

③ 印度《宪法》第269条。

④ 印度《宪法》第268条。

对个人收入征收和收回税款。对收入征税的“人”一词包括个人、印度教徒未分割家族、企业（包括 LLP）、公司、人事协会、个人团体、地方当局以及所有其他人工法人。如果这些人在一个财政年度的总收入超过不应征税的最高数额，即 25 万印度卢比，按照 1944 年《财政法》修正的税率法规定的税率征收。

因此，在间接税的结构下，《货物和服务税（GST）法》是一种基于目的地 / 消费的间接税，对印度的商品和服务供应征税。按照 2017 年《中央商品和服务税法》《国家商品和服务税法》《综合商品和服务税法》委托的方式，征收商品及服务税的权力由中心和国家承担。

（2）印度收入和货物和服务供应税的可征税性。

根据《所得税法》（ITA）对个人征税的收费标准取决于个人的居住状态。ITA 对术语居民进行了定义，它规定了不同的测试，根据一个人在印度停留的几天来确定一个人的居住状态。

例如，根据印度法律，公司被视为印度居民。当实体有效管理的地点位于印度时，即实体的主要业务决策实质上是在印度制定的，其也有资格作为居民。而当一个人在财政年度在印度逗留的时间超过 182 天时，他就有资格成为居民。

一旦建立了积极的居民身份，那么这些居民印度收入以及全球收入就会在印度纳税。另外，非居民仅对在印度收到或被视为收到的收入征税，即在印度累计或出现或认为应计或产生的收入。

在间接税制下，即 GST，印度所有供应品均适用三项税收：中央商品和服务税（CGST）、国家商品和服务税（STGST）、商品和服务综合税（IGST）。

CGST 由中央对国内货物和服务的供应进行征收，国家内部供应的 STGST 归邦政府所有，国家间货物和服务供应的 IGST 由中央政府收取。值得注意的是，石油产品暂时被排除在消费税的范围之外，因为它们仍然是一个吸引征收国家消费税的邦议题。

（3）税率。

每年的税率都是由“年度金融法”规定的，并且总是以预期的方式确定。收入的适用税率取决于实体类型和纳税人的居住状况。例如，居民公司征税 30%。收入超过 2000 印度卢比和 5 万印度卢比的个人必须缴税 5%、20% 和

30%，而非居民公司则按 40% 统一税率征税。

在计算非居民收入时，应考虑印度与居住国之间避免双重征税协定（DTAA）的规定。如果 DTAA 的条款与 ITA 的条款相比更有利，则非居民可以参照 DTAA 的规定选择纳税。

个人的收入在各种收入项下确定，即工资、房产收入、企业或专业的利润和收益、资本收益，以及其他来源的收入。

根据 GST 法律，商品和服务供应的税率分别为 5%、12%、18% 和 28%。大约 81% 的产品和服务吸引了 18% 的税收，而只有 19% 的服务吸引了更高的税率，即 28%。

（4）声明和报告。

在印度需要缴税的人需要在特定的到期日内向所得税主管部门申报收入。外国公司的联络处也需要向所得税当局提交其业务活动报告。

所有经营业务的应纳税人员均须备存账簿，如收入超过 50 印度卢比的从业人员须依法由特许会计师审计其账簿，并向所得税当局提交税务审计报告。

GST 制度还规定供应商和接收方提交退货单。《消费税法》规定提交每月申报表和一份年度申报表。根据组合计划注册的纳税人、非本地纳税人及注册为输入服务分销商的纳税人，可分别获得报税表。值得注意的是，纳税人需要根据他们所从事的活动提交报税表。

（5）争议解决。

一般来说，收入评估是根据评估年度收入回报进行的。但是，所得税当局也有权要求提供文件和财务账目，以便对个人收入进行进一步评估。

印度的《所得税法》还规定，在应纳税的收入逃避摊款的情况下，重新开放摊款。入息税专员有广泛权力，可在命令错误或有损收入利益的情况下，修订评税。

可以直接向第二个上诉当局，即所得税上诉法庭（所得税上诉法庭），对 Income 税务官员的命令提出上诉。纳税人也可根据最后命令，向税务局提出上诉后，向税务处申请暂缓执行评核人员提出的要求。

根据间接税制度，根据《消费税法》任命的适当官员通过的命令可向上级当局提出上诉。任何人如因裁决当局对他作出的决定或命令而感到受屈，可向上诉当局（AA）提出上诉。当事人向 AA 提出上诉的期限为自被指控的命令发出之日起 3 个月。AA 须遵循自然公义的原则，如听取上诉人的意见、容许合理的延期（不超过 3 次）、容许额外的理由（如认为合理）等。

审裁处是上诉的第二级，可就 AA 所通过的上诉令或修订当局作出的修订令，由任何因上诉令 / 修订令而感到受屈的人提出上诉。法律规定了一个两级法庭，即国家法官 / 地区法官和国家法官 / 区域法官。

如果供应地是争议的问题之一，那么法庭的国家法官 / 地区法官有权审理上诉。如果争议涉及供应地以外的问题，那么邦 / 地区法院有权审理上诉。对国家法官的裁决提出的上诉直接提交最高法院，邦法院对法律实质性问题作出的判决，向司法高级法院提出上诉。

法律规定，任何一方（部门或当事方）如果对法庭的国家法官或地区法官通过的任何命令感到受屈，可向高等法院提出上诉，高等法院如信纳案件涉及重大的法律问题可受理这类上诉。应当指出，就事实而言，法庭是最终权威。向高等法院提出的上诉应在 180 天内提出，但最高法院有权宽恕拖延，以满足提出上诉的充分理由。

（6）预先裁决—预防措施。

ITA 规定了对某些合格申请人的预先裁决。法规要求预先裁决管理局在收到符合资格的申请人的申请后 6 个月内作出裁决。这些裁决对纳税人和税收都有约束力。

建立先期裁决机制的大目标是：就申请人拟进行的活动预先提供税务责任的确定性；吸引外国直接投资（FDI）减少诉讼；以透明和廉价的方式迅速宣布裁决。

根据《消费税法》，纳税人可在下列情况下利用预先裁决：任何货物或服务的分类，或两者兼而有之；根据《商品和服务税法》的规定发出的通知的适用性；定货物或服务或两者的供应时间和价值；进口税收抵免的可接受性；确定对任何商品或服务或两者都支付税款的责任；是否要求申请人注册；以及申请人对任何商品或服务或两者作出的任何特定事情是否构成供应商的意义内的商品或服务的供应或两者兼有的结果。

三、贸易

（一）部门监管贸易部

部门监管贸易部包括商务部、进出口部及其首席执行官、对外贸易总监（DGFT）。

（二）贸易法简介

印度是 1948 年 GATT 的创始成员，随后参加了贸易谈判。印度是《世界贸易组织协定》和其他贸易协定的签字国，如与贸易有关的知识产权、与贸易有关的服务、2008 年关贸总协定等。以下是与印度货物进出口交易有关的法律框架。

印度政府每 5 年制定一次对外贸易政策。目前的政策将涵盖到 2020 年 3 月 31 日，主要法律框架由 1992 年《对外贸易（发展和管理）法》规定，该法于 2010 年进行了重大修订。外贸总干事（DGFT）通知程序手册和附件，规定进出口程序。此外，还需要就具体的贸易问题制定法律。例如，《茶或咖啡特别法》，如果有任何特定的商品，也将是必要的。根据该法案，印度政府通知具体的出入境口岸，这些港口也是海关站。海关部门在以清关令清除货物前，保留进出口货物的区域称为海关区。有海关经纪人作为海关中介机构，由海关当局认证和许可。根据贸易政策，出口商 / 进口商必须从 DGFT 获得进口商 / 出口商代码（IEC）。还要求出口商必须是出口促进委员会的成员。会员登记证明书由理事会发给。

（三）贸易管理

根据 1992 年全面修订的《对外贸易（发展和管理）法》和贸易政策，贸易管理当局由 DGFT 组成。通知进出口岸，这些口岸也是海关签发结关证书和放行货物的站。管理包括以下步骤：货物到货、仓储、检疫令和检验、海关清关。

（四）检验检疫进出口商品

2003 年《植物检疫令（PQ）》附表 5 和附表 6 所列任何农产品的进口，进口商必须以规定的形式向农业和农民福利部下属的农业部植物保护、检疫和储存局申请许可证。在根据 PQ 命令组成的每个通知条目或存在港口中都有指定的检验机构。

进口清关涉及从海关收到参考书到向海关建议放行或以其他方式向海关提出建议的各种步骤，包括抽样、在 PEQ 设施下的进口商处所进行详细测试。这类种植材料的进口许可证是根据有关管辖区的指定检验当局（DIA）颁发的证书颁发的，证明进口商拥有进口种植材料的 PEQ 设施。进口材料仅在 PEQ 检验的最终证书上发布。涉及的法律包括《环境保护法》《农药法》国际标准处方规定的标准和 ISI 标准。

有关畜牧业和畜产品的法律规定于 1953 年和 2001 年修订的 1898 年《畜产品进口法》中。印度政府规定了动物检疫和认证服务（AQCS）。AQCS 在德里、钦奈、加尔各答、孟买、班加罗尔和海德拉巴设立了六个动物检疫站。AQCS 需要防止包括人畜共患病在内的外来疾病进入国家。这些站有标准的设施，如住房设施、隔离棚、配药和敷料、验尸设施等。如果动物进口有任何外来疾病，就要检查和发布拒绝释放令。该政策是预防胜于治疗。因此，DGFT 非常严格地提供进口许可证，包括要求疾病（如果有的话）及其状态，以及要求 DAHDF 的卫生进口许可证（SIP）。牲畜和牲畜产品通过机场 / 海港和 ICD 作为行李和货物进口。上述货物由海关以进口印度政府的检疫健康规则通过动物检疫许可进口。在允许进入印度之前，货物将随同随附的健康证书和其他文件一起检查。如果托运的货物不符合印度政府规定的保健议定书，则根据国家利益的需要采取适当行动。进口牲畜按照规定的规范进行检疫观察和检验。畜产品也按照卫生议定书进行检查和测试。

四、海关管理

经济特区（SEZ）是一个专门区域，企业享有更简单的税收和法律规定。经济特区位于一个国家的国界内，但从税收角度看，它们被视为外国领土。

为了促进企业家在这些经济区建立单位，各种有吸引力的财政政策已经建立。这些政策包括促销优惠和简单的投资、税收、贸易、配额、海关和劳动法规。此外，在这些地区设立的单位提供特别的免税期。

出口企业根据《所得税法》第 80 条 -IAB 的规定，对特区发展业务所得收入免征 10 年所得税，根据《所得税法》第 115JB 条免除最低替代税，并根据《所得税法》第 1150 条免除股息分配税。

根据《GST 法》，经济特区被豁免 GST，并被视为印度以外的出口国，同时也受益于货物和服务采购时所支付的商品和服务输入税的简单退款程序、最低限度的遵守要求和退货申报程序。

五、劳动

（一）劳动法律法规简介

劳工属于印度《宪法》规定的“并行清单”，中央政府和邦政府都是有权制定法律的立法主体，但是，某些事项是保留给中央政府的。

《劳动法》的制定通常涉及员工和他们的就业条件，主要有三类员工：政府雇员、政府控制的公共机构（PSU）和私营部门雇员。公共部门的雇员受其自身的服务规定管辖，这些规定对法定公司而言具有法定效力，或者以法定命令为基础。在私营部门，员工可以分为两大类，即管理人员和工人。没有关于管理、行政或监督员的法定条款。因此，就管理和监督人员/雇员而言，就业条件受各自就业合同约束，他们的服务可以根据其就业合同履行。

许多劳动和就业法律也适用于无组织部门，即由于就业的随意性质、无知或文盲、雇主的优势或联合等限制因素，无法组织起来追求共同目标的劳动力。这些工人可能包括建筑工人、从事家庭手工业的工人、手摇织机/强力织机工人、清扫工人和拾荒者、比迪烟和雪茄工人等。这一部门有下列立法：1996 年《建筑和建筑工人法》、1976 年《保税劳动制度（废除）法》、1979 年《邦际移徙工人法》、1986 年《码头工人法》、1951 年《人工劳动法》《运输工人法》、1966 年《比迪烟和雪茄工人法》、1986 年《童工（禁止和管制）法》，以及 1952 年《矿山法》。

《劳动法》的分类如表 3 所示。

表 3 《劳动法》的分类

序号	《劳动法》
1.	与劳资关系有关的法律，如：
	1926 年《工会法》
	1946 年《工业就业常规法和规则》
	1947 年《工业纠纷法和规则》
2.	与工资有关的法律，如：
	1936 年《工资支付法和规则》
	1948 年《最低工资法案和规则》
	1965 年《奖金支付法》、1975 年《奖金支付规则》
	1958 年《工作记者（固定工资率）法》、1958 年《工作记者（固定工资率）规则》
3.	与工作时间、服务条件和就业有关的法律，如：
	1948 年《工厂法》
	1951 年《种植园劳动法》
	1952 年《矿业法》
	1955 年《工作新闻工作者和其他报纸雇员（服务条件和其他规定）法》
	1958 年《商船法》
	1961 年《汽车运输工人法》
	1966 年《比迪烟和雪茄工人（就业条件）法》
	1970 年《合同劳工（管制和废除）法》
	1976 年《促销员工法》
	1979 年《国家间移徙工人（就业和服务条件条例）法》
	1986 年《码头工人（安全、健康和福利）法案》
	1996 年《建筑和其他建筑工人（就业条件和服务条件）法》
	1996 年《建筑和其他建筑工人福利法》
	1981 年《电影工作者和电影戏剧工作者（就业条例）法令》
	1983 年《危险机器（管理）法案》

续表

序号	《劳动法》
	1948 年《码头工人（就业条例）法令》
	1997 年《码头工人（就业规定）（不适用于主要港口）法令》
	1993 年《使用人工清道夫和建造干厕所（禁止）法案》
	1946 年《工业就业（常规）法》
	1957 年《矿业与矿产（发展与管理）法》
	2005 年《私人安全机构（管理）法》
4.	与平等和赋予妇女权力有关的法律，如：
	1961 年《产妇福利法》
	1976 年《同酬法》
	2013 年《对工作场所妇女的性骚扰（预防、禁止和补救）法》
5.	与社会弱势群体有关的法律，如：
	1976 年《保税劳动制度（废除）法》
	1986 年《童工（禁止和管制）法》
6.	与社会保障有关的法律，如：
	1923 年《工人赔偿法》《雇员补偿法》
	1948 年《雇员国家保险法》
	1952 年《雇员公积金及杂项规定法》
	1972 年《支付酬金法案》
	1938 年《雇员责任法》
	1976 年《比迪烟工人福利法》
	1976 年《比迪烟工人福利基金法》
	1981 年《电影工作者福利法》
	1981 年《电影工作者福利基金法》
	1855 年《致命事故法》
	1976 年《铁矿石矿、锰矿矿山和铬矿矿山劳动福利法》
	1976 年《铁矿石矿、锰矿矿山和铬矿矿山劳动福利基金法》

续表

序号	《劳动法》
	1972 年《石灰石和白云石矿山劳动福利基金法案》
	1946 年《云母矿山劳动福利基金法案》
	1963 年《个人伤害（赔偿保险）法》
	1962 年《人身伤害（紧急规定）法》
	2008 年《无组织工人社会保障法》

（二）劳动法律类别

印度《劳动法》可以大致分为两类：一类是《工业法》，如工厂、商店和商业机构；另一类是《劳动法》，包括有关工资、社会保障和福利、工会等的法律。

1. 工厂和商店

工厂受 1948 年《工厂法》规定的约束，该法仅适用于雇用 10 名或 10 名以上工人的工厂，如果它在制造过程中使用电力。但是，如果工厂在其制造过程中不使用电力，则该法只适用于该工厂雇用 20 名或 20 名以上工人的情况。该法规定了工厂工人的健康、安全、福利、工作时间和休假。它由邦政府通过其“工厂”视察员予以执行，并授权邦政府制定规则，以便在执行过程中适当反映国家的当地情况。该法有助于加强有关工作安全和健康的规定，规定进行法定健康调查，要求任命安全官员，在大型工厂设立食堂、托儿所和福利委员会等。此外，该法还规定了工厂占用者使用和处理有害物质的具体安全措施，并制定了应急标准和措施。

其他最重要的劳动立法是《商店和企业法》，该法主要适用于工厂以外的商业机构。它规定商店、商业机构、住宅酒店餐厅、餐厅、剧院和其他公共娱乐场所的就业。在印度，没有中央商店和企业法案。每个国家都制定了自己的《商店和企业法》。《商店和企业法》规定了几乎类似的条款，如《工厂法》，涉及商业机构登记、工作时间、每周假期、加班工作、带薪工资等。

2. 1926 年《工会法》

《工会法》承认结社自由，该法的重要条款之一规定，任何 7 个或更多的工人可以组建和注册一个工会。但是，雇主没有义务承认工会，其主要规定涉及工会的注册、工会的注销和解散以及注册工会的权利和义务。

3. 1946 年《工业就业常设法令及其规则》

《工业就业常设法令及其规则》规定雇用超过 100 名工人的工业企业的服务条件。根据该法的规定，雇用 100 名或更多工人的工业企业的每个雇主都必须确定雇佣条件，并根据该法第 3 条获得相同的认证，这种认证服务条件优先于就业合同条款。

4. 1948 年《最低工资法案及其规则》

《最低工资法案及其规则》规定，雇主有义务按计划就业支付一定数额的最低工资。该法案只处理工资的数量，并不涉及工资的支付方式。根据该法，政府确定应付给任何预定就业人员的工人的最低工资标准。政府还定期修改最低工资。

（三）对外国雇员的雇用要求

印度法律不以员工公民身份为基础进行区分。根据相关法律，在印度公司工作的外国公民有资格享受与适用于印度公民有关的福利和保护。无论就业合同中的法律选择如何，印度法律都将继续适用。但是，如果一些外国公民在印度工作，但不在印度就业，则《劳动法》可能不适用。印度国民必须参加 1952 年《雇员储蓄基金和杂项规定法》（EPFA），但以基薪为上限。然而，外国国民不论其工资如何，都必须缴纳会费，但须遵守印度与外国国民的母国签署的任何社会保障协定的条款。

印度的社会保障体系为在该系统覆盖的工厂或其他机构工作的雇员提供退休和保险福利，该制度受 1952 年《雇员公积金和杂项规定法》（PF 法）及其下的计划管理，即雇员公积金计划（EPF）和雇员养老金计划（EPS）。雇员公积金组织（EPFO）是由印度政府成立的法定机构，负责管理印度的社会保障条例。

2008 年 10 月，印度政府通过引入一种新的雇员类别——“国际工人”，并将外国国民纳入 EPF 和 EPS 的范围，对跨境工人实行了强制性社会保障计划。如果一名外国国民来印度为印度社会保障条例适用的机构工作，他 / 她就有资格成为“国际工人”。同样，如果一名印度国民已经或将要在与印度签订社会保障协定的国家工作，并有资格根据有关的 SSA 的规定享受东道国社会保障方案规定的福利，则他 / 她有资格成为“国际工人”。

国际工人在以下情况下可免除印度社会保障条例：来自与印度有互惠的 SSA 的国家；作为公民或居民，为其祖国的社会保障作出贡献；他或她在此期间享有“独立工人”的地位，并按照有关 SSA 规定的条件行事。

1. 外国人所需的许可证

（1）外国人需要工作签证（EV）才能在印度工作。EV 一般发给印度公司根据合同或就业基础任命的高技能和 / 或合格专业人员。印度最近重新定义了其移民法，并澄清了可以颁发 EV 的活动的性质。

（2）IT 和 ITES 部门。为了在印度推广这些行业，EV 仅授予技能熟练的外国公民，他们的最低年薪为 25000 美元（截至 2010 年 8 月 1 日，1 美元约合 0.8 欧元）。

（3）其他部门。印度公司可以在公司或项目中聘用的外国公民的数量：不得超过员工总数的 1%；至少可以雇用 5 名员工，最多可以雇用 20 名员工。

如果 EV 或在印度逗留的时间超过 180 天，外国人必须在抵达印度后的 14 天内向外国人地区注册办事处（FRRO）注册。

2. 申请许可证的申请程序

外国人可以向其本国的印度领事馆或大使馆申请 EV，即他的护照已经发出；他在申请日期之前至少居住过两年。

申请电动汽车的过程包括填写签证申请表并提交某些文件，包括就业要约函和委任函以及印度公司的要求函和某些声明。

（四）社会保险 / 社会保障

印度的社会保障体系由遍布许多法律法规的一系列计划和方案组成。但是，印度政府控制的社会保障制度只适用于一小部分人口。此外，印度的社会保障体系不仅包括向政府基金（如中国那样）支付保险费，还包括一次性支付的雇主义务。

一般来说，印度的社会保障计划涵盖以下类型的社会保险：养老金、健康保险和医疗福利、残疾福利、产妇福利、酬金。

尽管大部分印度人处于无组织部门，可能没有机会参与这些计划，但有组织部门的印度公民（包括外国投资者雇用的印度公民）及其雇主有权参与上述计划。强制性缴款对社会保险的适用性各不相同。一些社会保险需要所有公司的雇主供款，一些来自雇员不少于10人以上的公司，另一些来自拥有20人以上雇员的公司。

1. 退休金或雇员公积金

劳动和就业部下属的雇员公积金组织确保在工作期间死亡时领取退休金和家庭养恤金。雇员公积金组织的计划适用于至少有20名雇员的企业，员工每月赚取15000印度卢比时，雇主和雇员都必须缴纳雇员公积金计划的供款，当雇员的收入超过这个数额时，自愿缴纳雇员公积金计划供款。雇员公积金组织包括三项计划：1952年雇员公积金计划、1995年雇员养老金计划，以及1976年员工存款链接保险计划。

2. 健康保险和医疗福利

《雇员国家保险法》设立了一项基金，向雇员及其家属提供医疗服务，并在生病和分娩期间提供现金福利，并对在有10名或10名以上雇员的工厂和机构工作的工人，每月支付死亡或残疾津贴。

ESI（中央）修订规则扩大了覆盖范围，包括从2017年1月1日起一个月内收入在21000印度卢比或以下的员工；随后，2017年的《雇员国家保险（中央）修订规则》于1月20日公布，详细介绍了有保险妇女的新产妇福利。

3. 残疾福利

1923年的《雇员补偿法》，以前称为1923年《工人赔偿法》，要求雇主在导致死亡或伤残的工伤事故中向雇员或其家属支付赔偿金。根据该法，患有职业病的工人被视为在就业过程中发生事故，雇主有责任为此支付赔偿。造成永久完全和部分残疾的伤害列于《雇员赔偿法》附表1第一、第二部分，而职业病则在《雇员赔偿法》附表3A、B和C部分中作了定义。

4. 产妇福利

2017年《产假福利（修正案）法》于2017年4月1日生效，并增加了先前1961年《产妇福利法》规定的一些关键福利。经修订的法律规定，有组织部门的妇女有26周的带薪产假，高于前两个孩子的12周，而第三个孩子的产假为12周。

在其他条款中，法律规定，每一家雇员超过50人的机构都必须在方便的距离内提供托儿所设施，母亲一天最多可以参观四次。出于合规目的，公司应该注意到，这一特定条款将于2017年7月1日生效。《产妇津贴（修正案）法》规定，如果妇女在产假结束后与雇主谈判达成一致，则可选择在家中进行工作。

5. 酬金的支付

1972年《支付酬金法》规定，有10名或10名以上雇员的机构，每年向在公司工作5年或5年以上的雇员支付15天的额外工资。

酬金是由公司一次性支付的。如果员工死亡或残疾，酬金仍然必须支付给被提名人或雇员的继承人。但是，如果个人由于任何不当行为而被终止了工作，雇主可以拒绝向雇员支付酬金。在这种没收的情况下，必须有一份终止令，载明指控事项和雇员的不当行为。

小费通过以下公式计算：小费 = 最后所定工资 ×15/26× 服务年数，其中，比率15/26代表一个月中26个工作日中的15天；最后薪资 = 基本工资 + 物价津贴；服务年数四舍五入到最近的全年，例如，如果员工的总服务年限为10年10个月25天，则计算时将考虑为11年。

（五）劳动争议

1947年《工业纠纷法》（以下简称法案）下的争议解决程序如下。

1. 法案介绍

根据法案第2（k）条，工业纠纷是“雇主与雇主之间或雇主与工人之间的任何争议或分歧；或与工人或工人之间的关系，这与就业或非就业或就业条件或与任何人的劳动条件有关”。因此，法案所涉及的工业纠纷的范围非常广泛，有一个强大的机制来规范和解决这种争端是必要的。

法案和其他相应的国家法律通过设定工作委员会、调解官员、调解委员会、劳工法院、工业法庭和国家法庭等当局，规定了以和平与和谐的方式管理和解决劳资纠纷的机制。法案对以下列方式解决争端作出了规定：通过谈判和调解进行集体谈判；如果上述程序失败，则争议解决应通过自愿仲裁或强制裁定解决。

2. 纠纷解决方法

（1）集体谈判。集体谈判是一种以自愿方式解决工会与管理层之间争端的技术。法案第18条规定了两种解决方式：一是和解是在当局进行调解程序的过程中达成的。这种解决方案对签署工会成员和非成员，以及管理层现在和未来的所有员工均具有约束力。二是和解不是在调解程序中达成的，而是由和解各方独立签署的，只有这些成员是和解协议的签字人或当事方，才有约束力。

法案第 19 条规定了解决办法开始实施的时间，法案规定，和解应在争议各方商定的日期开始实施。如果没有约定日期，则在争议双方签署和解备忘录之日。

（2）斡旋和调解。法案提供了一个有效的调解机制，可以自行或者通过接触争端的任何一方来认识现有的和已经发生的争端。法案使大多数争议的调解成为强制性的。法案规定政府任命调解官员，以调解劳资纠纷各方之间的关系。调解官员被赋予民事法院的权力，在民事法院，他被授权传唤当事方宣誓作证。

在任何工业机构发生争议时，工人或雇主都可以向政府指定的调解员提问。调解官试图通过调解来解决雇主和工人之间的问题。如果调解员成功地使双方达成共识，那么雇主与工人之间达成协议，称为和解，并且该协议对有关各方具有约束力。如果调解干事在作出一切合理努力后未能成功解决雇主和工人之间的和解，那么他将编写一份调停失败调查报告，并将此报告送交政府。此后，政府将分析调解官的报告，并决定该案是否适合提交劳动法院或法庭进行裁决。

（3）自愿仲裁。在上述调解程序未能解决争端的情况下，调解官可以说服当事人将争议提交给自愿仲裁员。自愿仲裁是指当事人双方自愿选择的独立争议解决纠纷的方式。法案第 10 条规定了通过仲裁解决工业纠纷的规定，从而形成了最终的有约束力的裁决。一旦仲裁员作出了裁决，就必须提交政府，然后政府将在其提交后的 30 日内公布裁决，裁决将在公布 30 日后对裁决各方具有约束力。

（4）调查法庭的调查。法案第 6 条授权政府组成调查法庭，以调查与工业纠纷有关的任何事宜。法案第 11 条规定了调查法庭的程序。虽然法院的报告对当事方没有约束力，但很多时候它为双方之间的协议铺平了道路。

（5）裁决。在这一过程中，争端由劳动法院、工业法庭或国家法庭（裁决机构）以法案规定的方式解决。这是一种强制性解决方式，一旦政府提到裁决当局解决争端，由裁决当局解决争端的进程就开始了。裁决当局通过裁决解决提交给它的工业纠纷，该裁决对此类裁决的当事方具有约束力。

（6）裁决当局的上诉。没有关于对裁决当局作出的裁决提出上诉的规定。然而，根据印度《宪法》第 226 条和第 227 条，这些裁决可根据印度《宪法》第 136 条以令状形式向有关高等法院或最高法院提出上诉。

（六）争议解决

1. 争议解决方法和机构：印度有一个混合司法制度

（1）印度有普通法的传统，但没有像美国那样的司法联邦制。印度最高法院是印度的最高法院，拥有原令状管辖权和上诉管辖权，可就民事、商业和刑事事项提出最后上诉。法院允许在特别请愿（SLP）管辖范围内允许特殊休假。国家最高法院是国家高等法院，对于地方法院在民事和刑事事务方面的决定既具有原始的令状管辖权，又具有上诉管辖权。最高法院有两级上诉，即第一上诉和第二上诉。在基层一级，有地区法院和开庭法院。每个地区都有一名地区法官。地方法院论坛是审判和备案的法庭。在地区法院有民事和刑事审判管辖权，该法院有两个明确的分类，如民事法院和刑事法院。法官有三个等级，即在民事方面有地区法官、附加地区法官、高级副法官，然后是初级分法官或初级民事法官。在刑事方面，主审法官也是区域法院法官，然后是附加地区法官，下面是首席司法行政官、分庭治安法官，在第一级有一级治安法官或大都会治安法官。管辖权既有涉案金额的限制，又有地理管辖的限制。法院在所有民事案件中遵循《民事诉讼法》，《刑事诉讼法》也适用于所有刑事事项。此外，每个高等法院都有自己的判案规则，印度最高法院则拥有印度最高法院规则。

（2）印度设有几个特殊法庭，最古老的是土地租金审裁处和所得税审裁处，随后是劳资审裁处及决定政府和中心政府雇员事项的法庭。后来印度又增加了若干衡平法庭，如 SEBI 上诉法庭、技术上诉审裁处、竞争委员会上诉法庭、国家公司法法庭、保险监管上诉法庭、机动车事故法庭。除去可能被印度最高法院对特许申诉进行司法改判的裁决，大多数上诉法庭裁判对其专职案件具有终审效力。例外的是，针对税务上诉法庭判决提起的再次上诉可交由高级法院处理。每一个特别法庭都能决定自己的审判程序，以确保司法透明度和自然公正。

（3）印度设置有地方和/或内部争端解决机制，如消费者申诉救济委员会、监察员，也有银行监察员、保险监察员等。监察员遵循他们自己的程序提供快速补救措施。这些地方性救济论坛根据自然正义原则制定自己的程序。

（4）在公司和商业合同主体中，当事人可以将仲裁引为他们的争端解决机制。仲裁员在第一次会议上与当事人决定应遵循的程序。他们经常遵循依据 ICC 规则制定的程序。印度的跨国诉讼要求在涉诉合同中约定强制性仲裁条款，约定仲裁所涉地点、语言、程序以及适用的法律。

2. 法律适用

在民事案件中，有《民事诉讼法》规定的民事诉讼程序；在刑事案件中，有《刑事诉讼法》规定的刑事诉讼程序。此外，地区法院还有民法典规则和命令。每个高等法院都有高等法院的规定，最高法院也有最高法院规则。实体法是以标的物为基础的。州律师在州一级设有总检察长。除此之外，每个地区都有刑事检察官和政府民事诉讼辩护人。每一方都有不同级别的各种律师，如 APP、AGP 等国家指定的律师和为私人当事人订立合同的律师。没有能力任命律师的当事方可根据《法律援助法》向法律援助局寻求法律援助，法律援助局为无力聘请律师代表其案件的人指定律师。

阿根廷投融资法律研究篇

阿根廷投融资法律研究

Augusto Vechio

几十年来，阿根廷都不是商业发达的地区，不过，它在区域和全球市场上的战略地位正在不断增强。这不仅是因为阿根廷庞大的经济规模，而且还因为阿根廷的自然资源和合格劳动力的种类及数量都有潜力。在阿根廷进行投资是有挑战性的，投资者在分析其在阿根廷不同行动方针时的一点不小心往往就是马虎失职了。但从长期发展的国际视角来看，毫无疑问，阿根廷是一个拥有着极强存在感并随时准备行动的地方，因为阿根廷已经再次证明了它是拉丁美洲创新方法和商业革新的宝贵来源之一，并且为那些精明的人们提供了充足的以待挖掘的经济机会。专业领域的监管，如劳工、税务和合规，应该是任何投资者分析的中心焦点，因为它们是我们复杂的当地法律框架的组成部分。

从 2015 年 12 月开始，在毛里西奥·马克里就任总统之后，阿根廷开始向全世界敞开大门，与前政府的政策相比，新政策出现了许多积极的变化。

一、阿根廷地理及政治体系概览

（一）地理和经济基础

阿根廷坐落于南美洲南锥地区，其拥有的 280 万平方公里的领土使之成为世界第八大国以及世界上领土面积最大的西班牙语国家，其领土面积在拉丁美洲仅次于巴西，与乌拉圭、巴西、巴拉圭、玻利维亚、智利和大西洋毗邻。它是该地区最重要的经济体之一，并且还是美洲大陆所有发达国家的重要商业合作伙伴。

阿根廷具有多变和较大差异的独特地理环境，中部是广阔无垠的平原（该国 53% 的国土都是适于耕作的土地）；令人印象深刻的安第斯山脉则雄踞于西方，处于与智利的邻界位置；东北方有瀑布，西北方有高原，帕塔哥尼亚地区则有湖泊、森林和冰川。阿根廷蕴藏着丰富的资源，包括食物、水和能源（石油和天然气、风力、太阳能和矿藏），预示着探索和投资开发的巨大机遇。

阿根廷也具有多种多样的气候类型：北部是亚热带气候，帕塔哥尼亚南部是亚南极气候，潘帕斯平原气候则温和湿润。

阿根廷是拉丁美洲仅次于巴西和墨西哥的第三大经济体，GDP 达 5000 亿美元。该国目前人口超过4000万人，全国人口密度为每平方公里10.7个居民。然而，其人口并非是均匀分布的：布宜诺斯艾利斯城市地区拥有超过每平方公里 14000 人的人口密度，与此同时，南方的圣克鲁斯地区人口密度在每平方公里却不足一人。阿根廷除布宜诺斯艾利斯之外，在发达地区中最重要的一些城市包括科尔多瓦、萨尔塔、内乌肯、圣路易斯、拉普拉塔和马德普拉塔。

尽管在阿根廷许多人说英语，美元也被广泛接受，但阿根廷的官方语言是西班牙语，官方货币是阿根廷比索。

阿根廷经常处于拉丁美洲人口发展和教育指数的顶尖位置，该国识字率为 98%，高等教育毕业生每年约有 11 万人。

阿根廷是若干双边条约的缔约国，是 20 国集团、南方共同市场、拉美一体化协会、南美洲国家联盟等机构的成员。在过去 35 年里，阿根廷都保持了民主政府，但在那段时光的大部分时间里出现了经济动荡，其特点是高通货膨胀率、主权债务违约和法律制度的削弱。然而，毛里西奥 · 马克里在 2015 年底就任总统，为阿根廷开启了一个新的时期，许多现有的法律和监管障碍已经消除，以促使外国投资者信任阿根廷及其法律制度。阿根廷目前正在进一步深入完善上述方面的工作。在这方面，马克里总统政府的执政重点是强化国家机构，提高阿根廷经济的信誉和稳定性，同时促进该国旨在改善生活水平的可持续、长期的发展。

为达成该目的，马克里总统政府已经采取的措施包括但不限于如下：取消遣返限制；允许自由浮动汇率；在其主权债务重组的长期争议中与抵制债权人达成合意，作为获取国际信贷的途径；以减小通货膨胀率为主要目标；取消出口税和进口限制；同意批准一项新的制度，与政府实体联合促进私人投资用于基础设施部门；重新启动国家统计局。

现任政府一直在积极推动外资投资，这些行动的基础是改善商业环境，强调法治，并通过振兴该国的区域经济来释放阿根廷的潜力。

（二）《宪法》和政府

阿根廷于 1810 年开始从西班牙分离独立，并于 1816 年宣布独立。

阿根廷《宪法》第 5 条和第 123 条规定，各省应根据“国家宪法”“确保司法运作”的原则，陈述和保证制定自己的《宪法》。每个省都被视为先于国家，因此，其有权在未明确授权给联邦政府负责的所有事项中进行自主管理。

阿根廷《宪法》于 1853 年通过，最后一次修订于 1994 年，根据代议制和联邦制建立了一个共和国，由三个独立的政府部门组成：行政部门、立法部门、司法部门。

行政部门：联邦政府行政部门的权力主体是国家的总统和副总统，任期四年，他们可以再连任四年。

立法部门：立法部门由两院制全国代表大会组成，由参议院和众议院组成，他们来自全国各省，每省为数三名的参议员和布宜诺斯艾利斯市的三名参议员组成了参议院的72名成员。众议院则由257名按每个地区的人口比例直接选举产生的代表组成。参议员的任期为六年（该院每两年更替一次），而众议院代表任期四年，其中一半每两年更换一次。在每个司法管辖区，两名参议员通过民众普选从主政党中产生，第三名参议员则来自第二大政党。他们可以在没有时间限制的情况下再次当选。过去，参议员由各省当局任命。

司法机构：司法机构由五人组成的最高法院和下级法院组成。

作为一个联邦共和国，阿根廷分为 24 个辖区：23 个省和联邦首都布宜诺斯艾利斯自治市。每个省都有自己的《宪法》，且其须始终符合国家《宪法》。

各省也分为三个独立的部门：行政、立法和司法。

根据《宪法》序言，阿根廷《宪法》旨在保障正义，促进普遍福利，确保居住在这片土地上的所有人获得自由。它还规定了基本权利，如法律面前人人平等；言论、集会和私有财产的自由；阿根廷境内的过境自由和依照国家制定的法律经营业务的权利。

（三）阿根廷法院系统

由于阿根廷是一个联邦国家，联邦和地方都有司法系统。前者由联邦最高法院和下级联邦法院组成，后者由省级和地方法院组成。

两个法院系统由三个层级组成：下级法院，通常由一名法官主持；上诉法院以及省（或国家）最高法院，通常由一组法官组成。在某些司法管辖区，特别是在《刑法》问题上，一些特殊的上诉法院的处理会作为将案件最终交由最高法院处理的先决条件，这些上诉法院审查下级法院决定中的任何错误或不一致。在阿根廷，尽管早在1853年，陪审团的审判已经是国家《宪法》的一个特点，但该制度从未得到充分执行。因此，专业法官负责在司法案件中作出决定。该规则的例外是在23个司法管辖区中的三个（布宜诺斯艾利斯、科尔多瓦和内乌肯省），上述三个辖区在过去的15年中，已经在某些案件的刑事案件中采用陪审团的审判。

阿根廷《宪法》用以下条文描述联邦管辖权：

第116条最高法院和国家下级法院有权审理和裁决根据《宪法》和国家法律产生的所有案件，所有涉及大使、公共部长和外国领事的案件，与海事和海事管辖有关的案件，国家作为当事方的事件，两个或多个省之间、一个省与另一个省的居民之间、不同省份的居民之间以及一个省或其居民与外国国民或公民之间发生的案件，但第75条第12款和外国条约规定下的案件例外。

上述“联邦事务”的处理通常取决于联邦最高法院的最终决定。但是，根据《宪法》第117条的规定，某些事项受联邦最高法院的原始、排他的管辖权的约束，“在涉及外国大使、部长和领事的所有事项中，以及在一个省属于当事方的情况下，法院应具有原始和专属管辖权”。在这些案件中，最高法院是作出决定的唯一（初始和最终）法院。这意味着联邦最高法院可以管辖：通过 Recurso Extraordinario Federal（例外补救措施）上诉的案件，以及根据《宪法》第117条产生的案件。最高法院是阿根廷《宪法》的最终守护者，并且可以介入《宪法》保护的所有权利事项。

有资格获得 Recurso Extraordinario Federal 的案件的一般要求是：（1）对

受《宪法》保护的权利存在实际损害，可以通过司法判决进行修复；（2）该争议是基于联邦法律（caso federal）的问题以及不涉及普通法规范解释的事实和证据问题；（3）该联邦案件指向影响已被授予联邦法律级别的法律制度的相关问题，或者可能直接或间接损害已被承认为具有《宪法》地位的规则的法律不一致问题。判例法还确定了另外两种类型的caso federal：影响《宪法》权利的判决的任意性（arbitrariedad desentencia）和造成严重的体制影响的事项（gravedad institucional）。其他必要条件包括：最高法院审查的决定是由最高权力级别（上诉级别已经用尽）发布的，以及所有程序均已得到适当遵守。最高法院有权自行决定是否对作为Recurso Extraordinario Federal提交的案件作出判定。

对双重审判（上诉法院审查司法裁决的机会）的保障完全是在刑事事项上确立的，作为从下级法院提出的上诉的权利的一项《宪法》保护。虽然《1853/1860年国家宪法》没有明确规定双重审判的保障，但在1994年的修正案之后，由于某些国际人权条约的《宪法》地位，它间接地被纳入阿根廷立法。在许多情况下，上诉法院也作为二审机构来审查政府或其他行政机构通过的决定。

在1994年的修正案之前，法官是在得到参议院同意的情况下，由行政部门酌情选举和任命的。1994年的修正案将法官的甄选置于治安委员会的控制之下，治安委员会成员必须进行公开竞选，以便形成一份候选人名单，总统必须从中选出候选人。治安法官理事会由13名成员组成：3名法官由同行任命、6名国民议会成员、2名律师协会代表、1名行政部门代表、1名由学术界任命。最高法院和下级法院的法官只要在75岁退休前保持良好的品行，就可以连续任职。

关于地方司法系统，各省有义务规定在其领土内执行普通判决（不具有较高联邦地位的法），并适用国家《宪法》第75条第12分节：《民商法》《刑事法典》《劳工法典》和《社会保障法》。这类法典不是上述意义上的联邦立法，因此由全国各地联邦和地方法院无例外地适用和解释（如各省颁布的《刑法》并无不同），这与地方立法机构颁布的程序法形成了鲜明对比。后者因其制定、颁布程序，导致各省之间存在差异，有时还可能导致完全不同的结果，在刑事案件中尤其如此。

根据各省的组织情况，最常见的司法权限分为如下几种：民事和商业法院、行政诉讼法院、劳工法院和刑事法院，上述分类并不妨碍其他可能存在的特别司法管辖区，如采矿、社会保障和选举等。通常，在人口较少的省份，一些上诉法院被赋予不止一个上述的专项管辖权能，这意味着会有几个法律领域的事项集中在同一法院。各省的具体情况各不相同，而联邦法院没有这种专门的司法权限分配。

在布宜诺斯艾利斯市（以及一些省份）有一项强制性的调解法。这项法律是提出任何诉讼的先决条件，但如下几类案件除外：刑事事项；离婚、婚姻分离和无效、子女关系认定、收养或亲权事项（由此产生的财务事项除外）；涉及国家或政府机构的案件；与宣布丧失法律行为能力有关的程序；要求宪法保护令；预防措施；初步交付和预期证据程序；遗嘱认证程序；破产和重组程序；召集不动产业主会议；受劳动法管辖的冲突；自愿诉讼。调解对于行政征收和驱逐程序都是可选的。当事各方必须得到其律师的协助，并可同意选择某一调解员，或可个别向对此事具有管辖权的法院总办事处提出请求，在后一种情况下，调解人将通过抽签的方式选出，法官将在调解失败时审理案件。启动诉讼程序将中止相应诉讼时效。如果被传唤的任何一方在没有正当理由的情况下未能出席听证，另一方可认为调解失败，因此，司法通道就开启了。当事方在调解中达成的协议可以类似于司法裁决的方式强制执行。调解员的费用受一项特别规定的约束。

（四）新《民商法》

新《民商法》于 2015 年 8 月在阿根廷生效，它取代了 1871 年由法学家 Velez Sarsfield 编写的《民法典》，该法经过必要的修正，保持了以欧洲民法传统为基础的结构和基本概念。在 2015 年之前，有一部单独的《商法典》，该法典于 1862 年首次在布宜诺斯艾利斯省实施，并在整个 20 世纪得到大量补充立法的修订。新《民商法》将两者结合起来，并根据以前的判例法和法律学说作出了大量的修改，它处理了以前的法典中没有具体规定的商业和日常生活的新情况。现行的《公司法》和《破产法》，以及商业文件和其他现有的特别立法与新《民商法》分开，并未进行重大修改，因此，新法典的商业影响主要体现在合同事项、侵权行为、诉讼时效以及某些过去在民商事法

律概念上不同的概念统一上。

新《民商法》的组织架构更加合理，其辞令更为趋近于日常用词，其中最重要的几点是：

（1）表现出一种明确的决定性结论，即总体上保护处于弱势的一方。这取代了先前法律中的一项假定规则，即除非以其他方式证明，否则所有私人主体都是平等的。这一改动影响了对预先处置协议的解释，限制了放弃协议的可接受性，产生了对消费者法律的更彻底的监管，并强化了行使权力之滥用权力的观念（现在包括意在反制应对市场支配地位的保护），以及界定哪些规则被认定为公共政策。

（2）更多地关注合同谈判，以及因此可能存在的合同前责任风险。

（3）明确集体利益，明确规定个人权利，除受制于适用的行政立法外，不得影响环境、文化价值等。土著社区享有特殊的保护地位。这些和其他“开放式”条款在《宪法》中比普通立法中更常见，对法官来说是一种重要的赋权。

（4）民事责任已经超出了传统义务并将扩展至防止损害的义务。法官可决定采用惩罚措施，并发出先行命令。现在已经解决了特定情况下的损害赔偿责任（在其他情况下，公司对其职员在其职能范围内所造成的损害负有责任）。所有者的责任包括那些从损害对象获利的人。

（5）包含了分销协议（代理、特许权、供应）、融资租赁、特许经营、保理、合作、信托、银行协议以及其他协议。仲裁作为另一种解决争端的手段，已被规定为当事方之间的一项协议。

（6）增加了新的物权，如地上权、土著社区财产、房地产开发、私人墓地和分时有关的权利。共管公寓被承认为法律实体，并进行了详细的规制。

（7）制定了时效规则，规定了五年的违约期和三年的民事责任期限。

（8）国际私法为确定适用的法律和管辖权提供了一套系统的规则。

（9）在非商业性民事法规中引入了深刻的改革，其中一些，特别是在家庭法领域，对其渐进性 / 自由性的性质引起了一些争议，如赋予未成年人和青少年决定某些个人事务的权利（在 16 岁未成年人有权对健康问题作出永久决定，即使成年年龄定为 18 岁）；在性别平等方面，对子女姓氏的规定变得灵活，并与父母双方平等；父母的权利已转化为父母的责任，未成年人在法庭上提出申诉的权力有所增加。

两种不同婚姻制度，即允许财产单独所有或共同所有；婚姻忠诚作为一项法律义务已被取消；离婚规则旨在尽量减少纠纷或减少对这种情况的原因的指责；婚姻约定已得到法律许可；同居（异性或同性）的出现引发了一些对分手时共同住所的保护规则；为了配合辅助人类生殖技术制定了一套如何确立父母身份的规则，生育意愿也纳入了法律规定；改进了规则以助于实现快速和安全收养；儿童有权就其权利发表意见。先前的继承规则规定，有后代的立遗嘱人可以自由决定其遗产的 20% 的去向；根据新《民商法》，这一比例现在已经增加到 33%。

总的来说，法官比之前处于旧民法典框架时拥有更大的决策权。总体而言，商业律师认为新《民商法》代表了合同事项的改进。在《财产法》和某些技术问题上，同时存在积极和消极的评论，一些批评人士指出了一些法律中的不一致之处。在判例法得到发展和法院的解释解决不确定因素之前，就新《民商法》的价值发表意见为时尚早。

二、外商投资与外汇

阿根廷与下列国家缔结了一系列双边投资条约：阿尔及利亚、奥地利、亚美尼亚、澳大利亚、玻利维亚、保加利亚、比利时、加拿大、捷克共和国、哥斯达黎加、克罗地亚、古巴、智利、中国、丹麦、厄瓜多尔、埃及、萨尔瓦多、芬兰、法国、德国、希腊、危地马拉、匈牙利、印度尼西亚、以色列、意大利、牙买加、立陶宛、马来西亚、墨西哥、摩洛哥、荷兰、新西兰、尼加拉瓜、巴拿马、秘鲁、波兰、葡萄牙、菲律宾、罗马尼亚、俄罗斯、塞内加尔、南非、韩国、西班牙、瑞典、瑞士、泰国、突尼斯、土耳其、乌克兰、英国、美利坚合众国、越南和委内瑞拉。双边投资条约规定签署国的外国投资者与阿根廷国民享有平等待遇，在某些情况下还包括最惠国待遇。

阿根廷于 1994 年成为解决投资争端国际中心的成员，并成为世界银行集团的成员。

此外，阿根廷是将阿根廷、巴西、巴拉圭、乌拉圭和委内瑞拉联合起来的区域联盟——南方共同市场的关键成员。依托南锥体共同市场，阿根廷成为该区域贸易和投资网络的一部分。

阿根廷具有一个关于外国投资的具体法律框架，主要是在第21382号《外国投资法》中作了规定。

根据《外国投资法》，外国投资是指对该国发展的经济活动作出的任何资本贡献,以及对当地公司的任何参与的、由外国投资者投入的资本。此外,《外国投资法》还将外国投资者定义为“在阿根廷拥有外国资本投资的所有在国外定居的个人或实体”。不仅如此，《外国投资法》第2.3条还将外国投资者定义为在阿根廷境外直接或间接拥有任何在阿根廷注册的公司股本的49%以上或直接或间接控制在该公司股东会议上通过决议或作出决定所需票数的任何个人或实体。

在这一框架内，外国投资者可以：（1）未经事先批准或登记要求进行投资；（2）与当地投资者一样有机会获得奖励方案；（3）不受限制地进入所有经济部门（大众媒体除外）；（4）采用第19550号《普通公司法》所允许的任何法律实体形式；（5）与当地公司一样获得信贷。

货币兑换受到行政机关和阿根廷中央银行（ACB）颁布的一系列行政命令和通信的管制，所有这些都是根据第19359号法律（经修正）的规定，被称为刑事外汇制度。虽然阿根廷有一个自由的外汇市场，但上述制度规定了完成外汇交易的某些条件。如果不符合这些条件，则应受到刑事外汇制度规定的制裁。

外汇交易只能通过ACB授权的实体在外汇市场运作，此类实体必须根据ACB条例核实申请人（包括其居民或非居民性质）的身份。

所有外汇交易（包括资金流入和流出）必须根据ACB的规定通过ACB向当地银行（或被授权与客户进行外汇交易的其他金融实体）登记。每一笔交易都将根据ACB公布的概念列表中的一个概念代码进行登记，以确定交易的类型（如资本贡献、金融贷款、货物或服务出口应收款项等）。

所有个人或法人（公司）、继承人和其他财产集团均可自由进入外汇市场。财产继承人和其他财产集团包括但不限于信托、共同基金、合资企业、不可分割的继承、所有者财团和其他多边联合协议。

只有在货物出口应收款的情况下，资金进入阿根廷（以及资金兑换成当地货币）才是强制性的，并且必须在特定的时间框架内（目前为10年）完成。在其他交易中没有这种义务（如对当地公司的股本捐款、金融贷款等），在这种情况下，资金可以收到并存入离岸账户，也可以用当地或外币的当地账户。

此外，当地居民可以向海外（非居民和其他阿根廷居民或他们自己的国外银行账户）付款，而不需要ACB的事先批准，包括但不限于分红。

干预性金融机构可以根据《反洗钱和恐怖主义融资条例》（如“了解您的客户”或KYC政策），请求其认为相关的任何文件或信息进行外汇交易。尽管在阿根廷的监管框架内，目前不需要提交特殊文件来执行这些交易，但中间银行或外汇代理机构可以根据上述规定请求支持性信息和文件。

应当指出，外国投资可能受到双边投资条约的管制，这在2001—2002年阿根廷经济危机之后具有根本上的重要性。阿根廷政府为应对2001年的经济和政治危机而采取的行动导致了外国投资者对一个东道国提出的近代历史上最大的一波索赔。在这场危机之后根据双边投资条约迄今对阿根廷提出的40多项索赔中，现已作出了一些仲裁裁决。其中，包括美国投资者对阿根廷天然气运输和分销公司的四项索赔，即CMS、Enron、Sempra和LG的索赔。在所有四个案件中，根据世界银行国际投资争端解决中心（投资争端解决中心）规则设立的特设法庭都认为阿根廷对其行为负有责任。损害赔偿金超过1亿美元，是ICSID法庭有史以来最高的裁决之一。

虽然所有这些决定都解释和适用同一条约，且美国和阿根廷1991年《关于相互鼓励和保护投资的条约》对类似的事实作出了解释，但迄今作出的五项判决在若干问题上存在分歧，特别是对该条约“不排除的措施”条款的解释有所不同。

三、海关和对外贸易

关税及贸易总协定和世界贸易组织

1994年，随着《马拉喀什法案》的签署，关税及贸易总协定（关贸总协定，GATT）的“乌拉圭回合”谈判以许多重要的体制和规章改进而结束，并成立了世界贸易组织（WTO）。

1994年12月7日，阿根廷批准了最后文件，其中纳入了乌拉圭方的条款以及《马拉喀什法案》第24425号法律（《多边商业协议法》，MECAL），除其他外，还引入了关于执行 1994 年关贸总协定第 6 条（反倾销）的协定、关于保障措施的协定以及关于阿根廷法律制度的补贴和反补贴税的协定。

根据第 1393/08 号[①] 监管令，经济和生产部部长（现为生产部）及其附属行政机构已被指定为本法令和任何相关行政机构的执行机构。

阿根廷可能因减少关税和其他自由贸易壁垒，以及当地生产者使用世界贸易组织规则规定的补救办法而面临损害性竞争。但是，阿根廷仍然允许反倾销措施和反补贴税手段打击定价不公平的损害性进口产品，并允许在有害进口品定价不公平的情况下采取保障行动。

1. 关于实施 GATT1994 第 6 条的协定（反倾销）

关于适用 GATT1994 第 6 条的多边国际协定（以下简称反倾销协定）阐述，原则上而言，倾销是指在正常商业运作过程中以低于同一制造商 / 卖方 / 出口商在其国内市场上确定的价格出口的同一产品。这就是说，该产品以低于在原产国或其制造地的国内市场消费的该类产品或其他类似产品的“正常价格”的“出口价格”进入另一个国家的市场。

在国家层面，内政部第 1393/08 号法令规定了一项行政程序，规定了反倾销调查的背景。

尽管如此，即使有明确证据表明进口产品是倾销战略的对象，也需要有其他两个法律条件的证据才能适用任何反倾销措施。有必要证明：（1）因价格差异而产生的倾销幅度对有关产品的国家工业部门造成“实际或潜在损害”；（2）倾销行为与所声称的损害之间存在“因果关系”，也就是说，对民族工业的损害是倾销策略的结果。

在阿根廷进行反倾销调查的程序由下列行政机构负责，它们依托于生产部商业部秘书处：

（1）不正当竞争局：这是外国贸易分秘书处下属的一个机构，它是决定假定倾销幅度是否存在的机构。

（2）国家对外贸易委员会：这一委员会负责进行调查，对进口被认定为调查目标的对象所造成的所谓对阿根廷国家生产的破坏进行评估，并且出具倾销与估定损害之间存在因果关系的调查分析报告。

① 该法令规定了反倾销或补贴调查的程序和进行，以确定这些调查是否损害或可能损害国内生产者和国家市场。

2. 关于保障措施的协定

保障协定规定了适用保障措施的规则，这是GATT1994第19条所允许的。

在阿根廷，生产部（及其附属机构、反不正当竞争局和国家外贸委员会）根据第1059/96号法令，负责遵照执行该部关于保障措施内容的协定。第1059/96号法令还规定了行政程序，以便开始及跟踪与保障职责有关的调查。

保障措施是指在某些特定情况下，WTO成员国可采取向本国工业提供保护期的手段，使其能够通过上述调整程序在国际市场上获得更好的竞争力。由于保障措施不是针对某一特定国家的不公平贸易做法而采取的措施，因此无论对某一特定产品的所有进口，都适用这些措施。保障协定规定的此类措施的适用，在满足某些要求时受到限制：

（1）阿根廷当局必须按照预先确定的程序进行调查，调查结果必须确定下列事项：

① 被调查产品的进口量有所增加；

② 阿根廷某一工业部门受到实际或威胁的物质损害；有关产品进口增加与严重损害或严重损害威胁之间存在因果关系。

（2）阿根廷有关工业部门必须遵守旨在提高竞争力的调整方案不同阶段规定的目标，这一方案必须与适用保障措施的请求一并提出。

（3）阿根廷必须保持对受保障措施影响的出口国有利的津贴水平和其他承诺。

（4）阿根廷必须给予出口国事先协商时间，以便在调查期间审查数据，就有关措施交换意见，并就如何实现维持上一段所述津贴的目标达成协议。

3. 关于补贴和反补贴措施的协定

根据补贴和反补贴措施协定，如果政府或任何公共机构在成员国领土内提供财政补助，或有1994年关贸总协定第16条意义上的任何形式的收入或价格支持，并由此获得利益，则应视为存在补贴。

依据98/08号管制令，经济和生产部（现为生产部）及其附属行政机构反不正当竞争局和国家外贸委员会已被指定为执行补贴和反补贴措施协定的执行机构。

4. 南方共同市场

1991年阿根廷、巴西、巴拉圭和乌拉圭（成员国）签署的《亚松森条约》

（成员国）在成员国之间建立了共同市场，具有共同的外部关税，随后，玻利维亚（2015年，目前正在适应南锥体共同市场标准）和委内瑞拉（2012年，但自2016年起暂停）被纳入共同市场。

通过《亚松森条约》，成员国承诺通过以下方式实现货物、服务、人员和资本的自由过境，也就是说，它们承诺建立一个自由贸易区：

（1）取消对货物过境的关税和非关税限制，以及具有类似效果的其他措施；

（2）确定共同对外关税和对非成员国采取共同贸易政策；

（3）成员国在对外贸易、农业、工业、税收、货币汇率、资本投资、服务、运输和通信等方面协调宏观经济和部门政策，以确保成员国之间的适当竞争；

（4）承诺各成员国调整其立法，以加强一体化进程。

南方共同市场内外商业交易的增加，大大增加了在与产品进出口有关的事项上对法律咨询的需求，例如，南方共同市场各技术委员会修改区外对外关税的问题；在不同市场实施技术壁垒，即自由贸易的障碍；输入旧资本资产等。

目前，南方共同市场任何成员国的全部商品供应都享有零进口税的优惠政策。

还应指出的是，为了获得南方共同市场的利益，必须遵守第18号补充经济协定第44号附加议定书目前规定的所谓的原产地制度。

5. 拉丁美洲一体化协会（以下简称协会或ALADI）

1980年8月12日，阿根廷、玻利维亚、巴西、智利、哥伦比亚、厄瓜多尔、墨西哥、巴拉圭、秘鲁、乌拉圭和委内瑞拉等国政府在乌拉圭共和国蒙得维的亚签署了《蒙得维的亚条约》，形成拉丁美洲一体化协会。随后古巴（1999年）和帕纳马（2012年）被纳入该协会，尼加拉瓜目前正在遵守成为该协会成员的条件，尽管它尚未成为其成员。

通过拉丁美洲一体化协会条约，成员国商定适用于每个国家具体情况的差别区域关税优惠。

适用的优惠将取决于：是否在从事国际销售交易的国家之间签署的任何协定中就特定商品的关税进行谈判，以及是否实现了由拉丁美洲一体化协会建立并受代表委员会第78号决议管制的原产地制度。

目前，许多协定已经由该协会全体或部分国家签订完成，这些协定有不同的目标（有部分范围的协议、商业协议、补充的经济协议、农业协定和促进），这取决于它们所监管的问题。

6. 海关条例

（1）进口。向阿根廷进口货物存在三种不同的制度，取决于货物的原产地：一般制度；南方共同市场；拉丁美洲一体化协会。生产部第5/2015号决议还建立了进口许可证制度，将进口商分为两类，即拥有自动进口许可证的进口商和持有非自动进口许可证的进口商。许可证类型之间的主要区别是，持有非自动进口许可证的进口商必须在输入特定信息之前提交比持有自动进口许可证的进口商必须提交的更具体的信息。

（2）一般制度。一般制度适用于从南方共同市场或拉丁美洲一体化协会集团以外的国家进口产品。阿根廷采用了南方共同市场制度，其中规定了每一种情况下必须根据进口商品支付的税率百分比，如进口税、统计税率、增值税及增值税、预缴所得税和毛额税构成的自留总保费。

（3）出口。阿根廷出口管制的规定与进口管制有着根本性的区别。阿根廷政府通过经济部第11/02号决议征收出口关税。适用的税率一般从5%到20%不等，视商品类型而定。

因此，南方共同市场或拉丁美洲一体化协会给予的好处不适用于货物出口，因为出口业务中的关税没有减少。

尽管如此，《海关法》第820条至第833条、第1011/91号和第1012/91号法令以及修正案规定了某些出口利益。

7. 有利于进出口商的制度

在过去的几年里，当局引入了不同的进出口制度，使某些商品的进口商和出口商受益。下面我们列出其中的一些，尽管有其他更特定的制度来进行某些活动。

（1）进口二手资本资产。作为总体规则，阿根廷禁止进口废旧资本资产。尽管有这一般性限制，阿根廷当局（原经济、公共工程和服务部）已颁布第909/94号决议，该决议为那些历史不超过20年并已重建或重新调整的资本资产规定了具体的进口制度。这些货物将根据具体情况征收6%、14%或28%的进口税。

（2）进口二手生产线。2016年，生产部通过了第1174/16号决议，旨在鼓励投资，利用旧机器提高工业化产品的竞争力，为此，该决议规定，根据该进口制度进口的二手货应按进口时相应的正常进口税的25%征税，并进一步免除进口关税。该进口制度还要求获得该项目新的国家资本资产总价值的30%。

（3）为大型投资项目进口货物。尽管这一进口制度也是旨在鼓励投资以提高使用旧机器的工业化产品的竞争力的促进措施，但在这种情况下，经济部第 256/00 号决议对构成新的完全自主生产线一部分的所有新产品规定了零进口税，并免除了它们支付目的地验证费用。部件也可进口，但不得超过拟进口货物总值的 5%。该进口制度还要求获得该项目新的国家资本资产价值的 20%。

（4）进口货物—供生产和再出口—不缴纳关税。第 1330/04 号法令规定了“临时进口的类型化证书”（CTIT 为西班牙缩写），允许进口商在阿根廷完善原材料或产品并重新出口。这一制度的一个主要好处是，只要进口的原材料或货物是完善和再出口过程的一部分，就不需要支付任何费用。

（5）退税。退税制度是一种促销激励，允许出口商获得进口关税、统计税率和增值税，它们为进口投入支付，然后用于出口产品的生产和包装。受该制度影响的商品不得在正式许可证生效之日以外的最终出口。

（6）安全认证。为了遵守当地标准，国内贸易局要求几种特定产品在阿根廷进行商业销售需要安全认证，包括钢铁、电梯、节能产品、打火机、玩具、电气产品、工业安全、纺织和鞋类、墨水。

四、投资工具 / 公司

尽管外国投资者可以使用许多工具在阿根廷设立和管理其项目，但最受欢迎的是：股份公司、有限责任公司和分公司。以下是最常用的投资工具的简介。

（一）公司运转模式

在阿根廷，获得法律行为能力的机构数目有限，即被承认为与其成员不同的实体。其中，最常见的类型是《普通公司法》规定的 8 种不同的公司类型。外国公司也可以在不创建当地公司的情况下开展其商业活动：它们可以自己直接或通过当地分支机构从事商业活动。

根据《普通公司法》第 123 条，为了参与阿根廷的法人机构，外国实体必须在阿根廷任何一个省的商业公共登记处登记。在一些省份，这种登记是由一个特别法院管理的，而在另一些省则是政府机构。然而，大多数是在布宜诺斯艾利斯市登记的，因为它不仅是国家的首都，而且也是主要的金融中心。尽管如此，有些省份的登记更容易、更便宜，但有时（主要是由于目前的官僚作风）并不一定更快。

1. 股份公司（Sociedad Anónima）

股份公司目前是阿根廷最常见的商业组织形式，不仅因为其管理相对简单，而且因为它是股东对第三方责任限制于其股权参与范围内的公司种类之一（除去如下文所述的个别法律实体可能被忽视的特殊情况外）。

（1）股东。股份公司可以有一个或多个股东、个人或公司，作为其成立公司的门槛。除统一个人（AnóNima）外，在股份公司的整个生命周期内，应保持多个股东的多元化，使其保持良好的地位。

在两家或两家以上的股东公司中，布宜诺斯艾利斯市监管当局的一般做法是要求小股东至少拥有 2% 的股本，这被认为是相当多的。在剩下的大多数阿根廷省，不存在实质性的多元化门槛。但是，如果股东的出资来自国外，由于这些条例的联邦性质，10% 的门槛不仅适用于在布宜诺斯艾利斯市注册的公司，而且也适用于全国各地的公司和公司的每一位股东（即使是有两名以上股东的公司也是如此）。如果任何股东是外国公司，它必须首先向相应的监督机构登记其公司文件，以证明该公司是按照其公司所在国的法律合理组织的。布宜诺斯艾利斯市规定的要求比各省的要求更严格，但登记通常更快。

（2）资本。一家股份公司必须拥有至少 10 万阿根廷比索（约合 5000 美元）[①] 的最低公司资本。在布宜诺斯艾利斯市，这一最低限额必须根据公司目标的范围提高，直到监督当局审慎地认为前者足以使公司完成后者。该股本必须以面值相等的股份代表，以阿根廷比索计值。资本必须全数认购，如在

① 截至 2018 年 5 月，美元兑澳大利亚元汇率约为 25 美元。

成立时被裁定须以现金支付，则须在成立法团时缴付该股本的至少25%。余下的必须在其后两年内支付。

发行不同类别的股票是可能的，而附则必须提供每一类股票所享有的权利，发行不同类别的股票可以为保护小股东提供一种非常有效的途径。附则还可以包括对股权转让的限制，这些限制是在附则提交商业公共登记处批准时加以监督的，因此通常会在股东协议中列入可能经不起官方审查的更严格限制。此类协议在当事人中有效，但对第三方不能强制执行，这是法律规定的情况。要确定何种限度的灰色地带才能通过登记处的审查的标准是，股份/配额的转让可以受到法律的限制，但不受法律的禁止。例如，规定向第三方转让股份/配额需要一致或多数同意的条款，或给予合伙人或公司优先拒绝或优先权的条款可被视为有效，只要这种合同规则在实践中并不意味着（由于其性质或范围）禁止转让。

最近制定的简化股份公司对股份转让作出了特别规定，因为注册文书可包括最长10年的转让禁止条款。列入这一禁止条款必须得到代表全部股本的股东的批准。

在支付股东认购的股份时，允许进行实物投资，法律规定了评估这种投资价值的具体方法。①

（3）公司目的。股份公司必须定义其公司目标，这必须是单一和独特的，尽管与这种主要目的相关的辅助活动也可以考虑纳入其中。

任何股份公司，除纯粹为金融或投资目的而成立的公司外，不得取得或维持一间或多于一间公司的权益，其数额超过其可自由动用的储备金及其资本及法定储备的一半，但如因股票分红或储备资本化而造成超额，则属例外。任何超额必须在批准之日起计6个月内出售。年度财务报表，如有这种超额证明，则处罚为暂时丧失表决权以及任何可能使其有权获得的利润。股利分配给股东的有效条件是，其产生的已实现利润和已清算利润与常规、核准的财务报表相对应。

任何股份公司，除为金融或投资目的组建的公司外，不得在一家或多家公司，获取或维持数额超过其可自由支配的准备金及其资本和法定准备金的

① 如果资本是实物支付的，则必须在成立时支付100%。

一半，但如超额是股票红利或准备金资本化的结果，则不在此限。

任何超额必须在反映这种超额证明的年度财务报表被批准之日起计 6 个月内出售，并对超额公司处以惩罚，暂时剥夺其表决权以及由这种超额行为可能带来的任何利润。

股利分配给股东是有效的，只要它们处于定期的、核准的财务报表所示已实现利润和清算利润范围内。

（4）管理。股份公司由股东任命的一名或多名成员组成的董事会管理。董事会成员的最长任期为三个财政年度。股份公司的法定代表权授予董事会主席，这意味着，一般而言，他 / 她以这种身份所做的工作对公司有约束力。

非居民可获委任为董事，但必须注意如下事项：

① 董事会多数成员必须是阿根廷居民。如果董事会只有一名成员，则该成员必须是阿根廷居民。

② 董事会必须定期举行会议，至少每三个月举行一次。

③ 产生有效的董事会决定所需的最低法定人数是其成员的绝对多数，这一最低限度可在章程或股东协议中增加。

④ 董事可以由代理人代为出席，但这仅在不计入该董事时的出席人数已经达到最低法定限定人数的情况下才被允许。

⑤ 所有董事会成员，无一例外，必须向税务机关登记，以获得税务登记号码，他们还必须作为独立工作者向社会保障机构登记。

⑥ 布宜诺斯艾利斯市的董事会成员必须提供担保，以保证他们的业绩，这种担保必须至少在个人基础上为 1 万美元。保险政策是最符合这一要求的手段。

（5）内部控制人员。董事会的业绩由一名控制人员监督，他必须是注册会计师或律师。他的主要职责是签署资产负债表，代表股东监督公司的活动，并核实董事照顾公司利益的责任。私营公司不需要长期雇用控制人员。由于他们的公司资本低于 1000 万里亚尔（约合 40 万美元），他们不得从事公共特许经营，也不参与银行或金融服务有关的活动。

（6）股东会议。年度普通股东大会必须审议和批准上一个财政年度的财务报表、董事会成员和控制人的业绩，以及必要时任命董事和 / 或控制人。这一强制性会议必须在每个财政年度结束后 5 个月内举行。

除普通股东大会外，特别股东大会可随时召开，主要审议所有其他事项。

普通股东大会涉及公司的一般行政事项，包括任命董事和高级人员、批准财务报表等。决定资本增加或资本减少、兼并和分拆、章程修正案或一般业务以外的其他决定等事项则由特别股东大会决定。

表 1　股东会议的分类

		法定人数（最低出席率）	多数（作出有效决定所需人数）
普通股东大会	第一次召集	50%+1votingshares 50% 股份代表 +1 股有表决权股份（对应代表）	出席人数占多数（除非附例规定更高的百分比）
	第二次召集	无法定最低出席人数	出席人数占多数（除非附例规定更高的百分比）
特别股东大会	第一次召集	60% 有表决权股份代表（除非附例规定更高的百分比）	出席人数占多数（除非附例规定更高的百分比）
	第二次召集	30% 有表决权股份代表（除非附例规定更高的百分比）	出席人数占多数（除非附例规定更高的百分比）

（7）根据阿根廷法律，公司住所应是其主要活动的所在地，每次变更住所均应在《政府公报》上公布，以便监督当局能够监督其管辖范围内的公司活动。

2. 单一人公司（Unifad）

单一人公司是一种股份公司，其他商业实体不得由单一股东注册。因此，适用于股份公司的所有规定都适用于单一成员公司。但是，单一人公司也须遵守以下要求：由相应的控制人机构审计；必须指定一名代表代理人从事业务。

3. 有限责任公司（Sociedadde Responsabilidad Limitada）

有限责任公司是继股份公司之后阿根廷第二受欢迎的公司形式，它与股份公司都有易于管理的好处（有限责任公司的管理很可能甚至更容易，成本也更便宜），并将合伙人相对于第三方的责任限制在各自的股权参与范围内。

有限责任公司的一些缺点是规模有限（允许成员不超过 50 人），需要向监督机构登记任何资本转让，以及不能参与公开发行股票或债务，这与股份公司不同。有限责任公司通常用于旨在尽量减少经营成本的中小型企业。

（1）有限责任公司的特征与股份有限公司的特征相当相似，但有限责任公司的股本是以配额而不是股份来代表的，合伙人的数量最少为 2 人，最多为 50 人。这两种公司对外国实体成为股东的要求是相同的。

有限责任公司成立，在法律上并不需要最低限度的公司资本。不过，一般情况下，这类公司成立的最低资本为 3 万阿根廷比索。全数认购及最低实缴出资的规定，与股份公司的相同。

同样，关于不可撤销出资和公司住所的规定与股份公司相同。

（2）管理和监督。有限责任公司有一个管理委员会，其无须如股份公司一样每三个月举行一次经理会议。经理的任期可能不明确。公司的法定代表权属于一个或多个经理。在后一种情况下，大多数经理必须居住在阿根廷。

在布宜诺斯艾利斯市，每一位经理必须提供 1 万阿根廷比索的最低担保，视公司资本而定。无论如何，这种担保也可以通过保险政策来履行。

与股份公司一样，非上市有限责任公司不需要雇用控制人员，只要其公司资本低于 1000 万阿根廷比索，它们不从事公共特许权或从事与银行或金融服务有关的活动，但必须有一名控制人。

（3）有限责任公司“快车道”注册。商业公共登记处最近建立了有限责任公司注册的“快车道”程序，该程序允许公司成立、签署和盖章，并在初始提交后 24 小时内签发税号。

4. 简化股份公司（Sociedadpor Acciones Simplificada）

简化股份公司是阿根廷法律制度最近采用的一种工具，其目的是支持阿根廷的创业精神，因为它为没有广泛经验的新的和不那么成熟的投资者提供了一种简化的工具。这种工具意味着股东的有限责任，因为他们的责任仅限于他们所持有的股份的百分比范围内。

（1）资本。一家简化的股份公司的资本分成股份。最低资本相当于公司最低工资的两倍，其中至少 25% 在公司成立之时支付。资本应在公司成立之日起两年内完成实缴。

（2）公司目的。简化股份公司的公司目的可以是多元的，并应明确描述公司将要进行的活动。

（3）管理。简化股份公司的管理应确定一人或多人、股东或非股东，特定或非特定范围内承担责任。

（4）股份转让的限制。公司成立文书可以包括长达10年的禁止转让条

款，该禁止条款必须得到代表股本总额的股东的批准。

5. 分支机构（Sucursal）

分支机构在阿根廷也颇受欢迎。它们的主要特点是责任不限于分支机构自身，而是母公司对分支机构进行的所有交易承担无限责任。与相对独立的子公司相比，这可能被视为一个缺点。

分支机构的管理和代表由母公司董事会任命的人负责。一般而言，分支机构的代表与股份公司董事会成员负有同样的责任。

子公司和分支机构有类似的会计要求，因为它们必须为阿根廷业务保持单独的会计记录。然而，在分支机构的情况下，公司控制更为简单。股份公司的法定报告要求和控制使它们比分支机构运行起来更加复杂和昂贵。此外，分支机构的管理比股份公司更简单，因为分支机构没有董事会，不召开股东会议。

6. 外国公司的直接活动

外国公司在阿根廷可以在没有向有关当局登记的情况下在阿根廷采取行动，但这种活动仅限于出庭和进行孤立的活动。当地法律没有明确界定什么是孤立的活动，但人们普遍认为，比如说，购买单一的房地产尚可算处于其定义范围内。因此，外国公司无论其是子公司抑或者是分支机构，其任何进一步活动（出租或以任意方式挖掘房地产价值）都将引发强制注册，从而导致所有外国公司的行为无法（自主）执行。

《一般公司法》第118条有关部分规定：惯常业务为履行其公司目的所包含的惯常行为，为设立分支机构、营业场所或任何其他类型的常驻代表（外国实体），必须：（1）证明公司是根据阿根廷法律存在的；（2）在阿根廷共和国设立住所，遵守本法对在阿根廷共和国注册的公司的公布和登记要求；（3）就设立上述代表人的决定提供证据，并指定受委托的人。

此外，就某一分支机构而言，在特殊法律要求下，必须确定赋予它的资本。这一要求的根本要点是，阿根廷的永久商业活动被要求采用当地立法规定的外国公司在阿根廷经营的一种形式（如果这种经营超出“孤立行为”的概念）：分支机构将被视为外国实体在当地的延伸，而附属公司将具有不同的身份。规则不仅适用于建立正式的法律代表，而且适用于在地方一级发展任何类型的常设活动，如在阿根廷提供服务，包括参加合资企业和一般的其他合作协定那样。

7. 揭开公司面纱

揭开公司面纱，或无视法律实体，仅在一家公司被用作其股东的欺诈工具时才适用。因此，只要公司以法律允许的方式运作，阿根廷法律就保证合伙人的有限责任。这一解释源于两项法律规定：

《一般公司法》第 54 条第 3 款规定："公司企图隐瞒对社会目标的追求，充当违反法律的工具，违反强制性的公共基础、诚信原则或阻挠第三方权利的行为，将直接归咎于使这种行为成为可能的股东或控制人，由其各自承担连带责任。"

《破产法》第 161 条规定："破产影响应扩大到破产公司的实际控制人，条件是他们违背受控公司的公司利益行事，为了控制人或控制人所属的经济集团的利益，将受控公司置于统一管理之下。"

由于上述原因，有三个必要要素来触发无视例外的应用：公司控制、欺诈或不当行为，以及对第三方造成的损害或不当损失。这一理论的法理建构是有严格限制的，也就是说，当有要素是否具备存疑时，不予适用该项规则。

8. 法律发展：企业支持法

2017 年颁布了第 27349 号《创业法》，目的是支持阿根廷境内的创业活动和实现国际增长。它还为新投资者通过简化交易开发自己的项目提供了一种手段。此外，该法还规定了税收优惠，即资本投资可以从所得税中扣除。

（二）非法人机构组织

本节专门讨论缺乏法律行为能力的组织形式，即被认定为与构成该组织形式的成员没有不同的组织形式。然而，使用这些组织架构能为企业带来某些好处，如管理简单、成本较低和二级市场充足等。

1. 信托

信托的优点包括其简单性（仅以信托协议的方式组织）、对不同项目和计划的适应性以及它们给予的保护，因为信托资产不能由信托债权人以外的任何债权人获得。信托的主要缺点是受托人有严格的责任制度，信托的时间限制最多 30 年。至于它们是否能自动延长到类似或更短的时间，目前存疑。

如前所述，信托是通过信托协议设立的，但信托转让的资产必须按照其性质办理转让手续。例如，不动产必须通过订立公共转让契据并向有关房地产登记处登记所有权变更而转让。

信托有三种类型：行政信托、担保信托和金融信托。前两种信托所追求的是不同的：行政信托是根据信托创建者的具体和详细的指示为受托人创建的，而担保信托是通过抵押品设立的，受托人通常被迫将资产让与债权人。无论何时发生违约事件。在这个意义上，担保信托非常类似于托管协议。金融信托拥有一种非常不同的性质。它们是作为一种证券化工具创建的，通过这种方式，受托人对他所信托的资产发行股票和债务证书，用于偿还这些证券。这一工具的优点是，公募和私募都可采用这种形式。

应当指出，在阿根廷，信托的受托人和创造者必须是不同的个人或公司。信托的创造者和受益人也必须如此。

2. 联合体

（1）联合体（Agrupacionesde Colboración Empresaria，ACE）：居所地在阿根廷的当地公司和企业家可通过一项分组合同，建立一个共同组织，以促进或发展其成员的某些商业活动，或改善或增加这种活动的成果。

外国公司若要参加联合体，就必须在阿根廷注册分支机构或子公司。前述机构本身不能为谋取利润进行活动，但该集团可能产生的任何收入应直接惠及集团或集团的公司。联合体不与第三方进行任何活动，只监督其成员的内部活动，为其成员谋取利益。

联合体的管理是由集团合同中指定的一名或多名个人或由联合体成员通过的一项决议进行的。参与者的捐款和由此获得的资产构成联合体业务的共同财产。

联合体成员对其代表以团体名义承担的义务，对第三方负有连带责任。但是只有在要求联合体经理支付未获成功的付款后，才可对任何参与者采取追责行动。

当联合体代表以某一特定参与者的名义承担义务，并已通知所涉第三方时，则该参与者应（以自身财产）与联合体共同运作资金一起承担连带责任。

（2）临时公司联盟（Uniones Transitoriasde Empresas，UTE）。住所地在阿根廷的当地公司和企业家可以根据 UTE 合同在阿根廷境内或境外加入开展特定目标或服务的合同。它们可以发展或开展补充与支持主要目标的工程和服务。在国外组织的公司可以以当地注册的分支机构资格参加此类协议。

这些联盟既不是公司，也不是法人，其权利和义务受一般公司法的规定管辖。这种联盟的合同必须符合一般公司法，并在商业公共登记处登记。

（3）合作联盟（Consorciode Cooperación，CC）合作财团是由第 26005 号法律创建的一种相对较新的商业协会形式。该组织的结构与临时公司工会的结构十分相似，其成员不承担连带责任，其责任范围以其在合作联盟中的份额为限。然而，决定应由大多数成员作出。

合作联盟还需要一个业务基金，在这种合作联盟的整个有效期内不可分割。

（三）商业渠道：分销和代理协议

新《民商法》载有关于代理、分销和销售代表协议的广泛而详细的规定（虽然有些判例法已经存在并被用作指南，但在当地法律之前没有加以规定），虽然新《民商法》的许多条款是缺省规定（除非双方另有协议，否则它们将适用于任何协议），但其中有些规定已被确立为强制性规定以及公共政策事项。后者适用于所有代理或分配协议，而不论合同各方可能另有约定或选择适用外国法律这一事实。

就代理协议而言，《民商法》第 1492 条规定，协议生效后，每年无理由终止合同，需提前一个月通知；换而言之，一项已生效六年的协议的终止需要提前六个月的通知。该条还规定，不遵守事先通知的要求使不终止协议的一方获得就代理人在法律规定的通知期内本应获得的利润获得赔偿的权利。该规则遵循阿根廷关于这一问题的现行判例法。

随着对这类协议的新规定，人们普遍怀疑当事人是否可以对关于通知期的规定不予理会，即如果当事各方可以设定较之第 1492 条规定的通知期而言更短的通知期，因为《民商法》生效以来的时间较短，法院还尚未有机会规制此事项。第 1497 条也赋予代理人在协议终止后获得赔偿的权利，条件是代理人在协议过程中的行动为委托人带来重大利益。这种客户补偿须由法院决定，除非双方自主成功解决该问题。

五、资本市场

（一）概览

阿根廷的资本市场主要受第 26831 号法律（《资本市场法》，以下简称 CML），第 23576 号法律（承付款项，LON）、第 24083 号法律（共同投资基金和封闭式投资基金，MCIF）、《民商法》和其他相应颁布的条例和规则的管制。对资本市场的控制和监督是由一个单一的专门机构——国家证券委员会（SNC）进行的。

CML 有着最重要的规则，包含有关整个资本市场环境的主要和最重要的条款。LON 包括对最受欢迎的地方债券可转让债务的一项具体规定。MICF 规范了当地的共有、开放式和封闭式基金。《民商法》载有关于金融信托的规定，金融信托是实现证券化目的最常见的工具。最后，SNC 规则载有本地资本市场内任何类型活动的具体和详细规定。

尽管行政当局是由行政部门任命的，但委员会是一个自主的机构，它发布自己的内部规则，并有自己的独立预算。SNC 的董事、官员和雇员在该领域应具备资格和经验，并通常有业务重点方针。尽管如此，政治变化通常影响到 SNC 董事会的组成及其业务方向。

SNC 负责执行 CML，提出新的条例，控制股票和衍生品交易所，批准自己的规则，对在当地资本市场内活动的实体（经纪人、托管代理人、结算机构等）发放许可证和进行登记，并对任何违反证券规则的实体或个人实施处罚。

SNC 的规定受到美国证券交易委员会的条例和西班牙王国的《民族议会条例》的很大启发，最近于 2012 年颁布，CML 深受 IOSCO 建议的影响，代表了当地资本市场的一种新的“强有力的控制”倾向。阿根廷的资本市场由于不同的规则的批准，特别是在关系最紧密的股票市场之间进行了某些收购之后，正在不断地演变。

新一届政府于 2015 年 12 月就职，为了吸引外国投资者和建立明确而简单的指导方针，几乎没有批准新的规则，从而使当地资本市场保持强劲和持续的增长[①]。

阿根廷的股票市场是私人实体，它们发布自己的规则和规章。然而，这些条例需要事先得到 SNC 的批准才能强制执行。

最重要的地方股票市场是：Bolsas y Mercados Argentinos S.A.（ByMA，是 the Bolsa de Comercio de Buenos Aires and the Mercado de Valores de Buenos Aires S.A 的合并体）；电子公开市场（西班牙语中的 Mercado Abierto Electrónico or MAE）；Mercado a Término de Buenos Aires S.A.（MATBA，主要进行农业衍生品交易）；ROFEX，这是罗萨里奥市（Rosario）的股票交易所，衍生品（货币等）主要在那里交易。

尽管当地资本市场仍未充分发挥其潜力，但主要参与者非常有创造力，因此能够开发有助于市场发展的新产品。[②]

（二）公开发售和许可证

在阿根廷境内公开发行证券或相关服务应事先在 SNC 之前注册。公开发行的定义见 CML 第 2 节，范围极为广泛。涵盖可能提供的任何手段（包括但不限于，一对一会议、电话或电子邮件通信等），并且没有提供针对目标公众的含义的唯一定义。

CML 既没有私人配售豁免，也没有安全港制度，也没有注册豁免制度。尽管一些学者和当地律师的个案指导可能有助于制定具体规则以规避公开发行条例，但目前尚无任何可接受或可容忍的市场操作得到 SNC 的正式或非正式批准。

在阿根廷境内未经许可公开发行证券可能导致行政或刑事制裁和民事责任。

1. 公开发售注册及上市程序

在进行任何类型的证券公开发行之前，都需要在证券公司登记之前进行登记。通常情况下，证券公司的登记过程从第一次申请起不少于 3 个月。这一登记将使发价人进入一种具体的控制制度，即所谓的公开发行制度。在公

① 与巴西等 500 多家公司在股票市场上市的其他国家不同，BIMA（当地主要股票市场）的上市公司不到 100 家。

② 根据标准普尔，阿根廷市场仍然是前沿市场。

开发行制度下登记的任何实体都将成为受 SNC 监督的实体，且其应遵守某些具体规定（如披露义务、提交某些财务信息等）。

一旦进入公开发行制度，任何随后发行的证券也必须登记。通常，这种进一步的登记要短得多，而且容易得多。

授权证券不会自动在股票市场上市。在（进入）相关市场之前，必须遵循采用不同但更简单的程序。

特定的 SNC 和股票市场规则可根据所提供和上市的证券种类而适用。

2. 许可过程

任何单位如欲在本地资本市场内进行任何构成公开提供服务的活动，应事先获发代理商执照。根据活动类型不同，可适用不同类别的许可证。主要代理类别如下：

（1）补偿和清算代理人：有权与有关市场结算其交易的经纪人。

（2）谈判代理人：为获得结算服务而与赔偿和清算代理人有联系的经纪人。

（3）综合存款代理：也提供保管和登记服务的清关实体。

（4）托管和登记代理人：只提供托管和登记服务的实体。

（5）全球投资顾问：私人银行交易商。

如同公开发行制度一样，一旦获得许可证，实体将受到 SNC 的严格控制，并适用具体规则。大多数公开发行制度规则也适用于被许可实体。任何被许可实体只能从事其许可范围内的活动，其必须特别考虑可能适用的具体禁止事项。

在阿根廷领土内进行未经许可的活动可能导致行政制裁和民事责任。

（三）上市公司

公司希望上市的，应当事先进入公开发行制度，取得首次公开发行的具体登记，并在有关市场进行上市手续。如上所述，适用公开发行制度的规定。

任何上市公司在公开发行制度范围内均受 SNC 最严格的控制。最重要的一些规定适用于董事独立性、相关实体交易、投标报价制度、股份回购、不披露重要信息、审计委员会等方面。

财务报表必须按年度和季度公布，并按 NIIF 编制。股东和董事会会议可由 SNC 的监督人员任命。另外，上市公司一旦进入公开发行制度，应遵循特定的规范化程序，逐步完成相关事项并最终退出这一制度。

请注意，未上市的实体受更宽松的公开发行制度约束。

（四）许可的实体

被许可的实体，如经纪人—交易商代理人，一旦注册，应遵守国家统计局颁布的某些具体规则，除其他外，他们应保持最低净值（其中的部分应纳入流动资产），任命一名管理人员和公共关系官员等，向客户收取的任何费用应予以公布，在某些情况下，应事先得到 SNC 的批准。

获得许可证可能需要支付初始费用和年费，具体取决于许可证类型。被许可的实体的宣传活动必须明确提及其拥有的许可证类型，并披露登记号。

（五）一级市场

任何进入一级市场的实体都应获得登记或许可证，这取决于所要进行的活动。一旦公开发行在 SNC 登记后，一级市场只能由注册实体或通常是经纪人—交易商代理的特许代理人进入。

预登记活动只有在备案后，根据某些严格的披露规则才能得到授权。任何预登记活动都应限于特定的目标，任何相关的文件都应妥善保存。

一旦发行被批准，营销前期适用于发行结束之前。这类前期营销可能会因交易类型和实体而有所不同。

招股说明书和其他文件应提交、授权并随后发布为投资者信息。此类文件必须包括任何相关的商业、法律和财务信息。

可以采用不同的定价方法（造书、固定价格、投标等），通常使用SICOLP（由BIMA提供）和SIOPEL（由MAE提供）IT系统来组织、构建和完成整个募集过程。结算通常通过主要的清关实体（Caja de Valores S.A.）完成。

例如，在 SICOLP 的情况下，它的主要功能是[①]：

（1）配售管理：该系统允许市场管理主要配售投标事项、更改一般配售信息、查询和列出一般配售细节、公布招股说明书和文件、计算截止价值和

① 根据 http：/www.merval.sba.com.ar 提供的信息。

关闭配售渠道。

（2）对用户的管理：这一系统允许市场管理用户，允许或禁止他们与单一、多个或全部市场位置产生联系。

（3）要约管理：只要其报价状态是公开的，系统就允许用户记录特定价位的报价信息。因此，用户可以接受要约或提出自己的要约。

（4）公布自己的出价信息。

目前，阿根廷一级市场正在增长，特别是最近推出了新的、重大的首次公开发行（IPO），使市场略有扩大。过去 10 ~ 15 年，阿根廷初级市场只用于公债（以弥补财政赤字和其他公共开支）和私人债券（主要用于为营运资本融资），但最近出现了一种新的趋势，使新产品能够激励基础设施项目的融资。

（六）二级市场

与一级市场一样，禁止未经许可的实体或个人直接进入交易所（QIB 除外）。任何个人或实体如果打算在任何交易所进行交易，必须事先与被许可实体联系，开立账户，并通过该被许可实体的代理进行操作。

最重要的地方交易所有各种实体可以经营的部分。通常情况下，交易是通过担保部分进行的，在这部分交易中，交易所作为交易双方的中间交易对接方，交易由交易所担保。

该部门依靠一个基于计算机的平台进行公共或私人证券的交易，该平台允许实时进入投标 / 报价计划，从而能够执行交易（Sinac）；它以价格—时间优先级为基础以及要约的介入运行。

没有市场中介的被许可实体也可以使用其他无担保部分，例如，在 ByMA 的情况下，这种部分被称为双边部分，它允许通过被许可实体或 QIB 之间的直接安排进行证券交易。

在这种情况下，任何已执行的命令都应在相关市场和自己的实体账簿中登记。其他要求可根据市场情况适用。

目前，阿根廷二级市场体量不深，主要集中在股票或公债交易上，其他产品的二级市场，如私人债券、共同基金配额和金融信托发行的证券，一般都不存在。

六、税务

在阿根廷，有两级政府可以征税：联邦政府和省政府。所述税收管辖权的界限由国家《宪法》和《联邦税务共同参与法》第 23548 号规定。此外，各省内的不同市政厅也可以根据相应的省《宪法》规定的限额征税。

各级政府应在其管辖范围内制定相应的税收立法，从而对在其领土内征收的每项税收的不同要素作出规定。

（一）在阿根廷成立公司或分支机构

股份公司或有限责任公司的成立须向联邦公共收入管理局（AFIP）登记，并向公司提供税务识别号码（cuit），以供 AFIP 和其他纳税人识别。此外，该公司还将获得一个税务密码，以便进入 AFIP 的在线系统进行报税及办理其他税务事务。

公司必须在 AFIP 注册为所得税、推定最低所得税和增值税的纳税人。

此外，为了雇用雇员，公司必须在 AFIP 登记为雇主、社保缴纳义务人、扣缴义务人，以便代表其雇员遵守社会保障制度。

在省级税务方面，公司还必须向省税务机关登记，并与其纳税地址相对应。

外国公司的分支机构必须遵守与当地公司相同的税收规定。因此，它们必须遵守上述所有登记要求。

（二）主要国家税

1. 所得税

所得税是对阿根廷个人、法人实体和外国实体的阿根廷分支机构的全球收入征收的国家税。在阿根廷，没有常设机构的非居民个人或法人实体仅通过预扣税系统对其阿根廷收入来源征税。

所得税是根据每个财政年度取得的净收入缴纳的。一般情况下，如果是法人或企业，应将收入分配给应计财政年度。

适用于法人的税率为 35%，亏损可结转至接下来 5 个财政年度。

截至 2016 年 7 月，公用事业费用或利润的支付不需缴纳所得税，因此，当地公司向外国股东支付的股息不在所得税预扣缴范围内。

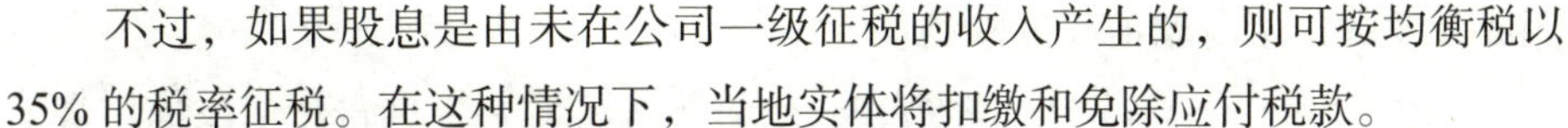

不过，如果股息是由未在公司一级征税的收入产生的，则可按均衡税以35%的税率征税。在这种情况下，当地实体将扣缴和免除应付税款。

2. 所得税预扣缴制度

根据《所得税法》（ITL）第91条，当地当事方在发出付款之前，必须扣缴应缴税款。

一般情况下，外国居民不得扣除获取和维持收入来源的费用。相反，推定净收入（应纳税基数）将由ITL确定。应纳税基础将根据交易类型而有所不同。有些例外可能因交易类型（如出售股份）而适用。

3. 转移定价

从税收的角度来看，关联方之间的交易必须遵守转移定价规则。这些交易所商定的价格必须遵循一定的原则：关联方商定的价格和条件应像各个独立主体协商议定的价格与条件一样。阿根廷转移定价条例规定了确定这一价格的六种潜在方法［可比较的无管制价格（CUP）］、转售价格、成本添加、利润分割和交易净利润率（TNM）和第六种仅适用于商品的方法。根据ITL，必须使用最佳方法规则对给定操作的转让价格进行合理调整。

因此，阿根廷公司、信托或常设机构与相关实体——甚至是在低税或无税管辖区（避税地）注册或位于其中的无关实体（避税地）进行的交易，如果不符合上文所述的标准，可受到税务当局的质疑。

4. 双重征税政策

阿根廷是许多双重征税条约的缔约国，其中有18项条约目前正在生效，包括与德国、澳大利亚、比利时、玻利维亚、巴西、加拿大、智利、丹麦、西班牙、芬兰、法国、英国、意大利、挪威、荷兰、俄罗斯、瑞士、瑞典和乌拉圭签署的条约。此外，阿根廷最近签署了执行税收条约有关措施的多边公约，以防止经济合作与发展组织推动的税基侵蚀和利润转移，尽管该公约目前尚未得到批准并生效。

目前生效的大多数条约都是按照经济合作与发展组织公约的方针制定的。

5. 增值税（VAT）

增值税是对销售货物、提供服务和进口货物征收的一种联邦税。一方面，在某些情况下，在阿根廷境内被有效使用或开发，并在该国境外提供的服务也必受增值税规制。另一方面，在阿根廷境内提供的服务被认为是在国外使用或开发的，不受增值税的限制。

增值税是在生产或分配货物或服务的每一阶段，根据每一阶段的增加值支付的，并按所谓的税收借方（出售给客户的货物或服务的产出增值税）和税收抵免（从供应商收到的货物或服务的输入增值税）之间的差额征收。税收借方和税收抵免的差额，如果是正值，则就是向税务机关支付的金额。

现在的一般增值税税率为 21%，但如某些资本货品的买卖和进口，以及外国及国内银行贷款的利息，则须按 10.5% 的特别税率征收；而对于大部分公用事业服务，特别是天然气、电力、水和电讯的服务，则征收第三类增值税，税率为 27%。

6. 假定最低所得税（PMIT）

PMIT 适用于阿根廷公司以及外国实体和个人在阿根廷的所有资产，利率为 1%，条件是该实体的资产总值在其财政年度（财政期）结束时超过 20 万阿根廷比索。支付的税款可视为以后 10 年的所得税抵免。

请注意，根据联邦法律第 27260 条，从 2019 年 1 月 1 日起，该税将自动被废除。

7. 个人资产税（TPA）

自每个财政年度的 12 月 31 日起，对纳税人拥有的资产征收。所有阿根廷居民对其全球超过 80 万阿根廷比索的资产征收这一税。根据联邦法律第 27260 条，这一税基在 2017 年将提高到 95 万阿根廷比索，到 2008 年将提高到 105 万阿根廷比索。目前，阿根廷居民适用的税率为 0.75%，这一税率将在 2017 年财政年度降低为 0.50%，2018 年及其后财政年度进一步降为 0.25%。

当地法律实体不受 TPA 约束，它们的资产受 PMIT 约束。

然而，非阿根廷居民只对其位于阿根廷的资产征收此项税。持有当地公司股份和 / 或其他股权参与的外国法律实体须按当地公司净资产的 0.25% 的税率征收。在这种情况下，必须由当地公司代表股东缴纳税款。当地公司可在此之后要求由相应的股东或权益所有人偿还这些款项。

根据国家最高法院 2014 年 12 月 16 日就东京三菱 UFJ 银行有限公司一案作出的裁决，就 TPA 而言，分支机构不应被视为与其总部分开的实体。因此，就分支机构而言，外国总部对当地分支机构的所有权并不等同于外国总部持有的分支机构股权。因此，总部并不应被征收此项税，而本地分支机构也不应扣缴此税项。

8. 银行账户借记和贷计税（TDCBA）

TDCBA 根据阿根廷金融机构账户中的借项和贷项以及用于替代银行账户的其他交易进行评估。具体而言，每项借方和贷方的分摊率为 0.6%。某些不是通过银行账户进行的资金转账可按 1.2% 的此项税税率缴纳。

此外，特别支票账户的登记变动在以外国人名义开立并专门用于阿根廷的金融投资时免征本税。

（三）主要省税

这些税收要求存在领土联系，以便适用，因此，各省只能征收与其管辖范围有关的应税事件。省级主要税种有以下两种。

1. 营业税（TT）

TT 是对在各自省管辖范围内进行的商业、工业、农业、金融或专业活动和繁重活动所产生的毛收入总额征收的地方税。每个省和布宜诺斯艾利斯市对不同的活动适用不同的税率（通常从 1% 到 4%，在一些非常特别的情况下高达 7%）。布宜诺斯艾利斯签署了一项多边协定，以避免对在跨管辖范围进行的活动实行双重征税。

根据纳税人获得的总收入情况，可以适用较低的税率。

2. 印花税（ST）

印花税是由各省和布宜诺斯艾利斯市征收的一种地方税。每一司法管辖区征收此项税务，基于：（1）在其领土内执行协定；（2）执行虽然在其管辖范围之外实施但在其管辖范围内产生效果的协定（因为它涉及位于该管辖区内的资产或提供的服务）。一般来说，这项税是根据协定的经济价值估计的，人们普遍认为，每个管辖区都可以依据其领土内受合同工影响的经济价值向合同征税（尽管在这方面没有任何具体规定，各省之间也没有就如何计算影响达成普遍一致，因此这个问题仍然存在一些不确定性）。

尽管印花税是一种地方税，而且每个管辖区都有自己的规则，但联邦税务共同参与法规定了各省和布宜诺斯艾利斯市在颁布关于这一税收的立法时应遵循的某些准则。印花税主要只适用于“文件”，即具有独立性并可被当事各方执行的文件。

一般来说，印花税税率为 1.2%，尽管不同司法管辖区的税收可能不同，也可能因交易种类不同而有所不同。

根据国家最高法院目前支持的标准，使用要约文件机制执行的协议（一方发送一份提议，然后由默示的接受行为或一封未提及协议内容的普通接受函作为回应）不能被视为联邦税务共同参与法界定的文书。因此，根据最高法院的判例，要约函件形式协议不受此税规制。

（四）市政税

市政税需要有领土联系才能适用，因此，市政厅只能征收与其管辖范围有关的应税活动，主要是阿根廷的几个市政厅以及布宜诺斯艾利斯市征收提供公共服务的费用。

七、反贿赂

（一）反腐败立法概述

阿根廷《刑法》（ACC）是管理和惩处与贿赂和腐败有关的行为的主要法律部门，惩处外国和国内贿赂的主要法律规定是 2018 年 3 月颁布的《刑事责任法》（第 27401 号法律）第 256 条至第 259 条。

1. 涉外贿赂

ACC 第 258 条第 2 款对贿赂外国政府官员的行为作了规定，该条规定的外方贿赂的定义为："任何外国或国际公共组织的个人，不适当地以个人名义或通过中间人提供、许诺或给予公职人员金钱、任何具有金钱价值的物体或其他利益，如馈赠、恩惠、许诺或利益，目的是使该官员实行或不实行与其职务有关的行为，或利用他 / 她在经济、金融或商业交易中担任的职务所产生的影响，意在为该人或第三方谋取利益。"对于这类行为，可处以 1 ~ 6 年的监禁，并剥夺担任任何公职的终身资格。在这方面请注意，提供礼物，例如，向外国官员提供旅费、膳食或娱乐等可能构成贿赂外国公职人员的罪行。

为避免产生疑问，《行政程序法》规定了外国公职人员的定义，或阿根廷共和国承认的任何领土实体的公职人员的定义，即在阿根廷共和国政府的任何级别或领土区划中，或在任何类型的、受外国施加的直接或间接影响的机构、组织或上市公司中，被指定或当选履行公共职能的任何人。

2. 国内贿赂

阿根廷政府官员的国内贿赂由《刑法典》第258条涵盖，该条规定，任何人如亲自或通过中间人向公职人员提供金钱或礼物，目的是让该公职人员实施、拖延或不实施与其职责有关的事项，应处以1 ~ 6年徒刑，并采取终身不得担任公职的特殊资格禁止。

此外，如果在司法机关或国家检察机构为谋求非法使用任何影响力而给予或提供任何金钱或礼物，目的是让相关公职人员就其管辖范围内的任何事项发布、判令、拖延或删漏任何决议或判决，则最高刑期应增加至12年。

《宪法》规定，公职人员的定义是“任何长期或临时担任公职的人，无论是通过公共选举还是通过任命任公职”。

3. 疏通费

阿根廷反腐败立法没有具体规定便利支付，因此，在指控中，它们可能被视为贿赂犯罪。没有安全港或豁免，疏通费（用于日常政府行动）是受到禁止的。

4. 通过中间人或第三方付款

阿根廷法律禁止通过中间人或第三方付款。直接或间接贿赂外国或阿根廷公职人员都会被认定为犯罪（ACC第258条第2款）。

5. 公司刑事责任法律

为了使阿根廷反腐败立法与国际标准相一致，并符合经济合作与发展组织的要求，阿根廷国会于3月1日起生效了第27401号法律（《公司刑事责任法》），该法负责规制某些违反ACC条款的、负有刑事法律责任实体。根据《公司刑事责任法》规定的法定犯罪，法律实体对下列犯罪主体承担刑事责任：

（1）国家或国际贿赂和不当游说（ACC第258条和第258条第2款）；

（2）禁止公职人员进行交易（ACC第265条）；

（3）非法勒索（ACC第268条）；

（4）公职人员和雇员的非法致富（ACC第268条）；

（5）严重伪造资产负债表罪（ACC第300条第2款）。

6.《公司刑事责任法》下的后继责任

《公司刑事责任法》还规定了继承责任，这意味着在根据本制度负有责任的法律实体涉及合并、拆分或任何其他修改的情况下，由此产生的实体仍然负有刑事责任。

7.《公司刑事责任法》规定的制裁

对于贿赂外国和（或）阿根廷公职人员，个人和公司均可承担刑事、行政和民事责任。《公司刑事责任法》规定，法律实体对“已直接或间接在其干预下或以其名义，为利益或好处实施的”，被法律规定的罪行负有刑事责任。如果任何为其利益或好处行事的人是没有代表法律实体行事的权力的第三方，法律实体也应承担责任，条件是该法人实体已批准由该第三方进行相关管理，即使是默许的。

根据《公司刑事责任法》第7条，对法人的刑事处罚可包括：

（1）处以2 ~ 5倍的法律实体所获得或本可获得的不当利益的罚款；

（2）全部或部分中止活动，在任何情况下均不得超过10年；

（3）暂停参与公共招标、公共工程或服务邀请书或与国家有关的任何其他活动，该禁止事项在任何情况下不得超过10年；

（4）仅为实施犯罪或构成该实体主要活动的行为而成立的法人实体的解散和清算；

（5）国家性福利利益的丧失或中止；

（6）由犯罪法律实体承担成本费用发布认罪摘录。

《公司刑事责任法》还规定了行动标准的独立性，在第6条中规定，即使不可能查明或定罪参与犯罪的个人、法律实体也可以被定罪，条件是确定该案的情况下，如果没有法律实体的默认，犯罪不可能发生。

关于上文所列的制裁措施，《反腐败法》规定，在第6章（贿赂和影响贩卖）和第11章（危害公共行政罪）中规定的犯罪行为的情况下，应处以2 ~ 5倍的罚款，数额是赠与金额或价值、给予或最终给予（给予外国的）不适当的利益或好处总体数额的2 ~ 5倍（该项处罚对于外国或国内公职人员贿赂都适用）。

另外，根据ACC第22条第2款，如果外国贿赂犯罪是为了金钱利益实施的，则可处以最高达90000阿根廷比索的罚款，并可判处徒刑；此外，个

人一经定罪，将被没收贿赂财物和贿赂所得（ACC 第 233 条）。

8.《公司刑事责任法》规定的免予处罚

《公司刑事责任法》规定的违法犯罪行为，可以依法免除处罚责任和行政责任：（1）因内部侦破和侦查自发性自发报告有关犯罪的；（2）在被调查的事实发生之前，已经建立了适当的控制和监督制度，且违法者必须耗费精力打破该制度；（3）返还犯罪所得的不当利益。上述要求中的所有这些理由必须同时满足。如果尚未全部满足，它们中的一个或多个的发生可能仍然被视为考虑调整处罚的理由。

9. 争端解决——《公司刑事责任法》规定的有效合作协议

根据阿根廷法律，民事案件可以（以诉讼以外的方式）解决，但刑事案件必须受到刑事起诉，不能像在美国那样通过和解或认罪协议得到解决。根据《刑事诉讼法》（CPC）第 71 条，除《刑事诉讼法》允许外，检察官不具有自由裁量权。在这方面，《刑事诉讼法》第 431 条第 2 款规定了简化审判。检方和被告在口头审判阶段开始时就有罪和判刑达成协议的案件，条件是所指控的罪行所涉刑罚不超过 6 年监禁，被告接受指控并同意以这种方式进行诉讼。

《刑事诉讼法》规定，ACC 指出，任何被判犯有可根据法院动议起诉的，且可能被判处最高不超过 3 年监禁刑的罪行的人都可以要求进行暂停审判测试。与其他国家众所周知的缓刑不同，该请求并不意味着被指控者认罪或承认民事责任。提出该申请的被指控者应当尽可能修复其造成的损害，法院也必须确定其所提申请的合理性。在执行本机构规则期间，刑事诉讼的时效会中止。如果新的罪行发生在上一次测试期届满后的 8 年之后，可以准予两次暂停审判测试。新的审判测试不得适用于不遵守前一次暂停规定的行为规则的人。公职人员在任职期间参与实施犯罪或可被取消任职资格的罪行时，不得给予这种暂停测试的许可。

然而，有一些类似于最近的《公司刑事责任法》制定的宽大处理方案，包括但不限于，反腐败调查中的诉辩交易。在这方面，《公司刑事责任法》第 16 条描述了一种称为有效合作协议的新机制（ECA）。总检察长办公室（AGO）和一个法律实体可以进入 ECA，该法律实体有义务通过披露下列资料或准确、有用和可核查的数据进行合作：

（1）实施澄清；

（2）始作俑者或参与者的识别；

（3）犯罪所得的追缴。

在这样做时，实体必须遵守下文所述的《公司刑事责任法》规定的条件。在被告被传唤受审之前，任何时候都可以签署进行 ECA。《公司刑事责任法》规定，该实体与 ECA 之间的谈判，以及在协议核准之前在谈判框架内交换的信息，必须在被告被传唤审判之前签署。严格保密，违反行为构成犯罪。根据法律，ECA 机制必须满足下列条件才能有效：

（1）支付相当于适用的最低罚款的一半的数额；

（2）归还犯罪所得；

（3）放弃可能在定罪时被没收的资产，以造福国家。

此外，还可对牵连方施加下列任择条件：

（1）损害赔偿；

（2）确定有利于社区的服务；

（3）对参与犯罪行为的人采取纪律约束措施；

（4）适用一套完整程序或对现有程序进行改进。

ECA 协议必须由该实体的法律代表、辩护方和 AGO 的代表签字，并必须提交给评估商定条件的合法性或合理性的法官，交由其决定维持或否决该 ECA。如果 ECA 不成功或被法官推翻，谈判期间该实体的资料和佐证将不得扣留副本。除非 AGO 独立了解该信息和文件，或在协议之前对某一案件的现有调查过程中可能获得知识，否则禁止使用谈判期间该法律实体的资料和文件来确定该实体的责任。

10. 账簿和记录

阿根廷法律要求法律实体保持准确的账簿和记录。要求准确的公司账簿和记录、有效的公司内部控制、定期财务报表或外部审计的主要法律规则如下：

（1）ACC 第 300 条及第 300 条之二；

（2）阿根廷《民商法》第 320 条至第 327 条；

（3）关于国有公司的第 19550 号《普通公司法》和第 24156 号《财务管理法》；

（4）第 26831 号《资本市场法》。

11. 个人商业贿赂

目前，贿赂犯罪不适用于私人之间的贿赂，但只有在涉及政府官员和雇员的情况下才适用。该罪的例外是最近引入的针对规制雇员或金融机构官员实施的贿赂犯罪（ACC 第 312 条）。该法规定触犯该罪的，在证券交易所运作的金融机构雇员或实体，以个人名义或通过中介获得资金或任何其他利益，以作为提供贷款、金融或证券交易所交易的条件，则应受到 1 ～ 6 年的有期徒刑惩罚，以及最长达 6 年的任职从业资格禁止。

（二）法律和建议的控制环境对公司反腐败政策和程序的要求

根据目前的反腐败立法，除非是与联邦政府签订合同的情况下，否则公司没有强制执行任何具体的反腐败政策 / 程序的义务。

尽管如前所述，《公司刑事责任法》规定了法律实体实施合规方案的可能性，即由旨在促进廉洁、监督和控制的行动、机制和内部程序组成的方案，重点是防止、发现和纠正违规行为和非法行为（合规方案）。这些方案已成为中心，因为考虑到一家公司可免除刑事责任必须满足的要求之一恰恰是合规计划已经生效。

根据《公司刑事责任法》，合规方案，必须适合公司所执行活动的具体风险、公司规模和公司经济能力，必须至少包含以下要素：

（1）道德守则或行为守则，或适用于每名董事、经理和雇员的合规政策和程序，而无论其担任何种职务或职能，以指导其职责或任务的规划和执行，防止犯下违反公司刑事责任法规定的罪行；

（2）防止在公开招标范围内、在执行行政合同或与公共部门的任何其他互动中的非法行为的具体规则和程序；

（3）定期为董事、经理及雇员提供有关合规的培训。

此外，《公司刑事责任法》还提供了一些指导，说明了一个强有力的合规方案也可以包括哪些其他要素，但是这些要素仅仅是选择性的：（1）定期风险分析和后续对该方案的修正；（2）最高管理层对该方案的明显和明确的支持；（3）向第三方开放并适当促进的内部报告渠道；（4）保护举报人免遭报复的政策；（5）尊重被调查者的权利的内部调查机制，并对违反道德守则的行为实行制裁；（6）对第三方或业务合作伙伴（包括供应商、分销商、服务提供商、代理商和中介机构）在承揽服务时进行背景调查；（7）M&A交易中进行尽职调查，以评估其中任何潜在的非法行为或者违法情况；（8）不断监测和评价遵守方案的有效性；（9）一名内部合规干事，负责制定、协调和监督遵约方案；（10）遵守由联邦、省、市或社区当局发布的对法律实体进行的活动具有强制权的程序中相关规定。

请注意，如果公司打算与联邦政府签订合同，《公司刑事责任法》规定，相关法律实体制定符合上述（强制性）要求的合规方案是一个先决条件。

（三）反腐败立法的域外影响

阿根廷《刑法》的一般原则规定，《刑法》只能适用于在阿根廷共和国境内或在其管辖下的任何其他领土内犯下或产生效力的罪行。

尽管如此，最近颁布的《公司刑事责任法》已经指出了例外情况。新修订的《刑事责任法》第1条确定，阿根廷公民或在阿根廷共和国拥有合法住所的法律实体在境外犯下的根据《反腐败法》第285条之二所犯的罪行（向公职人员行贿），应受阿根廷法院管辖：阿根廷公民或在阿根廷共和国拥有合法住所的法律实体在国外犯下的罪行。依据规定，在阿根廷领土上设立分支机构或拥有法定住所的法律实体，若犯所涉罪行，都在阿根廷域外司法管辖范围内。

八、环境条例

（一）《环境法》的《宪法》方面

阿根廷有三种法律制度：联邦、省和市立法。1994年修订的《宪法》第41条规定，这三类政府当局有义务保护环境，并根据其管辖权赋予每种政府不同的权力。第41条规定如下：

“阿根廷所有居民都有权享有一个适合人类发展和生产活动的健康和平衡的环境，在不损害子孙后代需要的情况下满足目前的需要；他们有义务维护这种环境。当局应确保这一权利得到保护，合理利用自然资源，保护国家的自然和文化遗产和生物多样性，并向人民提供环境信息和教育。国家应颁布载有最低环境保护标准的法律和条例，而各省应颁布必要的法律和条例来补充这些法律和条例；任何国家法律不得改变地方司法管辖。”

因此，很明显，根据阿根廷《宪法》，与环境有关的义务如下：

（1）联邦政府对环境问题拥有一般立法权。国家有责任颁布基本的保护法律和法规。

（2）各省（或其各市）必须颁布补充基本保护联邦法律的法律和条例，并可根据具体情况在各自管辖范围内制定更严格的环境保护要求。应当指出的是，省政府可根据其各自省《宪法》的规定，将某些权力下放给各自的市镇。

（二）《一般环境法》

第25675号《一般环境法》（GEL）于2002年颁布，它为阿根廷全境建立了一些基本的环境保护原则。基于《宪法》第41条的规定，任何联邦或省级环境法都必须遵守GEL的指导方针。另外，GEL还确认了所有省份都参加的两个省际协定：产生环境联邦委员会的协议（COFEMA，1990年）和环境联邦协议（1993年）。

GEL的主要特点为：

（1）适用于全国；

（2）使环境成为法律保护的利益；

（3）为环境和生物多样性的可持续和充分管理创造了某些基本条件；

（4）给予了当地法院以职权管理GEL，但是只要违反GEL属于跨管辖权，联邦法院就会参与其中[①]；

（5）体现了国家环境政策；

（6）规定了强制性的环境影响研究；

（7）提出了一种评价项目环境影响的听证制度。这是采矿活动最需要考虑的部分之一；

（8）描述了环境损害，并设立了一个环境补救基金。

现在应该提到GEL中提到的两个重要问题：环境影响研究和环境损害。

根据GEL，环境影响研究是强制性的，必须在“在阿根廷领土内从事可

---

① 如果违法行为超出了一个省的范围，涉及两个或两个以上省份，则属跨司法管辖范围。

能对环境或其任何组成部分或人民生活水平产生负面和实质性影响的任何工作或活动之前进行（第 11 条）。因此，应根据各省适用的要求，向有关当局提交一份环境影响研究报告，包括一份关于该项目是否将对环境产生影响的说明。当局会进行一项环境影响研究，然后发出一份环境影响报告书，批准或不批准先前提交的研究报告。这些研究至少应包括“详细说明项目及其对环境的影响，并说明为减轻任何负面影响而采取的行动”（第 13 条）。

GEL 将环境破坏定义为对环境、自然资源、生态系统平衡或集体利益或价值观产生负面影响的任何相关改变。GEL 还规定，无论是谁造成环境损害，都将对恢复损害发生前的状况负有严格责任。环境损害赔偿责任既包括民事责任，也包括刑事责任，独立于行政责任。这意味着，除了行政当局规定的支付任何罚款的义务之外，无论谁造成损害，都可能受到第三方的民事和刑事索赔。根据 GEL，造成环境损害的人必须恢复损害发生前的普遍情况；如果在技术上不可能这样做，责任方将向由执法当局管理的环境赔偿基金支付一笔由法院确定的赔偿金（第 27 条）。

颁布 GEL 的第 2413/2002 号行政命令反对 GEL 的某些规定，它基本上规定 GEL 的规定不起作用，这意味着政府行政部门必须在事后对其适用作出规定。同一行政命令还反对 GEL 中凡被裁定违反行政环境条例的人，均应承担环境损害赔偿责任的规定。行政命令还反对法院审理环境损害案件，将其判决范围扩大到当事方所要求的范围之外。

尽管 GEL 最终将如何实施的指导方针不多，但 GEL 不仅因为它所建立的权利和义务有矛盾，而且因为它在某些方面似乎与国家《宪法》不一致而受到批评。

重要的是要指出，GEL 的某些方面，例如，“环境破坏”的概念不符合特定采矿环境法规考虑的相同标准和标准。因此，大多数 GEL 条款的未来应用将不得不密切关注，因为它们无疑将对采矿活动有非常相关的影响。

（三）《水环境管理法》

《水环境管理法》第 25688 号（WEML）规定了与阿根廷境内水有关的某些基本环境保护条件。WEML 涵盖自然和人工河流中的水以及其他水体、地表水和地下水，以及水库、地下河流和大气中的水（第 2 条）。

WEML 规定，为了使用上述任何水，一方必须事先征得有关当局的同意（第 6 条）。WEML 进一步描述和规范了所谓的流域的运作，并建立了流域委员会来管理它们。作为批准使用公共用水的条件，WEML 规定此类使用必须得到相关流域委员会的批准。

值得注意的是，WEML 受到阿根廷几个专业领域的广泛批评。因此，政府行政部门尚未通过实施条例，因此，其适用范围目前有限。从环境的角度来看，WEML 主要是因未能充分保护相关资源而受到批评。

WEML 中发现的一些缺陷包括：

（1）它赋予联邦政府大部分相关决策权，从而干扰省级自治；

（2）其措辞使能够将未经省份授权的权力移交给联邦政府；

（3）它包括问题的某些非法律方面，在自然科学和社会科学之间没有适当的联系；

（4）它不涉及真正的环境问题，实际上只涉及水的政治管理。

1. 第 25612 号法：《工业废物和服务活动的综合管理法》

《工业废物和服务活动综合管理法》适用于整个阿根廷，它废除了以前的第24051号《危险废物法》的大部分规定，但《刑法》规定和有关致病废物的规定除外。在刑事责任方面，个人参与造成环境损害的行为的董事、经理、内部控制人员或公司代表将受到处罚：（1）在疏忽或不充分遵守适用条例的情况下，法律规定了1个月至2年的监禁，如果造成死亡或受伤，可判处3年有期徒刑；（2）如该等损害对公众健康或整体环境构成威胁，则可处以3~10年的罚款或监禁，如果导致死亡，则可处以10~25年监禁。

与以前的法律相反，第 24051 号法律、第 25612 号法律将危险废物制度适用于所有工业废物，无论其是否有危险。第 25612 号法律还要求确保特定的保险单，以涵盖由某些类型的废物造成的潜在损害。

现阶段尚不清楚新的第 25612 号法律将如何适用，因为它取代了原第 24051 号法律的大部分关键条款。将需要对第 24051 号法律和新的第 25612 号法律进行单独的具体分析。

2. 第 25348 号法：阿根廷对《京都议定书》（2001 年）的遵守情况

阿根廷通过第 25348 号法律正式通过了 1997 年 12 月 11 日在日本京都通过的《〈联合国气候变化公约〉京都议定书》。除其他外，这项国际条约规定签署国有义务减少温室气体排放。《京都议定书》自 2005 年 2 月起在阿根廷生效。

3. 第 25831 号法：《免费获取环境公共信息法》

2003 年颁布的第 25831 号法律允许任何个人获得任何公共机构或部门提供的环境公共记录。法律还定义了诸如“环境信息”之类的术语，并规定了有义务披露此类信息的个人或实体以及可获得该信息的程序。

该法还规定了《宪法》规定的最低限度要求，以保证保护所有各级政府机构，包括与公共服务有关的公司拥有的环境信息。

4. 第 26331 号法：《原始森林法》

《原始森林法》于 2007 年颁布，规范了阿根廷原始森林的使用，旨在促进可持续森林管理。它将森林分为以下区域：

（1）第一类（红色）：具有很高保护价值的部门不应被拆除或用于伐木，而应永远作为一片森林加以维护。这些部门包括具有突出生物价值的自然保护区及其周边地区和 / 或保护重要水域（河流和溪流）的地点。

（2）第二类（黄色）：具有较高或中等保护价值的部门，这些部门可能会退化，但如果恢复，则可能具有较高的保护价值。这些地区不能拆除，但可能受到下列用途的制约：可持续利用、旅游、收藏和科学研究。

（3）第三类（绿色）：具有低保护价值的部门，这些部门可以部分或全部地随着环境影响评估的事先执行情况而改变。

《原始森林法》第 10 条规定，负责执法的当局是国家政府、各省和布宜诺斯艾利斯市。

在过去的几年里，阿根廷几乎所有省份都制定了自己的具体立法，同时考虑到了这些联邦级别的标准。

九、劳工

（一）基本劳动条例

劳动关系主要由经修订的第 20744 号《劳动合同法》、国家《宪法》、国际条约、集体谈判协议和个人雇用合同条款规定。

劳资纠纷是阿根廷竞争力的致命弱点，因为立法具有特别的保护作用，法院通常对雇员对公司提出的索赔表示同情。因此，从劳工的角度来看，阿根廷被认为是一个容易发生冲突的国家。马克里政府已将解决这一问题列为优先事项。

以下是适用于就业合同的最突出条例的简要概述。

1. 雇用员工

法律对雇用外国雇员没有任何限制，也没有雇用当地雇员的任何法律义务。关于外国雇员，他们需要有工作签证才能在阿根廷就业。

为雇用雇员，雇主必须向税务局登记，并遵守雇员的登记条款。此外，雇主也须在雇员开始工作前为他们进行职前健康检查。

2. 延缓期间

雇员可按固定期限合同或无限期受雇。在后一种情况下，头 3 个月的就业是试用期。在此期间，任何一方均可终止雇用合同，提前 15 天通知雇主，而雇主没有义务支付遣散费。

3. 工作日

《劳动法》规定了每天 8 个小时和（或）每周 48 个小时的工作时间限制。超过最高限额的，应支付加班费，每周加班时加收 50% 的附加费，星期六下午 1 时、周日和国定假日后加收 100% 的附加费。董事和经理不受工作日限制。

4. 报酬

报酬可按月、每日或两周支付，可采取工资、销售佣金、参与利润等形式。报酬必须在有关月份结束后的 4 个工作日内或两周内支付，或在每周支付的 3 个工作日内支付。

5. 强制性奖金（第 13 笔工资）

强制性奖金每年 6 月 30 日和 12 月 18 日支付，相当于分别在上半年和下半年支付给工人的最高工资的 50%。当雇佣关系终止时，考虑到相应时段的工作时间，雇员有权按比例领取第 13 笔工资。

6. 休假

雇员有权享受年假，年假从 14 ~ 35 个工作日不等，视资历而定。在开始休假之前，雇员有权领取假期工资，其计算方法是将其实际工资除以 25，并将这一结果乘以假期天数。在终止雇佣关系时，考虑到过去一年的工作时间，雇员有权按比例领取所欠休假天数。

7. 特别假

雇员在子女出生、结婚、近亲死亡以及高中和大学考试时可享受短期特别假。特别休假时间的支付与休假时间的支付相同。集体谈判协议可以延长期限和（或）规定额外的休假。

女雇员还有权享受生产前45天和生产后45天的产假。在此期间，他们的工资由家庭津贴基金支付。

如果雇员生病或残疾（与工作无关），合同将继续完全有效，雇员有权根据雇员的年资和家庭义务（他或她是否供养近亲）领取3～12个月的正常工资。

8. 终止雇佣合同

（1）无理由解雇。在无限期合同中，雇主可随时通知雇员：①在试用期内解雇雇员，提前15日通知雇员；②提前一个月解雇服务满5年的雇员；③提前两个月通知资历较高的雇员。如果不发出任何此类通知，将导致支付相当于上述期间本应付给雇员的报酬的赔偿金。如果解雇发生在与当月最后一天不同的日期并且没有提前通知，则雇主还必须支付相当于解雇月剩余天数的工资的赔偿金。此外，《欧洲仲裁示范法》第245条规定，如果雇员在没有因由的情况下被解雇，雇主必须根据过去一年或较短期间累积的最佳一般月薪酬，为每一年或每一年适当部分的服务，支付相当于一份月工资的补偿金。考虑到适用的集体谈判协定和判例法，可适用这一数额的上限。在怀孕、工会代表和婚姻等特定情况下，雇员有权在一定时期内得到特别保护。在这些情况下，应作为遣散费的数额大幅度增加。

（2）有正当理由的解雇。雇主可能因严重不当行为而解雇员工。在这种情况下，不向雇员支付遣散费，但雇主有严重不当行为的举证责任，而劳动法官是有权决定这种决定是否合理的人。

（3）辞职。雇员可以通过辞职终止雇佣合同。雇员须提前15日发出终止合约通知书，并须将辞职通知书送交雇主。在这种情况下，不需支付遣散费。

（4）相互同意。双方可随时通过双方同意的协议终止合同。ECL明确规定，在这种情况下，终止的文档需要经过公证。ECL还允许当事人在劳动法院或劳工部终止合同。

（5）残疾。如果雇佣关系因雇员长期和完全残疾而终止，他/她有权领取相当于年资补偿的赔偿。

（6）退休。当雇员达到法律规定的领取普通退休福利的年龄时，可以终止雇佣合同。为此，雇主必须发出通知，通知雇员他有义务开始退休程序。一年后，或一旦雇员获得养恤金福利，以先发生者为准，雇主有权终止雇佣协议而不支付遣散费。

（7）死亡。如果雇员死亡，雇佣合同也可以终止。在这种情况下，某些家庭受抚养人有权获得相当于无故解雇资格的 50% 的特殊赔偿金。

（二）职工登记

1. 社会保障登记

根据 AFIP/DGI 的第 1891/2005 号决议，雇佣合同的每一个新的雇用和终止必须被传达给 AFIP/DGI，以便被纳入社会保障登记处。招聘的通知必须在有效工作开始前一天完成，每个劳动合同的终止必须在终止日期后的第 5 天内通知 AFIP/DGI。

2. 劳动手册

《劳动合同法》第 52 条规定，雇主必须保留一本《特别劳动手册》（有相关当局的名称），以便登记雇主和雇员的信息、工资和劳动合同的其他强制性方面。

3. 社会保障及相关出资

根据第 24241 号法律，向阿根廷雇员支付的任何金额均由雇员和雇主（按不同比例）支付社会保障金，并且由于所得税而须缴纳预扣税。

表 2 显示了雇主对社会保障制度缴款的百分比。

表 2　雇主对社会保障制度缴款的百分比

<table>
<tr><th></th><th colspan="4">退休金及退休制度</th><th>退休人员的医疗保障</th><th>家庭津贴基金</th><th>失业基金</th><th>医疗保险法</th><th>总额</th><th>人寿保险</th><th>职业风险保险</th></tr>
<tr><td>从雇员处扣缴的税款</td><td colspan="4">11%</td><td>3%</td><td>—</td><td>—</td><td>3%</td><td>17%</td><td>—</td><td>—</td></tr>
<tr><td rowspan="2">雇主供款</td><td colspan="4">主要活动是提供或雇用服务的雇主占 21%</td><td rowspan="2">6%</td><td rowspan="2">27%</td><td rowspan="2">0.027%</td><td rowspan="2">这个百分比因公司的活动而异</td><td rowspan="2"></td><td rowspan="2"></td><td rowspan="2"></td></tr>
<tr><td>12.71%</td><td>1.62%</td><td>5.56%</td><td>1.11%</td></tr>
</table>

续表

	退休金及退休制度				退休人员的医疗保障	家庭津贴基金	失业基金	医疗保险法	总额	人寿保险	职业风险保险
	以上未包括的其他雇主的 17%				6%	23%	0.027%	这个百分比因公司的活动而异			
	10.17%	1.5%	4.44%	0.89%							

（三）扣缴所得税

雇主有义务在年度税额超过 AFIP/DGI 规定的最低限额时，从其工人的薪酬中扣缴所得税。这些扣缴款项应支付给税务机关。在每个日历年结束时，工人必须向他 / 她的雇主提交一份表格，说明他 / 她的年度所得税的计算情况。本表格也可通过互联网递交税务机关。

十、知识产权

保护知识产权的第一个来源是阿根廷《宪法》第 17 条，其中规定保护所有作者或发明者在法律允许的一段时间内了解他们的作品、发明或发现。

关于国际条约，除其他外，阿根廷批准了下列知识产权条约：《巴黎公约》（第 17011 号法）《涉贸知识产权（与贸易有关的知识产权方面）协定》（通过第 24425 号法）和《伯尔尼公约》（第 22195 号法）。

（一）专利和实用新型

专利和实用新型在阿根廷受到第 24481 号法（PUML）和第 260/96 号法的特别管辖。

应该指出的是，阿根廷不是《专利合作条约》（PCT）的缔约方。

为保护植物，阿根廷遵守了《保护植物新品种国际公约》（UPOV 公约）。

1. 专利

PUML 第 4 条规定，涉及创造性步骤的产品或工艺的新发明以及导致工业结果的新发明可获得专利。

因此，专利申请的基本要求如下：新颖性、工业应用、创造步骤。

尽管如此，法律规定，发明人或发明人的继承者或受让人以任何通信手段披露发明不影响新颖性，包括在专利申请提交日期前一年内在展销会上展示，或对所要求的优先权（如有的话）予以披露。

专利授予所有者在自申请之日起计算的不可续约的20年期间内开发一项发明的专属权利。就产品专利而言，这一专有权利包括制造、使用、出售、销售或进口专利产品的专属权利。在工艺专利的情况下，这一专属权利包括使用专利程序的专属权利以及生产、使用、提供销售、销售或进口直接通过专利程序获得的产品的专属权利。

一旦专利被授予，年费必须支付才能使该专利继续有效。

PUML规定以下不被视为发明：（1）科学理论和数学方法；（2）文学或艺术作品或任何其他美学创作，以及科学作品；（3）开展智力活动、游戏或经济商业活动以及计算机程序的计划、规则和方法；（4）可提供资料的其他方式；（5）用于人类和与动物有关的手术、治疗或诊断治疗方法；（6）已知发明或已知产品的组合的并置，其形式、尺寸或组成材料的变化，除非所述的合并或合并使其组成部分不能分开运作，或当对其特性或功能进行修改以取得本领域专家不明显的工业结果时除外；（7）预先存在的任何生命物质和物质。

自PUML颁布以来，药品被特别列为可获得专利的发明，目前受阿根廷法律保护。然而，它们的规定得到了国家工业产权局、生产部和卫生部分别根据第118/2012号、第546/2012号和第107/2012号发布的联合决议的补充。联合决议严格限制了制药领域几类发明的可专利性。

在专利局发布第283/2015号条例后，类似的限制适用于生物技术发明。

关于软件专利，专利局发布的第318/2012号条例批准计算机程序本身不具有可专利性。然而，如果要获得专利的对象对现有技术做出技术贡献，则计算机程序涉及专利申请的事实可能不一定导致缺乏可专利性。相反，涉及计算机程序的专利申请，只要其提供技术领域中的特定问题的技术解决方案，如果符合新颖性、创造性和工业应用要求，则可以是专利的。

专利可以被许可和转让，但这种转让必须在专利局注册，以便可以对第三方强制执行。

如果专利在授予之日后的两年内未被使用，或者其使用被中断两年，则可应第三方的请求予以取消。

法律还规定了无效诉讼，向专利所有人提供补救办法，以对付那些在没有任何权利的情况下获得专利而违反法律规定的任何要求的人。

专利侵权补救措施也包括在 PUML 中。侵犯专利被视为一种犯罪，处以罚款或监禁。可获得法院命令，以防止继续侵权行为，并使收取损害赔偿。

2. 实用新型

PUML 第 53 条规定，在工具、工作工具、用具、装置或物体中获得或采用的用于实际工作的新安排或模式的发明者，只要涉及改进其目的对象的使用，可获得开发的专属权利，这应由所谓的实用新型证书(实用新型)加以证明。在已经生效的专利保护领域内，不得为实用新型授予证书。

本实用新型证书的有效期为 10 年，自申请提交之日起计算。

实用新型应用程序的基本要求如下：新颖性、工业应用。

与专利不同，实用新型不需要创造性的步骤。

实用新型可以被许可和转让，但是这种转让必须在专利局注册，以便可以对第三方强制执行。

（二）工业模型和设计

工业模型和设计受第 6673/63 号法令管辖、第 16478 号法律及其第 5682/65 号管理法令批准了该法令。

它们保护工业模型或设计工业产品的形状或外观，赋予它们装饰性，无论其功能如何。

工业模型是三维产品，如汽车或椅子；工业设计是二维产品，如图案。

工业模型或设计自申请之日起计算，有效期为 5 年，并可续期两次，每次延长 5 年。

工业模型或设计应用的基本要求是新颖性。

相关法律和法令规定对那些无权获得工业模型或设计或其工业模型或设计违反法律规定的任何要求的人采取取消注册。

侵权救济措施包含在法律中并受到罚款处罚，可以获得法院命令以防止继续侵权和获取损害赔偿。

（三）商标和贸易权

第 22362 号法律及其第 558/81 号法令管理与阿根廷商标和商标名称有关的所有事项（联合，TTL）。

1. 商标

TTL 规定了一种制度，在这种制度下，商标权及其专用权产生于注册，而不是使用，但规定了为续订目的而使用的要求。

阿根廷采用了国际商品和服务分类，将商标分类标准与发达国家统一起来。

关于哪些标志法规是允许作为商标申请的：特殊名称、标志、字母组合、广告标语、邮票、小插图、浮雕标记、带有图画、容器或标签的字母和数字，或用于区分所有者的其他标志产品与服务。目前，一些非传统商标，如声音、嗅觉、动作和三维（3D）商标也已被接受注册。

必要或通常的名称、描述性或通用的名称、常用的名称、产品的形状、产品的自然颜色、一种适用于产品的单一颜色、违反公共秩序或道德的欺骗性设计、官方符号、商标、第三方名称或化名，或与其他先前注册或适用于同一产品或服务的商标相同或类似的商标，以及非原创性的口号不能注册。

即使未在 TTL 中提及，我们的法院也已根据阿根廷批准的国际条约对驰名商标进行保护。

商标保护期限自注册之日起 10 年，并且可以无限期续订 10 年，只要商标在续订日期之前的最后 5 年内使用。为了更新商标，需要提交宣誓声明，其中所有者声明该商标已在该国用于产品或服务的商业化和 / 或至少作为贸易或公司名称的一部分。

商标可以转让，但这种转让只有在与国家工业产权局一起记录后才对第三方有效。

通过对那些知道或应该知道该商标属于其他人的法院诉讼，或者如果被授予的商标与法规的任何规定相抵触，可以宣布商标无效。

如果该商标在提起撤销诉讼之日之前的 5 年内未在该国使用，也可应一方当事人的请求予以取消。将商标用于销售产品或提供其他类别的服务，或作为一项活动的一部分，可能有助于防止被取消。

还可采取商标侵权补救措施。侵犯商标被视为一种犯罪，处以罚款或监禁。

可获得法院命令，以防止继续侵权和收取损害赔偿。

2. 商号

根据阿根廷法律，商品名称是区分具有或不具有利润目的的活动的名称或标志。与商标相反，商标名称的所有权是通过其使用而获得的，并且仅与使用商标的商业类型有关，且不得与同一类型商业中已有的商品名称混淆相似。

商标名称的权利随着指定活动的终止而到期。

3. 域名

域名由阿根廷法律和技术秘书（国家主席）颁布的第110/2016号决议（《阿根廷互联网域名管理条例》）规定。NICArgentina是以先到先得的方式授予域名的政府机构，它已发布了几条建立在线域名注册程序的规则。

可以注册以下区域名：com.ar;net.ar;tur.ar;gob.ar;gov.ar;org.ar;mil.ar;int.ar;musicar.ar。

只要域名可用，任何利益相关方都可以在com.ar和net.ar区域下申请域名注册。在其余区域内访问注册表必须满足特殊要求。

此外，对于域名争议，存在争议程序，争议各方可以证明其对域名的合法和更大的利益。然后，NICArgentina将根据诉讼程序中的证据解决争议。

必须支付费用才能获得域名注册。

（四）版权

第11723号法律对阿根廷的版权作了规定。该法律规定的保护包括科学、文学、艺术或教育作品，无论其复制过程如何。有许多作品可以受到版权保护，如绘画、雕塑、书籍、杂志、绘画、服装设计、家具设计、汇编、摄影作品、电影和视听作品、数据库和计算机程序等。

思想不受保护，但这些思想的实现方式受保护。保护的一般保护期是作者的生命加上他 / 她死后70年，但有些作品具有特殊的保护期限。

外国作品必须符合作品首次出版国家规定的手续，才能受到保护。

版权赋予作者经济和精神权利，后者包括父权和完整性。

版权可能会被转让，但此类转让只有在与版权局一起记录后才能对第三方强制执行。

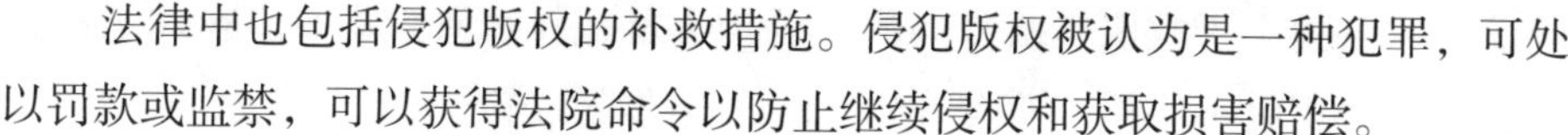

法律中也包括侵犯版权的补救措施。侵犯版权被认为是一种犯罪，可处以罚款或监禁，可以获得法院命令以防止继续侵权和获取损害赔偿。

（五）原产地标志和地理标志

原产地和地理标志由第 25163 号法律及其关于葡萄酒和基于葡萄酒的酒精饮料的第 57/2004 号条例和经修正的第 25380 号法律以及关于农产品和食品的第 556/2009 号条例（不包括葡萄酒和烈酒）管辖。

没有其他原产地或地理标志法。

（六）技术转让

经修正的第 22426 号法律及其第 580/1981 号法令规定了一种技术转让制度，通过该制度，外国许可人和当地的被许可人之间的技术或知识产权转让，转让或许可的登记可以获得某些财政收益。无政府协议被排除在该制度之外。

十一、反垄断

（一）法律框架

阿根廷《反托拉斯法》（AAL）已于 2018 年 5 月颁布，它以国家《宪法》第 42 条为基础，该条款确定当局必须为防止市场中各种形式的扭曲提供辩护，并且必须控制自然和合法的垄断。

其他相关条例包括《刑事诉讼法》（第 23984 号法），这是一个默认的程序平台；第 480/2018 号行政令是提供有关《刑事诉讼法》的细节和澄清的主要机构。

（二）机构结构

截至 2018 年 5 月，根据先前的第 25156 号法律，所有补充规则和对审咨委的澄清都是由生产部下属的一个机构和所有竞争事务的法律主管机构 Comercio 发布的，反托拉斯委员会（Competencia）目前是临时权力机构，该委员会属于 Competencia 秘书处，直到新的 AAL 当局建立。《反托拉斯法》规定，应设立一个独立于政府行政部门的新机构（反托拉斯管理局）。在此之前，Comercio 秘书处和反托拉斯委员会继续负责执法工作。

目前，该委员会由一名主席和四名正式成员（目前包括三名经济学家，包括总统和两名律师）组成，四个不同的专业领域协助这一结构，每个领域都有不同的侧重点：反竞争行为；合并管制；经济和法律研究；促进竞争。

新的反托拉斯局在执行时，应包括一个由 5 名成员组成的竞争法院，负责作出与执法和合并管制有关的决定（他们的任期为 5 年，只有在他们违反职责时才被撤职）。两个秘书处应分别负责评估或起诉与合并有关的事项，并对反竞争行为进行调查。

（三）反竞争行为

AAL 第 1 条规定了一般原则，因为它禁止与商品和服务的生产或贸易有关的行为，限制、伪造或扭曲竞争，或构成滥用市场支配地位的行为，以可能损害一般经济利益的任何方式进行；第 2 条列出了具体的行为，这些行为会引起竞争对手之间的协议串通行为，被认为是对竞争的绝对限制，并被认为损害了一般的经济利益。该条提到下列行为：

（1）固定价格；

（2）限制或生产商品和服务的做法；

（3）确定最小数量或区域、市场、客户和供应来源的横向分配的做法；

（4）在公开招标中同意或协调投标。

上述行为被视为无效协议，因此被剥夺了任何和所有法律效力。

AAL 第 3 条列举了一份非详尽无遗的行为清单，如果属于第 1 条的规定范围，则可能是反竞争行为。该条提到下列行为：

（1）固定价格；

（2）限制或控制技术发展或生产货物和服务的做法；

（3）确定最低数量或横向分配区域、市场、客户和供应来源的做法；

（4）排除、阻碍一个或多个竞争对手进入市场的；

（5）以购买另一商品或服务为条件出售货物，或将提供服务的条件限定为使用另一种服务或购买货物；

（6）限制购买或销售，以避免使用、购买、销售或供应由第三方生产、加工、分销或商业开发的商品或服务；

（7）无条件拒绝履行现有市场条件下的货物或者服务的买卖订单；

（8）对非基于现有商业惯例的货物或服务的购买或销售施加歧视性条件；

（9）暂停向公共服务提供者或公共利益服务提供者提供市场上占主导地位的垄断服务；

（10）掠夺性定价（这一术语在法律中有广泛的定义）；

（11）参与竞争公司的连锁董事会。

有大量的法律和行政判例，根据上述法律规定对上述行为类别进行了审查。如果一种行为，无论其名称如何，都符合第 1 条的规定，则构成侵权。第 2 条和第 3 条中的清单只是说明性的。

滥用支配地位。对于特定类型的产品或服务，AAL 认为实体在市场中占据主导地位：此类参与者是国内市场或世界上一个或多个地区的唯一供应商或买方；或者尽管不是唯一的供应商，但它能够独立于竞争对手。

支配地位本身不受禁止或惩罚，但禁止滥用支配地位影响一般经济利益。

补救措施和权力。委员会依职权或应当事方的请求拥有广泛的调查权力，并可命令停止或弃绝反竞争行为；命令履行特定条件（如处置某些资产）；下令采取预防性补救措施，以防止对竞争造成严重损害；发布不具约束力的意见和建议；实施制裁（通常包括罚款）；采取法律行动。

罚款和其他处罚。可通过以下方式对违反《行政法庭法》规定的个人或实体进行制裁：

（1）停止有害活动或行为及补救其影响的命令（如有的话）。

（2）罚款最多违反法律的阿根廷的经济集团上个财政年度业务所产生的收入的 30%（乘以公司违规的年数），但仅限于总收入的 30%；或违规产生的双重利益。如果以前的计算都不能执行，最高罚款将达到 2 亿单位（或截至 2018 年 6 月为 1.6 亿美元）。如果该公司在过去 10 年中已经因违反《反托拉斯法》而被定罪，则罚款将加倍。罚款的确定将考虑以下因素：违规行为的严重性；对所有受影响方造成的损害；违规时违法者的资产价值；意图；持续时间；所涉公司的市场份额；受影响市场的规模；与调查的合作程度。

（3）除可能适用的任何其他制裁外，还向不遵守委员会命令的各方处以相当于阿根廷经济集团在上一个财政年度总收入 0.1% 的每日罚款，或者如果无法计算总收入，最高罚款 75 万个单位（约合 60 万美元）。

（4）如果公司滥用其支配地位或达到侵犯 AAL 的垄断或寡头垄断地位，竞争管理局可以施加条件以改变这种情况或要求法官下令解散，分割或清算公司。

（5）每天对阻碍调查或不响应委员会要求的人处以最多 500 个单位（约 400 美元）的罚款。

法律实体可以在法人实体的帮助下或为法律实体的利益而以其名义行事的个人行为为由起诉。

当 AAL 违法行为由法律实体承担时，如果通过他们的行为证明，该罚款也将在其起诉时向其母公司及其董事、经理、管理人员、联合组织或法律实体的法律代表共同和分别适用。或者由于他们在控制、监督或审查职责方面的疏忽，他们被视为已经提供，鼓励或允许实施违法行为。此外，可以对从 1 ~ 10 年的商业活动取消资格进行额外的制裁。为了实施这种处罚，必须遵循单独的程序。

司法审查。施加罚款的决议；拒绝批准或在有条件的情况下批准交易；停止和制止命令；拒绝申请宽大处理的请求；对指控的驳回可向联邦民事和商业上诉法院或各省的联邦主管上诉法院提出上诉。上诉必须在 15 个工作日内提出。

宽恕规定。任何参与第 2 部分 AAL 中包含的任何反竞争行为的个人或公司都可以申请其参加宽大计划的资格。宽恕请求必须在竞争法庭对请求方发出任何指控之前提出。为了完全免除罚款，请求方必须：（1）提交证据，允许竞争法庭证明存在反竞争行为；（2）在调查开始之前或当局没有足够的行为证据时提交此类证据；（3）首先参与要求宽大处理并提交此类证据的行为；（4）停止并制止行为（除非竞争法庭另有指示进行调查）；（5）在整个调查过程中与竞争法庭充分合作；（6）避免破坏、没收或隐藏行为的证据（之前也没有这样做）；（7）没有公开披露其申请宽大处理的意图（除非此类披露是在其他竞争管理机构之前）。

如果公司或个人未能遵守（1）~（3）中关于全额免除罚款的任何要求，若该公司或人士提交对竞争法庭有用的补充证据，只要该公司或人士符合其余的规定，便有资格获得20%～50%的罚款减免。此外，不符合关于被调查行为的第1条至第3条规定的个人或公司，如果提交了当局不知道并遵守（1）～（3）规定的另一种行为的证据，则可请求宽大处理，可完全免除对此类行为的罚款，并可将最初调查的行为减少三分之一。

请求方的身份将保密，如果拒绝宽大处理的请求，这种请求将不被视为供词，也不会将提交的证据用于调查。

两个或多个反竞争行为的参与者不可能共同要求宽大处理。公司要求与公司共同宽大处理的人员（如董事、经理、管理人员、联合组织和法律代表）是例外。这些人在履行强制性要求后，在其控制、监督或审查职责方面的行为或疏忽将被免除任何制裁，他们被视为已经提供，鼓励或允许违反此类反竞争行为。

（四）合并控制

《反洗钱法》第 8 条禁止目的或效果是或可能是为了减少、限制或扭曲竞争而损害一般经济利益的集中交易。一般而言，如果经济集中度能够降低产品或服务的产量、提高市场价格或阻碍创新，那么，如果经济集中度创造或增加了一个参与者的市场力量，那么它可能会损害一般的经济利益。经济集中可以通过合并，转移资产或转让授予业务单位控制权的股份来进行。在这方面，AAL 确定哪些合并被认为足够相关，以便进行强制性备案：

（1）控制权的改变[①] 必须发生在阿根廷有活动或资产的公司或公司的一部分；

（2）必须满足以下两个门槛：

在扣除与营业额直接相关的销售退税和税收后，收购集团的阿根廷营业额加上上一财年的阿根廷营业额[②]（包括销售产品和 / 或提供服务）必须相

① 就 AAL 而言，控制权一词是指对一项或多项企业行使决定性影响的能力，包括法律上的控制和事实上的控制，可由一项企业（唯一或实际的）行使，或由两个或两个以上的企业（共同承诺）共同控制。这一术语既适用于法人实体的购置，也适用于资产的购置。控制结构的变化和给予小股东否决权的权利应由律师审查，因为他们可能需要向竞争管理当局发出通知。

② 在购买者的情况下，要考虑的销售是由该方所属的整个集团所做出的销售（最终母公司实体和由该第一实体直接和间接控制的实体）。就目标而言，要考虑的销售是由目标和由目标直接或间接控制的所有实体进行的销售。

等——截至 2018 年 6 月，超过 1 亿单位为 20 亿越南盾（约 8000 万美元）；交易价格[①] 或所购阿根廷资产的价值必须等于（或超过）2000 万单位，截至 2018 年 6 月，这些单位为 4 亿 AR（约 1600 万美元）。

该股的换算率每年更新一次（2018 年的换算率为 1 个单位等于 20 美元），在审查集中交易时，竞争管理机构应评估这种交易是否以会计准则所规定的相关方式影响竞争，而且由于这一评估，它可能对交易提出质疑，批准以满足某些要求为条件的交易，或给予完全的许可。如果买方集团和目标群体的总营业额不超过营业额测试的总门槛，则交易不必向委员会提交。尽管如此，请注意竞争管理机构有权对所有交易提出质疑，包括那些不受强制申报限制的交易，因为这些交易违反了对集中的禁止，其目的或效果是或可能是为了减少、限制或扭曲竞争，从而损害一般的经济利益。

通知豁免。审咨委考虑对满足周转率标准的交易通知委员会的义务给予各种豁免，其中包括：（1）如果要支付的价格和将要转移或控制的阿根廷资产价值不超过 2000 万单位，此类交易免于强制备案；但是，如果双方已进行了与相同相关市场相关的交易在过去 12 个月内总计超过 2000 万单位，或在过去 36 个月内，总计超过 6000 万单位，此豁免不适用。

（2）如果交易涉及单一外国企业通过在阿根廷拥有资产或股份（ “首次登陆” ）而没有商业活动的单一企业收购，则该交易免予强制申报。以下问题与评估在任何特定情况下是否可获得首次登陆豁免有关：①收购人是否直接或间接通过其附属公司在阿根廷持有企业；②购买方（或其任何附属公司）是否向阿根廷进行销售（出口）活动[②]，以及这样的销售是否具有实质性和经常性；如果上述任何问题的答案都是肯定的，豁免的可行性将取决于对阿根廷所持股份的信息的评估，以及涉及这类阿根廷企业的关键信息，包括过去三年所涉及的产品、数量和数量。

（3）收购清算公司（上一年不活跃的）也不需要强制提交。

集中的有效性。根据 AAL，经向委员会发出强制性通知的交易仅在竞争管理局明确或暗示授权后，才能在当事人之间或对第三方有效。

---

① 交易价值应解释为“阿根廷的交易价值”，从而允许各方计算可分配给交易阿根廷部分的购买价格部分。

② 竞争管理机构有一些先例表明，对阿根廷的大量定期出口相当于在阿根廷持有资产。

提交文件。这对买方是强制性的，对卖方是可选的。但是，管理局可以要求卖方提交文件成为诉讼程序的一部分。任何情况下，双方可以选择单独或联合以单一形式发出通知。

根据 AAL 第 9 条，通知必须在关闭日期前提交。尽管如此，作为一项临时规则，在新的竞争管理机构成立之前，可以在关闭之日之前或一周内提交通知。

批准程序。审咨委的审批程序分为三个阶段，分别要求填写表格 F-1、F-2 和 F-3，每一阶段都涉及更详细的交易及其竞争效果，表格 F-1 是强制性的通知手段，缔约方在认为交易值得进行这种审查时，可选择同时提交表格 F-2。F-3 不是标准表格，由竞争管理委员会逐案编写，只在复杂的交易中才需要。

实际上，目前一项在相关市场没有重大影响的非复杂交易通常需要 6 个月左右才能获得清算。

此外，在涉及受监管市场的交易中，根据 AAL 第 17 条，反垄断委员会必须要求相关监管机构就拟议交易对该特定（受管制）市场竞争的影响以及买方遵守监管框架的情况发表意见。

尽管有关监管机构发表的意见对反托拉斯委员会没有约束力，但从实际角度来看，竞争分析将考虑到这一意见。

从程序上看，反托拉斯委员会应自提交通知之日起 3 天内征求监管机构的意见，监管部门答复的截止日期为 15 个工作日。

如果监管机构在截止日期前未提出答复或延期请求，则 AAL 可以假定该机构对该交易没有异议。根据 AAL，对此意见的请求不会中止 AAL 必须通过其最终决议的 45 个工作日期限。

如果不能及时向竞争管理机构提交交易通知，则可能导致阿根廷经济集团被处以上一个财政年度总收入 0.1% 的日罚款，在总收入无法计算的情况下，罚款从提交之日起算，最高为 750000 个单位（约合 75 万美元），但不影响根据会计准则规定可能适用的其他后果。

目前，申报费可从 5000 ~ 20000 个单位（4000 ~ 16000 美元），但仍有待进一步管制。

十二、商业国际管辖权

（一）法律的选择

根据阿根廷《民商法》第2651条，合同各方可选择适用于这种关系的法律，但消费者协议除外。如果没有作出这种规定，阿根廷《民法》规定，合同由合同履行地的现行法律管辖。无法确定该地点的，适用协议执行地的法律。

当事人对合同适用法律的选择权受到阿根廷法律所规定的国际公共秩序条款的限制，以及强制性的国际申请规则。特别规则适用于证券、继承、家庭事务、法律手续和消费者关系。

（二）司法管辖权的选择

阿根廷《民法典》第2605条允许商业协定的当事方选择阿根廷境外的外国法院或仲裁，但条件是法律没有规定阿根廷法官的专属管辖权，或者法律没有明确禁止这种选择。如果当事各方未就审理其争议的法院达成协议，并且在没有条约的情况下，任何一方可向被告住所法院或履行义务的法院提出其主张。

在房地产事项、与公共记录登记处有关的纠纷以及商标和专利注册的案件中，专属管辖权被分配给国家法院。破产程序和其他制度须遵守具体规则，根据所涉当事人的住所和其他方面提供差别待遇。

阿根廷《民商法》第2610条保障国民与在国外永久居留的人，包括根据外国立法注册的实体之间的平等待遇。不得对在阿根廷提起诉讼的外国当事人施加任何担保。

在使用仲裁或当地法院系统解决争端之间，仲裁通常被认为是处理复杂商业安排中争端的一种更快和更专门的方式，使当事各方普遍期望在决策方面达到最低质量标准，尽管仲裁的适当性应视具体情况而定。

（三）外国判决的执行

在没有关于执行外国法院判决的具体条约的情况下，阿根廷程序法为这种执行以及仲裁庭的裁决提供了规则（我们认为，在与外国投资者打交道时，这是解决争端的建议方法）。要使阿根廷法院执行外国裁决，必须符合下列要求：

（1）判决必须是由主管法院根据阿根廷关于管辖权的法律冲突规则作出的，并且必须是由个人诉讼而作出的管辖范围内的最终判决；如果判决涉及个人财产，则争议中的货物或动产必须在起诉外国行动期间或之后移交给阿根廷。

（2）申诉必须适当送达正在执行判决的被告，而且根据正当法律程序，被告还必须有机会为自己辩护。

（3）判决应在其通过的管辖区内有效，并根据阿根廷法律的要求予以批准。

（4）判决不应违反阿根廷法律的任何公共秩序原则，不得与阿根廷法院事先或同时作出的判决相冲突。

（5）阿根廷加入了关于承认和执行外国判决的各种国际条约，其中包括：

① 1961 年 10 月 5 日《海牙公约》废除了阿根廷于 1987 年批准的外国公共文件合法化的要求，根据该公约，认证程序被该条约所规定的 Apostille 程序所取代；

② 1889 年和 1940 年《蒙得维的亚条约》；

③ 1958 年《承认及执行外国仲裁裁决纽约公约》（1988 年批准）；

④ 阿根廷 1983 年签署的《美洲外国判决和仲裁裁决域外效力公约》。

墨西哥投融资法律研究篇

墨西哥投融资法律研究

Vidaur Mora
Viktoria Von Mirbach
G.Angelica Juárez

一、墨西哥基本概况

墨西哥是由 31 个州和墨西哥城的联邦区组成的民主联邦共和国。墨西哥拥有约 1.2 亿人口。西班牙语是其官方语言。大部分人是罗马天主教徒。

（一）分权

墨西哥《宪法》是在 1917 年墨西哥革命之后制定的，从那时起它就经历了几次改革。它界定了权力的划分：立法、司法和行政权力。

1. 立法权

墨西哥议会（Congresodela Union）是墨西哥的立法组织。它由两院组成：议会和参议院。议会议员每三年由人民选举产生，不得连任。国会负责颁布法律、经济和政治组织、劳动法等。

2. 司法权

墨西哥有联邦和地方法院的制度。墨西哥的最高法院是墨西哥最高法院（Suprema Corte），它由 11 位由总统提议的联邦法官组成。除最高法院外，还有几个专门的法庭和仲裁法庭。根据每个联邦州的《宪法》，每个省都有自己的省级和市级法院。通常每个联邦州都有其高等法院、一审法院和市法院，即所谓的“和平法院”。墨西哥法庭和法官是独立的。

3. 行政权

墨西哥总统是联邦政府的首脑，由墨西哥人民每六年直接选举一次，总统不能连任。除其他职责外，总统还负责颁布和执行法律，可以任命几名工作人员并执行外交政策。

（二）墨西哥法律

墨西哥的法律制度以罗马法律制度为基础。墨西哥的合法来源是立法、判例、习惯法、个人规范和一般原则。联邦政府以及州和市政府可以通过法案，具体取决于授予法律的权限。

墨西哥有不同的法律部门：公法、私法、社会法等。每个部门都有独立的法律体系。

除国家法律外，墨西哥还签署同意了几项国际公约，如《自由贸易协定》《京都议定书》等。

总检察长是执行《刑法》的最高公共权力机关。总检察长是该当局的主任。除联邦办公室外，每个州都有总检察机关。检察机关是警察的负责人。经过2016年生效的刑罚改革后，执法变得更快，效率更高。

为了执行民事诉讼请求，申诉人必须向责任法院提交正式申诉，以执行其权利。在合同关系中，通常会同意仲裁条款，以避免烦琐的流程。

二、与中国企业合作的现状和方向

墨西哥驻华使馆官方数据表明，中国是墨西哥的第二大贸易伙伴，2016年贸易额为75亿美元；同时中国也是墨西哥的第二大进口国和第三大出口国。另外，墨西哥仍是中国在拉丁美洲的首要贸易伙伴。

2014年，墨西哥总统恩里克·培尼亚·涅托和中国国家主席习近平签署了14项协议，以促进投资和商业、投资和金融合作的可持续发展，特别是在能源、资源、基础设施、农业、制造业、汽车和通信技术等领域。

值得特别强调的协议是中国国家开发银行与Bancomext的协议；Pemex将与中国石油（Cnooc）和中国工商银行（ICBC）合作开展石油项目。

实际上，一些协议已经实现：

（1）2016 年，墨西哥总统恩里克·培尼亚·涅托和中国国家主席习近平将投资基金中国—墨西哥正式化，以支持 5000 多万美元的多元投资项目。

（2）2016 年 6 月，中国工商银行在墨西哥开始运营是一个资本项目，将促进墨西哥和中国之间的贸易和投资流动。

（3）2017 年，在高层商业集团（GANE）第五次全体会议上，墨西哥和中国证实了其促进能源、基础设施和汽车合作的承诺。

新签署的双边协议旨在增加贸易和投资，这得益于公共和私营部门通过战略和举措实现两国关系的一体化，以及优先进入中国市场。这方面的例子包括中国公司运营的众多基础设施项目，为外国人提供的签证便利服务和增加的航空联系——这得益于墨西哥航空公司所开辟的墨西哥城与上海、广州之间直飞航班的南航新航线，以及从 2018 年 3 月 21 日起，中国航空公司海航开辟了从北京到墨西哥城的新航线，巩固了两国的双边关系。

三、投资

在墨西哥，《外国投资法》第 2 条指出了三种被认为是外国投资的情况：外国投资者以任何比例参与墨西哥公司的股本；大部分为外资的墨西哥公司；外国投资者参与本法规定的活动和行为。

另外，外国直接投资是外国投资者在东道国建立的具有长期经济和商业目的的长期债券。

（一）市场准入

1. 监督投资部门

在墨西哥，有三个机构负责监督和支持外国投资。

（1）国家外国投资委员会。根据《外国投资法》第 23 条，国家外国投资委员会是一个秘书处间机构，由政府秘书、对外关系、财政和公共信贷、社会发展、自然资源和渔业、能源、商业和工业发展、通信和运输以及劳工和社会保障及旅游业组成。

① 结构。

• 主席：经济部长。

• 代表委员会：由秘书任命的副部长。

• 执行秘书：竞争和管理事务副国务卿。

• 技术秘书：外商投资总监。

② 特征。

•制定关于外国投资和设计机制的政策指导方针，以促进在墨西哥的投资。

• 通过秘书处解决外国投资参与的来源、条款和条件。

• 外商投资咨询机构。

• 为联邦公共行政机构的附属机构和实体制定适用法律条款的标准。

（2）外国投资总办公室。外国投资总办公室是经济秘书处的行政单位，负责根据《外国投资法》颁布行政决议；管理和运营国家外国投资注册局（RNIE）；编制和公布关于外国直接投资在本国境内的行为的统计资料；担任国家外国投资委员会的技术秘书处；助力推动促进和吸引投资；传播关于墨西哥投资环境的信息和研究，并执行关于外国直接投资的公共政策指导方针。

（3）国家外国投资登记处。国家外国投资登记处隶属于经济秘书处外国投资总部；外国投资流入墨西哥是联邦政府负责会计和监督的领域；抵达墨西哥的外国投资记录在 RNIE 中；此外，RNIE 对其收到的信息进行分组，并根据有关墨西哥境内外国直接投资行为的国际标准编制统计数据。

为了组织和运作，书记官处分为三个部分：第一部分为个人和公司；第二部分为社团；第三部分为信托。

该结构基于《外国投资法》第31条和《国家外国投资注册局条例》第31条。

2. 投资行业法律法规

《墨西哥合众国政治宪法》第 73 条第 XXIX-F 条规定，外国投资管理法律问题是国际电联大会的一项职责。

作为墨西哥新经济环境的一部分，《外国投资法》于 1993 年出版，它规定，其目的是确定规则，将外国投资引入该国并促使其为国家发展作出贡献。

《外国投资法》和《国家外国投资注册管理办法》是对《外商投资法》在外商直接投资开放和监管方面的补充手段，它们描述了如何执行相应的程序，此外，它们还为全国外商投资委员会（CNIE）和国家外国投资登记处提

供了权限范围。

3. 投资形式

根据《外国投资法》第 2 条第 2 款，外国投资理解为外国投资者以任何比例参与墨西哥公司的股本；由拥有大部分外资的墨西哥公司进行的投资以及外国投资者参与《外国投资法》所规定的活动和行为。

除《外国投资法》规定的情况外，外国投资可参与墨西哥公司资本存量的任何比例、购置固定资产、进入新的经济活动领域或制造新的产品线、开设和经营企业以及扩大或迁移现有企业。

有三种类型的投资：

（1）直接投资。墨西哥是最容易接受外国直接投资的新兴国家之一。根据联合国贸发会议发布的《2016 年世界投资报告》，墨西哥是世界上第十五个最重要的外国直接投资接受国。

（2）间接投资。如果参与是通过墨西哥资本的大部分墨西哥公司进行的，并且如果这些公司不受外国投资控制，则间接外国投资将不会被计算出来，以确定受最大参与限制的外国投资在经济活动中的比例。

（3）中性投资。中性投资是在墨西哥公司或授权信托中进行的；这一投资不用于确定外国投资在墨西哥公司资本存量中所占的百分比；对没有表决权或仅具有有限公司权利的股票的投资被视为中立投资；为了进行这类投资，必须事先获得经济秘书处的批准，并在适用情况下获得国家银行和证券委员会的批准。

① 以受托机构发行的工具为代表的中立投资。这种模式针对的是打算将股份转让给中立投资信托的墨西哥公司以及旨在创建或修改中立投资信托的信托机构。同时，这种模式需要经由法律事务厅和国家外国投资委员会在外国投资总局处理的授权。此外，打算在信托合同中作为信托机构行事的信托机构也可以请求授权。同样用于已经拥有中立的投资授权，打算修改先前授权的信托协议或计划的墨西哥公司或信托机构。

② 以特殊系列股票为代表的中性投资。这种模式针对的是旨在通过发行仅授予金钱权利的特殊股份或在适用情况下有限公司权利的情形下收集外国资金以扩大其业务的墨西哥公司（拟成立或即将成立）。

③ 国际金融社会对发展的中立投资。这种模式针对的是国际金融社会的

被视为外国法律实体的发展，其主要目标是促进发展中国家的经济和社会发展，通过临时风险投资，提供优惠融资或技术支持。这种模式需要通过外国投资总部在国家外国投资委员会处理的授权。

《外国投资法》第 4 条规定，外国投资可以参与墨西哥公司股本的任何比例；外商投资比例没有限制；公司的资本可能完全是外来的，至少由两个合作伙伴（可以是国内公司或外国公司）合并。但是，在外资限于以下百分比时，在下列特定行业中有一些例外：

• 外国投资参与率超过 49%，并获得国家外国投资委员会事先授权：内河航道服务；为公众提供机场许可证的公司或持有人；民办教育服务；法律服务和铁路的建设、运营和开发。

• 最高 49%：制造和销售火药衍生物和枪支；在国内印刷和出版专用流通报纸；拥有农业、畜牧业和林业用地的公司的股份；在淡水、沿海和专属经济区捕鱼；港口管理；从事商业开发的船公司；为船舶、飞机和铁路设备供应燃料；广播；空运服务。

• 最高 10%：生产商合作社公司。

另外，《外国投资法》第 5 条和第 6 条规定了经济活动和社团，这些活动和社团只限于：

• 具有外国人排除条款的墨西哥或墨西哥公司（国家旅客、旅游和装载运输，开发银行机构以及提供某些专业和技术服务）。

• 国家（石油和碳氢化合物的勘探和开采；电能的规划、控制和分配；核能发电；放射性矿物；电报；邮政；钞票的发行；硬币造币；港口的控制和监督、机场和直升机场）。

2014 年，出现了几项改革，将墨西哥变成一个对外国投资更加开放的国家，原因是消除了对不同部门的外国投资的若干限制。最近有利于外国投资的改革是：

• 石化部门：取消基本石化行业的国家独占权，允许外国人零售汽油和分销液化石油气，参与以油气井钻井为目的的活动或公司，以及在施工中用于运输石油及其衍生物的管道。

• 电信部门：允许外国人提供广播和电视服务，以及参与经济活动或手机公司。

• 机构和公司：允许外国人参加保险或债券机构的经济活动，货币兑换，一般仓库，退休基金管理人员，评估值机构，保险代理人和股票市场推广公司或信用信息公司。

（二）融资

1. 主要融资机构

（1）开发银行。开发银行是墨西哥银行体系的一部分，正如《信贷机构法》第 3 条所规定的那样。发展银行机构是联邦公共行政机构，具有法人资格和自有资产，由国家信用社组成，其主要目标是便利个人和公司的融资渠道，并提供技术援助和培训。

在“国家发展筹资方案”的框架内，已成立了开发银行，作为促进发展、解决获得金融服务的问题和改善对经济增长和就业作出突出贡献的部门的条件的基本经济政策工具。

开发银行由以下 9 个机构轮流集成：

① 国家农业、农村、林业和渔业发展融资（FND）。它有助于增加农村人口发生的任何经济活动的资金来源，并改善其居民的生活质量。

② 全国储蓄和金融服务银行。它促进储蓄、金融教育、金融普惠、性别观点以及金融工具和服务在获得这类产品的机会有限的人群中得到促进。其服务包括考虑到所需的期限、金额和流动性、满足每个人的投资需求的产品和服务。

③ 国家外贸银行。它是一家专门从事通过融资促进对外贸易的金融机构，它可以直接运营或间接通过商业银行和非银行金融中介机构授予贷款和担保来运营，以便墨西哥公司提高生产力和竞争力，它为超过 300 万美元（USD）的资金提供融资。

其服务目标包括：

• 墨西哥的外国投资者：具有商业活动的个人或墨西哥以外的国籍的公司在与外贸或外币相关的生产部门投资于墨西哥。

• 有外资的墨西哥公司：拥有商业活动的个人或墨西哥公司在其外资股中拥有外资份额，并参与与外贸或外汇有关的活动。

④ 国家工程和服务银行。墨西哥开发银行的领先机构，促进创造高社会

盈利能力的基础设施。

⑤ 陆军、空军和海军国家银行。它为墨西哥军队、空军和海军成员以及广大公众提供银行和信用服务。其产品包括金融服务和信托服务，如公共和私人资源、物品和权利的管理。

⑥ 国家金融。墨西哥开发银行机构负责为墨西哥的经济发展作出贡献，鼓励商业银行和信贷机构提供更多更便宜的贷款，从而促进公司、企业家和优先投资项目获得融资和其他业务发展服务，并为金融市场的形成作出贡献，并作为联邦政府的信托和金融代理人，从而促进创新，提高生产力、竞争力，创造就业机会和促进区域增长。

⑦ 联邦抵押协会。经营和住房银行业务融资基金，通过担保或各种金融工具促进住房市场的发展，目的在于建设、购置和改善住房。

⑧ 农村部门资本化和投资基金。它支持和补充农村生产者及其经济组织的经济能力，鼓励农村和农业工业企业的发展和巩固。

⑨ 设立与农业有关的信托。它向墨西哥的农业、农村和渔业部门提供信贷、担保、培训和技术援助。

（2）商业银行。在墨西哥提供融资的主要银行包括 BBVABancomer、Santander、CitiBanamex、Banorte、HSBC。

2. 外资企业融资条件

尽管各金融机构要求有所不同，但开立账户和申请融资的要求并不区分外国或国内公司。

（三）兼并与收购

1. 兼并

公司合并在《商业法》第 222 条至第 228 条中进行了规定。决定每一个决定合并的公司在股东大会上同意与每一个公司形式相对应的条款。

从公司角度来看，合并生效有两个不同时刻：首先，它在合并双方（合并公司和合并后的公司以及这些合并后的股东）之间生效；其次，它对第三方（参与合并的所有公司的债权人和债务人）生效。

公司合并可以在合并公司与被合并公司之间生效，合并时间由合并公司股东约定。一旦达成了协议，必须将其提交由公证人核证的公共契约，该公共契约将在公共登记处登记，并在经济秘书处的电子系统中公布。以同样的方式，合并的公司应公布其最后的余额，而不再存在的公司，应在为其债务的消失而设立的制度中公开，以便对第三方有效。在商业公共登记处登记后，需要等待 3 个月才能进行合并，从合并协议登记在商务公共注册处之日起算。在这 3 个月内，合并公司的债权人可以通过简易判决反对合并。在这种情况下，合并将被暂停，直到宣布反对方没有根据的判决。一旦这段时间过去了，没有任何反对意见，就可以进行合并，而且合并后的公司或合并公司应负责公司的权利和义务。

《商业法》第 225 条提出了合并立即生效的选项，无须等待 3 个月。在这种情况下，合并公司可以支付合并公司的所有债务，将其存入信用机构或获得所有债权人的同意。如果几家公司合并后会产生不同的公司，其章程将受有关组建相应公司形式的规定的约束。已经组建和合并的公司可能会采取新的公司形式，并将自己转变为可变资本公司，但合作公司和简体股份公司除外。

根据《联邦税法》第 14-B 条的规定，如果符合以下条件，财政部门有可能不会将合并视为转让：提交合并通知；合并后，在合并生效后至少一年内合并公司在合并之前继续执行合并和合并后的公司进行的活动；存在的公司提交待定税务申报，并且合并公司在合并后的一个月内在联邦纳税人登记处注销。

2. 收购

收购是由另一家公司（收购公司）购买一家公司（被收购公司）的股份，该公司获得了被收购公司的控制权。收购方通过购买股份获得被收购公司的公司控制权。收购可以通过仅获得一定比例的股份来获得全部股份来实现，如果获得大多数股份，则获得公司的多数票。作为合伙人的权利和义务按照投资于公司的资本成比例地获得。财政上，根据《联邦财政法》第 14 条，收购股份构成财产转让，导致纳税义务（增值税和 ISR）。

3. 劳工

从劳动力角度来看，并购可以等同于劳动替代，因为合并公司承担了雇主对合并后公司的责任。根据《联邦劳动法》第 41 条，雇主的替代不会影响公司的雇佣关系。被替换的雇主将承担新的责任，承担由替代日期之前设立的劳资关系和法律所产生的义务，直至6个月的期限；一旦完成，新雇主的责任将保持不变。

4. 在墨西哥的实体类型

墨西哥的公司受到《商业法》和《股市法》的监管。《商业法》第1条界定了公司的主要类型。

（1）股票公司。在股份公司，公司股份仅由至少两名股东持有，其责任仅限于其出资。

（2）有限责任公司。有限责任公司至少由两名合伙人组成，合伙人有义务支付其供款，他们的责任仅限于他们的参股。同样，《股票市场法》第12条也定义了其他公司形式。

（3）股票促进投资公司。股票促进投资公司是由两个或两个以上的个人或公司组成的公司，旨在开展允许其股东拥有公司和经济权利的商业活动。其组织章程采用与股份公司相同的规则，在其公司名称中增加"投资促进者"或其缩写"P.I."。它的显著特点是在墨西哥股市交易股票的可能性。

（4）子公司。根据《商业法》和《外国投资法》，在墨西哥设立子公司以执行商业行为或提供服务的外国公司应在公司所在国取得经济部颁发的许可证或授权书，以便外国公司的文件可以在商业登记册中注册，并且该子公司被视为已经建立。

重要的是要注意：子公司在墨西哥执行的所有活动和责任将以无限的方式直接转移到原产地公司。因此，它被认为是母公司法人人格的延伸。外国国籍的公司将具有作为外国人的所有约束、限制、义务和权利。应该注意的是，在墨西哥设立子公司并不常见，这会给日常业务带来困难。

（四）竞争规定

墨西哥的监管和竞争政策从20世纪90年代开始增加。墨西哥在自由竞争、经济竞争、垄断、垄断行为和集中的基础上制定了基于《墨西哥合众国政治宪法》第28条的竞争和监管政策。

1. 竞争规定监管部门

联邦经济竞争委员会是自治的宪法机构，由商业和工业发展秘书处（SECOFI）下放，该机构负责监督、促进和保证墨西哥市场的自由竞争和合作。

根据《联邦经济竞争法》，委员会拥有合法所有权和自有资产，可自由决策和运营，其业绩专业、行动公正，并拥有自主预算。

根据《联邦经济竞争法》，委员会于 1993 年 6 月 23 日开始活动。现在，其目标是保证自由竞争和经济竞争，并防止、调查和打击垄断行为、非法集中和对市场有效运作的其他限制。

2. 竞争法规简介

经济竞争立法起源于 1857 年的墨西哥《宪法》，《宪法》禁止垄断行为，并规定所有墨西哥人有权自由进入市场。20 世纪上半叶，颁布了 1917 年《宪法》第 28 条的三部法律。1992 年 12 月，《联邦经济竞争法》获得联盟大会批准并于 1993 年 6 月 23 日生效，同时联邦竞争委员会（CFC）开始履行其职责。

2014 年 5 月 23 日，新的《联邦经济竞争法》出台，目标是促进、保护和保障自由竞争和经济竞争，有效防范、调查、打击、起诉、严惩和消除垄断行为、非法集中、自由竞争和经济竞争的障碍以及对市场有效运作的其他限制。

3. 控制竞争的措施

《联邦经济竞争法》区分垄断做法、绝对做法和相关做法。第一种是严格禁止的，而第二种则需要通过经济分析证明这种做法影响竞争过程和扭曲市场。

根据相对的垄断做法，法律将以下活动区分开来，这些活动一般是指生产链的所有参与者之间的一项义务：

• 在同一市场的经济代理人中，他们不适当地取代了其他经济代理人，而偏袒另一部分人；

• 在不是竞争对手的经济代理商中，专门实施商业化；

• 强加价格；

• 以做或不做某些商业行为条件的销售；

• 拒绝向公众出售资产或服务；

• 经济代理人协议，迫使经济代理人朝某一方向行事；

• 销售低于其成本，但高于其可变的平均成本；

• 向买方提供供应商的折扣或福利，要求其与其他人作出或停止进行商业行为；

• 利用经济代理人的利润为另一资产或服务的损失提供资金；

• 在同等条件下为不同的买方或卖方确定不同的价格或销售或购买条件；

• 经济主体的行动，其目的是增加成本或阻碍生产进程或减少其他经济主体面临的需求；

• 限制在歧视性条件下获得基本投入的机会；

• 收窄价格利润率。

委员会通过调查当局防止和消除妨碍自由竞争和经济竞争的障碍，该机构是委员会负责调查委员会实现反竞争做法的案件机构，也是以审判形式遵循程序的一部分。

（五）土地和房地产

《墨西哥合众国政治宪法》第 27 条规定了三种财产：私有财产、公共财产和社会财产。

私有财产：《墨西哥合众国政治宪法》承认第 27 条第 1 款中的财产权，它规定国家领土内的土地和水域的所有权最初对应于国家，国家有权转让所有权归个人所有，因此构成私人财产。《民法》对私有财产作了规定。根据《民法典》第 984 条，财产是赋予其所有者使用、享有和处置财产的权力，具有法律规定的限制和方式。

公共财产：公共财产是一种财产，它不是商业的对象，它有两种形式：一是公有财产，国家规定的用于公共服务、历史古迹等的房地产；二是联邦的私有资产，它们是公共行政实体继承财产的一部分。

社会财产：社会财产是具有法人资格的法人及其自有资产，由一套称为公有财产的资产和权利组成，它受 1992 年 2 月 26 日《土地法》的管制，这是第 27 条第Ⅶ条的管理法，它承认公共财产和公共人口中心的法律人格，并保护他们的财产，无论是住宅区还是生产性活动。

为了出售社会财产，必须将其从社会财产转为私有财产，通过一项法律行动，由公有土地所有人大会授权改造，并要求取消国家土地登记处的土地认购权，然后在财产公共登记处登记所有权契据。

（六）税收

1. 主要税种和税率

（1）联邦税。

① 所得税。所得税是征收个人和公司收入的一般、个人和直接税。

• 主体：在下列情况下，所有个人和公司都是所得税主体：墨西哥的居民，无论其财富来源在何处，其全部收入如何；在该国有常设机构的海外居民，与上述机构的收入有关；以及在国外的居民，涉及在本国境内的财富来源的收入。

• 对象：所得税的目的是指人们以现金、实物或信贷方式获得的收入。就法人而言，这是指从事商业或工业活动所得的收入；就个人而言，则是从征税制度中获得的收入。

• 基数：所得税基数是应纳税所得之和减去相应扣减额的结果。

• 税率：根据《所得税法》第 152 条，公司的所得税税率为 30%，而个人所得税税率根据基数的下限而有所不同。

② 增值税——VAT。增值税是每购买一项资产或服务时产生的一般和间接税，并征收在其生产过程中添加到商品中的所有价值。通过它，主体转移到提供资产或服务的人身上。因此，谁纳税，谁就是最终消费者。

• 主体：指从事下列行为或活动的个人和公司，包括资产转让、提供独立服务、租赁资产、进口资产和服务。

• 目的：增值税的目的是对上述行为或活动征税。物质对象是在生产链的每个阶段向资产或服务添加的价值。

• 基数：增值税基数是法律对其征收的四类行为或活动所表示的价值。一般而言，增值税基数是行为或活动的价值。

• 税率：一般增值税税率为 16%；同样，还有一个特别的零税率，主要用于食品和药品。

③ 生产和服务特别税。IEPS是一项适用于资产和服务生产的特殊税收，通常会导致社会损害或其消费不受欢迎。另外，IEPS也是可以转移的税款。

• 主体：IEPS 的主体是从事下列行为或活动的个人和公司：在国家领土内转让或输入《IEPS 法》规定的资产或服务。

• 对象：根据《IEPS 法》第 2 条，该税的目的是对含酒精饮料、烟草、汽油和柴油、能源饮料、添加糖饮料、化石燃料、农药和高热量食品征收转让和进口税。

• 基数: IEPS 的基数是转让或进口的资产的价值; 或所提供的服务的价值。

• 税率：就 IEPS 而言，《IEPS 法》第 2 条中的每种商品或服务的费率和 / 或费用均不同。

④ 一般进口税。根据《对外贸易法》第 12 条的规定，一般进口税是根据进口产生的。这可以是：

• 从价，以商品关税价值的百分比表示。

• 具体，以每一计量单位的货币表示。

• 混合，是前两者的组合。

税收的价值应当与进口商品的关税项目相对应，按照《进出口总税法》或《自由贸易协定》规定的墨西哥税收减免表的税率进行分类。

（2）州税。每个州的代表大会负责规划州的收入和支出，并每年出版各国的收入法。这项法律决定每个州在每年 1 月 1 日至 12 月 31 日的财政年度的收入。国会决定的税只适用于每个州的边界，而不影响其他州，因此费用可能会有所不同。公司的州税为：对个人工作报酬的支出税，这一税将根据州的情况，适用 2% ~ 3% 的平均税率。

（3）市政税。各州的每个市镇都有一部市所得税法，其中规定州的收入在一个财政年度内确定。为市政府公司征收的税款如下：

① 财产税。

• 主体：位于本市的乡村或城市物业的所有者或持有人。

• 对象：位于本市的乡村或城市土地的所有权或拥有权。

• 基数：地籍总公司确定的地籍价值。

• 税率：根据财产类型，每年产生一次。

② 财产的取得。

• 主体：取得本市境内财产的个人或者法人。

• 对象：取得位于本市的、由土地或土地及其附属建筑物组成的不动产。

• 基数：这种贡献的基础是财产的价值，它必须是以下三种假设中的最高者：收购价值、地籍价值和由评估产生的价值。

• 税率：基数的 1.8%。

2. 税收制度和规则

公司的一般制度规定的法律实体有：商业协会，公司或民间协会，合作生产协会，信贷、保险和担保机构、一般存款仓库、金融和租赁公司、信用社和资本投资公司，资产或服务商业化的分散组织，以及与从事有利可图活动等商业活动有关的信托机构。

属于这一制度的法律实体负有下列义务：

• 在联邦纳税人登记处登记。

• 开具发票。

• 保存会计报表。

• 提交声明。

• 在联邦纳税人登记处更新数据。

3. 税收申报和优惠

在公司的一般制度中，提交的声明如下：

• 月度报表：所得税、增值税、生产和服务特殊税（取决于活动）。报表必须在与付款或声明相对应的月份的第 17 天之前作出。这一义务必须通过参考的付款方法来履行，使用申报和付款服务，可在税务管理处的门户网站上查阅。

• 年度报表必须不迟于所报告的财政年度之后的年度的 3 月完成。

• 与第三方的信息化运营声明。这是《增值税法》中规定的一项财政义务，其中包括在紧接相应信息之后的月份内向税务管理处（SAT）每月提供与其供应商的操作信息，并通过税务管理服务处在线门户网站的可下载格式提供。

• 多种信息性陈述。它们不迟于 2 月 15 日通过税务管理服务处在线门户网站上的多重信息声明（DIM）计划提交。

四、贸易

（一）贸易监管部门

在墨西哥，有各种监督和管理贸易的国家秘书处。最重要的部门如下。

1. 财务和公共信贷部门

财务和公共信贷秘书处是联邦行政权的附属机构，其任务是在财政、支出、收入和公共债务事项上提出、指导和控制联邦政府的经济政策，目的是巩固一个具有高质量经济增长的国家。

（1）税务管理部门。税务管理部门是财政和公共信贷部的下放机构，它是一个财政机构，负责实施个人和法人的税收和海关法规，为公共支出作出贡献并推动自愿遵守税法。

根据《海关法》第10条，税务管理部门负责批准从墨西哥领土入境或离境的资产，这些资产因其数量而无法发送，或为提高效率和通过发送货物来提高效率和提供便利。

（2）海关总署。国家税务总局分为几个行政部门，其中包括海关总署，负责监督海关、制定应遵循的政策和行动。海关总署是根据清关以及相应的制度、方法和程序适用立法的唯一主管当局。

2. 经济秘书处

经济秘书处是一个国家部门，负责管理产品的本地和出口税，以及相关的定价。此外，它还考虑到消费者对商业的防范。此外，它控制工业和商业财产数据库，并管理墨西哥官方标准和国际单位制的正确使用。其归属依据的是《联邦公共行政组织法》第34条。

经济秘书处有一个外贸事务的分秘书处。外贸部副部长是一个政府部委，受权对各项条约及国际贸易和投资协定进行谈判、管理和维护。

（二）贸易法律法规简介

墨西哥前总统马德里的政府经济政策（1982—1988年）提出了国家市场导向的结构性改革，他通过放开外贸来提高经济的外部竞争力。

1983年，墨西哥通过一项符合工业需要的关税政策、国际贸易协定谈判和对外国投资开放的政策，实现了自由贸易的增加。10年后，墨西哥通过了《对外贸易和海关法》，并且制定了配套的法律法规。

1. 《对外贸易法》

墨西哥《对外贸易法》于1993年7月发布。因此，贸易委员会批准废除《宪法》第131条旧监管法的法律。为了遵守世界贸易组织（WTO）争端解决机构发布的决议和建议，该法于 2006 年进行了改革。

目前，墨西哥《对外贸易法》的目标是规范和促进对外贸易，以提高墨西哥经济的竞争力，它的目标是促进有效利用该国的生产资源，使墨西哥经济与国际经济适当结合，保护生产工厂免受不正当的国际贸易侵害，并为提高人民的福祉作出贡献。

2.《海关法》

作为开放战略的一部分，1995 年首次公布的墨西哥《海关法》和《一般进出口税法》经过若干修改。后者管制墨西哥领土内的货物进出口。

（三）贸易管理

1. 对贸易的要求

（1）关税成分。关税项目是世界海关组织（WCO）统一制度（HS）规定的每种产品的编码。“统一制度”是一种术语，它将可以交易的产品分组，并根据某些特定规则加以编纂。

为了能够启动进出口程序，必须与海关代理联系，海关代理是财政和公共信贷部授权的唯一代理机构，代表公司推动必要的程序，其中包括确定与产品对应的关税项目以适应市场。

（2）关税分类。关税分类包括一般进出口税的关税中与其对应的部分商品的地点。负责分类的是海关经纪人，承包商必须就商品的识别和质量提供必要的信息，以便能够作出正确的分类，因为这取决于关税的支付和非关税规则和限制的遵守情况。

（3）进口商登记处。进口商向国家进口商品的义务之一是在税务管理服务之前在进口商登记处登记。

（4）特定行业进口商登记册。必须考虑到，某些商品，根据其关税项目，海关人员确定这些商品属于特定部门，因此必须在特定部门进口商登记册上登记，以防止和发现影响墨西哥各部门的做法，并保障公共卫生和国家安全。这些部门包括化学产品；放射性产品和核产品；火器或推力武器及其附件；爆炸物；雪茄；鞋类；纺织和服装；乙醇、碳氢化合物、钢铁产品和汽车。

另外，墨西哥有几个管理墨西哥贸易发展的条例，这些条例分为关税条例和非关税条例。

2. 关税条例

进口可造成的出资有：一般进口税（关税）、海关运送费、增值税（VAT）、生产和服务特别税（IEPS）和仓储权。

（1）一般进口税。根据《外贸法》第13条，这些关税可以采取下列方式：

• 关税配额，对出口或进口货物的一定数量或价值确定关税水平，并对超过上述数额的商品的进出口实行不同的税率。

• 季节性关税，在一年中的不同时期建立不同的关税水平。

• 联邦行政部门可能指出的其他方式。

该税款是根据海关价值（发票价值 + 保险和运费价值乘以汇率）计算得出的，结果将乘以《进出口法》规定的税率。

（2）海关运送费。《联邦权利法》第49条规定，在使用请求或海关文件开展海关业务时，将支付海关运送费。这一权利是通过将海关货物的价值乘以0.008来计算的。

（3）增值税。根据《增值税法》第1条和第27条，增值税是在国家领土内的个人和公司进口货物或服务的义务。税额按报关金额、IGI引起的税额和所造成的海关运输费之和计算，税率为16%。

（4）生产和服务特别税。税额将根据《IEPS法》中规定的产品按照海关价值、IGI和海关费用的总和计算。

（5）仓储权。在《联邦权利法》第41条规定的期限届满后，将支付在海关前存放商品的费用。

3. 非关税条例

根据经济部的规定，非关税条例是主管当局对通过国家领土进出口、流通或过境货物规定某些义务和要求的行政行为。

（1）出口或进口配额。

可出口或进口的商品的数量，无论是最高的还是在关税配额内的，都是理解的。

（2）打击国际贸易中反对价格歧视的不公平做法的措施，包括以低于正常价值的价格将货物引入国家领土，以及补贴，即外国政府给予生产公司或子公司并产生利润的财政捐助。

（3）墨西哥官方标准是由主管标准化单位根据《联邦计量和标准化法》

第 40 条通过国家标准化咨询委员会颁布的强制性遵守的技术条例。

（4）标记原籍国。根据《对外贸易法》第 9 条的规定，货物的原产地可根据关税优惠、原产地标识、反补贴税的适用、配额和可能制定的其他措施确定。

（5）质量标准（IOS's）。在墨西哥，经济部负责核证本国或国际产品的质量。

对政府而言，认证确保所有货物和服务符合与安全、健康、环境等有关的强制性要求。此外，认证还作为控制与其他国家进行的对外贸易的一种手段。

4. 促进出口的方案

墨西哥政府实施了促进出口、提高生产力和提高工艺质量的方案，以提高公司的竞争力，并使它们能够适当地融入全球市场，这些方案包括：制造业、纺织业和出口服务业（IMMEX），高出口公司（ALTEX），外贸公司（ECEX），向出口国退还进口税（DrawBack），部门推广计划（PROSEC）。

（1）制造业、纺织业和出口服务业。它是一种工具，允许生产商或公司出口、暂时进口原材料、供应品、零部件和包装以及机械和设备，用于准备出口产品，而无须缴纳进口税、增值税或补偿性付款。要进入这个项目，公司必须出口 50 万美元或占其总销售额的 10%。

（2）高出口公司。这是一个计划，旨在简化为产业出口产品所需的行政程序，并允许个人和公司退还增值税，这些增值税有利于商品出口，并有可能在 20 个工作日内获得这些余额。

（3）外贸公司。它是市场营销公司利用开发银行的行政设施和资金支持进入国际市场的一种手段，其目的是根据国际需求将国家商品报价结合起来。这个项目只针对那些只从事海外营销的公司。

（4）向出口国退回进口税。这是一项计划，出口商通过该计划偿还因进口和随后出口而产生的税款的价值：纳入出口产品的原材料、零部件、包装、燃料、润滑剂和其他材料；进口在国外进口的货物；为修理或改装而进口的货物。

（5）部门推广计划。这是一项旨在专门生产某些产品的公司的项目，无论产品是针对国外市场还是面向国内市场，它的主要好处是，在进口商生产其产品时，它们将有权享受从价税的进口优惠。

（四）进出口商品检验检疫

联邦预防卫生风险委员会是卫生秘书处的一个权力分散的机构，负责保护民众免受与使用和消费食品、饮料、药品、医疗设备、香水、美容和卫生产品、植物营养物质、农药及其他产品和物质有关的健康风险。

作为最低要求，这些产品应符合墨西哥国家标准化管理和卫生推广协商委员会的官方标准，该标准确立了适用于产品的规则、规格、属性、指导方针、特性或规定。此外，它还规定了程序、安装、系统、活动、服务、生产方法或操作，与术语、包装、标记或标签有关的程序，以及在控制和健康促进方面涉及其遵守或应用的程序。

根据墨西哥官方标准 nom-144-SEMARNAT-2012，关于国际植物检疫措施国际标准（NIMF 第 15 号），国际公认的木制包装植物检疫措施用于国际货物和商品贸易。因此，就木材包装而言，要求以甲基溴熏蒸为基础的处理只能按照标准中所示的数量和形式进行。

（五）海关管理

墨西哥海关是国家边境、海岸线和重要城市的公共行政办公室，负责收取国库进出口货物的权利。

海关管理是企业必须遵守的安全标准，允许企业记录与遵守海关和对外贸易义务相关的流程。

在墨西哥，海关管理由海关代理履行，海关代理根据《海关法》第 162 条的规定承担关于商品进入墨西哥领土的海关手续。这些程序可以通过综合海关管理系统来执行，这些系统旨在支持进出口流程，加速交易并降低国际贸易成本。

五、劳工

（一）劳动法律法规简介

墨西哥联邦劳工起源于《墨西哥合众国政治宪法》第 123 条“A”节。该报告于 1970 年发布，并进行了几次改革，最后一次是在 2015 年。法律包括工作的原则和条件，以及工作和劳资纠纷的个人和集体关系所产生的权利和义务。

《联邦劳动法》包括以下领域：

（1）个体劳动法：它规定了员工与雇主的关系。

（2）集体劳动法：它管理集体劳动关系，并将工会视为一个法律机构。

（3）程序劳动法：它规范了解决劳动法主体之间的冲突。

（4）社会保障法：社会保障法的目标是保障个人和集体福利所需的健康、医疗、保护生活资料和社会服务的人权。这包括：

① 健康权，受社会保障法管辖。

② 住房权，由国家住房基金会工作人员法律监管。

③ 由退休储蓄系统法管理的退休基金。

（二）雇用外籍雇员的规定

在墨西哥，对雇用外国雇员有某些限制。根据《联邦劳动法》第 7 条，外国雇员不得超过雇主工人总数的 10%。墨西哥《移民法》规定了外国人希望在墨西哥从事有偿活动时应遵守的要求。国家移民局是负责当局。根据《移民法条例》第 166 条的规定，为了雇用外国人员，公司必须向国家移民研究所申请“雇主登记证”，这一证书允许它们认可自己的法人资格和能力。作为一家注册公司，雇用外国雇员是可能的。证书应每年续签。

1. 工作许可

根据《移民法》第 3 条第 20 款，雇用要约是个人或公司向外国人提出的关于在墨西哥领土提供从属个人工作或提供专业服务的建议，其方式是支付工资或报偿。根据《移民法》第 3 条第 2 款的规定，外国工人应根据《移民法条例》第 115 条获得收入、工资或报酬。个体或公司承包外劳的，应向国家移民局提交工作要约。申请签证时，应当告知当局外国人的姓名和国籍，该人的职业、收入、工作时间和地点以及承担外国人旅费的表现。根据法律，雇用要约是个人或公司向外国人提出的建议，目的是在墨西哥领土上提供从属的个人工作或专业服务，支付工资或报酬。

2. 适用程序

一旦公司收到雇主证书，并向国家统计局提交外国人的就业机会，它就可以向外国人申请工作签证的批准。

对于希望在墨西哥工作的外国人来说，有两种不同的移民身份可供选择，具体取决于时间段：

（1）获准进行为期 180 天以下有偿活动的访客，自入境之日起计算，不得续签（《移民法》第 52 条第 2 款）；

（2）获得工作许可的临时居民，期限超过 180 天，可延长最长 4 年（《移民法》第 52 条第 7 款）。

根据墨西哥《移民法》第 54 条，外国人可以在 4 年临时居留后申请永久签证。此签证授权外国人在墨西哥无限期生活和工作。一般情况下，国家移民局会在批准后的 20 个工作日后发放签证。外国人一旦获得授权，就必须通过 MEXITEL 上的账户与雇员居住国的领事馆或大使馆预约，该账户可在外交部的官方网站上查阅。在任命时，外国人应到移民局报到，并提供签发移民证件所需的个人资料。

一旦外国人收到签证，他 / 她可以移民到墨西哥。在移民区，有兴趣的人应向移民代理人出示签证，移民代理人可向外国人颁发证明在该国合法逗留的多重移民表（FMM）。FMM 是请求交换临时居民身份证的必要条件，外国籍人可以在本国合法工作。证明暂住居留身份的卡与工作签证的有效期相同。

3. 社会保险

根据《社会保障法》，社会保障的目标是保障个人和集体福祉的健康权、医疗保健权、生计保护权和社会服务权，以及国家保障的养恤金。墨西哥社会保障协会向受益人提供的福利兼顾强制性制度和自愿制度。在强制性制度下，由于需要社会保险的雇佣关系，个人与雇主有关联，而自愿制度与社会保障的联系则是个人或集体的决定。

墨西哥社会保障所的工人登记包括下列风险：

（1）操作危险；

（2）疾病和生育；

（3）残废与死亡；

（4）养老金、老年失业；

（5）日间护理和社会福利。

此外，雇员有义务向 Infonavit 支付最低工资的 5%。Infonavit 是工人的资金，用于购买或翻新他们的房子。此外，工人工资的 2% 应存入 AFORE 账户，作为退休偿金。

（三）劳资纠纷

地方调解和仲裁委员会及联邦调解和仲裁委员会有权处理墨西哥的劳资纠纷。根据《墨西哥合众国政治宪法》第 123 条第 31 款，劳工管辖权属于联邦实体的主管部门，尽管存在某些问题，但联邦当局完全有权处理：工业子公司和服务、与联邦政府有关的公司和工会、雇主在教育和培训方面的义务、州间冲突和集体协议。

劳动争议的解决有两种程序：普通程序和特别程序。

1. 普通程序

一般程序适用于个人和集体劳动冲突。《联邦劳动法》第 870 条至第 891 条规定，普通程序分为以下三个阶段：

（1）调解、请求和例外听证。第一阶段是从向主管委员会当事方办公室提出诉讼开始。它规定了一项协议，规定了听证会的日期和时间。听证会进行调解，调解是委员会通过调解官员或其法律工作人员进行干预，与当事人进行讨论，敦促当事人设法达成和解的程序。如果双方不能达成协议，则将提出请求和例外，以及听取提供和接受证据的日期。

（2）证据提供与受理的听证。第二阶段是在提供和接受证据听证时，当事人向委员会提供证据（供词、文件、证词、专家、检查、推定和工具）供委员会分析。一旦确定证据，就确定提交证据听证的日期。

（3）提交证据听证。第三阶段是提交证据听证。理事会作出仲裁裁决，这是结束冲突的最终解决办法。

2. 特别程序

特别程序适用于下列劳动冲突：

（1）与工作日有关的冲突；

（2）工人居住空间；

（3）批准在本国领土内订约的墨西哥境外工人提供服务的个人工作合同；

（4）发展和培训；

（5）劳工资历和资历溢价；

（6）如属船舶工人；

（7）如属航空机组人员；

（8）就业集体合同的所有权；

（9）合同管理——法律；

（10）临时中止或集体终止不属于雇主的雇佣关系；

（11）依法申报破产或破产；

（12）由于采用新机器或工作程序而导致人员减少；

（13）工人死亡时的受益人声明和赔偿；

（14）冲突的目的是收集不超过三个月工资的福利。

在任何程序中，根据《联邦劳动法》第 48 条，工人可向调解和仲裁委员会提出申请恢复工作，或获得 3 个月的工资补偿，并根据最后的工资从解雇之日起至最长 12 个月期间领取工资。如果该程序在年底尚未完成，则还将向工人支付 15 个月工资的利息，按每月 2% 的费率计算。雇主应考虑到，尽管法律规定了每次听证的具体最后期限，但在实践中，从一次听证到另一次听讯的时间可能持续数月，因此裁决可能需要数年才能解决。

六、争议解决

在墨西哥，解决冲突可以通过普通法诉讼来解决，然而，过去几年制定的各种法律更容易解决冲突。

普通法诉讼。对抗性纠纷通常通过向主管法院提起诉讼来解决。一般而言，法官对争议作出决定和判决。

替代诉讼程序。有三种不同的争端解决方式：

（1）和解：在所有审判中，必须事先进行和解听证会，以便在正式启动审判之前达成协议。在和解中，如果达成协议，便具有与司法解决相同的效果。

（2）调解：调解是一个程序，由两个或两个以上的人参与，以自愿寻求解决他们的争议的方法，在公正和中立的称为调解员的第三方的帮助下，促进双方之间的沟通，达成令人满意的协议。

（3）仲裁：仲裁是通过将利害关系方提交第三方裁决来解决冲突的一种形式。在墨西哥，通常在劳动事务中指定专门的裁判机构。

（一）解决争端的方法和机构

1. 联邦级别

联邦的司法权力在墨西哥负责司法，并且是墨西哥的独立政权，以维持权力分配。联邦司法权力的一个最重要职能是维护《宪法》秩序。

《墨西哥合众国政治宪法》第 94 条规定了联邦司法权的行使。因此，司法权由下列独立法庭行使。

（1）国家最高法院。国家最高法院是墨西哥的最高法院，它由 11 位部长组成，其中一位是总统。

（2）联邦司法委员会。该委员会是一个独立的技术机构，负责管理和发布关于联邦司法部门的行政、监督、纪律和法律职业的决议，但涉及国家最高法院和联邦选举法院的事项除外。

（3）联邦选举法院。联邦选举法院是联邦司法权力的一个专门机构，它负责选举事宜，是选举问题的最高司法当局。

（4）合议庭。合议庭是由三名治安法官组成的联邦法院，其法院判决一致通过，或以其成员的多数表决通过。

（5）单一巡回法院。这些法院是由唯一的法官组成的联邦法院，这些法院审理民事、刑事或行政纠纷。

（6）地区法院。地区法院是联邦司法权初审的管辖机构。每个法院都由一名地区法官主持。联邦法院分布在墨西哥全境，但只能对其司法辖区内发生的法律纠纷作出裁决。此外，还有其他机构负责管辖，这些机构不是联邦司法权的一部分。

（7）联邦财政和行政法院。联邦财政和行政司法法院是一个行政法院，与联邦行政权力机构有关联。法院有充分的自主权作出裁决，它由一个上级办事处和分布在该国的地区办事处组成。

（8）高等农业法院。高等农业法院是一个联邦法院，拥有对农业事务作出裁决的充分管辖权和自主权。土地司法工作在全国范围内是一致的。

（9）联邦调解和仲裁委员会。这是一个具有充分管辖权的三方法院，由同等数量的工人和雇主代表以及一个政府组成，负责解决工人和雇主之间出现的劳资纠纷。

（10）联邦调解和仲裁法院。联邦调解和仲裁法院负责解决联邦权力机构与各自工人之间的劳资冲突。

2. 地方一级

每个州的政治宪法都规定了一个合议庭的司法权，即州最高法院和每个联邦实体的组织法所确定的法院的司法权。

各州的组织法规定了州司法权的行使。预计将有以下州司法实例。

（1）州司法高级法庭。州司法高级法庭是每个州的最高司法机关，它由地方法官组成，一般分成几个分庭。

（2）法院。这些地方法院是各州司法权的一部分，每个法院的首长都是一名法官，一审时作出判决。墨西哥设立了以下地方法院：

① 民事和商业；

② 家庭；

③ 刑事，控制和起诉；

④ 青少年与执行；

⑤ 默认行为；

⑥ 域名消灭法庭；

⑦ 市法院、仲裁法院、土著法院的编外法官。

（3）选举法院。选举法院负责解决各州选举事务中出现的冲突。其成员一般是治安法官。应当指出，在一些州，选举法院是地方司法权的一部分，而在另一些州，选举法院是自治的。

（4）诉讼行政法院。诉讼行政法院是解决国家和个人公共行政之间争端的自治机构，其名称和权力可能因州而异。

（5）地方调解和仲裁委员会。地方调解和仲裁委员会是解决在其领土内发生的不属于联邦调解和仲裁委员会专属职权范围内的劳资纠纷的州一级机构。

（6）地方调解和仲裁法院。这些法院解决州或市政府及其各自工作人员之间的冲突。其组织和派系因州而异。

（二）法律适用

墨西哥是一个具有分散式组织的联邦州，尽管在《宪法》中规定了法律的适用，但采用法律的方式通常各州不同。

法律制度的结构是建立在凯恩斯模型的基础上的，该模型主要考虑两个要素，通过法律之间的等级和法律效力的范围来确定能力。根据这一模式，墨西哥法律可以从另一个赋予其效力的法律中衍生出来。在墨西哥，他们的法律体系的等级是以下面的倒金字塔为图形代表的：

墨西哥的政治宪法和国际条约

联邦法律

地方宪法

当地法律

市政法律

条例

个性化的法律规则（法律行为判断和行政决议）在墨西哥，有四种不同维度的适用法律范围。

一是地理维度：根据地理范围，界定关于地域的法律适用范围。墨西哥的三个地理范围是联邦、地方和市政。

二是时间维度：该范围以时间段来定义范围，该法律是有效的。这可能是一个确定的或不确定的时间段。前者确定了一定的失效日期，后者在被明确或默认废除时变为无效。

三是物质维度：在物质范围方面，法律对有关事项作出规定时，适用法律。

四是个人范围维度：根据个人范围，如果法规是针对主体的，则适用法律。这可以分为两个适用范围：通用的，如果适用范围指的是社区；个性化的，如果适用范围是指一个或几个人。前者一般由法律规定，后者通常由法律行为或行政和司法决议确定。

媒体报道篇

中国企业赴欧洲投融资法律研讨会在沪举办

证券时报网（2017-03-20）

由上海上市公司协会、上海股权投资协会、上海国际服务贸易行业协会、金茂凯德律师事务所和上海大学法学院联合举办的中国企业赴欧洲投融资法律研讨会 2017 年 3 月 20 日在沪举行，上海市政协副主席周汉民、上海市政协常委及经济委员会副主任张宁、上海市黄浦区副区长陈卓夫、上海上市公司协会秘书长钱衡、锦江国际集团副总裁王国兴、黄浦区政协秘书长庄利平、黄浦区司法局局长刘辉及副局长杨冬雨、黄浦区金融服务办公室主任朱立新、上海国际服务贸易行业协会常务副会长吴根宝、上海大学法学院常务副院长李凤章和近百位中外企业家、金融家和法学法律工作者参加研讨会。

全国人大常委会副秘书长李飞发表视频讲话，民建中央副主席、上海市政协副主席周汉民做“一带一路”和中欧经贸关系主旨演讲。著名国际法律专家高仕林、孔宏德和环太平洋律师协会中国理事、黄浦区政协常委、金茂凯德律师事务所创始合伙人李志强律师，分别就比利时、荷兰、卢森堡、英国、法国、意大利等欧洲国家投融资法律实务和中国企业在欧洲进行并购融资的法律风险防范作专业分享。

与会专家指出，尽管在“走出去”的过程中我国企业面临各种法律风险和挑战，但是完备而高效的防范机制必然能够为其保驾护航。面对诸多的法律风险，国家、行业协会和企业三方应当成为构建中国企业赴欧洲投融资风险防范机制的重要参与者。

研讨会上举行了“一带一路”法律研究与服务中心德国站和金茂凯德律

师事务所日内瓦代表处等揭幕仪式，举行了由外滩金融创新试验区法律研究中心组织专家编撰，著名法学家、上海市人民政府原参事室主任李昌道教授主编的《外滩金融创新试验区法律研究》（2017 年版）首发式，该书点评了 2016 年金融市场 20 例经典案例，聚焦互联网金融、金融控股与创新金融、企业融资与投资贸易、并购重组与争端解决、“一带一路”研究等多领域前沿问题，书中多篇中外文论著宣传和传播了中国法律制度和法律文化，有利于金融市场监管者和立法者借鉴总结，有利于金融法律研究和服务者从鲜活的市场元素中提炼升华，有利于中外金融家和法学家切磋交流，为推进上海国际金融中心建设的国家战略添砖加瓦。

据悉，中国企业赴欧洲投融资法律研讨会是继 2016 年 5 月中国企业赴日本投融资法律研讨会和 2016 年 11 月中国企业赴美洲投融资法律研讨会后，又一次专业法律服务机构联合行业协会和高等院校等举办的专题研讨会，是服务国家“一带一路”倡议的务实举措。

中国企业赴亚洲投融资法律研讨会在上海举办

证券时报网（2017-05-23）

2017 年 5 月 23 日，由上海上市公司协会、上海股权投资协会、上海国际服务贸易行业协会、金茂凯德律师事务所和上海政法学院联合举办的中国企业赴亚洲投融资法律研讨会在上海举行。

上海国际仲裁中心副主任兼秘书长马屹，环太平洋律师协会、香港国际仲裁中心和香港律师会前主席王桂埙，亚洲国际仲裁中心仲裁员、金茂凯德律师事务所创始合伙人李志强，马来西亚律师范晓钧分别就亚太地区争议解决机构的最新发展、中企海外融资及投资法律问题、中国企业在亚洲进行并购融资的法律风险防范及中企在马来西亚投资案例做分享。

与会专家指出，亚洲国家在世界版图中影响巨大，在“一带一路”发展格局中影响深远，在习近平总书记治国理政新理念、新思想和新战略引领下，中国企业赴亚洲投融资的浪潮势不可当。尽管在“走出去”的过程中我国企业面临各种法律风险，但是完备而高效的防范机制必然能够为其保驾护航。面对诸多的法律风险，国家、行业协会和企业三方应当成为构建中国企业赴亚洲投融资风险防范机制的重要参与者，中外法律工作者应当携手合作打造人类法律服务共同体。

研讨会举行了上海政法学院教学科研学术实践基地、金茂凯德律师事务所“一带一路”法律研究与服务中心新加坡站和越南站及代表处的揭幕仪式。

全国人大常委会副秘书长李飞和上海市人民政府原参事室主任李昌道分别发表视频讲话；全国政协常委、民建中央副主席、上海市政协副主席周汉民发表主旨演讲；上海市政协常委及经济委员会副主任张宁，中共上海市黄浦区区委常委、政法委书记吕南停，上海上市公司协会秘书长钱衡及副秘书长史美健，上海政法学院校长、国际商会仲裁与多元化纠纷解决机制委员会副主席刘晓红，锦江国际集团副总裁王国兴，上海市黄浦区司法局局长刘辉，上海国际仲裁中心副主任兼秘书长马屹，环太平洋律师协会和香港国际仲裁中心前主席王桂埙，上海国际服务贸易行业协会常务副会长吴根宝，黄浦区金融服务办公室副主任陈功，上海市人民政府参事徐静琳等和近百位中外企业家、金融家和法学法律工作者参加研讨会。

据悉，中国企业赴亚洲投融资法律研讨会是继 2016 年 5 月中国企业赴日本投融资法律研讨会、2016 年 11 月中国企业赴美洲投融资法律研讨会和 2017 年 3 月中国企业赴欧洲投融资法律研讨会之后的又一次专题研讨会。

后 记

2017年5月14日，中国政府在北京成功举办“一带一路”国际合作高峰论坛，由习近平总书记提出的“一带一路”倡议得到国际社会的广泛响应，并写入联合国的法律文件，法律界也积极参与“一带一路”倡议的宏伟事业。2016年2月18日，上海市专业服务贸易重点单位金茂凯德律师事务所成立了“一带一路”法律研究与服务中心，截至2018年10月1日，已在亚洲、欧洲、美洲、大洋洲和非洲设立了56个站点，广泛传播中国法律制度和法律文化的正能量，联合各有关国家和地区的优秀法律专业人士潜心研究各国投融资法律制度，以期为中国企业“走出去”提供优质、高效的法律服务。

2017年10月召开的党的十九大提出了习近平新时代中国特色社会主义思想，将“一带一路”倡议写入党章，为新时代法学法律界人士继续不忘初心和牢记使命指明了路径和方向。

《中国企业海外投融资法律研究》是“中国企业海外投融资法律研究”系列丛书之四，全书由英国、意大利、比利时、荷兰、卢森堡、新西兰、印度、阿根廷和墨西哥九国的顶尖律师、国际仲裁员和专家学者担任撰稿人，聚焦论述九国的投融资法律及相关法律问题。

本书作为系列丛书之一，承蒙德高望重的司法部原部长、中国法学会会长、中国政法大学校长和中华全国律师协会首任会长邹瑜为丛书题写书名；承蒙全国人大宪法和法律委员会主任李飞百忙中作总序；著名法学家、上海市人民政府原参事室主任李昌道教授审定本书并作序；司法部党组成员、副部长熊选国，中共上海市委常委、上海市人民政府常务副市长周波，上海市政协副主席周汉民、徐逸波任总指导；一批著名的金融家、法学家和企业家担任本书指导和编委；中国金融出版社编辑贾真为本书的出版给予了细致的指导，对各方面专家的鼎力支持在此一并致谢！

“长风破浪会有时，直挂云帆济沧海。”“一带一路”倡议的伟大事业需要一批又一批法律人不懈努力，由于丰富多彩的法律实践发展迅速，对中国企业海外投融资法律研究的相关总结也是阶段性的。书中疏漏不当之处还请领导、专家和同仁批评指正。

李志强

2018 年 10 月 7 日于上海

Postscript

On May 14, 2017, the Chinese government successfully held the "Belt and Road"Forum for International Cooperation in Beijing. The "Belt and Road" Initiative proposed by General Secretary Xi Jinping received extensive response from the international community and was written into the UN legal documents. The legal industry actively participates in the grand cause of the "Belt and Road" Initiative. On February 18, 2016, Jin Mao Partners, the key professional service provider for trade, established the "Belt and Road"Initiative legal research and service center in Shanghai. As of October 1, 2018, this center has established 56 stations in Asia, Europe, America, Oceania and Africa, widely disseminating the positive energy of China's legal system and legal culture, and uniting outstanding legal professionals from relevant countries and regions to study the investment and financing legal systems of various countries in order to provide quality and efficient legal services for Chinese enterprises to go global.

The 19th National Congress of the Communist Party of China held in October 2017 put forward Xi Jinping's thought of socialism with Chinese characteristics in the new era. The "Belt and Road" Initiative was written into the Party Constitution, which pointed out the path and direction for the people of the legal and law circles in the new era to continue to remain true to our original aspiration and keep our mission firmly in mind.

Legal Research on Investment and Financing for Chinese Enterprises in the Overseas Countries, the fourth series of *Legal Research on overseas Investment and Financing for Chinese Enterprises*, is written by the top lawyers, international arbitrators and experts and scholars from nine countries including the United Kingdom, Italy, Belgium, the Netherlands, Luxembourg, New Zealand, India, Argentina and Mexico, focusing on the investment and financing laws and related legal issues of the aforementioned nine countries.

As one of the series of books, the title of this book is written by Zou Yu, the former Minister of Justice, the President of the Chinese Law Society, the President of the Chinese University of Political Science and Law and the first President of the All-China Lawyers Association. Li Fei, the Director of the Constitution and Law Committee of the National People's Congress, wrote the preface despite his busy work. Professor Li Changdao, the famous jurist and the former director of the Counsellors' Office of Shanghai Municipal People's Government, examined and wrote the preface. Xiong Xuanguo, the members of the Party Team and Vice Minister of the Ministry of Justice; Zhou Bo, member of the Standing Committee of the CPC Shanghai Municipal Committee, executive deputy mayor of the Shanghai Municipal People's Government；Zhou Hanmin and Xu Yibo, vice chairman of the CPPCC Shanghai Commission act as the chief director. A number of well-known financiers, jurists and entrepreneurs act as directors and editors of this book. Jia Zhen, the editor of Financial Publishing House, gave meticulous guidance for the publication of this book, and I would like to thank all the experts for their support!

"*A time will come to ride the wind and cleave the waves to cross the sea.*" The great cause of the "Belt and Road" Initiative requires the unremitting efforts of a group of legal persons. Due to the rapid development of rich and colorful legal practices, the relevant summary of the law on overseas investment and financing for Chinese enterprises is also phased. Leaders, experts and colleagues, please criticized and corrected the mistakes in the book if any, thank you.

Li Zhiqiang（Jack Li）
October 7, 2018 in Shanghai